D1710334

# The
# Punitive
# Turn

CARTER G. WOODSON INSTITUTE SERIES
Deborah E. McDowell, Editor

# The Punitive Turn

New Approaches to
Race and Incarceration

Edited by
Deborah E. McDowell,
Claudrena N. Harold,
and Juan Battle

University of Virginia Press    *Charlottesville and London*

University of Virginia Press
© 2013 by the Rector and Visitors of the University of Virginia
All rights reserved
Printed in the United States of America on acid-free paper

*First published 2013*

9 8 7 6 5 4 3 2 1

Library of Congress Cataloging-in-Publication Data
The punitive turn : new approaches to race and incarceration / edited by Deborah E.
    McDowell, Claudrena N. Harold, and Juan Battle.
        pages cm. — (Carter G. Woodson Institute series)
    Includes bibliographical references and index.
    ISBN 978-0-8139-3520-1 (cloth : alk. paper) — ISBN 978-0-8139-3521-8 (e-book)
    1. Imprisonment—United States.  2. Corrections—United States.  3. Criminal
justice, Administration of—United States.  4. Discrimination in criminal justice
administration—United States.  5. African American prisoners.  I. McDowell,
Deborah E., 1951–  II. Harold, Claudrena N.  III. Battle, Juan, 1968–
    HV9471.P865 2013
    365'.608996073—dc23
                                                                2013011739

# Contents

# Foreword: Challenging Mass Incarceration

MARC MAUER

> I didn't know jack weenie about what people were going through in here
> [federal prison].
> —RANDY "DUKE" CUNNINGHAM, *former "tough on crime" member of Congress,*
> *imprisoned for eight years on conspiracy and tax-evasion charges*

It is now commonplace to note that the United States, with its more than 2 million people behind bars, has become the world's leading jailer, incarcerating far more of its citizens than do other industrialized nations. Criminologists and political theorists have produced a broad range of scholarship assessing the unique political culture, social structure, and racial dynamics that have produced this phenomenon.

While these analyses have been enlightening, it is important to note that mass incarceration is no longer a new development. As far back as 1991, the Sentencing Project issued a report documenting that the United States had become the world leader in its use of imprisonment, outpacing its former Cold War rival Russia as well as apartheid South Africa.[1] The combined prison and jail population of 1.2 million at that time dwarfed the incarcerated population of 330,000 in the early 1970s, at the inception of the race to incarcerate.

Faced in 1991 with the data regarding this dubious distinction, U.S. policy makers could have paused to assess the results of the two-decade-long "experiment" in the use of massive incarceration as a mechanism of crime control. Such an assessment would have proved quite sobering. The most recent seven-year period of 1984–91 would have indicated a 17 percent rise in crime despite a 65 percent increase in the number of people in prison.[2] The racial/ethnic makeup of the imprisoned population had become impossible to ignore, with nearly one in four young black males living under some form of criminal justice supervision. And prison cells supposedly reserved for the "worst of the worst" were increasingly being filled by young men and women of color caught up in the rapidly expanding set of law enforcement and sentencing policies enshrined under the aggressive launch of the "War on Drugs."

But little assessment of these developments occurred at the highest levels of power. Instead, policy makers embarked on a program of enhanced punishment at all levels that virtually institutionalized the system of mass incarceration. At the federal level, this included the adoption of the Clinton administration's federal crime bill in 1994, a $30 billion measure loaded with $8 billion for new state prison construction, enhanced federal sentencing penalties, and only modest resources for prevention initiatives. State-level policy makers jumped on board as well, with half the states adopting "three strikes and you're out" policies by the mid-1990s. The most notorious of these, the California law defining any felony as a third strike, produced such bizarre outcomes as a golf-club thief being sentenced to twenty-five years to life[3] and a videotape thief being sentenced to fifty years to life,[4] sentences that the U.S. Supreme Court upheld in 2003.

In the area of juvenile justice, the long-standing mission of a distinct juvenile court established to recognize the diminished culpability of children and their unique capacity to change was upended by a slew of policy decisions designed to have young people tried in the adult court system. In the early 1990s, virtually every state amended its statutes to expand the variety of ways in which juveniles could be tried in adult court and face sanctions historically reserved for adults; consequently, the number of such cases rose significantly in the succeeding years.

Promoting and implementing punitive criminal justice policies has seemed like a "no-brainer" to many political leaders in recent decades. Since the late 1960s, public support for harsh sentencing policies has made it a virtual article of faith that one can never be too tough on crime. Sensationalized media coverage of crime has helped to prime an audience to respond positively to such initiatives.

Political dynamics also play a part in generating tough-on-crime policies. Legislative sessions primarily focused on budgetary decisions for a single year lead to a focus on short-term solutions. Thus, public policies such as investments in preschool education that hold the potential for long-term approaches to issues of public safety, but do not necessarily produce short-term crime-control benefits, are not seen as politically expedient.

Public policy making is not focused on serving the interests of low-income people in general, and even less so of persons with criminal convictions. In an era when moneyed interests are arguably more influential than ever in determining legislative outcomes, those at the bottom rungs of the income ladder are hardly competitive in this realm.

So, in 2013, we live with a prison population almost double that of 1991. Not until 2009 did the state prison population decline slightly, for the first time in nearly four decades.[5] And while the population has been steadying in recent years, there is as yet no sign of a sustained national reduction.

## An Alternative Scenario Rejected

It did not have to turn out this way. Political and civic leaders could have embraced a more comprehensive, and compassionate, approach to problems of crime and substance abuse, one that relied on evidence-based research on better measures to address these problems. In the area of substance abuse, for example, policy makers could have reversed the funding allocation that prioritized law enforcement and incarceration over prevention and treatment. A wealth of research over time and through various drug epidemics demonstrates that reducing demand for drugs is a more effective strategy than continued efforts to interrupt the supply chain.

Initiatives to support families in raising healthy children could have built on the findings from early Head Start programs that demonstrated the benefits of preschool education. Policy makers could have looked abroad as well for varying approaches to these issues: the industrialized nations of western Europe, as well as Canada, incarcerate their citizens at a fraction of the U.S. scale. The reasons for these differences are complex, but they involve the presence of a broader social safety net, less inequality of wealth, and a greater cultural skepticism regarding the value of punishment.

Why, then, were these arguably very sensible alternative policies not adopted twenty years ago? The proximate causes are many. First, the institutionalization of the system of mass incarceration makes it very difficult to change course. With police, prosecutors, judges, prison guards, and entire communities often dependent on the wages and presumed economic benefits of a vast criminal justice apparatus, there is great resistance to any proposed shift in course.

Even were there to be a shift in the political consensus around dealing with problems of public safety, the nature of funding within the system would make it very challenging to reallocate resources. Suppose, for example, a new drug court is able to divert fifty people to treatment rather than incarceration, a welcome outcome for many reasons. Yet reducing the population of a given prison by fifty saves very little money. Given the enormous fixed costs of operating a prison system, the small savings in this case derive primarily from the food and health-care costs for each diverted person. Only when we reach a point of closing an entire prison are substantial cost savings realized. In the interim, however, overall costs actually increase since the fixed costs of the prison remain, and additional treatment resources are necessary for the drug-court services.

Over time, sentencing policies have also contributed to institutionalizing a massive prison population. With the advent of widespread use of mandatory sentencing, "three strikes" policies, and the like, record numbers of people are now serving long-term prison sentences for which no relief is available in the form of parole, and in which the role of executive clemency has diminished considerably, largely due to the political winds.

## The Racial Dynamics of Mass Incarceration

While these impediments to change are substantial, we can also trace their origins to a broader political and social dynamic, one in which race remains as a dividing line in the twenty-first century. During the past half century, opportunities have opened up to many people of color that had been closed to them for three centuries. Political and public discourse has changed as well, and in polite company it is no longer acceptable to express racist beliefs. Yet while there are surface changes in the ways in which race permeates societal relationships, within the criminal justice system, racial outcomes are now markedly worse for African Americans in particular.

Race produces criminal justice policy in two broad ways. First, we see the consequences of the vast economic changes of the past three decades, a period in which the rich have gotten richer and the poor have gotten poorer. With rampant globalization causing a decline in the United States' manufacturing economy and its replacement in large part by a low-wage service economy, urban communities of color have been particularly hard hit. The union-wage jobs that previously enabled working-class blacks and whites to support a family have now frequently been replaced by nonunion entry-level positions, with severe implications for family and community stability. Related to this is the still prevalent pattern of housing segregation in which disadvantaged communities are both spatially and psychologically isolated from middle-class America. Such patterns translate into educational segregation, in which children in these communities grow up in low-functioning schools, with boys in particular recognizing that their future is more likely to involve spending time in prison than in a college classroom.

As a result of these shifts, for the largely black and brown working-class communities left out of the new economy, opportunity declines and social problems proliferate. These manifest themselves in part through substance abuse and crime, further contributing to destabilized neighborhoods.

The other means by which racial considerations impact criminal justice policy is through the framing of the "crime problem" by media and political leadership. Stretching back to the late 1960s and political initiatives highlighting "crime in the streets" as part of the backlash to the advances of the civil rights movement, crime has come to be defined and perceived largely as a "black problem." One only has to reflect on the infamous Willie Horton case that inflamed the 1988 presidential campaign or the dynamics of the crack cocaine sentencing legislation in the late 1980s to recognize that the face of the "crime problem" was inevitably that of a black male.

Once this image of the problem becomes pervasive, the political discussion about policy options becomes very constricted. Rather than engage in a broad consideration of the varied ways in which public safety can be produced—which might include mentoring young people, training in parenting skills, creating economic opportunity, providing prevention and treatment approaches for problems of substance abuse and mental health, and yes, criminal justice initiatives—the public conversation instead focuses primarily on criminal justice responses to the problem, and punitive ones in particular.

Thus, for example, the harsh federal crack cocaine mandatory-sentencing policies were adopted in the 1980s in near-record time, with virtually no consideration of any other approach to the problem. There was no attempt to examine the source of the emerging drug issue, the amenability of crack abusers to treatment, or lessons learned from the history of previous drug epidemics, all of which may have produced a more balanced approach. While this is admittedly one of the more stark examples of such narrow thinking, we can trace similar approaches in a host of policy initiatives promoting the adoption of "get tough" sentencing laws. So while the overt racism of the past century may now be largely absent, the outcomes of criminal justice policy look strikingly similar to those of the Jim Crow era.

### The Impact of Mass Incarceration

Looking back at the expansion of the prison population in recent decades, some would draw a more positive conclusion about the impact of this strategy. They would point to the sustained decline in crime since the early 1990s and conclude that this trend is a direct result of rising incarceration. While such a conclusion seems intuitively obvious to some, in fact the relationship between crime and incarceration is far more complex. Crime rates rise and fall for a host of reasons. These include the relative health of the economy, the proportion of fifteen- to twenty-four-year-olds in the population, the presence of drug markets, the availability of illegal weapons, policing initiatives, and the level of incarceration. Research to date suggests that rising imprisonment explains only a small part of the decline in crime beginning in the 1990s, and that factors unrelated to criminal justice produced the bulk of the change. Further, given the present scale of incarceration, any crime-reducing effect of imprisonment is very much one of diminishing returns due to the excessive incarceration of drug and nonviolent offenders.

But suppose for the moment we assume that most of the decline in crime since the early 1990s has in fact been a result of mass incarceration. Would that suggest that this had been a necessary and effective policy? Certainly not. Consider what a bleak perspective this represents. Essentially, it suggests that in order to control crime, it is necessary to imprison one of every three black males and one of every six Latino males born today. Are there really no other ways to promote public safety? Imagine what the response would be if we were told by political leaders that public safety required locking up one in three white males during his lifetime? Such a scenario is of course beyond imagination.

## Seeking a New Direction for Public Safety

Given the distressing dynamics of criminal justice policy, is there any reason to believe we can create a movement to reverse course? This is a tall order, but there are some reasons for cautious optimism.

Although the prison population in the United States remains at record high levels, the public climate around public safety issues has in fact shifted in recent years. While punishment remains a guiding theme for public policy, it now also coexists uneasily with steadily increasing support for a mix of policies that are both evidence-based and fiscally sound. For example, both liberal and conservative political leaders have embraced the need to provide supportive services to people transitioning back to the community from prison. In the realm of drug policy, mandatory sentences still abound, but so too do drug courts and other forms of diversion to treatment that hold the promise of a more compassionate and effective approach to the underlying problem of substance abuse. Even in regard to sentencing policy, in 2010 the notorious disparity in sentencing between federal penalties for crack and powder cocaine was substantially reduced.

While we approach these problems grounded in a sense of history and an understanding of social movements, it is also important to remain cognizant of the complexity of social change. Who, for example, could have predicted even in the year 2000 that within a decade we would have an African American man as president? Such an outcome does not suggest that we should ignore an analytical framework, only that we recognize that social change is a complicated process. And as all successful social movements have demonstrated, we need to be both visionary and practical at the same time—visionary in order to inspire people to create a better community, and practical to provide a road map to get there. This volume represents an important contribution toward grappling with these challenges. Hopefully, it can help to shape our intellectual understanding of these issues as well as contribute to the process of engagement for social justice.

## Notes

1. Marc Mauer, *Americans Behind Bars: A Comparison of International Rates of Incarceration*, The Sentencing Project, 1991.

2. Jenni Gainsborough and Marc Mauer, *Diminishing Returns: Crime and Incarceration in the 1990s*, The Sentencing Project, 2000.

3. Ewing v. California, 538 U.S. 11 (2003).

4. Lockyer v. Andrade, 538 U.S. 63 (2003).

5. Heather C. West, *Prisoners at Yearend 2009—Advance Counts*, Bureau of Justice Statistics, June 2010.

# Acknowledgments

This collection of essays grew out of a three-day symposium held at the University of Virginia during the spring of 2009. Sponsored by the Carter G. Woodson Institute for African-American and African Studies, the symposium's theme was "The Problem of Punishment: Race, Inequality, and Justice." The vast majority of essays collected in this volume were given as short papers and then expanded and revised for publication. The editors wish to acknowledge a generous grant in support of the symposium from the University of Virginia's Page-Barbour and James W. Richard lecture series, as well as the close involvement of Professor Vesla M. Weaver in organizing the event.

The editors also wish to acknowledge the support of various individuals and institutions at the University of Virginia without whose assistance this publication would have proved an impossible task: Cheryll Lewis, Deborah Best, and Nicole Marrs, administrative staff at the Woodson Institute; the Department of English; the Corcoran Department of History; and the Woodrow Wilson Department of Politics. Thanks are due to the student interns, fellows, and former fellows of the Carter G. Woodson Institute who participated in various aspects of the production process, including Sandy Alexandre, Safiya Sinclair, and Eden Zekarias, who assisted—ably and cheerfully—at the very end, enabling us to push the production to the finish line.

Thanks also to the staff at the University of Virginia Press. Richard Holway, our acquisitions editor, believed in the project from the very start and steered it through some rocky patches. Raennah Mitchell, Morgan Myers, and Ellen Satrom each deserve a special crown for exemplary patience and professionalism—and for incalculable grace.

Thank you, finally, to all the contributors.

# Introduction

The prison is considered an inevitable and permanent feature of our social lives.

—Angela Davis

The prison has become a looming presence in our society to an extent unparalleled in our history—or that of any other industrial democracy. Short of major wars, mass incarceration has been the most thoroughly implemented government social program of our time.

—Elliot Currie

Whatever accrues to formal citizenship depreciates under the pressure of inegalitarian distribution and is remanded under the auspices of excessive policing and punishment.

—Nikhil Pal Singh

When Alexis de Tocqueville and Gustave de Beaumont journeyed to the United States in 1831 to tour its prisons, they immediately described the "monomania of the penitentiary system," noting that "while society in the U.S. gives the example of the most extended liberty," its penitentiaries "offered the spectacle of the most complete despotism," evidence of a mistaken belief that prisons were a "remedy for all the evils of society." The observations of Tocqueville and Beaumont still retain their relevance. The alarms they sounded in the early decades of the nineteenth century have only grown. Indeed, many at the forefront of prison studies would argue that the "monomania" Tocqueville and Beaumont observed has brought us to the point where this country's swelling inmate population has made it difficult for some to fathom.

For those who track the escalating rates of imprisonment in the United States and note their disproportionate effect on African Americans, it has become increasingly commonplace to summon some version of the assertion that Michelle Alexander has made so popular: "More African Americans are under correctional control today—in prison or jail, on probation or parole—than were enslaved in 1850, a decade before the Civil War began."[1] Such assertions are offered to explain the growing signs of inequality  in wealth, income, employment, life expectancy, educational achievement—and the diminished prospects overall for social and economic advancement, particularly for African Americans, even as some optimists herald the arrival of a "postracial" America. A recent book by Becky Pettit suggests that current assessments of racial inequalities would be far worse if the roughly nine hundred thousand African American men in prison figured into the statistics tracking the social standing of African Americans in the United States.[2] While African American men—as well as people of color broadly speaking—certainly figure disproportionately among incarcerated populations, the untrammeled growth of the prison system in the United States has created, notes Kim Gilmore, "a level of human bondage, unparalleled in the 20th century," inspiring Angela Davis, among others, to designate the last forty years as the "era of the prison industrial complex."[3]

The contributors to this volume collectively explore multiple aspects of mass incarceration: its historical, political, economic, and sociocultural roots; as well as its collateral costs and consequences, the exacting toll incarceration takes on inmates, their families, their communities, and the society at large. The volume has its genesis in a two-day symposium held at the University of Virginia in April 2009. Organized by faculty members in the Departments of English, History, and Politics, and sponsored by the Carter G. Woodson Institute for African American and African Studies, the symposium brought together academics, policy makers, political organizers, social activists, and former inmates to consider the massive and seemingly unstoppable expansion of the U.S. carceral state.

In the keynote speech Angela Davis delivered at the symposium, she advanced the claim that the prison, an institution that emerged at the time of the American Revolution, "has proven to be a failed experiment in democracy and an institution of racial injustice, especially when we consider that one in 100 Americans is behind bars."[4] Participants wrestled throughout the symposium with this and other alarming statistics concerning the escalating rates of incarceration:

- The United States is the world's leader in incarceration and death-row inmates, with 25 percent of the world's prison population but only 5 percent of the world's people.
- Since 1973, incarceration rates have risen by a factor of six, even as crime statistics have fallen. There are now three times as many offenders released each year as compared to the entire prison population in 1973.
- The prison industry is one of the most rapidly growing industries in the

United States, now employing more than Wal-Mart, General Motors, and Ford combined.

- Expenditures on the criminal justice system have quadrupled over the past four decades, absorbing an ever-increasing share of public resources. State spending on corrections has doubled over the past two decades. Today, government contributes more to the criminal justice system than to all income-maintenance and unemployment programs combined. For example, in 2008, federal, state, and municipal governments spent a combined $68 billion on corrections.

This data set tells but a fraction of the story; it fails to account for the role that race has played in the formation of the contemporary prison industrial complex.[5] Once again, the statistics prove instructive:

- In 2010, while African Americans constituted 13.6 percent of the U.S. population, they comprised 37.4 percent of the nation's prison inmates.
- The incarceration rate among black men ages thirty to thirty-four years old, a significant wage-earning group, was 7,265 per 100,000 in 2010.
- Thirty percent of those African American males not incarcerated are under correctional supervision—on probation or parole.
- While males continue to dominate these statistics, African American girls and women have become the fastest-growing population among the incarcerated.

These statistical trends establish nothing more profoundly than that the link between crime and punishment has become emphatically racialized.[6] While African Americans are certainly not the only category of the U.S. population affected by this crisis, policy makers, academics, and grassroots activists alike agree that the collateral damage of the nation's carceral crisis on African American communities has been especially severe. The contributors to this volume thus appropriately focus their attention on this community, examining the troubling relationship between race and crime and raising a range of critical questions central to the burgeoning field of carceral studies: How has the disproportionate representation of African Americans in the penal system deepened racial inequalities within the political, economic, and social structures of our nation? What are the political implications when incarceration becomes a "systematic aspect of community members' family affairs, economic prospects, political engagements, and childhood expectations for the future"?[7] What are the historical connections between the contemporary prison crisis and earlier forms of racialized bondage, servitude, and civic exclusion? And last, given our nation's growing attentiveness

to the problem of mass imprisonment, why have movements geared toward decarceration proven ineffective in generating substantive policy change?

The essays collected here demonstrate the analytical benefits, if not the necessity, of a multidisciplinary approach to the history, politics, and culture of the
U.S. carceral state. Structured along thematic rather than chronological lines, this
volume is divided into four major sections. The first includes essays that focus on
the historical context or origins of the current carceral crisis; the second, on the
collateral consequences of mass incarceration; the third, on the prison as cultural
commodity, the imagery of which is marketed for mass consumption. The fourth
and final section features interviews and reflections from selected activists and
former inmates whose theoretical insights into mass incarceration must be incor-
porated into any analysis of the contested history of the nation's carceral system.

The first section, which spans the years between the close of the Civil War and
the peak of the Black Power era, locates the origins of the current carceral crisis in
the penal practices and white-supremacist initiatives of the postemancipation era
(rather than in the law-and-order politics of the 1960s). As Heather Thompson
notes in section 1, the current mass-incarceration crisis had its analogue in a crisis
of the mid-1870s, one equally racialized and transparently brutal. Then, as now,
African Americans were subjected to hyperpolicing, but Thompson discusses
how and to what effect they—in their families, their communities, and political
movements—confronted and resisted such policing. By "walking more carefully
through the prison horrors of the past," Thompson suggests, and exploring the
multiple responses engendered at that time, "we get much closer to eradicating
the horrors of the present."

The contributors to section 2 focus on the "horrors of the present," examining both the causes and consequences of mass incarceration, demonstrating
how the expansion of the carceral state has fundamentally redefined the social,
economic, and political citizenship of millions of racial minorities, particularly
African Americans. These essays share a simple but important claim: punishment
for ex-offenders, their families, and their communities persists and reverberates
long after an individual's period behind bars.

Pushing the interdisciplinary boundaries of the volume still further, section 3
includes essays exploring the place of punishment and prison in the aesthetic
imagination. Not lost upon many of these contributors is the necessity of confronting the normalization of mass incarceration in popular culture, whose
highly seductive productions have arrested our political imagination in ways that
weaken the development of progressive alternatives to the prevailing system of
punishment and incarceration. Despite the allure of television shows and movies
focused on the prison industry, many in marginalized communities have relied on

lyrical and artistic practices to expose the undemocratic forces and dehumanizing objectives shaping this country's criminal justice system.

No volume on the history and consequences of the U.S. criminal justice system would be complete without the intellectual contributions of the formerly incarcerated, and thus we conclude this volume with interviews with former inmates. Their responses extend the insights of the essays in this volume, particularly those concerning the collateral consequences of mass incarceration on families and children, the denial of human rights to ex-offenders, and the assaults on the democratic process, particularly for ex-felons, for most of whom "time served" is a misnomer. As Jim Shea, one respondent, notes, "I know people who were convicted twenty-five or thirty years ago, who still when they go for a job . . . have to check that box indicating they've been convicted of a felony." The terms of their probation place them at heightened risk of reoffending, and such a cycle repeats generation after generation.

Despite its wide disciplinary spectrum, this volume is unified by the commitment of each essay to examining the formation and evolution of the U.S. carceral state within the larger context of U.S. political, social, legal, and cultural history. The end result is a collection that generates critical questions not simply about the penal system, but also, implicitly, about the inner workings, failings, and future of American democracy. As Angela Davis suggests, if "democratic rights are defined in relation to what is denied people in prison . . . we might ask, what kind of democracy do we currently inhabit?"

## Historical Context

As many readers are well aware, historical research on crime and punishment in the United States has proliferated in the past fifteen years.[8] Scholars in the subfields of African American, urban, southern, and gender history have combined archival research with the theoretical insights of radical criminology, sociology, and critical race theory to deepen our understanding of the evolution of the U.S. carceral state. Among the most influential of such scholars are Kali N. Gross, Rebecca McLellan, Khalil Muhammad, David Oshinsky, Alex Lichtenstein, Robert Perkinson, and Douglas Blackmon. These historians, among others, have forced scholars to think more critically about a range of pertinent issues, including but not limited to the historical origins of the nation's mass incarceration crisis. While many have traced the rise in rates of incarceration—climbing steeply since the 1970s—to several important policy changes connected to the "War on Crime" and the "War on Drugs," others understand the necessity of placing the current crisis in a historical context that looks as far back as slavery. Indeed, as Loïc Wacquant argues, "Slavery and mass imprisonment are genealogically linked," and thus "one cannot understand the latter—its timing and smooth onset . . . without return-ing to the former as historical starting point and functional analogue."[9] While it is important to establish such linkages, Kim Gilmore's caveat is useful: "the point of retracing this history is not to argue that prisons have been a direct outgrowth of slavery, but to interrogate the persistent connections between racism and the global economy," to which the economy of slavery was integral.[10]

Taken together, the essays in section 1 trace the origins of the contempo-rary prison crisis, along with its reverberating consequences. While the era of slavery and its aftermath figure prominently in these essays, they center on the postemancipation era, when the black prison population exploded and the white-supremacist structures of Jim Crow tightened their grip, relegating the formerly enslaved, to borrow David Oshinsky's resonant phrasing, to a penal system "worse than slavery."[11]

On the eve of Reconstruction's tragic demise, the rapid expansion of the black prison population weighed heavily on the minds of African Americans through-out the nation. As state and local governments designed new ways to criminalize African Americans who transgressed racial, class, and gender norms, the black prison population doubled from 8,056 in 1870 to 16,748 in 1880.[12] A decade later, as the number of incarcerated African Americans reached the 25,000 mark, blacks' representation in the nation's penal system hovered close to 30 percent. Comparatively speaking, the rate of incarceration among African Americans was three times that of white Americans. Though constituting only 12 percent of the U.S. population, African Americans had clearly become a dominant fixture in the nation's penal system by the close of the nineteenth century. Not just in the Jim Crow South, but also in the urban North, glaring racial disparities in the U.S. penal system garnered the attention of politicians, public policy advocates, and social scientists. Particularly after the publication of the 1890 census and the appearance of Frederick L. Hoffman's *Race Traits and Tendencies of the American Negro* six years later, conversations on black incarceration, the disproportionate number of African Americans in the penal system, and the alleged linkages be-tween blackness and criminality came to occupy a central place in national de-bates on the so-called "Negro Problem." As Khalil Muhammad notes in his recent study *The Condemnation of Blackness,* "prison statistics for the first time became the basis of national discussion about blacks as a distinct and dangerous criminal population."[13]

As historians trace the genealogical roots of contemporary carceral studies, it is important that they acknowledge the field's intellectual links, as well as its indebtedness to an earlier body of sociological research also centrally concerned with the problem of crime and punishment. The writings of W. E. B. Du Bois, Frances Kellor, Monroe Work, and Guy Johnson come immediately to mind.[14] By situating conversations on the problem of mass imprisonment within this broader history of black prison growth in late-nineteenth-century America and the scholarly literature that emerged in its wake, we do not intend to minimize the distinctive features (whether demographic or political) of today's carceral crisis, but rather to acknowledge that our current prison crisis not only mirrors but also bears the weight of our nation's turbulent postemancipation past.

In "Please Hear Our Cries: The Hidden History of Black Prisoners in America," Mary Ellen Curtin looks back to that past, building on her influential study of convict life in the New South, *Black Prisoners and Their World, Alabama, 1865–1900*. Unlike that previous study, which focused on the inner workings of the convict lease system in Alabama's coal mines, this essay moves beyond state archives to consider the possibility of writing prison history from a national perspective. Curtin turns to a set of papers of the National Association for the Advancement of Colored People (NAACP) entitled "Discrimination in the Criminal Justice System from 1910–1955." Such papers, she argues, establish not only the pervasiveness of racial segregation within northern prison systems, but also how deeply gender discrimination ran against black women. Within these documents, Curtin argues, can also be found one source of the "hidden history" of black prisoners in America: the letters they directed to NAACP lawyers appealing for investigations into the brutal treatment they received behind bars. Curtin illuminates how African American prisoners' labor was central to the industrialization and modernization of the New South.[15] She concedes that the worst abuses and practices of the postbellum prison have been abolished—the convict lease system, for example—but argues that "the modern prison bears the mark of the past."[16]

Heather Thompson's essay, "The Race to Incarcerate: America's Second Prison Crisis and Its Echoes in the First," poses a completely different set of historiographical challenges. Simultaneously historical and prescriptive, Thompson's analysis brings a fresh perspective to the political conversation on the problem of mass imprisonment by asserting that a critical step in "ending today's incarceration crisis" is acknowledging that it is not the "first, nor the first staggeringly racialized, prison crisis that this nation has witnessed." Noting the record number of African Americans incarcerated in the wake of the Civil War, Thompson calls into question the theme of exceptionality that runs through much of the social science literature on the current mass incarceration crisis. Working against this discursive grain, she insists that the nation's *first* prison crisis, as well as the forces that contributed to its demise, be considered in tandem. Such an approach will provide scholars and activists with much-needed historical perspective on the origins of the nation's *second* prison crisis, as well as important political lessons on how to hasten its end.

To this end, Thompson's essay engages three important historical developments in the history of the modern prison system: the rapid expansion of the African American prison population during the Gilded Age; the rise and fall of the convict lease system; and the upsurge in prison activism and reform legislation during the transitional period (1930–75) between the nation's first and second carceral crisis. She focuses on the political actors and organized movements that brought an end to the convict lease system (and the first carceral crisis) while working tirelessly to transform/humanize America's penal system. By interweaving social, labor, and political history, Thompson demonstrates how progressive politicians, labor leaders, and civil rights agitators pushed forward important prison reform legislation during the first half of the twentieth century. To the extent that history can serve as a useful guide for solving our current problem of mass incarceration, Thompson helps us identify social forces and movements that have contributed to transformative public policy reform. One of the greatest lessons to be gleaned from Thompson's story is how the success of any grassroots movement geared toward meaningful transformation of the penal system depends upon the existence of a vibrant American Left with deep political anchors in organized labor.

Thompson's essay avoids the simplistic generalizations that tend to flatten many historical overviews of the U.S. penal system. For example, she, like Curtin, is particularly attentive to the temporal and spatial distinctions in the nation's "prison crises" as they played out in South and North alike. In other words, criminal justice, Jim Crow style, had its counterpart well north of the Mason-Dixon Line. Cheryl Hicks also challenges these regional distinctions in "'Bright and Good Looking Colored Girl': Black Women's Sexuality and 'Harmful Intimacy' in Early-Twentieth-Century New York." Hicks demonstrates how critical inquiry into the history of crime and punishment can facilitate new approaches to subject matter that at first glance may have only a tangential relationship to the field of carceral studies. In the only essay in this volume to focus on female offenders and on youthful offenders, Hicks ventures into the interiority of black working-class life in Progressive Era New York. Drawing on prison dockets, court cases, and warden journals, she deepens our understanding of the worldview of black working women, their material desires, their family connections, and their struggles to navigate the travails of urban life.[17]

Hicks gives needed attention to three important yet underexplored issues in carceral studies: (1) the significant role of the urban North in constructing modern ideas about the presumed intersections of race, crime, and punishment;[18]

(2) the historical roots of black women's complex relationship to the criminal justice system; and (3) the urgent need for critical reflection on how youth crisis narratives within black urban communities have and continue to serve the legal arm of the state. Looking specifically at the varied experiences of African American women who served time at the New York State Reformatory for Women in Bedford Hills, she covers topics ranging from urban reformers' struggles to regulate black working women's social lives to black women inmates' complicated relationship to their families, prison officials, and white inmates. She also serves notice that the ideological work of constructing African Americans as the criminological other has never been an exclusively southern endeavor. "Centuries-old images that defined black women as immoral and pathological," Hicks explains, had considerable political currency among white reformers and law enforcement officials in the North. Thus, many African American women living above the Mason-Dixon Line were subjected to constant police harassment and surveillance, unfair convictions, and excessive sentences.

Hicks details the varied ways African American communities navigated these complex political realities. Her essay gives voice to African American working-class women who illuminated the pervasive racism of the criminal justice system, as well as African American reformers and parents concerned about the waywardness of black urban youth. Among the most valuable aspects of Hicks's essay is her observation that certain discourses within African American families, social institutions, and political organizations consciously and unconsciously buttressed hegemonic narratives and institutions that circumscribed—then and now—the freedoms of African Americans, particularly black youth. For example, one case at Bedford involved the heartbreaking story of how a mother's attempt to regulate her seventeen-year-old daughter's "youthful waywardness" resulted in her child's confinement at the reformatory. As Hicks notes, this unfortunate situation reveals the dangers involved in dealing with a state that viewed troubled black youth—particularly those from working-class communities—not as "people with problems" but as an irredeemably "problematic people." Here, Hicks's engagement with the adverse effects of social reformers and the state's construction of black women as incorrigible and deviant complements Jonathan Simon's essay, which appears in section 2. He, too, details how contemporary constructions of black urbanites—both offenders and nonoffenders—as irredeemably deviant and criminal continue to inform public policy discussions and to determine which groups deserve the protection of the state, rehabilitation opportunities, and/or the privileges of citizenship. In short, the significance of Hicks's essay lies not just in its comprehensive analysis of black women's struggles with an ever-evolving and complex criminal justice system but also in its engagement with a political and existential issue that has long concerned African American activists and scholars: "How does one study problems faced by a people without collapsing them into the problems themselves?"[19]

While detailing the contested legacy of the nation's penitentiary system, other essays in section 1 provide strong critiques of liberal penal theory, particularly the rehabilitative ideal undergirding many prison reform initiatives. Especially illuminating in this regard is Ethan Blue's chapter, "Abject Correction and Penal Medical Photography in the Early Twentieth Century." While analyzing the medical photography of Dr. Leo Stanley, resident physician at San Quentin Prison from 1913 to 1951, Blue casts a critical eye on the correctional techniques employed by liberal penologists of the Progressive Era. His examination of Dr. Stanley's medical treatment of San Quentin inmates exposes the brutal underside of the prison's attempt to "normalize" inmates and transform them into ideal/subject citizens. Under the pretext of not only reforming the prisoner but also strengthening the nation, Dr. Stanley relied on modern science and its technologies to strip inmates of their personhood in order to correct what he perceived to be their physiological and behavioral abnormalities.

Stanley maintained a visual record of the medical examinations and corrective surgeries he performed on inmates during his first seven years at San Quentin. According to Blue, this visual archive "both reflected and produced state prisoners as abjected beings whose poverty, criminal conviction, racialized status, bodily differences, and illness forced them into a threshold space between health and death, between normalized citizenship and the exclusion that imprisonment entailed." Like other prison reforms of the Progressive Era (that is, the sanitization of cellblocks, the abolition of the lockstep march, and the implementation of the case-history system), Stanley's biomedical techniques were seen by many penologists as evidence of a more humane prison system that offered convicts a route to personal rehabilitation and reintegration into society. Challenging such assumptions, Blue reminds us that, despite the perception that Stanley devoted his practice to creating a "humane prison system," his technology of "corrections" was not only fundamentally dehumanizing; it also hovered at the boundaries of barbarism.

Anoop Mirpuri's essay, which concludes the historical section of the volume, echoes Ethan Blue's in significant aspects. While Blue provides a specific examination of the sexualized violence at the heart of Stanley's medical practice and "treatment" of inmates, Mirpuri sees violence—including sexualized violence—as endemic to the prison system, in general. In "Mass Incarceration, Prisoner Rights, and the Legacy of the Radical Prison Movement," Mirpuri suggests that, at the level of both structure and practice, prison legitimizes violence. Indeed, he argues, "how we choose to understand and define violence [and] its relation to punishment" cannot fail to take into account the ways in which the prison, an institution existing at the "margins of the law," has played a significant role historically in "constructing the imagined boundaries between civilization and barbarism" and in casting the prisoner outside the law's imperative of protection, as well as society's normalization of human rights.

Mirpuri poses questions raised, both explicitly and implicitly, by other contributors to the volume: Why have critical discourses surrounding the prison so permeated our intellectual and cultural landscape while rendering society seemingly powerless to reverse the relentless growth of the prison itself? And why has the broad acknowledgment of mass incarceration as a crisis and scandal done relatively little to challenge its legitimacy? While Mirpuri readily concedes that recent trends in public and scholarly awareness of mass incarceration represent a critical development, the potential impact of which should not be underestimated, he asserts that any effort to fully understand just why such awareness has not challenged the legitimacy of the incarceration crisis demands that we seriously engage with the agency of prisoners, particularly those who initiated the "radical prison movement." Personified most iconically by George Jackson and Angela Y. Davis, this movement should be credited with formulating an insurgent critique of the modern history of captivity and punishment. This critique underlay a surge in prison revolts in the late 1960s and early 1970s at such institutions as Attica, Folsom, Auburn, San Quentin, Soledad, and the Tombs. Those at the forefront of the radical prison movement, Mirpuri argues, must be credited with contributing to the then emerging prison knowledge formation, much of which defines current critical theory regarding the relation between the prison and the larger society. Inmates at Folsom, and later Attica, fully understood that the modern prison was but the latter-day manifestation of a long history of black captivity, itself the "operative ground of capitalist property relations." In other words, the culture of punishment defining the United States, these inmates argued, was not a "state of exception," but a phenomenon central to the history of this nation-state.

While the names of Jackson and Davis loom large in any insurgent critique of mass incarceration, less known are the imprisoned men who constructed the Folsom and Attica manifestos, which have had an enduring, if often unacknowledged, intellectual impact on philosophical, activist, and cultural representations of incarceration since the 1970s. "The Folsom Prisoners' Manifesto of Demands and Anti-Oppression Platform," the template for the Attica manifesto that followed, has been most frequently read—when read at all—as a progressive appeal to the ideals of prison reform. On the contrary, argues Mirpuri, both

manifestos staunchly resisted those very ideals, undoubtedly because those who
penned their demands understood that prisons are meant to protect and police
the boundaries of the *human*, from which the very category "prisoners" has been
historically excluded.[20] Mirpuri concludes that resistance to prison growth cannot then be waged through appeals to notions of shared identity, humanity, and
human rights, for such appeals are not in themselves progressive. In other words,
"human rights," invoked on behalf of prisoners, functions as little more than an
empty concept, especially since it is typically uncoupled from questions concerning "material inequality," the very inequality that often leads to incarceration.[21] It
is precisely this relationship between incarceration and material inequality that
the chapters in the following section vigorously pursue.

### Incarceration and Social Inequality

That "incarceration deepens inequality," as Bruce Western and Katherine Beckett
note, is now axiomatic in discussions of the prison industrial complex.[22] Indeed,
it could be argued that the essays in this section extend the insight—shared by
many others—that "incarceration is a dramatic life-changing event that creates
a variety of challenges for those who experience it," especially minorities, for
whom the penal system has a particularly devastating and reverberating effect.[23]
"Those who experience it," note Western and Beckett, should not be taken to
refer exclusively to those who have actually spent time behind bars, for the effects (and aftereffects) of incarceration extend to a vast network of individuals
on the "outside" who experience what Marc Mauer and others have termed the
"collateral consequence of mass imprisonment": children, siblings, parents, local
communities, and ultimately, members of society as a whole.[24] The incarceration
of any offender, notes Donald Braman, "is not simply the sanctioning of an individual, but part of a broader corrosion of social bonds, bonds that sustain people,
particularly people in difficult circumstances."[25]

    In one form or another, the authors in this section pose questions fundamen-
tal to understanding the collateral consequences of imprisonment: what effects
does mass incarceration have on the economic prospects, as well as the relational
possibilities, of those formerly imprisoned? What are the effects of parental imprisonment on the health and cohesiveness of families, particularly the health
and well-being of children? What are the long-term consequences of mass imprisonment for persistent rates of racialized inequality? What penalties do the
formerly incarcerated continue to experience long after they have served their
time? Charles E. Lewis Jr. pursues a combination of such questions in his essay,
"Economic and Relational Penalties of Incarceration," noting, as do so many other

contributors to this volume, that African Americans experience such penalties at disproportionate rates. Indeed, Lewis asserts straightforwardly, their disproportionate involvement in the criminal justice system is "arguably the most vexing civil rights issue confronting African Americans today."

Using research data from the "Fragile Families and Child Well-Being Study," Lewis examines the effects of incarceration on the health and well-being of families, concluding, not surprisingly, that imprisonment clearly contributes to the fragility of families and compromises their viability. But such conclusions assume that families have actually developed to the point that makes such assessment possible. Focusing on the relationship between incarceration and employment outlook, Lewis's findings corroborate the research of Bruce Western and Devah Pager, who examine the relation between incarceration and poor labor market outcomes.[26] While other variables explain poor labor market outcomes, including family background, educational levels, and substance abuse, incarceration has a clear and significant impact on one's labor market outcomes. Specifically, incarceration reduces work probability, labor market earnings, as well as the market capital derived from on-the-job training and consistent work experience.

For the formerly incarcerated, poor labor market prospects also adversely affect marriage rates, stable unions, and family formation. Because men who are gainfully employed, or whose earnings come from the "underground" economy, are often regarded as less desirable mates and fathers, the formation of healthy families is thus impeded. Whether or not incarcerated persons can actually form "healthy" families, they are nevertheless—and frequently—the parents of children who suffer the "collateral consequences" of their parents' detention.[27]

Christopher Wildeman, Anna Haskins, and Christopher Muller explore the range of such consequences in "Implications of Mass Imprisonment for Inequality among American Children." Their research represents a "new frontier" in carceral studies, for as they note, "If the negative consequences of imprisonment for adults are only beginning to be documented, research on the effects of parental imprisonment on children has barely begun." But even the provisional findings of their research constitute cause for alarm, not least because these findings add to the mounting evidence that the range of penalties that accrue to the incarcerated, as well as their children, are dramatically compounded by race and class.

Working, like Charles Lewis, with the "Fragile Families" survey data, Wildeman and his colleagues report that, while one in twenty-five white children born in 1990 are at risk of experiencing parental imprisonment, the rate for black children is one in four. Children of incarcerated parents are likely to experience a constellation of socioeconomic disadvantages, including, but not limited to, homelessness, higher rates of poverty, family instability, and poor physical and

mental health. Such children are particularly prone to behavioral problems, stemming from the stresses, strains, and trauma of being separated from a parent, to
say nothing of the social stigmas resulting from having a parent in prison. Not
surprisingly, children of incarcerated parents face diminished prospects for academic success, and thus the likelihood of a dismal future. But even such prognos-
tications hold a paradoxical shred of optimism, in that they assume a future for
these children, an assumption challenged by Wildeman and his colleagues, whose
research establishes a connection between parental imprisonment and infant
mortality. Further, while their research focuses on children, Wildeman and his
coauthors would perhaps be the first to acknowledge that the link they establish
between mass imprisonment and childhood inequality is but one in a possible
chain extending from childhood to adulthood. Indeed, since, as Charles Lewis
notes in his contribution to this section, "families begin with kids, who are future
husbands, wives, mothers, and fathers," the experience of inequality in childhood
is often a harbinger of what lies ahead. In other words, it is entirely reasonable
to suppose that children of incarcerated parents may well grow up themselves
to become parents of incarcerated children, reproducing the cycle of inequality
across generations.

Wildeman and his coauthors include data on both maternal and paternal
rates of incarceration, uncovering, in the process, yet another stunning statistic:
"black children have nearly as high a risk of experiencing maternal imprisonment (3.3 percent) as white children have of experiencing paternal imprisonment
(3.6 percent)." When we allow for the fact that men constitute the vast majority of
U.S. prisoners, this finding is especially noteworthy. The effects of maternal imprisonment on children and families seem only likely to intensify, when we consider that women, particularly women of color, account for the fastest-growing
population in prison.

Recent studies of mass incarceration have detailed the challenges to reentry
that women offenders face, challenges that frequently result from policy changes
and political developments connected to the "War on Drugs" and the "War on
Crime." The growing arsenal of shorthand slogans for these policies is suggestive
of the ballooning rates of incarceration in which they are likely to result: "soft on
crime," "get tough," "three strikes," "zero tolerance," "mandatory minimums," "Do
the crime; do the time" are among the most familiar. Jonathan Simon also turns
his attention to the policies and politics that have fueled the engines driving mass
incarceration; unlike many who analyze this phenomenon, however, he discusses
the effects of such policies on the psychology of the public.

In "The 'Hard Back' of Mass Incarceration: Fear, Structural Racism, and
the Overpunishment of Violent Crime," Simon discusses the ways in which

the "fear of violent crime," uniting conservatives and liberals alike, has actually "animate[d] the larger cultural project of the "War on Drugs" and the "War on Crime."[28] This fear, he continues, not only intensifies the growing pressure to incarcerate, but also the pressure to mete out ever more punitive sentences for all crimes, regardless of their nature or severity. Those committing violent crimes in the United States—comprising the group that Simon terms the "hard back"—spend five to ten times as long in prison as do those committing such crimes in France. But for nonviolent offenders—forming the group that Simon terms the "soft underbelly"—the sentences, while "shorter," are no less extreme. Indeed, Simon argues, penalties for violent crimes provide a "reference price for crime that makes extreme but less severe punishments for other crimes seem appropriate." Simon makes it clear that because the "underbelly" and the "hard back" are symbiotically connected as "factors in the production of mass incarceration," the drug reduction strategies gaining increasing currency in debates about mass imprisonment hold limited promise for "decarceration efforts." At best, Simon continues, "the drug reduction strategy will produce an incarceration rate in America that is 25 to 45 percent lower than it is now, but that remains two or three times the norm for the twentieth century." Further, such excessive rates would do nothing to alter the intractable "racial imperative" of mass incarceration.[29]

Simon closes his essay by linking the racial imperatives of the penal system to spatial patterns of urban development. Drawing on the work of Mike Davis, Simon notes suggestively that mass imprisonment thrives alongside the middle-class flight to presumably "safer" and "crime-free" development zones and "gated communities," supposedly secure from the threat of the violent crime associated reflexively with inner cities. While Simon stops short of suggesting that "fear of crime" drove the middle class out of cities, he is not reluctant to note that the city is the site "where the relationship between mass imprisonment and structural racism is at its most salient." If the city is to be reborn, and mass imprisonment curbed, the gated-community mind-set, along with the residential patterns of racial segregation to which it gives rise, cannot be sustained.

## Race, Punishment, and the Aesthetic Imagination

The preceding sections of this volume have focused on various aspects of what Marlon Ross terms a "macro-narrative of the institutional, discursive, and historical development of the prison as an apparatus of state power or dominant ideology," as well as on the material consequences and forms of inequality resulting from mass imprisonment. In "Law and Dis/Order: The Banefully Alluring Arts of the Carceral Imaginary," included in section 3, Ross rightly suggests that such a focus, while necessary, can "easily eviscerate any sense of social agency on the part of prisoners." In various aspects, the two essays here seek to give voice to that agency, to document, notes Ross, "the ineradicable will" of the imprisoned to "create culture," which creations have historically had an impact palpably felt by those across the carceral divide.

No discussion of the place of prison in the aesthetic imagination would be complete without a consideration of music, which Claudrena Harold takes up in "'Rage against the Machine': African American Music and the Evolution of the Penitentiary Blues, 1961–2000." Harold looks at three critical historical stages: the civil rights era, the Black Power period, and the current age of mass incarceration, in each of which, she argues rightly, "music has . . . function[ed] as a critical site of protest against legal and extralegal forms of racial punishment." Musicians, especially blues singers, have used their music to protest the discriminatory policies of the criminal justice system. Lead Belly, Robert Johnson, Bessie Smith, Blind Lemon Jefferson, John Lee Hooker, among a host of others recorded music dominated by the thematics of prisons and prisoners. The enduring legacy of the penitentiary blues tradition can be found in the music of a range of contemporary musicians whose work gives voice to political communities frequently silenced within scholarly discourses that examine the racial politics of punishment. Indeed, notes Harold, such artists as Meshell Ndegeocello, Immortal Technique, dead prez, and the Roots have increasingly used their music to detail and challenge the racism embedded in mainstream discourses of criminology, within which black bodies—especially male bodies—are marked as "inherently and irredeemably criminal." But even as certain hip-hop artists reject this mass-mediated image, others can be charged with being complicit in the global marketing of African Americans as criminals.

While a range of musicians across the historical spectrum have sung the "penitentiary blues" in one form or another, Harold concludes by identifying one of the greatest challenges facing contemporary black musicians: to create "new systems of justice in the United States." To do so, they must be committed to mobilizing their communities to make meaningful changes at the level of public policy.

In "Law and Dis/Order: The Banefully Alluring Arts of the Carceral Imaginary," the second essay of section 3, Marlon Ross examines the global reach and cultural popularity of incarceration and "criminality" as marketable commodities. He makes the bold claim that the "profits of the incarceration industry are intimately tied to the profits of the carceral imagination." In other words, he continues, "the global mass media that profits on carceral imagery needs the prison industry to sell its wares."[30] The power and popularity of such imagery makes it virtually impossible to imagine any solution to the crisis of mass incarceration, for the "imagination itself has become structured through the carceral and its racially violent sexual seductions."

Ross goes on to remind us that, while the nature of incarceration is to erase the imprisoned as a collective body marked as deviant, different, and permanently fenced off "behind bars" from the nonincarcerated, in fact the lives of those supposedly "free" are subject to a markedly securitized way of life. In other words, every moment of existence for those who presumably roam unfettered outside prison walls is monitored or videotaped: "Whether on the street, in department stores, going through traffic lights in our cars, in airports, or in our homes—we are subject to a privatized security industry often subsidiary to the same companies marketing incarceration services for those 'behind bars.'" In other words, Ross concludes, those of us on the "outside" live in an attenuated version of the brutal regime directed against those on the "inside."

While Ross acknowledges that the dominant media play a major role in sustaining a "national culture of incarceration," this is but half of the question, he suggests. The other half must account for the impact of imprisonment and or prisoners on creative culture, a component noticeably absent from the national discourse. Reinforcing aspects of Harold's essay, Ross sees the importance of considering prisoners as "producers, creators, and interpreters of culture." He turns to the long tradition within African American writing that has either emerged from behind prison walls or has concerned itself with the experience and impact of incarceration, crime and punishment on black communities. Importantly, writers in this long tradition, which includes Claude McKay, Richard Wright, William Attaway, James Baldwin, Chester Himes, Eldridge Cleaver, George Jackson, Etheridge Knight, Bob Kaufman, Gayl Jones, among numerous others, deconstruct the "inside"/"outside" divide, which supposedly separates the imprisoned from the "free." Their work forms a counterpoint to the paradigm of ethnographic penology, which insists on preserving a carceral divide that does not hold. With great fluidity, this barrier continues to be worried and crisscrossed, binding together— though clearly not on equal terms—the imprisoned and the "free," who possess a "common culture across and despite the carceral divide."

## Life after Prison

Like other symposia sponsored annually by the Carter G. Woodson Institute, "The Problem of Punishment" in 2009 included a focus on matters with both historical and contemporary implications for the Commonwealth of Virginia. The final section in this volume thus includes interviews with Jim Shea, Eddie Harris, Debbie Walker, and Harold Folley—four citizens and three former inmates of the

Commonwealth. As we indicated at the outset, one of our objectives in compiling this volume was to involve former inmates in the process of contemplating the complexities and consequences of mass incarceration. Inasmuch as some of them participated in the symposium, we thought it only fitting that their voices be included here. Many of their observations corroborate the insights of other contributors who have detailed the effects of mass incarceration, not only on the inmates, but on their families and communities. As Jim Shea notes, former inmates, whom he describes as "state-certified victim[s] of discrimination for life," are tried and tried again in a "de facto kangaroo court" that says to ex-offenders: "you did your time, you paid your debt to society . . . but that's not good enough. We think you need to be punished further and so we consign you to the margins of society to live in poverty and you can take your children there with you, too, because, of course, if you can't get a job, your children suffer too, and this has a way of perpetuating, creating cycles, generational cycles."

Shea, along with Folley, Walker, and Harris, echo many other observations made by the contributors to this volume: that social policies play a strong hand not only in perpetuating cycles of incarceration but also in perpetuating forms of social and economic inequality. Each interviewee describes in one form or another being deprived of basic political rights, sometimes decades after completing their sentences, voting rights especially. High rates of felon disenfranchisement, as Vanessa Barker notes, are among "the most striking examples of [our] new political order. By denying many former and current inmates . . . the rights and duties of full citizenship, felon disenfranchisement excludes an entire class of people from the benefits of and commitments to a shared political community."[31]

While these interviews document such legalized forms of discrimination that track and "re-confine" ex-offenders, they clearly realize that merely documenting these realities is insufficient; they must simultaneously engage in various forms of collective organizing against mass incarceration and its effects. Both Harold Folley and Jim Shea are active in campaigns to restore voting rights to felons, and have recorded some successes on this front. Eddie Harris works with formerly incarcerated fathers to reconnect with their children from whom they've become estranged. Debbie Walker is similarly involved with helping female ex-offenders reconnect with their children. Walker describes the unique challenges women face as they seek to reenter communities already in crisis—substance abuse, family instability, underemployment—from the effects of mass incarceration. Collectively, these interviews point to the necessity of multiple interventions if the reverberating consequences of incarceration are to be reversed. Their postincarceration experiences provide examples of the kind of sustained action that can lead to change.

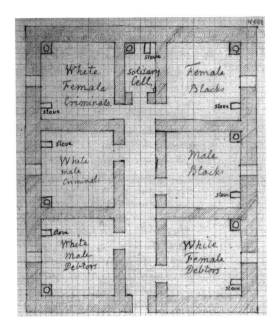

**Figure 1.**
Prison plan by Thomas Jefferson, with a cell for solitary confinement, undated. (Original manuscript from the Coolidge Collection of Thomas Jefferson Manuscripts, Massachusetts Historical Society; N488)

It is instructive to consider these interviews with former inmates against the broader context of the birth of the prison in Virginia. While historians consider Philadelphia's Walnut Street Jail (constructed in 1790) as the first prison in the United States, Virginia must figure centrally in any genealogy of the prison as an institution. As Paul Keve observes in *The History of Corrections in Virginia*, "In 1796 the creation of a penitentiary by the General assembly represented a radical new concept of how to promote a more humane society." In Keve's estimation, "If [Thomas] Jefferson had made no other impact on his state or nation, he would have been well worth remembering for his contribution to the profound redirection of Virginia's criminal code and the related inception of the penitentiary."[32] Jefferson acted as consultant and advisor to Benjamin Latrobe, who designed the first prison built in Virginia. Jefferson championed the construction of a state "penitentiary house" soon after the end of the Revolutionary War, but it was twenty years before Latrobe was hired in 1796 to design the building. Along with Pennsylvania, Virginia was among the first states credited with building "model prisons," in that convicts were sentenced, notes Caleb Smith, "to a discipline of penitence in solitary confinement."[33]

We include these obscure historical details, perhaps of interest only to historians and Jefferson scholars, because they form a contrast to what incarceration would go on to become in the Commonwealth and beyond. As the interviews plainly establish, whatever its original ambitions to "promote a more humane society" by "rehabilitating" inmates, the penitentiary has long since abandoned what Vanessa Barker terms "the rehabilitative ideal."[34] Instead, we have been in the iron grip of a decades-long "program of enhanced punishment," as Marc Mauer notes in his foreword to this volume. Executive Director of the Sentencing Project, Mauer offers a sobering reminder that the institutionalization of mass incarceration is the result of clear and traceable social policies and federal legislation. Like many contributors to this volume, he highlights the racial dynamics of mass incarceration, which are rooted in past and present forms of discrimination (particularly in housing), as well as economic decline. As Mauer notes, rampant globalization has produced a "decline in the United States' manufacturing economy[,] and its replacement in large part by a low-wage service economy" has hit urban communities of color particularly hard. "The union-wage jobs that previously enabled working-class blacks and whites to support a family have now frequently been replaced by non-union entry-level positions, with severe implications for family and community stability." Perhaps more sobering about Mauer's review of how we arrived here are his dismal predictions of the prospects for reversing course. As he notes, what "with police, prosecutors, judges, prison guards, and entire communities often dependent on the wages and presumed economic benefits of a vast criminal justice apparatus, there is great resistance to any proposed shift in course."

Perhaps this is the moment to recall Heather Thompson's essay in this volume, in which she discusses the movement of forces that contributed to the demise of this nation's first crisis of mass incarceration. As some readers are well aware, critical to the abolition of the convict leasing system, which factored significantly in the rapid expansion of the U.S. prison population during the Gilded Age and Progressive Era, were the collective engagements of such trade unions as the Knights of Labor, the American Federation of Labor, and the Industrial Workers of America. Convinced that the practice of hiring or leasing out prisoners had an adverse affect on the wage scale and working conditions of some of the nation's most vital industries, these labor bodies, along with other left-wing organizations, orchestrated remarkably successful campaigns against the convict lease system, which was abolished completely in 1923. Nearly forty years later, a coalition of activists affiliated with the civil rights movement, the Black Power revolt, and the New Left sought not only to eliminate the worst abuses of the criminal justice system, but also to raise fundamental questions about the moral and political legitimacy of legal punishment. On the litigation front, prison rights activists within and beyond the U.S. penal system engaged in successful legal battles that resulted in the passage of several important court cases that protected and extended the constitutional claims and rights of prisoners. The most notable among these cases are *Wolff v. McDonnell, Monroe v. Pape, Robinson v. California,* and *Morrissey v. Brewer.* Today, as federal and state budgetary concerns open lawmakers on both sides of the political aisle to the possibility of prison downsizing, contemporary activists committed to mass decarceration would do well to study closely the organizational lessons and theoretical insights of earlier generations of activists.

As noted throughout the volume, the institutional linkages and historical ties that bind our current political struggles to the past are many and varied. Necessarily then, scholars, activists, and ordinary citizens committed to creating an alternative system of justice must move with a deliberate sense of purpose and a keen sense of history. Here it is useful to bear in mind Vanessa Barker's observation that "societies make choices about how and why they punish, choices . . . bound up in changing historical conditions and cultural and political processes." Such choices are alterable. As Barker continues, "the history of American social movements tells us that sustained collective action that is strategic and morally pressing has successfully brought about radical social change in American public life."[35] We can only hope that such collective action, inspiration for the scholarly research in this volume, along with that to come, provides a road map for those striving to build not simply a new criminal justice system but also a more egalitarian world.

## Notes

1. Norval Morrison and David Rothman, eds., *Oxford History of the Prison: The Practice of Punishment in Western Society* (New York: Oxford University Press, 1995).

2. See Becky Pettit, *Invisible Men: Mass Incarceration and the Myth of Black Progress* (New York: Russell Sage Foundation, 2012).

3. Kim Gilmore, "Slavery and Prisons—Understanding the Connections: Critical Resistance to the Prison Industrial Complex," *Social Justice* 27, no. 3 (2000): 195; Angela Davis, *Are Prisons Obsolete?* (New York: Seven Stories Press, 2003), 12, 16. Discussions and definitions of the "prison industrial complex" date back to the early 1990s. The term commonly refers to what Eric Schlosser describes as a "set of bureaucratic, political, and economic interests that encourage increased spending on imprisonment, regardless of the actual need. . . . It is a confluence of special interests that has given prison construction in the United States a seemingly unstoppable momentum" (see Eric Schlosser, "The Prison Industrial Complex," *Atlantic,* December 1998, 3). See also Mike Davis, "A Prison Industrial Complex: Hell Factories in the Field," *Nation,* February 20, 1995, 229–34.

4. Angela Davis, "Surveillance, Imprisonment and the Quotidian Work of Race," keynote address at "The Problem of Punishment: Race, Inequality, and Justice," a symposium sponsored by the Carter G. Woodson Institute, April 16, 2009.

5. For discussions of the racialization of crime, see Angela Davis's *Are Prisons Obsolete?* See also Glenn C. Loury *Race, Incarceration, and American Values* (Cambridge: MIT Press,

2008); and Michelle Alexander, *The New Jim Crow: Mass Incarceration in the Age of Color-blindness* (New York: New Press, 2010)

6. As Robert Perkinson notes, the development of the prison has been influenced if not determined by the nation's "troubled history of racial conflict and social stratification" (Robert Perkinson, *Texas Tough: The Rise of America's Prison Empire* [New York: Henry Holt, 2010]).

7. Dorothy E. Roberts, "The Social and Moral Cost of Mass Incarceration in African American Communities," *Stanford Law Review* 56, no. 5 (April 2004): 1276.

8. To properly contextualize historians' growing interest in the racial politics of crime and punishment, one must consider developments within the historical profession and the larger society. In many ways, the United States' carceral boom has had a noticeable, and perhaps predictable, impact on the direction of historical writing. Indeed, several historians have acknowledged the ways in which the nation's "unprecedented experiment in mass incarceration" has informed their intellectual trajectory. Others have described their early encounters with the crime-and-punishment literature of the 1990s and credited it with solidifying in their minds the necessity of adopting not only a historical approach to the mass-incarceration crisis but also an approach sensitive to the inextricability of punishment and race. For example, in his recent study *Texas Tough: The Rise of America's Prison Empire*, Robert Perkinson writes: "In graduate school at Yale, I learned a great deal from this growing body of literature, but I felt increasingly dissatisfied. Many commentators agreed that race plays an important role in the justice system, but relatively few were making the entwined histories of criminal punishment and racial subjugation a central category of analysis. Fewer still carried the story further back than Barry Goldwater's 1964 presidential campaign, one of the first to make law and order a polarizing partisan issue" (4).

It should be noted that the analytical shortcomings and historical lacunae in the 1990s literature on the mass incarceration crisis were not the only factors in the upsurge in scholarship focused on the historical roots of the modern prison and the white-supremacist logics of the American judicial system. Other important factors included, but were not limited to: the mounting interest in black working-class history following the publication of Robin D. G. Kelley's *Race Rebels* and Tera Hunter's *To 'Joy My Freedom;* cultural and gender historians' increased emphasis on marginalized communities whose actions defied bourgeois notions of respectability; and scholars' shifting methodological approach to criminal justice matters, particularly their growing tendency to view 'crime' as a social prism through which to interrogate the worldview of marginalized populations.

9. Loïc Wacquant, "From Slavery to Mass Incarceration: Rethinking the 'Race Question' in the U.S.," *New Left Review* 13 (January-February 2002): 42. As Kim Gilmore notes, "African American prisoners have frequently used the language and narrative of slavery to describe the condition of their imprisonment" (see Kim Gilmore, "Slavery and Prisons—Understanding the Connections: Critical Resistance to the Prison Industrial Complex," *Social Justice* 27, no. 3 [2000]: 195). In a recent essay, the literary scholar Dennis Childs asserts that "the modern prison did not begin with Jeremy Bentham's panopticon, the Walnut Street Jail, or the Auburn system, but with the coffles barracoons, slave ships, and slave 'pens' of the Middle Passage" (see Dennis Childs, "'You Ain't Seen Nothin' Yet': *Beloved,* the American Chain Gang and the Middle Passage Remix," *American Quarterly* 61, no. 2 [June 2009]: 275). In "Maroon Abolitionists," Julia Sudbury argues that the "slavery/prison analogy tends to erase the presence of non-black prisoners" (*Meridians* 9, no. 1: 13).

10. See Gilmore, "Slavery and Prisons," 195.

11. See David M. Oshinsky, *"Worse Than Slavery": Parchman Farm and the Ordeal of Jim Crow Justice* (New York: Free Press, 1996).

12. See W. E. B. Du Bois, *Some Notes on Negro Crime, Particularly in Georgia* (Atlanta: Atlanta University Press), 11.

13. Khalil Gibran Muhammad, *The Condemnation of Blackness: Race, Crime, and the Making of Modern Urban America* (Cambridge: Harvard University Press, 2010), 3.

14. See W. E. B. Du Bois, "The Negro and Crime," *Independent* 51 (May 18, 1899), 1355–57; as well as "The Problem of Negro Crime," *Bulletin of Atlanta University,* February 1900; "Crime and Our Colored Population," *Nation,* December 25, 1902, 499); and *Some Notes on Negro Crime, Particularly in Georgia* (Atlanta: Atlanta University Press, 1904). For a discussion of Du Bois's research on the differential justice for Negroes and their over-representation in the statistics of prison populations in turn-of-the-nineteenth-century America, see Shaun L. Gabbidon, "W. E. B. Du Bois and the Atlanta School of Social Scientific Research, 1897–1931," *Journal of Criminal Justice Education* 10, no. 1: 21–38. See also the work of Du Bois's contemporaries in the field of sociology: Monroe Work, "The Negro and Crime," in *American Journal of Sociology* (1901); and Monroe Work, "Negro Criminality in the South," *Annals of the American Academy of Political and Social Sciences* 49 (1913): 74–80.

15. See Mary Ellen Curtin, *Black Prisoners and Their World, Alabama, 1865–1900* (Charlottesville: University Press of Virginia, 2000).

16. The literature linking past penal practices to those of the present is voluminous. Angela Davis has made much of this link. For example, in an interview by Avery Gordon, Davis observes that "the rampant exploitation of prison labor in an increasingly privatized context is a modern-day form of convict leasing" (see Avery Gordon, "Globalism and the Prison Industrial Complex: An Interview with Angela Davis, *Race and Class* 40 (1999): 154.

17. This essay is a slightly revised version of a chapter in Hicks's book-length study, *Talk with You Like a Woman: Urban Reform, Criminal Justice, and African American Women in New York, 1890–1935* (Chapel Hill: University of North Carolina Press, 2010). For further discussion of black women and criminal justice, also see Kali Gross, *Colored Amazons.*

18. Muhammad is one of few exceptions in this regard (see his *The Condemnation of Blackness,* 4).

19. Lewis Gordon, *Existentia Africana: Understanding Africana Existential Thought* (New York: Routledge University Press, 2000), 69.

20. For further discussion of this idea, see Caleb Smith's *The Prison and the American Imagination* (New Haven: Yale University Press, 2009). According to Smith, "the deepest allure of the prison as an object of inquiry is not its place in the history of crime and punishment, but its function as a central institution in modernity's redefinition of the human" (22).

21. The literature on the relationship between punishment and inequality is substantial. See Mary Patillo, David Weiman, and Bruce Western, *Imprisoning America: The Social Effects of Mass Incarceration* (New York: Russell-Sage Foundation, 2006); and Bruce Western, *Punishment and Inequality in America* (New York: Russell-Sage Foundation, 2006).

22. Bruce Western and Katherine Beckett, "How Unregulated Is the U.S. Labor Market? The Penal System as a Labor Market Institution," *American Journal of Sociology* 104, no. 4 (January 1999): 1031. As Western and Beckett note, racial disparities characterize

incarceration, particularly labor market inequality. Characterizing incarceration as a form of "hidden joblessness," they suggest that "sustained low unemployment in the future will depend on continuing expansion of the penal system" (1032, 1031). See also Bruce Western and Becky Pettit, "Incarceration: Racial Inequality in Men's Employment," *Industrial and Labor Relations Review* 54, no. 1 (October 2000).

23. See also Western and Pettit, "Incarceration: Racial Inequality in Men's Employment"; and Western and Beckett, "How Unregulated Is the U.S. Labor Market?"

24. Marc Mauer and Meda Chesney-Lind, eds. *Invisible Punishment: The Collateral Consequences of Mass Imprisonment* (New York: New Press, 2002).

25. Donald Braman, "Families and Incarceration," in *Invisible Punishment*, ed. Mauer and Chesney-Lind, 135. See also Dylan Rodriquez, who argues that "prison is less a 'destination' point for 'the duly convicted' than a point of massive human departure—from civil society, the free world, and the mess of affective social bonds and relations that produce varieties of 'human' family and community" (see *Forced Passages: Imprisoned Radical Intellectuals and the U.S. Prison* [Minneapolis: University of Minnesota, 2006], 227).

26. See Western, *Punishment and Inequality;* as well as Western's coauthored articles cited above. See also Devah Pager, *Marked: Race, Crime, and Finding Work in an Era of Mass Incarceration* (Chicago: University of Chicago Press, 2007).

27. See Marc Mauer and Meda Chesney-Lind, eds., *Invisible Punishment: The Collateral Consequences of Mass Imprisonment* (New York: New Press, 2002).

28. In discussing the "fear of crime," Simon builds on the work of Mike Davis in *The Ecology of Fear: Los Angeles and the Imagination of Disaster* (New York: Henry Holt, 1998), among others, including Angela Davis, who writes: "Fear has always been an integral component of racism. The ideological reproduction of a fear of black people, whether economically or sexually grounded, is rapidly gravitating toward and being grounded in a fear of crime. A question to be raised in this context is whether and how the increasing fear of crime—this ideologically produced fear of crime—serves to render racism simultaneously more invisible and more virulent" (see Angela Davis, "Race and Criminalization: Black Americans and the Punishment Industry," in *The House That Race Built: Black Americans, U.S. Terrain,* ed. Waneema Lubiano [New York: Pantheon, 1997], 269). See also Mumia Abu-Jamal, who writes "Any strategy that sees itself as challenging the prison-industrial complex must meet the pervasive and powerful fear industry—a convergence of economic, political and psychosocial interests" (see Mumia Abu-Jamal, "The Industry of Fear," *Social Text* 27, no. 3 [Fall 2000]: 23). See also Richard Delgado's discussion of the "social construction of threat" in "Rodrigo's Eighth Chronicle: Black Crime, White Fears—On the Social Construction of Threat," *Virginia Law Review* 80 (1994).

29. For more on this issue, see James Forman Jr., "Racial Critiques of Mass Incarceration: Beyond the New Jim Crow," *New York University Law Review* 21 (April 2012): 101–45.

30. Julia Sudbury points to the "plethora of economic interests [that] benefit from mass incarceration and the associated public obsession with crime and punishment. These include feature films and television shows, including MTV's latest Reality TV show featuring a first-time offender in a Texas prison, websites such as 'Prison Cam,' which includes video footage of women prisoners in Arizona, and products that cash in on the tough chic of the prison, from Prison Blues jeans to hip-hop videos that glamorize the 'thug life' inside" (see Julia Sudbury, "A World without Prisons: Resisting Militarism, Globalized

Punishment and Empire," *Social Justice* 31 [2004]: 9–30). See also Melissa Scrift's discussion of the circulation of prison art outside the penitentiary, which, she argues, "represents yet another example of contemporary popular culture's intrigue with criminality" (see Melissa Schrift, "Angola Prison Arts," *Journal of American Folklore* 119 [2006]: 258). Finally, Paul Wright discusses still other ways in which prison culture is marketed and sold for mass consumption. In Alpharetta, Georgia, men pay two thousand dollars to spend a weekend "in prison," being "abused, humiliated and mistreated." Wright also mentions the "latest fad among well-to-do homeowners and interior designers: stainless steel plumbing fixtures used in prison and jail and cells. Wright concludes that "by commodifying prison as pop culture, mass imprisonment is made socially acceptable and connected to blue jeans, theme parks, music, entertainment and resorts" (see Paul Wright, "The Cultural Commodification of Prisons," *Social Justice* 27, no. 3 [2000]: 17, 19).

31. See Vanessa Barker, *The Politics of Imprisonment: How the Democratic Process Shapes the Way America Punishes Offenders* (New York: Oxford University Press, 2009), 31. According to a report published by NAACP, 4 million Americans who have compleed prison sentences are ineligible to vote, 38 percent of whom are African American (see www.naacp.org/pages/defending-democracy). According to the Sentencing Project, 13 percent of African American men cannot vote due to criminal records, a rate seven times the national average (see www.sentencing project.org/detail/publication,cfm?publication id+15&id+131).

32. Paul Keve, *The History of Corrections in Virginia* (Charlottesville: University Press of Virginia, 1986), 7, 2.

33. Smith, The Prison and the American Imagination, 10. See also H. Bruce Franklin, "The Inside Stories of the Global American Prison," *Texas Studies in Literature and Language* 50 (Fall 2000): 238.

34 Barker, *The Politics of Imprisonment,* 7. Rehabilitation has been abandoned even for juvenile offenders. As more and more juveniles are being tried as adults and sentenced to life without parole, comments from Supreme Court Justice Antonin Scalia are telling. Writing for the majority in *Miller v. Alabama,* Justice Elena Kagan wrote to argue that "mandatory punishment [for juveniles] disregards the possibility of rehabilitation even when the circumstances most suggest it." This statement was meant to contradict Justice Scalia's quip during oral arguments of the case: "I thought that modern penology has abandoned that rehabilitation thing and they no longer call prisons reformatories" (see Liliana Segura, "Some Justice for Kids," *Nation,* July 16/23, 2012, 6).

35. Barker, *The Politics of Imprisonment,* 188.

# 1 Punishment in Historical Perspective

A genealogy of the contemporary prison regime awakens both the historical memory and the sociopolitical logic of the Middle Passage. The prison has come to form a hauntingly similar spatial and temporal continuum between social and biological notions of life and death, banal liberal civic freedom and totalizing unfreedom, community and alienation, agency and liquidation, the "human" and subhuman/nonhuman.

—DYLAN RODRIQUEZ

The overweening, defining event of the modern world is the mass movement of raced populations, beginning with the largest forced transfer of people in the history of the world: slavery. . . . The contemporary world's work has become policing, halting, forming policy regarding, and trying to administer the movement of people.

—TONI MORRISON

# "Please Hear Our Cries"

## The Hidden History of Black Prisoners in America

How should historians approach the history of the imprisoned, and how should the parameters of research be defined? A field largely dominated by social scientists, prison history remains fairly new terrain for historians who still seem to lack a central set of questions to explore or a methodology to employ. Is prison history the story of institutions or of convicts? When does it begin—at the moment of incarceration or the moment of arrest and trial? And when does it end—upon release or later? Should historians also attempt to trace the ripple effects of prison life on communities and families? What about the effects of prison on state and local economies, not to mention unemployment rates? From the perspective of convicts, how they became prisoners, and their life afterward, is as central to their story as their experiences as prisoners, but only rarely is this perspective included in institutional histories. Since the 1970s, detailed studies of African Americans, the law, vagrancy, peonage, and involuntary servitude have been penned by pioneering scholars such as Pete Daniel, William Cohen, Carl Harris, Mary Frances Berry, and Christopher Waldrep, to name but a few. Their work has transformed how scholars have come to understand the limits of emancipation, and the use of law as a tool of racial coercion.[1] Yet with some notable exceptions, the literature on modern prisons has tended to focus upon institutions; legal history, crime history, police history, and prison history remain largely separate fields of inquiry.[2]

Focusing on an individual's life story can illuminate the linkages in these fields. One person whose life demonstrates the complexity of American incarceration in the early twentieth century is a black Texan by the name of John Ed Patten. Patten's story includes a dubious conviction for attempted murder, a trial before a white jury, a rejected appeal, and then a lengthy sentence to work on sugar plantations operating under state control. He survived and was released back to his home in Houston, Texas, where he lived as a dealer in rags and junk. He refused to go to church, and most of his family regarded him as an eccentric loner. The one exception was his youngest granddaughter, to whom he remained particularly close until his death in the late 1950s. Patten's might seem a sad but unremarkable story were it not for the fact that this granddaughter grew up to be one of the greatest orators and best-known African American politicians of the twentieth century. Her name was Barbara Jordan, the first African American woman from the South elected to Congress. Her relationship with her grandfather, and his story of imprisonment, illuminates the tantalizing connections that undergird the hidden history of black prisoners in modern America.[3]

The legal enforcement of segregation in the South created a continuous tension between white police and black citizens that led to a lopsided number of black arrests and an overwhelmingly black prison population. And, as Patten's experience illustrates, African American victims of crimes found it nearly impossible to gain justice. At the time of his arrest in Houston in the spring of 1918, John Ed Patten was a thirty-nine-year-old migrant from rural east Texas. Married with three children, he owned a small shop in the city's Fourth Ward, a poor black neighborhood adjacent to the thriving, lively hub of downtown Houston. Patten was closing his store one evening when a stranger entered and took money from the register. Patten grabbed his gun, ran after the suspect, and chased him into the street. In the confusion, Patten was shot through his left hand. He picked up his weapon, took aim at a shadow, fired, and missed. Still, that misfire held dire consequences because the figure he shot at was a white police officer. Instead of chasing a criminal, Patten became the criminal: he was charged with attempted murder. The ordinary life of the man Barbara Jordan later knew as "Grandpa Patten" was turned upside down.[4]

Those in authority never seriously questioned Patten's intentions. They assumed that the white officer had been the store owner's intended target, even though Patten had no criminal record or motive. Enormous racial fear skewed judgment against him. It was well known that the police in Houston controlled black residents through humiliation, violence, intimidation, and arrests for petty crimes. But that pattern of power was momentarily disrupted during August 1917, when a fresh phalanx of black soldiers arrived at Camp Logan in Houston for training. These men had fought in Mexico; they were not from the South, and they were appalled at the rough treatment police meted out to black Houstonians and to black troops. One evening after the police had arrested and beaten a black woman and then also had arrested several black soldiers who had tried to intervene, 156 black soldiers responded with an unprecedented armed riot aimed at the local police. Four soldiers, four policemen, and a dozen civilians were killed in what the historian Robert Haynes called "a night of violence."[5] A total of nineteen black soldiers were executed.

The effect of the riot lingered, putting all black Houstonians under a cloud of suspicion. Several months later, John Ed Patten was arrested and tried; during the trial, his own victimization and even the injury to his left hand were ignored. His attorney and his witnesses could not persuade a white judge or jury that Patten had acted in self-defense and had not meant to harm the officer, let alone kill him. After a lengthy appeal, Patten received a ten-year sentence for attempted murder and was sent to a network of deadly state-run prison plantations to serve his time.

Patten entered the Texas prison system during a period of transition. After 1910, Texas began to phase out the convict-leasing system, in which prisoners were handed over to private contractors in exchange for revenue. This change began a route toward much-needed reforms. It is tempting to see the end of the leasing system as the start of something better. And yet, as Robert Perkinson has recently shown in his remarkable prison history *Texas Tough,* the Texas penitentiary system of the twentieth century set new standards in state-sanctioned cruelty.[6] Conditions remained uniquely bleak, especially for black and Mexican convicts, who were segregated to work on state-run plantations, mostly growing sugar for profit. Fewer guards and funds, a growing prisoner population, and the pressure to earn money led to new forms of institutionalized abuse and horror.[7] Physical force and torture were routine.

Despite the passage of new legislation that in theory limited working hours and improved treatment, the core of the old system in Texas remained intact well into the twentieth century. Racial segregation in prison was strengthened, and black prisoners remained at work in the fields. Guards were labor overseers as well as prison disciplinarians. They employed the "bat"—a long, thick leather whip—liberally and routinely. Prisoners rolled to fields "in cages mounted on flatbed trucks," shackled together by metal chokers fastened around their necks and legs attached by chains. Labor discipline depended on violence as "state authorities sought to wrest maximum exertion from convicts."[8] The workday began at sunup and ended at sundown. In Texas, state control of prisoners created an extensive network of prison plantations dedicated to keeping the largely black and Mexican labor force at work and under control for the least cost.[9]

Some of the worst abuse happened after the workday, when men were sent back to overcrowded shelters with dozens of bunks stacked close enough to touch. In these cramped "tanks," guards left the discipline to prison "tenders"— convicted men given the authority to rule. Tenders possessed weapons and exercised control through violence and rape. While the tenders established "order" inside, paid white prison guards stood outside and watched for escapees, who were summarily returned. Even the food was abysmal. At Ramsey State Prison Farm in 1927, a month of meals per prisoner cost the state $6.59, or 22 cents per day. Prisoners ate sow belly, peas, and spoiled cornbread. Slurry called stew—hard beans and moldy bread—was daily fare. The monotony and the filth spurred many riots over food, but such uprisings just encouraged more use of the bat. Brutal work, violence, humiliation, and fear characterized this system that remained largely unchallenged in its daily operations until the 1960s. After the end of leasing, according to Robert Perkinson, the lives of prisoners "scarcely changed—and sometimes for the worse."[10]

John Ed Patten survived. Between 1918 and 1924, he worked in a succession of four Texas sugar plantations. When he was pardoned, he returned to his home and family in downtown Houston. Sadly, his youngest son was dead, but his wife and daughters had earned a living by taking in boarders. John Ed began a fledgling business dealing in rags and junk, and looked on as his daughters grew up and married. He kept to himself until one gleam of hope entered his life: the birth of his granddaughter Barbara in 1936. The future congresswoman's first major attachment in life was to a man called a felon and an outcast by the outside world but who cared for her like no other person. "My mother tells me that she could leave me with him as a baby and I wouldn't whimper. . . . [S]o that attachment was formed at the beginning."[11]

John Ed Patten influenced Barbara Jordan in so many ways that it is difficult to imagine her character and personality without him. The rest of her family was extremely devout, while Patten never went to church. Jordan's father loved big cars and had many middle-class aspirations, but John Ed was frugal and valued his independence more than money. Jordan's mother and father wanted their daughters to be obedient and docile, but Grandpa Patten told her never to take a boss and to be skeptical of marriage. In their weekly talks in his junkyard, her grandfather's message, Barbara Jordan recalled, was overwhelmingly one of self-sufficiency. "Grandpa was saying the message of Jesus is: Don't get sidetracked and be like everybody else." The congresswoman's notably deep voice also bears traces of the older man's influence. Jordan's biographer, Shelby Hearon, observed Jordan as she described her memories of her Grandfather Patten. "Each time that Barbara recounts him, recreates him, brings his presence back into her own, the cadence and the timbre is what is known as 'the Barbara Jordan voice.' How did you learn to talk that way? At my grandfather's knee."[12] This ex-prisoner left a powerful legacy in his granddaughter.

Grandpa Patten's experiences also left Jordan to consider some hard truths about power and race in a nation that prided itself on its ideals. In her televised speech before the nation during the 1974 House Judiciary Committee's hearings on the Watergate scandal, Jordan forced the nation to recall that until recently, the rule of white supremacy always trumped the rule of law": "When that document [the Constitution] was completed on the seventeenth of September in 1787, I was not included in that 'we the people.'"[13] Jordan's limited understanding of her grandfather's ordeal brought home to her the violence endured by his generation. "I heard that he'd killed a white man," she said, "but I also know that back then he couldn't have killed a white man and lived. Now we know that. That would have been the end of him and I never would have known my grandfather."

Although privately Jordan felt proud of her grandfather, she was astute enough to know that she should not discuss his past with her parents. While she was a girl, her family never spoke about her grandfather's ordeal; the veil of secrecy and shame prevented a candid discussion of his alleged crime or his time in prison. When Jordan was a student, her grandfather stumbled over a railroad track while in a drunken haze and a train cut off his legs. He soon died, and she never learned the truth about his prison past until she became an adult. "There are some things about him I never got straight. I heard at one point that he'd been to prison. Not from my mother and father, no. But that's what I say; I just pick up these little things from various people." The stigma of Grandpa Patten's imprisonment and the gravity of his transgressions against white supremacy were so severe that the fact of his innocence simply became lost. Jordan reflected: "More recently I heard that he never killed anybody, that he shot at a white man. I don't know who's changing the real story."[14]

### Impediments to the "Real Story"

If we want to know the "real story" of men and women like John Ed Patten who were detained by white police officers, sentenced under Jim Crow laws, and incarcerated in segregated prisons, then deeply ingrained prejudices against those who have been convicted of crimes must be overcome. Shedding this prejudice is harder than it sounds. Prison history (as distinct from sociology) as a field has recently begun to come into its own, but it has eluded the profession, in part because prisoners are still stigmatized, even by their own families, and prison reformers—and historians—can easily be mischaracterized as the naïve defenders of guilty criminals. Historians cannot help but be defensive about their intellectual and ethical interest in the lives and fates of the unfree.[15] For most of the twentieth century, prejudice against African American prisoners was overwhelming and negative. African Americans were thought to be inherently immoral, and black prisoners doubly so. In the Progressive Era, criminals of all races were condemned as moral failures, and black prisoners suffered double ignominy.[16] Matthew Mancini has noted in his recent introduction to the prison classic *I Am a Fugitive from a Georgia Chain Gang* that, despite the popularity of the Hollywood film in the 1930s and the plethora of prison testimony and evidence about prison abuses, a massive outcry for reform never really occurred [17] The shame of being "unfree" in a free society remains enormous, and the stigma often comes from imprisonment, not from the crime.[18]

Another impediment to uncovering prison history is the fragmented nature of the sources. The prosecution of crime and punishment has been left largely in the hands of the states. It is true that state records contain many rich and detailed sources for studying imprisonment in the North and South. But it is also the case that the sheer volume of the material available at the state level makes a comparative or national approach daunting for a single scholar. As long as the best prison sources are state sources, it will be difficult for historians to get out of the narrow bind of state studies and address bigger questions with a more creative narrative. A plethora of state studies has presented numerous snapshots of the prison landscape, but how these works add up to a national picture that incorporates the full range of prison experiences in both the nineteenth and twentieth centuries remains unclear.[19]

A focus on institutional history has also hidden the experiences of prisoners. Since the late nineteenth century, state and federal penitentiaries have operated as fairly insular systems of control. Institutional decorum, as well as the nature of the documents, protected the bureaucracy in charge. Too often, American prison history has been presented as a chronicle of the evolution and reform of institutions. But as the historian Rebecca McLennan has shown, from their beginnings, prison institutions have been in perpetual crisis, a crisis that cannot be measured merely in terms of cycles of reform.[20] Of course, U.S. prisons have experienced their share of riots and uprisings, but historically the crisis has long been rooted in a disjunction between what prisons purport to do and how they actually operate. In the South especially, a gap loomed between the "official" story of reform and the "real" story of brutality. Prison bureaucracies kept records that preserved selected data such as the number of incarcerated individuals, their names, dates of birth, illnesses, deaths, and locations of trials, but they rarely show life as it was lived in prison. The political and financial pressures of running these ever-burgeoning institutions led to institutional opacity occasionally pierced by legislative investigations or muckraking. Still, however the reality deviated from their stated purpose, prisons endured. Now more than ever, the history of American prisons demands that the cries of the imprisoned be heard alongside those of their keepers.

### Overcoming a Fractured Past: The Papers of the NAACP

The papers of the National Association for the Advancement of Colored People (NAACP) entitled "Discrimination in the Criminal Justice System, 1910–1955" constitute one set of sources with the potential to allow a researcher to step back and focus on a broader, national picture of the prison experience, one not constrained by state limitations, bureaucratic niceties, race prejudice, or the artificial divorce between the courtroom experience and prison.[21] These documents provide a regional mix of evidence that allows a broad national picture during segregation to emerge. The papers consist of a variety of documents including court cases taken up by the NAACP as well as those cases the organization rejected; letters of urgency and complaint directed to the organization from prisoners throughout the nation, newspaper clippings detailing the imperfect workings of the justice system, and various and sundry correspondence from African Americans throughout the United States in trouble with the law. A snapshot of multifaceted conflicts faced by African Americans as they rubbed up against the criminal justice system, these documents show them escaping from prison, fleeing the threat of lynching, in trouble with the law, searching for lawyers, and as victims of police brutality.[22] Black prisoners and their advocates believed they had an ally in the NAACP, and the organization took their complaints seriously. Because of its inadequate budget and its operation under extreme political duress, however, the NAACP had to make difficult choices concerning how best to use its resources. While the complaints of the incarcerated often could not be addressed, they still made their mark on the early NAACP leaders.

In these documents, prisoners often emerge as the sanest voices in a corrupt, racist penitentiary system. State officials were more concerned with the appearance of compliance and legitimacy than with the truth of mismanagement and the realities of prison brutality. But prisoners were determined that their experiences be known. A letter smuggled out of Ramsey State Prison Farm in 1937 and sent to the NAACP described the terror inflicted on men by prison tenders at Ramsey, the same prison farm in Texas where John Ed Patten served time.

> To the NAACP: Please hear our cries. We are prisoners in the Texas State prison located on Ramsey Farm Camp #1. We are Negroes. Here as follows are some true facts which we are asking you all to investigate please. These officials are sure cruel to us. We have in each building two prisoners as building tenders they is allowed to kill you if they see fit. They have whips with iron handles and dirks knives. Each one of these building tenders are first grade students and they will do what the captains and guards tell them. On this camp No. 1, Otey Texas, Ramsey Farm, last year July 28th 1936 Boss JS Leigh the boss on building picket told Booker Smith to kill Dave Lamar. So he did stab him to the heart. It was claimed in self defense.[23]

From Florida, Texas, and Georgia, prisoners wrote to the NAACP to complain of torture in "Sweat boxes," whippings, and unlawful deaths. Witnesses to torture in Ramsey Prison in Texas wrote the following account to the NAACP:

a Negro convict was handcuffed and chained his hand also with a ¼ inch chain. This chain was fastened to this prisoner's feet and around his neck pulling his neck down to his knees he was made to sit on the concrete floor and this building tender Booker Smith whip this prisoner to death. This prisoner was James Brown. . . . Each night some poor prisoner are whip by the building tender unmerciable. This are the true things are now going on and the rules of the prison system don't allow it but that only a sham.

Prisoners kept careful accounts of the abuses meted out to them. In a letter from a camp in Valdosta, Georgia, JB Reynolds wrote: "Work till sundown, then on top of that they whip JB . . . he told the captain that he was tired and worn out they whip him with a stick of wood 3 feet × 4 long and 1 and ½ or 2 inches round. . . . I have been whip 14 times since 1930. I knows the date and month of every time they whip me.[24] Another letter from Jacksonville, Florida, complained of the poor treatment of women prisoners, segregation, and brutal beatings. The Raiford camp was described as "the worse place on earth."

Torture and beatings were hardly limited to the South. In 1929, the police commissioner of New York City denied that his officers used the "third degree" on suspects, but he did admit that police in New York beat suspects with nightsticks filled with lead. One complainant against police brutality felt outraged at such admissions, but also defensive: "I want no flowers or cream puffs for crime. Men who violate the law are not entitled to anything except fair conviction." However, the writer continued:

For policemen to take a man of whom they have no proof of his guilt but only suspicion and put him into a room and there pound him with clubs or keep him awake
and weary for hours in order to make him confess that he is guilty; cover his face
with a cap so he cannot see who is mauling him, that I say is the most cowardly and
damnable action that decent language can describe. . . . This "third degree" business
is making more criminals than it stops. It crystallizes the criminals' feeling against
the police and society. It hardens the innocent into contempt for a system that
violates his fundamental rights.[25]

The widespread nature of these complaints suggests that these acts of torture were sanctioned by criminal justice institutions in the North and South, and were not just the work of rogues.

Similarly, in the South, convicts were beaten as a matter of labor discipline and tortured to satisfy the primitive feelings of guards and prison tenders alike. During the 1880s, Alabama guards used "water torture": "A prisoner was strapped down on his back"; then "water was poured in his face on the upper lip, and effectually stops his breathing as long as there is a constant stream." Whipping was common, and often became torture. "I know we whopped niggers just to have fun," recalled a guard from an Alabama prison mine in the early twentieth century. "We'd pull their britches off and strop em across the Barr'l by their hands and feet so they couldn't move and then we'd lay it on em with a leather strop." Torture also included chaining men in awkward positions and lowering them into boiling water or sweat boxes. Some inmates were even murdered.

In Alabama, Ezekiel Archey wrote that he witnessed his mine boss "hit men 100 and 160 [times] with a ten prong strap and say they was not whipped. He would go off after an escaped man come one day with him and dig his grave the same day." Testimony from other southern states contains similar stories, leading Matthew Mancini to the rightful conclusion that the "distinction between punishment and torture started to blur" and was often nonexistent.[26] The outrage such torture provoked, and the actions taken by prisoners and others to subvert it, reflect not only a healthy sanity, but the seeds of a belief in justice that even the worse circumstances could not unhinge or lever out. Prisoners' consciousness of the immorality of torture is as much a part of the historical record as the abuse itself, and it deserves attention.

In the face of such evidence of torture, the NAACP took the controversial moral stance that the state had no right to engage in such practices against prisoners. In 1937, Thurgood Marshall reminded the governor of Texas that he should condemn the torture and murder happening under his watch: "We cannot too strongly urge upon you the seriousness of such offenses which, even though committed by persons in charge of a prison, are, nevertheless, brutal murders."[27] As at the Abu Ghraib prison in Iraq, this was not a case of a few rotten apples. The apple barrel was broken. The evidence suggests that torture was regularly practiced in American prisons. Such torture was not the work of extremists but a matter of institutional policy and practice. Historical research must investigate the details and implications of the uncomfortable truth that torture in prison was everyday fare.

The NAACP met with some success in convincing judges not to return prison runaways to the South because those accused were sure to meet with lynching, if not death. For a while, the NAACP focused on these extradition cases as both symbolic and substantive inroads into exposing the racism of Jim Crow justice in the South. For some individuals who had nowhere else to run, the organization made a difference. The NAACP represented in court only a few individuals from southern states who had fled the scene of a crime or who had escaped from a southern prison because of the fear of being lynched. They enjoyed a few victories. For example, in 1928, the organization prevented four extraditions on the grounds that the victims could be lynched if they returned.[28] The NAACP also became interested in police brutality, and took up several cases in Miami, Cincinnati, and

Jersey City.[29] Such victories, however, could not aid the quietly desperate majority of plaintiffs as they confronted the legal system and a return to southern justice.

At times, NAACP officials felt overwhelmed at the numbers of people who wrote to them, and were thus compelled to explain that the organization was not a "legal aid" society. They agreed to look at cases only where the person involved was unquestionably innocent. Hearsay from other attorneys would not suffice, for the organization did not want to be in the position of defending the guilty.[30] Over a dozen boxes of "cases rejected" files from all major states, including Florida, Texas, and New York, represented runaways from southern courts desperate for legal counsel.[31] Those boxes that remain in the record represent only a fraction of the complaints the organization received. These legal records could reveal many clues to the underside of black history under segregation, but the NAACP made the practical decision to act only where a legal challenge promoted the greater cause of antilynching.

While the NAACP could answer only a fraction of the petitions they received, the organization felt frustrated at the lack of public outrage concerning how individuals were treated in southern prisons. These documents show public indifference to prison conditions, even when the victims were white men. NAACP lawyers thought about using these cases to arouse public awareness. To that end, Charles H. Houston wrote to the NAACP's board of directors on October 11, 1937, suggesting that the organization sponsor a speaking tour by Paul Smith, the brother of the white man whose story was immortalized in the 1930s film *I Am a Fugitive from a Georgia Chain Gang.* Smith had escaped from a chain gang in Georgia and made his way to New York, where he was arrested and returned to Georgia. Houston thought this case might generate some controversy and tentatively suggested that Rev. Vincent Burns (Smith's brother and a popular minister) go on a preliminary speaking tour to see what "financial returns" might come from audiences. But the northern public failed to express any outrage about the conditions in southern prisons, even when the victims were white. Unfortunately, the NAACP's effort to link prison abuse to fund-raising strategies or public education campaigns did not attract the kind of positive responses or, for that matter, the kind of revenues the young organization needed to survive.[32] While the organization remained concerned with the issue of prison conditions, without revenue it could not continue to pursue the numerous court cases that came its way.

### Racism in the Courts and in Prison

There is no question that after emancipation the legal treatment of newly freed blacks and southern whites diverged dramatically. This difference, which began

with the Black Codes passed in southern states during "presidential reconstruction," continued long after the Fourteenth and Fifteenth Amendments to the
U.S. Constitution became law. The willingness of state appeals courts and the
Supreme Court to sanction racist treatment, despite the Equal Protection Clause
of the Fourteenth Amendment, and the Fifteenth Amendment's protection of the
black vote, had a major impact on how blacks were treated by law enforcement on
the ground. Blacks were far more likely than whites to be arrested, and far more
likely to be sent to prison to work. The extremes of this situation beggar belief. For
example, it is a known fact that thousands of black southerners were lynched in
this era, yet between 1877 and 1966, only one white man in Georgia was ever convicted of murdering an African American. In Alabama, over 90 percent of all state
prisoners and nearly 100 percent of county prisoners were African Americans.
"Everybody knows that the great bulk of convicts in the state are Negroes," stated
a future U.S. senator from Alabama, James Thomas Heflin, and "everybody knows
that there is no punishment in the world that can take the place of the lash with
him. He must be controlled in that way."[33] Numbers of similar disproportion, and
reflecting similar attitudes, could be found in the prisons of every southern state.

Despite gaps in the narrative, the southern story is better documented than
the northern and western legal attitudes toward African Americans. Evidence
suggests more similarities than differences in the racist practices of the regions.
One example from the NAACP files involves the case of a black man accused in
the winter of 1921 of murdering a New Jersey "choir girl" walking home from
church one evening. Local newspapers fanned the flames of public outrage by
running stories about the accused's sexual license with French women during
World War I. Threats to lynch the man were accompanied by descriptions bestial-
izing his appearance. The arrested man, one paper reported, "has [the] frame of a
gorilla. . . . He is a gorilla-like black if there ever was one." Only death would ap-
pease the public. The paper reported that the accused was to be "indicted Friday,
tried Monday, then walked to Chair."[34] Time and again, the NAACP was asked to
confront the reality of racism perpetuated by northern and western lawmakers
and police. For example, when the NAACP tried to collect factual information
from local law enforcement officials concerning the number of African Americans convicted of rape, one sheriff wrote back from Hardin, Illinois, to say "none"
since "we have no colored people in this county, they are not allowed here."[35]
Clearly, "the law" in the North practiced its own forms of white supremacy that
still need to be discerned and investigated in greater detail.

In addition to showing how deeply segregation pervaded the prison experience in the North, the NAACP Papers also show the gendered dimension to institutionalized prison racism. For example, it has long been noted that prison rein-

scribed gender inequality within the institutional setting, but racial segregation in prisons reinforced old racial hierarchies among women. For example, in one New York prison, white women received training and kind treatment, but black women were given no job training whatever, on the assumption that domestic work befitted their station in life, whether inside or outside prison. The NAACP gathered evidence that a female juvenile corrections facility in New York practiced blatant racial discrimination and segregation, and forced black women to wash the clothes of the white women inmates. They took the case straight to the governor.[36] Change did come eventually in this instance, but the case highlighted the lack of institutional oversight.

These cases establish nothing more profoundly than that organizations such as the NAACP faced tremendous burdens. It bears asking how one group could take up the plight of poor black defendants, argue the causes of the incarcerated, point out the illegality of police and prison brutality, and still be an effective lobbying and activist organization on behalf of civil rights? The larger point is not the limited efficacy of the NAACP (they did what they could) but the sheer number of people trapped within the legal system who needed help.

**Prisoners and Resistance**

Finally, it is neither redundant nor prosaic to use these papers to examine the humanity of prisoners and criminal defendants, as well as their resistance to efforts to dehumanize them. These documents suggest how prisoners themselves interpreted their status and their rights, and the steps they took to gain recognition from prison officials and from sympathizers on the outside. For example, one prisoner sent a letter to the NAACP from Parchman requesting an antilynching button. Historians need to mark such simple yet bold acts of defiance. Prisoners' letters of protest and complaint, and their insistence that torture was wrong, are important to record as such accounts constitute key pieces of evidence about the reality of prison life that contradict the official story of American innocence in these matters.[37] Indeed, historians of the prison need to revisit the theme of American innocence. The current shock over torture at Abu Ghraib led to much outrage because of the myth that, prior to these events, American prisons never tortured their inmates. One scholar summarized the thoughts that led him to write a lengthy analysis of torture at the Iraqi prison: "This is the United States of America[:] we are not supposed to do this." But he had to conclude that what happened at Abu Ghraib was an example of "systematic sadism."[38]

Documents and stories that provide flashes of insight showing these men and women at work, at play, in fear, or in danger call upon us to come to grips with deep and persistent prejudices against the incarcerated. A valuable topic of scholarly inquiry, such prejudice demands that we ask, for example, why lawbreakers who were never incarcerated garner respect and book deals, but the incarcerated (innocent or guilty) garner nothing but suspicion and shame? For example, the literary agent Bill Clegg recently received a $350,000 advance and plaudits in the *New York Times* for *Portrait of an Addict as a Young Man,* his memoir of crack addiction and solicitation of prostitutes. However, since he was never imprisoned for the crime of purchasing and consuming crack cocaine, he remains a free, employed, well-off, and sympathetic citizen.[39]

To be sure, prison history cannot be about historians rescuing the "humanity" of prisoners, for of course they are human. Nevertheless, criminal acts that lead to incarceration tend to make the public uneasy with scholarship or policy shifts that suggest the "unfree" might have something to tell us about our legal and criminal institutions. The historian Walter Johnson cautions against using evidence of ordinary human behavior on the part of slaves to simply mark the humanity of oppressed historical subjects and nothing more.[40] Historians should not call every ordinary act of enslaved men and women "resistance" and think that their work is done. The same is true of prison history. The situation of incarcerated men and women before, during, and after their imprisonment is often too complex to express with single words such as "guilty" or "innocent." Nevertheless, if Johnson is correct in suggesting that the stigma against slaves has been sufficiently lifted so that their humanity cannot be questioned, the same cannot be assumed of prisoners. As recent studies described in this volume show, the stigma of criminality remains and continues to have far-reaching implications not only for policy, but for how we see the prison past. Engaging in prison history and taking seriously the complaints and eyewitness accounts of prisoners from the past are key to dismantling the prejudices that still exist against the "unfree" in our free society, and that prevent us from uncovering what remains a largely hidden history of African American prisoners in America.

That hidden history has many untold and unknown influences in our shared past that need to be uncovered and known. At first glance, the story of Barbara Jordan would appear to have nothing to do with the unseemly topic of prisons, torture, and racism in the courts. Her history might be assumed to be simply that of a bright young black woman who broke race and sex barriers to prevail as a pioneer in American politics. But prison history seems to relate to almost every important aspect of African American history, and Jordan's case is no exception. Despite my best efforts to leave prison research behind me, the history of Jordan's own family and John Ed Patten drew me back. Jordan's history, and the nation's, demands a narrative that includes all of the facts of her family's past, even if those facts contradict cherished assumptions about how prisons and the law operated under segregation.

## Notes

1. Pete Daniel, *The Shadow of Slavery: Peonage in the South, 1901–1969* (Chicago: University of Illinois Press, 1972); Mary Frances Berry, *Black Resistance, White Law: A History of Constitutional Racism in America* (1971; New York: Penguin, 1995); William Cohen, *At Freedom's Edge: Black Mobility and the Southern White Quest for Racial Control, 1861–1915* (Baton Rouge: Louisiana State University Press, 1991); "Negro Involuntary Servitude in the South, 1865–1940: A Preliminary Analysis," *Journal of Southern History* 42, no. 1 (February 1976): 31–60; Carl V. Harris, "Reforms in Government Control of Negroes in Birmingham, Alabama, 1890–1920," *Journal of Southern History* 38, no. 4 (November 1972): 567–600; Leon Litwack, *Trouble in Mind: Black Southerners in the Age of Jim Crow* (New York: Knopf, 1998); Christopher Waldrep, *Roots of Disorder: Race and Criminal Justice in the American South, 1817–1880* (Champaign: University of Illinois Press, 1998).

2. There are several recent studies that emphasize the intersection of racist legal practices with incarceration, as well as the detrimental effects of prison on families, communities, the economy, and individual constitutional protections. See Michelle Alexander, *The New Jim Crow: Mass Incarceration in the Age of Color Blindness* (New York: New Press, 2010); Heather Thompson, "Why Mass Incarceration Matters: Rethinking Crisis, Decline, and Transformation in Postwar American History," *Journal of American History* 97, no. 3 (2010): 703–34; Douglass Blackmon, *Slavery by Another Name: The Re-Enslavement of African Americans from the Civil War to World War II* (New York: Anchor, 2009). See also Donald G Nieman, *Black Southerners and the Law, 1865–1900* (New York: Garland, 1994); Gail O'Brien, *The Color of the Law: Race, Violence, and Justice in the World War II South* (Chapel Hill: University of North Carolina Press, 1999); and Leon Litwack, *Trouble in Mind,* who approach the question of race and imprisonment from an angle wholly missing in classic prison histories such as Blake McKelvey's *American Prisons: A History of Good Intentions* (Montclair, N.J.: P. Smith, 1977).

3. Barbara Jordan and Shelby Hearon, *Barbara Jordan: A Self-Portrait* (New York: Doubleday, 1975).

4. Ibid., 13–24.

5. Robert V. Haynes, *A Night of Violence: The Houston Riot of 1917* (Baton Rouge: Louisiana State University Press, 1976), 83–89.

6. Robert Perkinson, *Texas Tough: The Rise of America's Prison Empire* (New York: Henry Holt, 2010), 179–90, 132–76.

7. Paul M. Lucko, "The Governor and the Bat: Prison Reform during the Oscar B. Colquitt Administration, 1911–1915," *Southwestern Historical Quarterly* 106, no. 3 (January 2003): 396–417; Paul M. Lucko, "A Missed Opportunity: Texas Prison Reform during the Dan Moody Administration, 1927–1931," *Southwestern Historical Quarterly* 96, no. 1 (July 1992): 27–52; Gary Brown, *Texas Gulag: The Chain Gang Years, 1875–1925* (Plano: Republic of Texas Press, 2002); Donald M. Walker, *Penology for Profit: A History of the Texas Prison System, 1867–1912* (College Station: Texas A&M University Press, 1988).

8. Perkinson, *Texas Tough*, 158–76, 179; Jordan, *Self-Portrait*, 29.

9. Theresa R. Jack, "'It's Hell in a Texas Pen': Life and Labor in the Texas Prison System, 1849–1929" (Ph.D. diss., University of Houston, Department of History, 2009), chaps. 6 7.

10. Perkinson (*Texas Tough*, 242–46) and Jack ("It's Hell in a Texas Pen," chap. 7) describe the "building tender" system. *Annual Report of the Texas Prison Board of the Texas Prison System, Fiscal Year ending Dec. 31, 1927*; Jordan, *Self-Portrait*, 20–21.

11. Jordan, *Self-Portrait*, 3.

12. Ibid., 10–11; Jordan interview by Hearon, Shelby Hearon Papers, Box 3, Folder 11, Ransom Center, University of Texas at Austin.

13. A full text and audio of Barbara Jordan's July 25, 1974, address to the House Judiciary Committee calling for the impeachment of Richard Nixon can be found at www .americanrhetoric.com/speeches/barbarajordanjudiciarystatement.htm.

14. Shelby Hearon Papers, Box 3, Folder 11, Harry Ransom Humanities Research Center, University of Texas at Austin.

15. Perkinson, introduction to *Texas Tough*; Michelle Alexander, introduction to *The New Jim Crow: Mass Incarceration in the Age of Colorblindness* (New York: New Press, 2010), 1–19.

16. For a typical article attempting to dislodge racist views of incarceration during the Progressive Era, see Otis D. Duncan, "An Analysis of the Population of the Texas Penitentiary from 1906 to 1924," *American Journal of Sociology* 36, no. 5 (March 1931): 770–81. Thomas Gossett, *Race: The History of an Idea in America* (New York: Schocken, 1965); Mary Ellen Curtin, *Black Prisoners and Their World: Alabama, 1865–1900* (Charlottesville: University Press of Virginia, 2000), 168–69; Khalil Gibran Muhammad, *The Condemnation of Blackness: Race, Crime, and the Making of Modern Urban America* (Cambridge: Harvard University Press, 2010).

17. Matthew Mancini, introduction to *I Am a Fugitive from a Georgia Chain Gang*, by Robert Burns (Athens: University of Georgia Press, 1997).

18. See, for example, the May 28, 2010, *New York Times* article about the literary agent Bill Clegg, who recently received a $350,000 advance and plaudits in the *New York Times* for *Portrait of an Addict as a Young Man*, his memoir of crack addiction and solicitation of prostitutes.

19. Recent state-based studies of convict leasing include Curtin, *Black Prisoners and Their World*; Alex Lichtenstein, *Twice the World of Free Labor: The Political Economy of Convict Labor in the American South* (London: Verso, 1996); Matthew Mancini, *One Dies, Get Another: Convict Leasing in the American South, 1866–1928* (Columbia: University of South Carolina Press, 1996); Karen Shapiro, *A New South Rebellion: The Battle against Convict Labor in the Tennessee Coalfields, 1871–1896* (Chapel Hill: University of North Carolina Press, 1998); Martha Meyers, *Race, Labor, and Punishment in the New South* (Columbus: University of Ohio Press, 1998); David Oshinsky, *Worse Than Slavery: Parchman Farm and the Ordeal of Jim Crow Justice* (New York, Free Press, 1996); Donald Walker, *Penology for Profit: A History of the Texas Prison System, 1867–1912* (College Station: Texas A&M Press, 1988); Vivien Miller, *Crime, Sexual Violence, and Clemency: Florida's Penal Board and Penal System in the Progressive Era* (Gainesville: University Press of Florida, 2000); and Talitha LeFlouria, "'The Hand that Rocks the Cradle Cuts the Cordwood': Exploring Black Wom-

en's Lives and Labor in Georgia's Convict Camps, 1865–1917," LABOR 8, no. 3 (2011): 47–63.

20. Rebecca McLennan, *The Crisis of Imprisonment: Protest, Politics and the Making of the American Penal State, 1776–1941* (Cambridge: Cambridge University Press, 2008).

21. Papers of the National Association for the Advancement of Colored People (NAACP; hereafter cited as NAACP Papers), Part 8, "Discrimination in the Criminal Justice System, 1910–1955," Manuscript Division, Library of Congress.

22. Ibid.

23. NAACP Papers, Group I, Box C280, f. 1.

24. JB Reynolds to the NAACP, September 29, 1936, NAACP Papers, Group 1, Box C279, f. 8

25. Clipping from *Yonkers Herald*; Dr. Alvah S. Hobart, letter, April 8, 1929, NAACP Papers, Group I, C265, f. 2; *New York World*, March 16, 1921, NAACP Papers, Group I, C265, f. 11.

26. Curtin, *Black Prisoners and Their World*, 69, 166–67; Mancini, *One Dies, Get Another*, 75.

27. Thurgood Marshall to James V. Alfred, Governor of Texas, July 31, 1937, NAACP Papers, Group I, Box C28, f. 1

28. The cases involved extraditions from Ohio to Mississippi; Montana to Alabama; and Michigan to Florida (NAACP Papers, Group I, Series C265, f. 1).

29. A typical press release dated March 8, 1929, is entitled, "Police Shoot Negroes in 2 Cities: N.A.A.C.P. Asking Justice" (NAACP Papers, Group I, C265, f. 1; and Group I, C265, f. 2).

30. NAACP Papers, Group I, Series C265, f. 1.

31. NAACP Papers, Group I, Series D, Boxes 26–40, "Cases Rejected, 1919–1939."

32. Charles H Houston to Board of Directors of the NAACP, October 11, 1937, NAACP Papers, Group I, C279, f. 10.

33. Blackmon, *Slavery by Another Name*, 122.

34. NAACP Papers, Group I, C265, f. 11.

35. NAACP Papers, Group I, C265 f. 12.

36. Marshall E Ross, M.D., to Walter White, July 14, 1936, and May 22, 1938; Ross to Governor Herbert Lehman, July 18, 1936, NAACP Papers, Group I, C279, f. 12 and f. 13.

37. Ennis Carter, Parchman, Mississippi, March 25, 1937, NAACP Papers, Group I, C279, f. 10.

38. James P. Pfiffner, *Torture as Public Policy: Restoring U.S. Credibility on the World Stage* (Boulder and London: Paradigm, 2010), vii.

39. *New York Times*, May 28, 2010.

40. Walter Johnson, "On Agency," *Journal of Social History* 37, no. 1 (2003): 113–24, 114.

# From Researching the Past to Reimagining the Future

*Locating Carceral Crisis and the Key to Its End,*

*in the Long Twentieth Century*

HEATHER ANN THOMPSON

By the first decade of the twenty-first century, the United States found itself in an unimaginable incarceration crisis. As the new millennium dawned, this country was locking up more of its citizens than any other country on the globe. By 2010, more than 7 million Americans had become trapped in the criminal justice system and more than 2 million of them were actually living behind bars. African Americans suffered this turn to mass incarceration most dramatically. Indeed, with one in nine black men aged twenty to thirty-four eventually imprisoned in America, as Lawrence Bobo and Victor Thompson recently pointed out, this nation is now not merely embroiled in a dramatic moment of "mass incarceration," but is in the grips of severely "racialized mass incarceration."[1] And America's embrace of such a vast and discriminatory carceral state has had a devastating impact—tearing at the social fabric of the poorest and most vulnerable communities, putting a serious strain on the economy, and even distorting the democratic process itself.[2] For these reasons, the question of how Americans might step back from such a reliance on imprisonment, and how they might undo the current carceral crisis, looms large for scholars and lay citizens alike. One cannot, however, change a system that one doesn't fully understand.

In fact, this is not the first, nor the first staggeringly racialized, prison crisis that this nation has witnessed. We have been here once before. In the wake of the Civil War, African Americans were also imprisoned in record numbers; then as now, prisons were the site of serious labor exploitation; then as now, the human rights as well as civil rights of prisoners were completely disregarded. By closely examining why the nation's *first* prison crisis came about, and by taking close note of how *it* was stemmed, scholars can derive new and necessary perspectives on the nation's *second*, and current, prison crisis—where it came from and how it, too, might eventually be ended. In short, by walking more carefully through the prison horrors of the past, we get closer to eradicating those of the present.

PRIOR TO THE AMERICAN CIVIL WAR, the majority of African Americans lived in bondage. With the Thirteenth Amendment came freedom, and with freedom came extraordinary African American hope for the future and possibilities for self-determination.[3] This very hopeful moment for the black community, however, also deeply threatened southern whites, who were determined to maintain complete control of the economy, the society, and the political sphere. In numerous ways, postbellum whites attempted to keep African Americans in positions of social and economic dependency, but arguably their most effective move was to completely overhaul the region's criminal justice system and to embrace a brand-new policy of mass imprisonment.[4]

According to the historian David Oshinsky, postbellum whites believed firmly that "bondage had been good for the negro . . . because the system kept his primitive instincts in check. And Freedom was bad because those checks had been removed."[5] Almost immediately after slavery ended, then, whites began using the criminal justice system as a new "dragnet for the negro," one that could keep African Americans in a state of fear much as had the Ku Klux Klan.[6] Indeed, white southerners quickly realized that one of the most effective ways to continue to dominate African Americans, and to make sure that they did not demand their share of the civic and economic pie, was to criminalize their behavior.

As the historian Mary Ellen Curtin has pointed out, when "African Americans asserted their freedom on the street, on election day, and in their efforts to buy and sell goods," such actions "generated a legal backlash."[7] This meant—in terms both immediate and practical—that after the Civil War, localities began to pass altogether new laws that converted certain behaviors, never before prosecuted as "crimes," into offenses punishable by incarceration. Unemployed blacks simply out seeking jobs, for example, could be charged with the crime of "vagrancy." Local and state governments also increased penalties for such crimes as stealing livestock or grain, knowing well that newly freed African Americans might have to resort to theft simply in order to eat.[8] For example, in 1876 the State of Mississippi "passed a major crime bill aimed directly at the Negro . . . [that] redefined grand larceny," and, thereafter, African American "arrests shot up dramatically."[9] More often, argues the journalist Douglas Blackmon, southern sheriffs arrested African Americans for countless "crimes" that they had never actually committed—trumping up charges so that they could secure cheap workers for local business elites.[10]

Such manipulations of the law meant that the South's "local jails and state prisons would grow darker by the year."[11] One jail in Columbus, Mississippi, that had incarcerated no blacks before the Civil War, held fifty-three blacks and no whites by 1866. Statistics from Georgia after the war are even more striking.[12] By 1871, 84 percent of the convicts in that state's penitentiary were black— already a shocking figure considering that there were *no* African Americans there in 1860—but by 1876, with an even greater criminalization of black spaces, a full 90 percent were African American.[13] In Alabama by 1890, whites comprised less than 4 percent of all county prisoners.[14]

Not only was the incarceration crisis of the mid-1870s deeply racialized, it was also defined by extraordinary brutality. As the historian Alex Lichtenstein has shown, black convicts were forced to eat food that "was bug-infested, rotten, and unvarying [and their] 'rest' was taken in unwashed bedding often in wheeled cages nine feet by twenty feet long containing eighteen beds."[15] In addition, "medical treatment and bathing facilities were unsanitary if available at all. And, above all, corporal punishment and outright torture—casual blows from rifle butts or clubs, whipping with a leather strap, confinement in a 'sweatbox' under the southern sun, and hanging from stocks or bars—was meted out for the most insignificant transgressions."[16]

Consider the fate of one inmate, Ed Turner, who was forced to labor for a Georgia company called Alexander, Grant & Co. after being sent to the state penitentiary in Atlanta. One evening in 1870, company officials charged Turner with poisoning one of their hounds, a charge he adamantly denied but to which he eventually confessed after being whipped for a solid hour from 8:00 until 9:00 p.m.[17] The next day Turner was forced outside and told to get to work. He simply could not. He would try to work a while and then collapse. Each time he fell, an overseer would take him out and give him another forty lashes. This happened repeatedly until the overseer finally called the company doctor to evaluate Turner's ability to labor. When the doctor arrived, he not only claimed that Turner could indeed work, but he gave him fifteen lashes himself for being so lazy. By the day's end, Turner had been beaten to death. According to the testimony of one John Christopher, a captain of the Eighteenth United States Infantry who located several prisoners willing to sign affidavits regarding Turner's fate, whereas Dr. S. G. White alleged that the "prisoner had died from sunstroke," in fact he died after receiving between 450 and 600 lashes at the hands of Captain Potts.[18]

As the above account illustrates, not only were the African Americans sentenced to prison in the wake of the Civil War commonly abused, but they were also exploited by private companies determined to work them nearly to death for their own profit. Southern whites' desire to maintain control of the region's newly freed black population clearly laid the groundwork for so many of them to be imprisoned, but, notably, it was their desire to rebuild the war-torn South on the cheap that ensured that they would continue to be targeted by the criminal justice system of the New South. Incarcerating blacks, they quickly learned, was not only socially useful, it was also highly profitable.

While the nation's first prison crisis was rooted in the South, it is important to note that this country's first carceral crisis was more broadly national than most assume. Recent scholars—Kali Gross, Cheryl Hicks, and Khalil Gibran Muhammad—have established that the North also severely criminalized black behavior, forced inmates to labor for private interests, and resorted to barbaric punishments to meet production quotas in the postbellum period.[19] What happened to Ed Turner and countless other convicts laboring for the State of Georgia happened as well to the inmates in the New Jersey State Prison, whose gruesome deaths, while usually attributed to other causes, had in reality resulted from "the cruel punishments inflicted."[20] Similarly, in Wisconsin, where, according to one report, inmate meals were "putrid"—prisoners were forced to eat "embryo calves, dogs, and glandered horses . . . furnished as meat"—men were also "beaten and put in a black hole . . . as filthy as a dog kennel, and five feet four inches by five in size. A man cannot lie at length in it. There is no ventilation. . . . Men have been placed there for 20 days, and two died."[21]

As the above descriptions make clear, inmate abuse knew no regional boundaries inasmuch as private companies came to profit mightily from prison labor in both regions. Because African Americans were locked up in such unprecedented and shocking numbers in the South of this period as well as in numbers disproportionate to their presence in the North, any contemporary observer could readily conclude that any reforms to the criminal justice system were highly unlikely. By the 1920s, however, many states had begun outlawing the worst abuses of the convict leasing system, and by the New Deal, barriers to private employers' unfettered access to prison labor for profit had finally been put in place at the federal level. To be sure, prisons were still terrible institutions and African Americans continued throughout the twentieth century to be incarcerated at rates disproportionate to whites. Indeed, it would take much more activism in future decades— particularly during the 1960s—to tackle many remaining vestiges of the abuse and exploitation that had fueled the criminal justice system of the postbellum period. Nevertheless, the nation's first racialized prison crisis—which emerged in the aftermath of the Civil War—did not continue unabated. This first carceral crisis, sparked by whites' desires to curtail black claims on freedom, and marked by teeming incarceration rates of African Americans, who were then horrifically treated, eventually netted enough scrutiny, and generated sufficient outrage, to invite serious censure and meaningful reforms. Exactly why and how this happened is well worth sorting out.

Three critical factors combined to stem the nation's first prison crisis. First, as the carceral crisis of the postbellum period deepened, not a few Americans in the free world eventually took it upon themselves to expose, and thus educate the public about, the human costs of this new move to mass imprisonment. Second, eventually some key groups of Americans in the free world realized that a policy of wholesale black incarceration hurt *them* economically, and they began to speak out against it for their own reasons and on their own behalf.[22] Third, prisoners themselves increasingly began to speak out against, and to physically resist, the horrors in the penal institutions that the policies of disproportionate and widespread incarceration had produced.[23]

The fact that convict leasing was brutal and depended on the unprecedented incarceration of African Americans should not have been news to anyone who took even the slightest notice of their surroundings in the postbellum period, least of all African Americans, who were, of course, acutely aware of the nightmare awaiting them should they wind up as convict lessees or members of a chain gang. There was plenty of ugliness in plain sight, for anyone to see. Human cages, literally crammed with men in chains on their way to forced labor camps, were routinely pulled down country roads across the South. Correspondingly, in the North there was an easily visible increase in the number of penal institutions being built to house the scores of similarly hapless people ensnared in the criminal justice system there.

African American activists and writers were some of the most diligently outspoken when it came to calling the nation's attention to this national, and deeply discriminatory, carceral crisis. By 1901, W. E. B. Du Bois was speaking out about the fact that "a new slavery and a new slave trade" had been established in America even while human bondage had been outlawed by the U.S. Constitution. As he made clear, in this new slavery, based as it was on the wholesale imprisonment of black men for their labor, "the innocent were made bad," and, because of this, too many human beings were once again suffering a horrific "death-rate from cruelty, exposure, and overwork."[24] Worse, Du Bois pointed out, "the state became a dealer in crime, profited by it so as to derive a net annual income for her prisoners."[25] Notably, Du Bois was not alone in calling attention to the horrors of the nation's first carceral crisis. Mary Church Terrell, Frederick Douglass, and even Booker T. Washington felt compelled to publicly delineate the many injustices being perpetrated in the name of the law.[26]

But while the message of black reformers like Du Bois reached many Americans, there remained many more living in both the South and the North—mostly the white residents of the nation—who gave little thought to the incarcerated and cared little about the conditions they faced either under the convict leasing system or locked in record numbers in the state penitentiaries of the North. That is, until the 1920s. In 1921, a story broke that brought home to whites just how draconian and abusive the nation's criminal justice system had become.

That year Martin Tabert, a white twenty-two-year-old from Munich, North Dakota, decided to seek adventure and hopped a ride on a freight train bound for Florida without paying his fare. To this stowaway's dismay, he was discovered, arrested, and subsequently sentenced to ninety days hard labor in Tallahassee—hired out to the Putnam Lumber Camp. Before he was able to complete his sentence, however, Tabert's parents were informed that he had expired from "malarial fever and other complications."[27] The problem for the Putnam Labor Camp, however, and ultimately for the State of Florida, was that his parents probed into their son's death and discovered that he had in fact been murdered. As a convict lessee, he had been "overworked, underfed, and beaten senseless."[28]

Thanks to their pressure, in 1923 the Florida Legislature voted to investigate Tabert's murder.[29] In the course of this inquiry, it became obvious that this boy had been forced to work in hip-deep muddy water fifteen hours a day. When he couldn't keep up, an overseer beat him with a thick strap that he repeatedly dragged through sand and sugar so that Tabert's open wounds would scathe. Witnesses testified that the overseer, Walter Higginbotham, struck Tabert with this lash more than one hundred times.[30] After two days of enduring such torture, Tabert died.[31] Because he was white, Talbert's death made national headlines, and such exposure dealt a serious blow to the practice of convict leasing in Florida, eventually leading to the outlawing of corporal punishment within that system.[32] Ultimately, educating the public had shined some needed light on the extreme abuse that defined the nation's first prison crisis.[33]

While calling national attention to the horrors of America's first racialized carceral crisis was important, it was alone insufficient to ameliorate it. Also needed was the mobilization of other Americans, those who perhaps cared little about what trauma the nation's prisoners endured, but who nevertheless recognized that they were being hurt economically by this dramatic rise in the rate of incarcerated African Americans. Indeed, by the late nineteenth century it was becoming increasingly clear to many citizens that convict leasing in particular, and prison labor more generally, posed unfair competition for their labor and, quite literally, took food from their tables.

For example, prior to the Civil War, many whites had worked the mines in southern states such as Tennessee and Kentucky. By the late 1800s, these same workers were finding it hard to feed their families because mining companies had determined that they could reap much higher profits by using their new and seemingly endless supply of black convicts.[34] Not only were convict laborers cheaper, but bosses could use extraordinary force to extract harder work from them without any repercussions. As the historian Karin Shapiro has chronicled, however, rather than accept the fact that the wholesale and record imprisonment of newly freed African Americans would lead to their own economic collapse, in 1891 free-world miners mobilized and launched "a rebellion against the use of convict labor in coal mines that would last over a year, involve thousands of Tennesseans and Kentuckians, and engulf five mining communities in east and mid-Tennessee."[35]

White southerners were not the only ones to see the connection between the rise of prison labor and the decline of jobs for them in the free world.[36] Workers across the North spent much energy in the late nineteenth and early twentieth centuries lobbying state legislatures to pass laws banning the use of prison labor.[37] Indeed, as the nineteenth century became the twentieth, American workers across the North, and the labor movement that sought to represent them, clearly recognized that they had a stake in what happened in the American justice system. Their self-interested activism in this regard proved a significant nuisance to those who sought unfettered access to prison labor and to the ability to sell goods made in prison on the national market. Indeed, determined agitation beginning in the 1880s and escalating dramatically during the Great Depression eventually garnered workers three very important pieces of federal legislation that directly limited private as well as public use of prison labor.[38]

While white laborers were instrumental in bringing an end to the nation's prison crisis, the activism of prisoners themselves was equally important. Not only did African American convict lessees protest the conditions they suffered as a result of indiscriminate racialized imprisonment in the South (for example, by maiming themselves so they could no longer net profits for either prison officials or private companies), but black inmates also rebelled in other, even more overt ways in other parts of the country. Consider, for example, that on June 20, 1927, a full 328 convict miners in Lansing, Kansas, went on strike to protest the inhumane conditions under which they were forced to labor. For four days they refused to come out of the mines and held fourteen prison guards hostage. Eventually hunger forced them to the surface, and many were injured in this protest, but actions such as this put state and private employers on notice that they could not treat prison laborers inhumanely without generating intense and unified resistance.[39]

Not coincidentally, as the controversy over the uses and abuses of prison labor escalated in the late nineteenth and early twentieth centuries, a new a discourse of rehabilitation over punishment began. There had always been corrections officials who argued that rehabilitation must be a central goal of incarceration, but for decades they were well on the outside of the corrections mainstream. For example, it was considered most newsworthy when prison official Zebulon Brockway announced plans to offer his inmates education programs, meaningful job training opportunities, and even some sort of parole incentive at the Elmira State Reformatory in 1876. By 1889, Brockway was still hoping to persuade the corrections community that "the punitive purpose" be "subverted by the improved conditions of prisoners, accorded them out of the humanity of modern Christian society."[40] But it wasn't until the early 1930s, and only after serious steps had already been taken to ameliorate the nation's first prison crisis, that Brockway's thoughts on the merits of rehabilitation over punishment were absorbed in a number of penal facilities, if only in the North. In 1932, for instance, the New York Legislature heard plans for bringing a serious educational program to that state's inmates. "The primary purpose of academic instruction," proponents explained, was "the eradication of illiteracy and the provision for each inmate of sufficient education to read newspapers fairly well, to write an adequate letter, and to be able to perform the commonplace arithmetic of everyday life."[41]

By the early 1940s, thanks to a range of developments—the publicity given the horrors of the convict leasing system by African American luminaries like Du Bois as well as ordinary white families such as the Taberts; the sustained agitation of workers in the free world from Tennessee to New York; and the endless protests launched by the incarcerated themselves—a great many of the worst aspects of the nation's first prison crisis had been put in check. In short, because "powerful interests had emerged to challenge the system on economic as well as humanitarian grounds," a new day had dawned in the nation's criminal justice system.[42] Notably, however, doing away with the most egregious abuses of the convict leasing system, and finally seeing serious attempts to rehabilitate rather than just punish the incarcerated, did not mean that injustice had been rooted out of the nation's criminal justice system completely.

The truth was that even while the worst of the nation's first prison crisis had been ameliorated, far too many American citizens—black and white, from South to North—were still trapped in the criminal justice system; far too many still faced horrific conditions. Even though the worst elements of the nation's post–Civil War carceral crisis had successfully been eradicated by the New Deal era, there was still much work to do over the subsequent two decades, singularly and collectively, to make that system more humane. As one inmate reported about conditions at Leavenworth Prison in 1930: "There are still brutalities in prisons—plenty of them . . . prisoners chained to the bars day after day until the blood oozed from their swollen fingertips. I have seen strong men broken and weak men hounded to madness."[43] Similarly, conditions were still so bad for inmates at the Eastern State Penitentiary in the early 1930s, particularly regarding how the guards treated them and their specific practice of locking prisoners in "punishment cells" for days and weeks on end, that the prisoners rioted in both 1933 and 1934. Upon investigation, the Pennsylvania Department of Welfare felt compelled subsequently to order "close supervision of the guards by the Warden and the Board of Trustees to obviate brutality" as well as "medical control of the punishment cells."[44]

Despite major efforts having been made to humanize penal institutions, they not only remained quite brutal for those detained in them, but African American inmates still bore the brunt of the prison system's worst abuses. In southern states from Arkansas to Texas, it was still an overwhelmingly black prison population being forced out into the prison's fields and worked to the point of collapse from dawn until dusk as late as the 1960s, And, as the historian Robert Chase has shown, southern states routinely placed the most violent and aggressive inmates in charge of the rest of the prisoners.[45] Called "trustee guards," these inmates ruled with an iron hand, using everything from extortion to terror to keep other prisoners in line. And whatever horrors these men did not experience at the hands of trustees, they suffered at the hands of the line overseers or administrators, who used various instruments of torture to keep them in line: "Black Annie" (a thick-strapped whip) on the prison farms of Arkansas, as well as the notorious "Tucker Telephone" (a telephone with live electric wires extending from it to be attached to inmates' genitals).[46]

The African Americans who lived in disproportionate numbers behind bars in the North also experienced terrible conditions well after the worst of the nation's first prison crisis had been stemmed.[47] For example, at New York City's largest jail, known as the Tombs, black inmates awaiting trial in the 1960s and early 1970s endured severe and inhumane overcrowding simply because too many of them could not afford to pay the exorbitant bails that judges set for them.[48] Designed to hold only 932 men, on the weekend of August 7–9, 1970, for example, this facility was jammed to 212 percent over capacity. There were four men crammed into each of the jail's tiny cells, and many Tombs detainees had nowhere to sleep but the concrete floor without so much as a blanket. Such overcrowded quarters meant that inmates lived in squalor and had to deal regularly with infestations of body lice and colonies of roaches and rats that skittered and nested in the facility's filthy cells.[49] One inmate who "hadn't showered in a week" noted that when guards finally allowed him to clean up, they subsequently told him to put on the same filthy clothes he had come in with.[50] It mattered not that he had been sleeping on the floor in these clothes every night. "They stunk," he said. "No matter how clean I was, I still stunk."[51]

All the while enduring conditions wholly unfit for human beings, the Tombs detainees were effectively barred from exercising their constitutional rights as U.S. citizens as well. There was, for starters, the issue of due process. It was a rare day when a Tombs inmate got to trial speedily.[52] In August 1970 eight thousand men were sitting in New York's city jails who had not yet gone to trial and who, therefore, had not been found guilty of any crime.[53] Being confined to the Tombs because one couldn't afford bail raised serious quality-of-life as well as constitutional issues. There existed no clear procedures for ensuring that a detainee had regular access to his family members, nor was there any easy mechanism for them to send or receive mail either personal or legal. Telephone access was completely out of the question. According to a later report, "a man who is presumed innocent should not be cut off from people who can help him raise bail, to secure witnesses, to obtain an attorney, or failing that, to lend him moral support during the time he is awaiting trial."[54]

New York's prisons weren't much better than its jails as the 1960s came to a close and the 1970s began. Attica, like the Tombs, had an overwhelmingly African American prison population. Inmates experienced significant hardships and discrimination while incarcerated. Even though only 37 percent of their population was white, for example, whites held 74 percent of the jobs in Attica's powerhouse, comprising 67 percent of the coveted clerk's positions and 62 percent of the staff in the officers' mess hall.[55] By contrast, 76 percent of the inmates in the dreaded and low-paid metal shop, and 80 percent in the grueling grading companies, were African Americans or Spanish-speaking.[56] It was common at Attica to have "white inmate[s] starting off at a higher pay grade in the same job."[57] What is more, "in 74 percent of the job categories, racial proportions are significantly different from the racial ratios of the general population."[58]

Racialized conditions at Attica were not simply restricted to prison labor. Attica's inmates in general and its black inmates in particular also had intensely felt grievances about the insufficient food they received. Of the meals they did get, pork was a mainstay despite the fact the Black Muslims could not eat it. Medical care for black inmates was substandard, and their medical needs, systematically ignored.[59] One inmate who had broken bones in his hand literally begged Dr. Sternberg, one of Attica's two staff physicians, to do something to help him because his pain had been "getting worse and worse" and his bones were actually "coming out."[60] But, according to another inmate who bunked near and overheard this conversation, Sternberg "turned around and said 'well, write a letter to another doctor.' He couldn't even move his fingers."[61]

Attica's prisoners found it hard to deal as well with the prison's all-white guards who could be hostile and even abusive and felt little compunction about using racial epithets and engaging in explicitly discriminatory behaviors. When guards felt slighted, it was not uncommon for them to retaliate violently such as happened when one corrections officer who had been cat-called by one black inmate "decided to frisk several of the inmates there and tear up their cells."[62] According to another guard, "it took days to get their cells reordered . . . [and the] individual [who had cat-called] got the shit kicked out of him."[63]

Notably, the same forces that, together, stemmed the nation's first prison crisis continued to work throughout the postwar period to improve the criminal justice system in both North and South. The first powerful force was, again, groups of citizens in the free world who committed themselves to exposing any continuing prison abuse. As had happened earlier in the century, for example, the prisoner mistreatments that continued to flourish on the penal plantations of the South came to light, and eventually were ended, because of men such as Tom Murton who were determined to end the horrors that they observed personally. Murton had come to Arkansas from a previous position as an assistant professor of criminology at the University of Illinois and, before that, as acting chief of corrections in Alaska. Asked by the governor merely to run the Cummins and Tucker prison farms, Murton felt compelled to completely overhaul them almost as soon as he arrived. In his best-selling book *Accomplices to Crime,* Murton informed the world just how bad conditions remained for black inmates in the South.[64] Similarly, the prison reformer Austin MacCormick, who directed the Osborne Association in New York, worked hard to investigate and expose conditions in the Texas system beginning in the 1940s. Indeed, according to the historian Robert Chase, "By the end of his sixty-five-year career as a penological expert, MacCormick had visited every state prison in the nation, and had served as an investigator and chief reformer for the prison systems in Alabama, Arkansas, Louisiana, Mississippi, North Carolina and Texas."[65]

As was the case with earlier efforts to ameliorate the nation's first prison crisis, though, efforts to educate the public needed to be wedded to other efforts on the part of free-world citizens to change the system. Notably, however, in the postwar period this group of citizens did not herald from the organized working class. From the moment that federal regulators had alleviated their fears about prison labor competition, America's working class appeared to care little about the fact that prisoners themselves were still being exploited and abused within the nation's penal institutions. And thus it took activists and organizations from the civil rights movement, as well as from other social movement struggles on the Left, to speak out loudly for additional prison reforms. From the NAACP, the Student

Nonviolent Coordinating Committee (SNCC), the Black Panther Party, and the Young Lords Party to the National Lawyers Guild, the ACLU, and various radical groups such as the Weather Underground, the Socialist Workers Party, and the Revolutionary Communist Party, prison rights became a galvanizing issue.

Civil rights activists in particular understood that their efforts to end oppression on the outside of prison walls would be greatly advanced if oppression was not allowed to flourish on the inside, and vice versa. The recognition that the racism of the free world and the racism within penal institutions were inexorably linked led 1960s activists to, among other things, file critically important "prisoner rights" lawsuits that markedly improved prison life for African American and white inmates alike. As one scholar has put it: "A platoon, eventually a phalanx, of prisoner rights lawyers, supported by federal and foundation funding, soon appeared and pressed claims. They initiated and won prisoner rights cases that implicated every aspect of prison governance."[66]

As a result of outside mobilization and concerted legal interventions, the "Hands Off" doctrine that had long determined America's internal prison policy finally weakened under the onslaught of two decades of significant legal decisions: *Bailleaux v. Holmes* (1961) established that prison officials could not restrict the study of law when it could be shown that such a practice impeded one's right of access to the courts); *Furman v. Georgia* (1972) ruled that the death penalty was applied in an arbitrary and discriminatory manner, which violated the Eighth and Fourteenth Amendments to the U.S. Constitution; *Estelle v. Gamble* (1976) established that officials who acted with deliberate indifference to an inmate's medical needs were violating that inmate's constitutional right not to endure cruel and unusual punishment; *Ruiz v. Estelle* (1980) ruled that the conditions of imprisonment within the Texas prison system constituted cruel and unusual punishment in violation of the U.S. Constitution. These cases established unequivocally that outsiders with their own guiding interests had finally established that prisoners did not in fact lose their humanity, or their constitutional rights, when they were imprisoned in America.[67]

Just as had occurred during the nation's first prison crisis in the wake of the Civil War, inmates' determined activism decades later was critical to generating further substantive changes within the criminal justice system of the 1960s. Although inmates had protested the conditions of their incarceration throughout the twentieth century, the most organized and politically effective inmate rebellions would have to wait until the late 1960s and early 1970s. In 1970, for example, the jail inmates who had been enduring such terrible conditions at the Tombs in Manhattan staged a dramatic rebellion that not only netted them much public attention and support, but also produced palpable changes in jail operations. Helping their protest tremendously was the fact that such exposés as Tom Murton's had made headlines. Added to this, radical lawyers across the country were now willing to file cases on inmates' behalves and activists were willing to launch protest after protest against the injustices that remained in the nation's prisons. Because of these broader efforts to humanize the American criminal justice system, in the case of the Tombs rebellion, Mayor John Lindsay not only acknowledged the legitimacy of the inmates' demands but also pledged to do something about them. As he told the inmates still held in the Tombs: "I am aware of your grievances and problems. I am prepared to deal with them positively, and to enlist the aid of the courts and the state."[68]

Just as the inmates at the Tombs launched a dramatic rebellion that netted them both great attention and a real opportunity to press for needed reforms, so did those at Attica. On September 9, 1971, more than 1,200 inmates took over the prison and took dozens of hostages as leverage so that state officials would negotiate with them. Notably, because these inmates also had the support of countless activists and reformers on the outside who were determined to expose the prisoners' miserable conditions for the American public, by September 11, 1971, they got the prison commissioner himself, Russell Oswald, to agree, at least in principle, to twenty-eight of the thirty-three demands that they had put forth. These included his agreement to "recommend the application of the New York State minimum wage law standards to all work done by inmates"; to "allow all New York State prisoners to be politically active, without intimidation or reprisal"; to "institute realistic, effective rehabilitation programs for all inmates according to their offense and personal needs"; and to "modernize the inmate education system, including the establishment of a Latin library."[69]

Despite the fact that negotiations were still under way, this particular rebellion ended horrifically. On September 13, 1971, Governor Nelson Rockefeller decided to retake Attica by sending in more than six hundred armed state troopers, who proceeded to shoot more than 2,400 bullets—many intended for large game and thus outlawed—into the 50′ × 50′ enclosure where inmates and hostages alike had gathered for the negotiations. Ultimately the bullets of troopers and corrections officers killed twenty-nine inmates and ten hostages while wounding and maiming hundreds of others.[70] Although the state's brutal reaction to the 1971 Attica rebellion lives on in infamy, it is important that the nature of the inmates' uprising not be forgotten. Their insistence on bettering the conditions under which they were incarcerated ultimately sparked other important prisoner rebellions that, together, netted substantial reforms to America's prisons.[71] Importantly, and specifically as a result of the Attica rebellion, eighty-five prison-reform bills were proposed to the New York State Legislature. By the end of 1972, not only had many of these bills been signed into law, but $12 million of public funds had been earmarked to make sure that key reforms were actually implemented.[72]

Ultimately, because of the powerful efforts of multiple parties—reformers who sought to expose prison abuses; civil rights and Left activists and organizations who challenged the criminal justice system from the outside; and inmates who risked everything they had to change the conditions in prison—the later 1960s and early 1970s represented a remarkable moment when reform, not crisis, defined the American justice system. In the immediate aftermath of the Attica uprising, for example, not only were prisons humanized in important ways, but ordinary Americans indicated a newfound sympathy for inmates and greater support for their basic human as well as civil rights. Significantly, soon after the Attica uprising, when Americans were asked whether they "would favor a policy of using armed force, such as in Attica, or not using force and sitting down with the prisoners to hear their complaints," only 10 percent responded, "use armed force, as at Attica."[73] And, according to a 1971 Roper Commercial Survey, when a random group of Americans was asked whether "there should be greater use of physical punishment in prisons," only 9 percent agreed,[74] whereas 92 percent agreed that "rehabilitation and job training should be greatly increased for prisoners," and 72 percent noted that "the guards should be more understanding and humane."[75] When asked whether they thought that "blacks breed crime," the vast majority of respondents answered no.[76]

Such data clearly suggest that the aftermath of the Attica uprising pointed toward significant reforms in the American criminal justice system, particularly those reforms that acknowledged that even prisoners were entitled to basic human rights. Why, then, one is compelled to ask, did this nation end up in yet another incarceration crisis—one more extensive and racialized than any that had come before it?

By the close of the twentieth century, the United States was indeed again in the midst of a severe carceral crisis—one that, like its predecessor, was characterized by a dramatic spike in the number of Americans who found themselves behind bars. The rates of imprisonment that came to mark the nation's second prison crisis, however, made those of the first pale in comparison. As the scholars Henry Ruth and Kevin Reitz note: "Over a one hundred year period, 1880 to 1980, the nation added a total of about 285,000 inmates to the prison systems. During the ensuing twenty years, from 1980 to 2000, the nation added about 1.1. million inmates."[77] This extraordinary jump in incarceration meant that, by 2006, one in every thirty-one Americans was either locked up, on probation, or on parole.[78]

The nation's second carceral crisis shared more with the first than imprisoning record numbers of Americans. It, too, was severely racialized from the start. To be sure, African Americans had always suffered disproportionate rates of incarceration throughout the nineteenth and twentieth centuries, but as the twentieth century wound down and the new prison crisis began, they once again found themselves particularly singled out by a battery of new laws that criminalized the urban spaces where most of them lived. Just as all-black rural spaces were criminalized in new ways after the Civil War, leading to record rates of African American incarceration at the end of the nineteenth century, so were overwhelmingly black urban spaces targeted in new ways in the wake of the civil rights advances of the 1960s, leading to even more staggering and disproportionate African American incarceration at the end of the twentieth century. Whereas in 1926, 21 percent of the Americans admitted to state and federal prisons were black (still an unacceptable figure given African Americans' percentage in the U.S. population as a whole), 44 percent of those admitted in 1986 were black.[79] While "the recorded number of black prisoners in 1986 was nearly 9 times larger than the number recorded in 1926[,] the recorded number of white prisoners was [only] 3 times larger."[80] By the close of 2007, a full 3,138 black males per 100,000 black males were sentenced prisoners compared with only 481 white males per 100,000 white males.[81] By 2006, one in fifteen African Americans, as compared with one in thirty-one Americans of every race, was in some way trapped in this nation's criminal justice system.[82]

As it did a hundred years earlier, the nation's turn to new levels of racialized mass incarceration after the 1960s devastated the black community. From orphaning more than a generation of black children, to eliminating needy Americans from eligibility for welfare and public housing, to reducing the lifetime income of black men and women, to eroding the public health in neighborhoods of color, to disproportionally disfranchising these same communities of color, the mass incarceration crisis of today is cataclysmic in its reach.[83]

Not only does today's turn to racialized mass imprisonment have a social impact fully as devastating as it did back in the late nineteenth and early twentieth centuries, but, just as alarmingly, it also signifies that Americans once again began gravitating toward a particularly punitive response to the potentiality and realities of crime. Note, for example, the extent to which public opinion had turned against the incarcerated by the last decade of the twentieth century and had retreated from the promises of the rehabilitative 1960s. According to one survey conducted in 1994, when respondents were asked, "Which best describes how you generally feel about punishment for criminals: "an eye for an eye" or "turn the other cheek"?, over 76 percent answered "an eye for an eye."[84] In a similar survey conducted by the Roper Center for Public Opinion Research, out of 1,517 people who were asked if they "agree or disagree that people who break the law should be given stiffer sentences," 532 "strongly agreed," and 607 "agreed."[85]

Unsurprisingly, with punitive attitudes on the rise as the twentieth century became the twenty-first, prisoners themselves grew newly and ever more vulnerable. Notably, for example, back in the 1960s virtually all Americans had come to agree that it was unethical and immoral for scientists to conduct medical experiments on inmates. By the close of the twentieth century, however, and as the nation's biomedical industry began facing a serious shortage of testing subjects for its new drug trials, the possibility of using prisoners was again up for debate with noticeable public support. Indeed, to cut costs in the 1980s, pharmaceutical companies like Merck and Pfizer had not done enough testing on some of its most touted new drugs such as Vioxx and Bextra, and, as a result, they were forced to pull these very lucrative drugs off the market at a great loss.[86] Remarkably, in the wake of this financial as well as public relations disaster, two esteemed scientific bodies, the Institute of Medicine and the National Academy of Sciences, agreed to conduct a new study on the ethics of medical testing in prisons. Ultimately, both scholarly bodies recommended that federal regulations be loosened so as to permit experiments imposing greater risks if they "had the potential to benefit prisoners." From the perspective of the inmates in question, however, such reasoning seemed ludicrous. As one prisoners' advocate put it, "It strikes me as pretty ridiculous to start talking about prisoners getting access to cutting-edge research and medications when they can't even get penicillin and high-blood-pressure pills."[87]

Notably, arguments for medical testing were only the tip of the new "prisoners are not to be coddled" iceberg. In addition to pharmaceutical companies seeking carte blanche to experiment with inmate bodies, the issue of whether inmates themselves might be able to sell their own organs to medical facilities in exchange for reduced time was now also on the table. One amendment to the National Transplant Act of 1984, for example, proposed that "an inmate could donate an organ for transplant, or for research, upon death" and that, if they wished to do this, "a contract would be drawn up between the inmate, the organ bank, the United Network of Organ Sharing (UNOS), and the Federal Bureau of Prisons."[88] The incentive for inmates, it went on, was that they "could pledge up to 3 organs upon death, for 60 days each of time suspended from his/her sentence—a maximum of 180 days." If any prisoner wanted "one year of suspended time," she/he could "pledge his/her entire body."[89] On the state level, politicians wrote similar legislation to allow inmate organ donation. South Carolina Democrat Ralph Anderson proposed two such bills. The first would allow inmates to leave prison two months early if they agreed to donate bone marrow.

The second would give up to a half year of "good-behavior credit" to "'any inmate who performs a particularly meritorious or humanitarian act,' which Anderson noted, could include living kidney donation."[90] Interestingly, and disturbingly, the senator decided to turn to the prison population to increase donor supplies because of "the shortage of black bone marrow donors" in the free-world population.[91]

Not only did the upsurge of coldly utilitarian laws affecting prisoners' lives indicate that free-world empathy for the incarcerated had waned dramatically, but the post–civil rights 1960s carceral moment had also entailed a revolution in the nature of imprisonment itself with the introduction, and wholesale embrace, of so-called "supermax" facilities. Just like the penitentiaries of the late nineteenth and early twentieth centuries that eventually were deemed "cruel and unusual," the supermax prisons of the early twenty-first century came to rely heavily on sensory deprivation as well as physical abuse to control their inmate populations. Rather than using the iron gag of yesteryear, by the year 2000 the four-point restraint was a favored device for keeping prisoners in line. One prisoner locked in an Indiana supermax prison "was held in four-point restraints for a total of fifteen days," and other prisoners were dying in similarly confining "restraint chairs."[92] And although Americans had already concluded that it was inhumane to keep human beings in indefinite solitary confinement after experimenting heavily with this practice a hundred years ago, by the dawn of the twenty-first century, supermax facilities such as Pelican Bay State Prison in northern California were once again keeping men in complete isolation for decades on end.[93] The modern version of isolation was no more humane. Indeed, one prisoner who had suffered "seizures and psychiatric symptoms since childhood" began having such severe panic attacks after being locked alone in a cell that he suffered "palpitations, sweating, difficulty breathing . . . and he mutilates himself . . . to relieve his anxiety and to be removed from his cell."[94] The mentally ill in particular suffered in the nation's reembrace of punitive penology.[95]

Young people in America also paid a high price as the nation became embroiled in yet another carceral crisis—characterized as it was by an excessive reliance on incarceration and harsher punishment. One of the most significant penal reform victories in the fight against the nation's first carceral crisis was that children became a protected class in the criminal justice system. Thanks to the United Nations Declaration on the Rights of the Child (1959) and cases such as re Gault (1967), juveniles who had been locked away, abused, and forgotten in the penal institutions of the nineteenth and early twentieth centuries had special legal representation and their own criminal justice facilities.[96] Just as adult penal facilities grew beyond capacity and were beginning to be run in more punitive ways as the second carceral crisis arrived and deepened, so did juvenile justice facilities become severely overcrowded and newly brutal. Consider the fact that, by the close of the twentieth century, some of the most notorious juvenile facilities were those run by private companies, for profit, that housed kids who had been convicted of crimes by local and state authorities. Some were set up to house children who had never been convicted of a crime but "might"—so-called "boot camps." Run like a combination of a forced labor camp and the harshest penal facility, such private facilities also made headlines for the shocking number of child fatalities that occurred there.[97]

But how did a nation that, by the mid-1960s, had turned so firmly in a reform-minded direction and against inhumane penal practices, once again find itself in the midst of such a deep carceral crisis? There are many interesting explanations for this punitive turn, but all of them tend to locate today's prison crisis, and the nation's embrace of mass incarceration, in the nation's turn to the political right more generally.[98] If one takes the time to unpack the origins of America's first prison crisis, it is clear that there is indeed an important relationship between the turn to a racialized system of mass incarceration and the simultaneous national turn to a conservative politics. Just as whites threatened with the loss of economic power and color privilege after the Civil War found the solution to their woes in the criminalization of black space back in 1865, it appears that similarly self-interested Americans "rediscovered" this solution after 1965. Discussing the 1880s, David Oshinsky observes that, by locking up newly freed African Americans en masse, southern Democrats were perceived to be "redeeming" their region "from the clutches of 'black power.'" Similarly, it would appear, those threatened and unnerved by the civil rights and Black Power activism of African Americans in the 1960s and 1970s also sought to regain and maintain control through the carceral state.[99]

If the origins of the most recent carceral crisis eerily resemble those of the late nineteenth century, so do the possibilities for ending it. As did their counterparts in the late nineteenth and early twentieth centuries, at least some segments of the American citizenry in the new twenty-first century began to recognize that their own fate and that of the nation's prisoners are intertwined. They once again began to take note of the brutality in the nation's penal facilities and to speak out against such cruelty; and, perhaps most important, prisoners once again began to act on their own behalf to change the system.

Although they had grown utterly complacent about the nation's criminal justice system once they had secured protections against wage competition from prison labor during the New Deal, America's workers once again are coming to realize that their fate is intimately tied to the carceral state and, more specifically, to the fact that there is now an endless supply of prisoners in the nation whom private employers can once again exploit for profit. While they paid no attention to what took place behind prison walls in the postwar period, private corporations, state governments, and the federal government itself were together seeking ways to weaken existing regulations on prison labor. In 1979, they succeeded in overhauling the most significant of these regulations, and by the new millennium, in states across the country, the durable goods that workers in the free world used to make, ranging from desks to eyeglasses, and the service jobs they used to do, ranging from taking phone orders for retailers to placing reservations for travel agencies, have increasingly gone to prisoners who can neither ask for a living wage nor demand that their workplaces be safe.[100] Although the largely white-led labor movement itself was slow to take up this issue—fearing that its criticism of the carceral state might alienate its members who must be "tough on crime"— noticeable movement in that direction was afoot by the close of the 1990s.[101] Increasing numbers of unions of color in particular began tackling this issue, but so did more traditional unions such as the American Federation of State, County and Municipal Employees (AFSCME), the Service Employees International Union (SEIU), and the American Federation of Government Employees (AFGE). As one journalist noted about labor efforts in the western United States in 1999: "The campaign against prison labor in Oregon is picking up steam. The fightback is headed by the Teamsters, the Building Trades unions and the American Federation of State, County and Municipal Employees, whose members include correction officers."[102]

Community activists, particularly activists of color less blinded by race privilege than much of the labor movement, also came increasingly to see that the most recent carceral crisis was their crisis, too. Organizations such as Critical Resistance, StopMax, Children of the Incarcerated, the Prison Activist Resource Center, Families of Prisoners, Families Against Mandatory Minimums (FAMM), to mention but a few, made it their full-time job to organize around the issue of mass incarceration and its myriad devastating effects. As FAMM explained its mission: "We shine a light on the human face of sentencing, advocate for state and federal sentencing reform, and mobilize thousands of individuals and families whose lives are adversely affected by unjust sentences" and "FAMM's vision is a nation in which sentencing is individualized, humane, and sufficient but not greater than necessary to impose just punishment, secure public safety, and support successful rehabilitation and reentry."[103]

Similarly, once again journalists, scholars, and other reformers began working hard to lift the veil on what was happening behind prison walls, trying to educate the public about the costs of mass incarceration, and trying to reform the nation's penal system. Indeed, by the first decade of the twenty-first century, there were countless articles being written on prisons and the abuses of prisoners within them. Scores of new books also emerged that sought to illuminate the collateral costs of the carceral state. Dozens of academic conferences were soon being devoted to ending mass incarceration and punitive criminal justice policies. One held at the University of Virginia in 2009, entitled "The Problem of Punishment: Race, Inequality, and Justice," made clear that "the aim of this symposium, therefore, is to promote a serious, informed dialogue that will contribute to a growing national debate on the growth of the carceral state. . . . [In this symposium] scholars will focus on the myriad implications of rising prison rates for forms of economic, social, and political exclusion in the United States."[104] Similarly, a conference at Princeton University in 2011, entitled "The Imprisonment of a Race," netted a huge audience of individuals from across the Northeast interested in hearing about "the prison system in a historical and present-day context through the lens of race."[105]

As important, there were soon numerous professional and philanthropic organizations devoting their time and resources to ending the most recent prison crisis as well. Consider, for example, that the Open Society Institute had, by the close of the twentieth century, dedicated an entire "Criminal Justice Fund" to aid "efforts to end the over-reliance on incarceration and harsh punishment in the United States." The institute explained: "The Fund supports advocacy, litigation, strategic research and analysis, public education, communications and organizing efforts to address institutional and structural inequality and reverse the policies and practices that criminalize race, poverty, mental illness, drug and alcohol dependency and youth; expose the destructive and costly impact of current policies on individuals and communities; stimulate rethinking about the appropriate role of prosecution, punishment, and prison in the 21st century; encourage participation and leadership of people with criminal convictions in justice reform; and assure equal access to quality representation and alternatives to incarceration."[106]

With such attention once again finally being trained on penal institutions, prisoners themselves could once again act on their own behalf in ways that made a policy difference as well. Indeed, when American citizens outside of prison walls began recognizing that prison labor harmed them, too, and when they began exposing the abuses again taking place in the nation's penal facilities, prisoners themselves had more public support for their attempts to eliminate the most abusive conditions of their confinement. Notably, it wasn't until groups such as Human Rights Watch and Amnesty International demanded access to supermax facilities in states such as Virginia, and organizations such as STOPMAX began educating the public on what inmates endured when placed in such severe isolation, that inmates could begin a legal assault on these Orwellian institutions.[107] Similarly, while organizations such as the American Friends Service Committee again began looking closely at the issue of prison reform, inmates in isolation units were then able to draw from international as well as constitutional law when they sought help. As Bonnie Kerness of the Newark AFSC office explained:

> The conditions and practices that the imprisoned testify to are in violation of the Universal Declaration of Human Rights, the United Nations Convention against Torture, and the United Nations Convention on the Elimination of All Forms of Racial Discrimination. U.S. prison practices also violate dozens of other international treaties and fit the United Nations definition of genocide. . . . The AFSC has been documenting human rights abuses in prisons for many years, and forwarded the documentation to appropriate U.N. committees, considering U.S. compliance with these agreements.[108]

As prisoners' experience throughout the first two-thirds of the twentieth century had already proved, when prisoners could be heard in courts of law, they could dramatically change their circumstances. Once again, the path toward improving penal conditions and, ultimately, to ending the most recent national carceral crisis, was paved by determined legal activism. Notably, even as the country grew more conservative in the 1980s and 1990s, inmates continued to look to the legal system to restore their human and civil rights. As Heather Schoenfeld points out, "By 1993, 40 states were under court order to reduce overcrowding and/or eliminate unconstitutional conditions of confinement."[109] Indeed, inmates filed so many suits in the late 1970s and into the 1990s that legislators passed the Prison Litigation Reform Act to limit their claims.[110] Nevertheless, even with restricted access to the courts, in the year 2000 inmates still filed 25,505 civil rights petitions. By 2005, they had won a critical civil rights victory when the U.S. Supreme Court ruled in *Garrison Johnson v. State of California* that prison officials could not segregate inmate housing on the basis of race when they entered a California prison.[111] Similarly, knowing that they might now be heard, prisoners filed two legal cases, *Plata v. Schwarzenegger* and *Coleman v. Schwarzenegger*, to fight the terrible health-care consequences of severe prison overcrowding.[112] In 2009, as a result of their activism, the Supreme Court of the State of California ruled that the state's Department of Corrections must release upwards of fifty thousand inmates, which is the equivalent of closing seven to nine prisons.[113] As such victories did a century ago, cumulatively, ameliorate the nation's first prison crisis, so might they end its second. While none of those victories was possible in isolation, collectively they made a substantial difference and could again.

Again, this nation has been here before, and the fact that the historical record shows clearly that even the most egregious carceral crisis could in fact be stemmed is good news, indeed. But this record carries bad news in tandem. Clearly, without constant vigilance from citizens in the free world, and without keeping the human and civil rights of the incarcerated protected, a racialized incarceration crisis can always again engulf this nation. History matters, and the only way to avoid repeating its worst offenses against humanity—even the humanity of inmates—is to return to "the scene of the crime," as it were. Uncovering the evidence of past abuses contributes to our knowledge of what to do, and not to do, now.

## Notes

1. Lawrence D. Bobo and Victor Thompson, "Racialized Mass Incarceration: Poverty, Prejudice, and Punishment," in *Doing Race: 21 Essays for the 21st Century,* ed. Hazel R. Markus and Paula Moya (New York: Norton, 2010), 329.

2. For more on this impact, see Heather Ann Thompson, "Why Mass Incarceration Matters: Rethinking Crisis, Decline, and Transformation in Postwar American History," *Journal of American History* (December 2010).

3. For a beautiful recapturing of this hope, see Jacqueline Jones, *Labor of Love, Labor of Sorrow* (New York: Basic, 2009); and Douglas Blackmon, *Slavery by Another Name: The Re-Enslavement of Black Americans from the Civil War to World War II* (New York: Doubleday, 2008).

4. I use the terms "mass imprisonment" and "mass incarceration" to describe even this earlier criminal justice moment that newly freed African Americans faced in the wake of the Civil War both to reflect the steep rise in the number of African Americans who were suddenly confined as prisoners by both state and private interests, and to indicate the scope of how many African Americans fell victim in this period to new laws intended to restrict their freedom and to labor poachers who operated a vast, and only newly appreciated, illegal operation of arresting and even kidnapping African Americans for crimes that had never been committed. On the dramatic and sudden rise in the numbers of incarcerated African Americans, see Mary Ellen Curtin, *Black Prisoners and Their World: Alabama 1865–1900* (Charlottesville: University Press of Virginia, 2000), 2; and Alexander Lichtenstein, *Twice the Work of Free Labor* (New York: Verso, 1996), 60, 180. On the scope of this imprisonment—some of which was itself illegal—see Blackmon, *Slavery by Another Name,* 127.

5. David Oshinsky, *Worse Than Slavery: Parchman Farm and the Ordeal of Jim Crow Justice* (New York: Free Press, 1996), 19, 29.

6. Ibid.

7. Curtin, *Black Prisoners and Their World,* 8.

8. There is a great deal of controversy surrounding how much crime newly freed African Americans committed in the wake of slavery. Whereas Oshinsky argues that there was a real crime problem in the postbellum South, albeit caused mostly by African American necessity, Douglas Blackmon argues that this crime problem was greatly exaggerated and was used merely as a pretense for securing a convict labor force. While there is little ques-

tion that food theft did occur because one white response to black freedom was to not provide food to those former slaves who refused to do their bidding, it is also clear that acts of food theft were hardly at crisis levels and cannot explain the white South's decision to incarcerate thousands of newly freed African Americans.

9. Oshinsky, *Worse Than Slavery*, 40.

10. Blackmon, *Slavery by Another Name*, 127.

11. Oshinsky, *Worse Than Slavery*, 39.

12. Ibid., 34.

13. Lichtenstein, *Twice the Work of Free Labor*, 60.

14. Curtin, *Black Prisoners and Their World*, 2.

15. Lichtenstein, *Twice the Work of Free Labor*, 183.

16. Ibid, 183. For more on the terrible treatments suffered by female convict lessees, see Talitha LaFlouria, "Convict Women and Their Quest for Humanity: Examining Patterns of Race, Class, and Gender in Georgia's Convict Lease and Chain Gang Systems, 1865–1917" (Ph.D. diss., Howard University, 2009).

17. *Penitentiary. Atlanta, Ga., May 5, 1870* (repr., New York: Arno Press, 1974), 111–14.

18. Ibid.

19. For a fascinating discussion of the ways in which, and the extent to which, African Americans were criminalized in the North, and, indeed, on the ways in which this manufactured association between blackness and crime reverberated both politically and in terms of policy, see Kali Gross, *Colored Amazons: Crime, Violence and Black Women in the City of Brotherly Love, 1880–1910* (Durham: Duke University Press, 2006); Cheryl Hicks, *Talk with You Like a Woman: Urban Reform, Criminal Justice, and African American Women in New York, 1890–1935* (Chapel Hill: University of North Carolina Press, 2010); and Khalil Gibran Muhammad, *The Condemnation of Blackness: Ideas about Race and Crime in the Making of Modern Urban America* (Cambridge: Harvard University Press, 2010). For more on prison labor in general, mostly white, see Rebecca McLennan, *The Crisis of Imprisonment: Protest, Politics, and the Making of the American Penal State, 1776–1941* (Cambridge: Cambridge University Press, 2008).

20. Henry Elmer Barnes, *A History of the Penal, Reformatory and Correctional Institutions of the State of New Jersey: Analytical and Documentary* (Trenton, N.J.: MacCrellish and Quigley, 1918; repr., New York: Arno Press, 1974), 133.

21. "A Revolting Story," *Massachusetts Ploughman and New England Journal of Agriculture* 39, no. 4 (October 25, 1879): 3

22. For more on the importance of labor movement activism to limiting prison labor abuses, see Heather Ann Thompson, "Rethinking Working-Class Struggle through the Lens of the Carceral State: Toward a Labor History of Inmates and Guards," *Labor: Studies in the Working-Class History of the Americas* (Fall 2011).

23. The historian David Oshinsky rightly notes another group whose eventual hostility toward the southern elites' unfettered access to a free workforce also led to the demise of this system: those poorer southern whites, racialized populists, who felt that planter and entrepreneur use of convict lessees only deepened the wealth and class divide in the New South (see Oshinsky, *Worse Than Slavery*, chap. 5).

24. Quoted in Shaun L. Gabbidon, *W. E. B. Du Bois on Crime and Justice: Laying the Foundations of Sociological Criminology* (Farnham, U.K.: Ashgate, 2007), 62.

25. Quoted ibid.

26. See Beverly W. Jones, "Mary Church Terrell and the National Association of Colored Women, 1896 to 1901," *Journal of Negro History* 67, no. 1 (Spring 1982): 20–33; Frederick Douglass on convict leasing in Ida B. Wells, ed., The Reason Why the Colored American Is Not in the World's Columbian Exposition: The Afro-American's Contribution to Columbian literature; and Louis R. Harlan, *Booker T. Washington Papers* (Urbana: University of Illinois Press, 1980).

27. "Grand Jury Today Gets Peonage Case: Witnesses to Tell of the Flogging of Tabert and Others in Lumber Camp," *New York Times*, April 11, 1923; Oshinsky, *Worse Than Slavery*, 74.

28. "Tells of Death Lash in Florida Camp: Ex-Convict Guard Asserts 'Whipping Boss' Gave 100 Strokes to Tabert," *New York Times*, April 18, 1923; Oshinsky, *Worse Than Slavery*, 74.

29. "Florida to Inquire into Peonage Charges," *New York Times*, April 4, 1923; "Two Inquires Start into Death of Tabert: Florida Grand Jury to Sift Circumstances and Legislature Names Joint Committee," *New York Times*, April 10, 1923.

30. "Tells of Death Lash in Florida Camp: Ex-Convict Guard Asserts 'Whipping Boss' Gave 100 Strokes to Tabert," *New York Times*, April 18, 1923.

31. Oshinsky, *Worse Than Slavery*, 75.

32. "Florida House Votes to End All Flogging in Convict Camps, But Keeps Leasing Plan, *New York Times*, April 19, 1923.

33. A similar exposé and trial took place in Arkansas: "Convict Ark. Officer of Slave Raids: Guilty on Seven Counts," *Pittsburgh Courier*, December 5, 1936.

34. "Strikers and Convict Labour in America, *Scotsman*, July 20, 1891.

35. Karin Shapiro, *New South Rebellion: The Battle against Convict Labor in the Tennessee Coalfields, 1871–1896*, 2.

36. "Hits Convict Road Labor: States Construction Council Contends It Adds to Unemployment, *New York Times*, July 11, 1932.

37. "Ban Goods Made by Prison Labor: United Drive by Garment Manufacturers against This Kind of Competition," *New York Times*, August 19, 1923.

38. Hawes-Cooper Act, 1929, c. 79, 1, 2, 45 Stat. 1084, title 49 U.S.C. 60 (49 U.S.C.A. 60); Walsh-Healey Public Contracts Act, as amended (41 U.S.C. 35–45); and Ashurst-Sumner Act, 1935, Public Law 215, 74th Cong. For more on the history of prison labor law and the labor history of inmates, guards, and the American working class, see Thompson, "Rethinking Working-Class Struggle through the Lens of the Carceral State."

39. "The Convict Miners' Strike," *Irish Times*, July 9, 1927.

40. Z. R. Brockway, "The Care of Criminals," *Chautauquan: A Weekly Newsmagazine*, March 1889.

41. *An Educational Program for the New York State's Penal System: Special Report by Commission to Investigate Prison Administration and Construction*, presented to the Legislature of the State of New York, January 1932, 24.

42. Oshinsky, *Worse Than Slavery*, 75.

43. Ralph Chaplin, "Prison Blight," *Forum*, March 1930.

44. Prison Report, Department of Welfare, *A Review of the Four-Year Period, 1931–34, Inclusive, in the Penal and Correctional Institutions of the Commonwealth and a Discussion of Objectives* (Harrisburg: Commonwealth of Pennsylvania, 1935), 46, 48.

45. For a brilliant account of the conditions of Texas prisons in the 1960s, see Robert Chase, "Civil Rights on the Cellblock: Race, Reform, and Violence in Texas Prisons and the Nation, 1945–1990" (Ph.D. diss., University of Maryland, 2009).

46. Tom Murton, *Accomplices to the Crime* (New York: Grove Press, 1969).

47. There are numerous examples of this, but for some particularly interesting treatments, see Bruce Jackson, "Our Prisons Are Criminal," *New York Times,* September 22, 1968; and Toussaint Losier, "'We Are One People': The 1970 New York City Jail Rebellions and the Practice of Solidarity," seminar paper, Department of History, University of Chicago.

48. See Public Law 89–465, 89th Cong., S–1357.

49. *New York Times*, August 13, 1970.

50. *Tombs Disturbance Report,* 1970, New York State Senate Committee on Crime and Correction, 31.

51. Ibid.

52. *The Hidden Society,* 1970, Annual Report, New York State Senate Committee on Crime and Correction, 10; *New York Times,* August 12, 1970.

53. *New York Times,* August 22, 1970.

54. *Tombs Disturbance Report,* 28.

55. *Attica: The Official Report of the New York State Special Commission on Attica,* 2nd printing (New York: Bantam, 1972), 39.

56. Ibid.

57. Testimony of David Addison, April 17, 1972, transcript, McKay Commission (New York State Special Commission on Attica Hearings), 57.

58. Ibid.

59. Testimony of Angel Martinez, April 13, 1972, transcript, McKay Commission, 57.

60. J. Rosenberg, interview, in *Voices from Inside: Seven Interviews with Attica Prisoners* (Great Jones Printing, 1972).

61. Ibid.

62. John Stockholm, interview by the author, July 1, 2005, Lehigh Acres, Florida.

63. Ibid.

64. For more on Murton's exposé, see Heather Ann Thompson, "'Blinded by the Barbaric South: Prison Horror, Inmate Abuse, and the Ironic Hisotry of American Penal Reform," in *The Myth of Southern Exceptionalism,"* ed. Matthew Lassiter and Joseph Crespino (New York: Oxford University Press, 2009).

65. Chase, "Civil Rights on the Cellblock," 62.

66. Quote from James B. Jacobs, *New Perspectives on Prisons and Imprisonment* (Ithaca: Cornell University Press, 1983), 39, in Joel Sahama, *Criminal Justice* (Stamford, Ct.: Wadsworth, 2002), 508.

67. All of these cases were crucially important, but for information on one of the most important and long-running of these, see Chase, "Civil Rights on the Cell Block," particularly chapters 7 and 8.

68. Linda Charlton, "Mayor Waits for Two Hours for Inmates to Respond," *New York Times,* October 5, 1970.

69. See original typed copy of "proposals acceptable to Oswald at this time" in the McKay Collection, #15855–90, box 84, New York State Archives, Albany.

70. For a comprehensive history of the Attica prison uprising of 1971 and its legacy, see

Heather Thompson, forthcoming from Pantheon. The material referring to Attica in this essay is drawn from research for this work.

71. For some other examples of crucial prisoner rights rebellions, see Daniel Berger, "'We Are the Revolutionaries': Visibility, Protest, and Racial Formation in 1970s Prison Radicalism" (Ph.D. diss., University of Pennsylvania, 2010). See also Alan Eladio Gómez, "Nuestras vidas corren casi paralelas": Chicanos, Independentistas, and the Prison Rebellion Years in Leavenworth, 1969–1972," *Latino Studies* 6 (2008): 64–96.

72. Alfonso A. Narvaez, "Prison Bills Fill Hopper in Albany: 85 Measures Await Action by the 1972 Legislature," *New York Times*, January 11, 1972; "Rockefeller Offers Package for Prison Reform," *New York Times*, April 2, 1972; Alfonso A. Narvaez, "Prison Reform Measures Are Signed by Rockefeller," *New York Times*, May 24, 1972.

73. Harris Poll, December 1971.

74. Roper Commercial Survey, conducted by Roper Organization, October 18– October 27, 1971, and based on personal interviews with a national adult sample of 1,499 (USROPER.524COM.R20E), Roper Center for Public Opinion Research, University of Connecticut.

75. See ibid.

76. Conducted by Louis Harris & Associates during July 1971, and based on personal interviews with a national adult sample of 1,600 (USHARRIS.71JUL.R26F). Data provided by the Roper Center for Public Opinion Research, University of Connecticut.

77. Henry Ruth and Kevin R. Reitz, *The Challenge of Crime: Rethinking Our Response* (Cambridge: Harvard University Press, 2006), 283.

78. Sourcebook of Criminal Justice Statistics Online, table 6.1, 2006, "Adults on Probation, in Jail or Prison, and on Parole 1980–2006," www.albany.edu/sourcebook/pdf/t61 2006.pdf.

79. Patrick A. Langan, Ph.D., *Race of Prisoners Admitted to State and Federal Institutions, 1926–86,* report, May 1991. U.S. Department of Justice, Office of Justice Programs, Bureau of Justice Statistics, www.ncjrs.gov/pdffiles1/nij/125618.pdf.

80. Ibid.

81. *Prisoners, 2007, Summary Findings,* report, Bureau of Justice Statistics, www.ojp .usdoj.gov/bjs/prisons.htm.

82. One in one hundred.

83. For specific information on all of the costs of racialized incarceration listed here, and cites to the broader literature on the same, see Thompson, "Why Mass Incarceration Matters."

84. "Crime, Punishments," Survey, September 1994, Wirthlin Group, McLean, Va., from "Polling the Nations" database.

85. "Crime, Punishments," General Social Surveys, 1992, Sample size 1,517, Roper Center for Public Opinion Research, from "Polling the Nations" database.

86. Timothy Weigand, "Captive Subjects: Pharmaceutical Testing and Prisoners," *Journal of Medical Toxicology* (September 25, 2009); Adriana Petryna, "Clinical Trials Offshored: On Private Sector Science and Public Health," *BioSocieties* 2 (2007): 21–40 (London School of Economics and Political Science).

87. Ian Urbina, "Panel Suggests Using Inmates in Drug Trials," *New York Times*, August 13, 2006.

88. Clifford Bartz, "Donation Inmate Organ Network (DION): Giving Inmates Time Off for Organ Donation," *Medicine and Health Rhode Island,* December 2005.

89. Ibid.

90. Quoted in Kevin B. O'Reilly, "Prisoner Organ Donation Proposal Worrisome," *American Medical News,* April 9, 2007.

91. Ibid.

92. "Cold Storage: Super-Maximum Security Confinement in Indiana," *Human Rights Watch Report,* October 1997, 30; Nick Wilkinson and Brett Cherry, "Death in the Restraint Chair," *Dayton City Paper,* September 17, 2004.

93. "Investigative Reports: Solitary Confinement," A&E Television (AAE-73200t).

94. "Cold Storage," 20.

95. Mary Beth Pfeiffer, *Crazy in America: The Hidden Tragedy of Our Criminalized Mentally Ill* (New York: Basic, 2007); Donald Specter, "Cruel and Unusual Punishment of the Mentally Ill in California's Prisons: A Case Study of a Class Action Suit," *Social Justice,* September 22, 1994.

96. re Gault, 387 U.S. 1 (1967); Declaration of the Rights of the Child (1959).G.A. res. 1386 (XIV), 14 U.N. GAOR. Supp. (No. 16) at 19, U.N. Doc. A/4354.

97. www.nospank.net/boot.htm; Tim Reid, "Torture, Starvation and Death: How American Boot Camps Abuse Boys," *London Times,* October 12, 2007; Melissa Sickmund, "Deaths of Juveniles in Custody, 2004," www.aca.org/research/pdf/Research_Notes03_07 .pdf; Catherine A. Gallagher and Adam Dobrin, "Bottom of Form Deaths in Juvenile Justice Residential Facilities," *Journal of Adolescent Health* 38, no. 6 (June 2006): 662–68

98. See, in particular, the work by Vesla Weaver, Michael Flamm, and David Garland on this topic. Vesla M. Weaver, "Frontlash: Race and the Development of Punitive Crime Policy," *Studies in American Political Development* 21 (Fall 2007): 230–65; Michael Flamm, *Law and Order: Street Crime, Civil Unrest, and the Crisis of Liberalism in the 1960s* (New York: Columbia University Press, 2005); David Garland, *The Culture of Control: Crime and Social Order in Contemporary Society* (Chicago: University of Chicago Press, 2001).

99. Oshinsky, *Worse Than Slavery,* 37. For more on the connection between mass incarceration and the shift in politics experienced in this country after the 1960s, see Thompson, "Why Mass Incarceration Matters."

100. For much more detail on the overhaul of New Deal–era restrictions on prison labor as well as on the impact of this overhaul on America's working class, see Thompson, "Rethinking Working Class Struggle through the Lens of the Carceral State."

101. There is one segment of the American working class that has been slow to see that a buildup of the carceral state is not in its interest: prison guard associations such as the California Peace Officers Association (CPOA) and the New York Safety and Correctional Officers Benevolence Association (NYSCOBA). Joshua Page has written extensively on the ways in which these organizations, which call themselves unions, acted to thwart efforts to reduce prison building and penal populations (see Joshua Page, *The Toughest Beat: Politics, Punishment, and the Prison Officers' Union in California* [Oxford: Oxford University Press, 2011]). Most guard labor unions, however, are not willing to see a wholesale buildup of the carceral state simply to safeguard their own jobs, and when they oppose closing prisons, it is often because of the severe crowding and speed up it causes at other prisons—in other words, those closings have not, in fact, reduced prison populations. For a critical

analysis of Page's argument about the prison guard unions, see Heather Ann Thompson, "Downsizing the Carceral State: The Policy Implications of Prison Guard Unions," *Criminology and Public Policy* (August 2011).

102. Victor Perlo, "Prison Labor in the U.S.," August 17, 1999, www.hartford-hwp.com /archives/45b/157.html.

103. Families against Mandatory Minimums, "About Us," www.famm.org/About FAMM.aspx.

104. "The Problem of Punishment: Race, Inequality and Justice," symposium, April 16–17, 2009, Carter G. Woodson Institute, University of Virginia, http://artsandsciences .virginia.edu/woodson/symposium/index.html.

105. "The Imprisonment of a Race," conference, March 25, 2011, Department of African American Studies, Princeton University, www.princeton.edu/africanamericanstudies /events/imprisonment/.

106. Specific projects include the Gideon Project, which focuses on the fair and equal administration of justice, including death penalty reform, improving public defense, and ending racial profiling; the Sentencing and Incarceration Alternatives Project, which focuses on sentencing reform, including mandatory minimums and crack-powder cocaine disparities, and limiting prison expansion and privatization; the After Prison Initiative, which focuses on reorienting policies and reinvesting resources of prison systems to maximize successful reentry and support the economic and political reenfranchisement of high incarceration communities; and the Soros Justice Fellowships Program, which provides one-year project fellowships to emerging and seasoned criminal justice advocates.

107. www.amnesty-volunteer.org/usa/group159/supermax.html; www.hrw.org/en /reports/2000/02/01/out-sight-super-maximum-security-confinement-us; Laura Magnani, *Buried Alive: Long-Term Isolation in California's Youth and Adult Prisons*, report, American Friends Service Committee, Oakland, May 2008, www.afsc.org/stopmax/ht/a /GetDocumentAction/i/38569%20

108. Magnani, *Buried Alive.*

109. Heather Schoenfeld, "Mass Incarceration and the Paradox of Prison Conditions Litigation," *Law & Society Review* 44, no. 3/4 (August 2010): 731–32.

110. For another take on prisoner rights litigation, and the controversial suggestion that it actually leads to greater incarceration, see Schoenfeld, "Mass Incarceration and the Paradox of Prison Conditions Litigation."

111. John Scalia, BJS statistician, "Prisoner Petitions Filed in U.S. District Courts, 2000, with Trends 1980–2000"; see Court decision in *Johnson v California,* www.usdoj .gov/osg/briefs/2003/3mer/1ami/2003–0636.mer.ami.pdf

112. See the order in these cases: www.prisonlaw.com/pdfs/Plata3JudgeOrder.pdf; and www.prisonlaw.com/pdfs/Coleman3JudgeOrder.pdf.

113. See three-judge panel ruling, www.prisonlaw.com/pdfs/Platatentativeruling.pdf.

# "Bright and Good Looking Colored Girl"

*Black Women's Sexuality and "Harmful Intimacy" in*
*Early-Twentieth-Century New York*

CHERYL D. HICKS

Mabel Hampton's experiences in early-twentieth-century Harlem never quite measured up to the popular image that many New Yorkers (and later the world) held of the black neighborhood. In 1924, as a twenty-one-year-old resident, she knew that visitors from other parts of the city would go to "the night-clubs . . . and dance to such jazz music as [could] be heard nowhere else," that the region's major thoroughfares like Lenox and Seventh Avenues were "never deserted," while various "crowds skipp[ed] from one place of amusement to another."[1] Those crowds of primarily middle-class white voyeurs, fulfilling their own ideas about the primitiveness and authenticity of black life, enjoyed and came to expect Harlem's "'hot' and 'barbaric' jazz, the risqué lyrics and the 'junglelike' dancing of its cabaret floor shows, and all its other 'wicked' delights."[2] As one black observer noted, after "a visit to Harlem at night," partygoers believed that the town "never sle[pt] and that the inhabitants . . . jazz[ed] through existence."[3] Hampton's everyday life, however, failed to coincide with these romanticized and essentialized stereotypes of black entertainment and urban life. A southern migrant, domestic worker, and occasional chorus line dancer, she understood Harlem's social and cultural complexities as she faced its pleasures, hardships, and dangers. Her time in Harlem also coincided with the historical moment when the neighborhood was touted by white New Yorkers as one of the most sexually liberated spaces in the city.

Like that of most working-class women, however, Hampton's social life, particularly her romantic attachments, faced more critical surveillance. With the increasing popularity of movies, dance halls, and amusement parks, community members and relatives became more concerned about how and with whom their young women spent their leisure time. Reformers and the police also attempted to regulate working-class women's social lives and especially their sexuality. During World War I, the federal government showed particular concern because of its fear that young women would spread venereal disease to soldiers, thereby physi-cally weakening the armed forces and thus endangering the country's war effort.[4] General concerns about working-class women's sexual behavior influenced the passing of numerous state laws that were shaped by reformers, approved by leg-islators, and enforced by police officers.[5] As such, young working-class women's interest in and pursuit of romance and sex caused various older adults unease not simply because such behavior rejected or ignored traditional courtship prac-tices but also because evidence of sexual expression and behavior outside of mar-riage and outside the parameters of prostitution eventually constituted criminal activity.

Even though all working-class women were scrutinized for their pursuit of social autonomy and sexual expression, race and ethnicity influenced the nature of reformers' and criminal justice administrators' interactions with their charges. Immigrant and native-born white working-class women certainly were targeted by reformers and the police for questionable moral behavior, but generally author-ity figures believed these women could be reformed. Rehabilitative efforts were less of a guarantee for women who were characterized as innately promiscuous because of long-standing negative stigmas associated with their African ancestry and the legacy of American enslavement. The fact that many African American women lived in Harlem, a neighborhood seen by white partygoers (and other New Yorkers) as a center of social and sexual abandon, reinforced the libidinous images of the neighborhood's residents and influenced how police officers and criminal justice administrators assessed black women's culpability in sexual of-fenses.

Young black women—incarcerated primarily for sex-related offenses, on charges that included vagrancy, disorderly conduct, and prostitution—usually rejected reformers' concerns and often believed they were unfairly targeted.[6] Ma-bel Hampton, for example, contended that her imprisonment at the New York State Reformatory for Women at Bedford Hills (hereafter Bedford) for solicitation stemmed from a false arrest. Other inmates revealed their own problems with law enforcement and, like Hampton, disagreed with the contention that their social behavior—in New York and especially Harlem—was criminal. One hundred Bed-ford case files show that between 1917 and 1928, a range of black women—from southern migrants to native-born New Yorkers—negotiated the urban terrain as well as their sexual desire. In particular, forty-nine southern migrants' experi-ences showed how they encountered and embraced a social and political free-dom unavailable to most black southerners. Yet many young working-class black women, regardless of their regional, religious, or familial background, grappled with the relentless surveillance of police officers, reformers, concerned relatives, and community members.

During admission interviews and throughout their association with Bedford, black women revealed how public perceptions of their sexual behavior failed to capture the complexity of their personal experiences.[7] Most importantly, their wide-ranging responses provide a lens through which we might understand how working-class black women whose imprisonment, in large part, stemmed from arrests for—alleged and admitted—sexual offenses dealt with urban sexuality. Like their white counterparts, they experimented with courting, treating (bartering sex for commercial goods or amusements rather than accepting money for intercourse), and the sex trade, but the "metalanguage of race" and especially "racial constructions of sexuality" influenced the distinct reactions they received from many authority figures. In particular, the prevalence of racial stereotypes meant that the police and Bedford administrators primarily viewed young black women's "sexual delinquency" as natural rather than judging the independent conduct of individuals.[8] Such essentialized renderings of their sexuality as well as black female reformers' concerted efforts to control such negative images by repressing discussions of sexual desire have obscured ordinary black women's complicated decisions and dilemmas regarding sex. While they enjoyed a greater range of choices regarding the conduct of their social lives, they also dealt with more restrictive treatment from both public officials and their own community. Their broader range of leisure options forced them to make difficult choices about how they would deal with their sexual desires as well as the consequences of their decisions and actions. Thus, black women's responses can offer a window into how they remembered past sexual encounters or, rather, how they chose to characterize them. This study privileges the ways in which working-class black women constructed their own narratives and the kinds of stories they chose to reveal about their sexual behavior. Focusing on early-twentieth-century New York, where moral panics about working-class female sexuality shaped urban reform and criminal justice initiatives, this work also shows how local and state officials' racialized conceptions of black women's sexual behavior influenced the dynamics of reform efforts in black communities as well as the tenor of Bedford's institutional policies.

Especially at this critical juncture in our nation's history, when public policy experts, academics, and grassroots activists grapple with the social consequences of the rising levels of incarceration among African American women, scholars in the field of carceral studies must attend to how the historical trajectory of U.S. criminal law and penal policy has been shaped by the intertwined politics of race, gender, and sexuality. More specifically, understanding the historical roots of the hyperpolicing and excessive punishing of African Americans requires critical engagement with the long history of state-sanctioned surveillance of black women and the carceral techniques employed to police their sexuality within and beyond prison walls. On this important front, the experiences of African American women in early-twentieth-century New York, particularly women housed at Bedford Reformatory, provide a useful case study for exploring how normative ideas regarding black women and their sexuality have informed and continue to inform their complex encounters with the criminal justice system.

### What Can Bedford's Prison Records Tell Us about Black Women's Sexuality?

Incarcerated women offer a perspective that places black working-class women's ideas about and experiences with sexuality at the center of discussions regarding early-twentieth-century urban life.[9] Using the cases of female offenders to address this issue, however, does not suggest that black working women were linked with criminality. Rather, this approach reflects the encounters of a particular segment of women who grew up and lived in certain black communities. Their experiences coincided with as well as diverged from those of other women but also vividly underscore the complexity of the black working class.[10] Such an inquiry emphasizes how some black women understood, experienced, and expressed heterosexual and same-sex desire while simultaneously dealing with how others perceived their sexuality, including police officers, prison administrators, black reformers, relatives, and white Americans generally.

Addressing black women's sexuality—which usually appears in literature or through the figure of the 1920s blues woman—from the perspective of a specific group of working-class women takes into account the directive of the scholar Evelynn Hammonds to consider "how differently located black women engage[d] in reclaiming the body and expressing desire."[11] Hammonds notes that scholarship on black women's sexuality typically focuses on how black women at the turn of the twentieth century refrained from discussing sexual desire and instead advocated behavior that rejected stereotypes that defined them as representatives of deviant sexuality. Black female activists, in particular, promoted what the scholar Evelyn Higginbotham has termed a "politics of respectability" in which appropriate behavior and decorum provided a defensive response to immoral images as well as corresponding civil and political inequalities.[12] Black women also enacted what the scholar Darlene Clark Hine calls a culture of dissemblance." In this sense, they "created the appearance of openness and disclosure but actually" fashioned a protective silence "from their oppressors" as it related to their personal and sexual lives.[13] While acknowledging the power of such theoretical concepts, Hammonds argues that using the "politics of silence" as a defensive strategy worked so successfully that black women eventually "lost the ability to articulate any conception of their sexuality"—with one exception: women performing the blues.[14] This scholarship, then, suggests that the most prominent and public articulation of black women's sexuality appeared through the experiences of early-twentieth-century blues singers who expressed sexual desire through explicit lyrics and performance.[15] Discussions about female entertainers, however, present one particular viewpoint on how black women addressed sexual desire.

Not solely representing black women enacting a "politics of silence" or blues women expressing a public identity as sexual beings, imprisoned Bedford women provide examples of both perspectives. Answering the explicit questions that Bedford administrators asked all women during the admissions process, black domestics, laundresses, factory workers, and children's nurses between the ages of sixteen and twenty-eight revealed sexual experiences that exemplified a variety of behaviors, including desire, ignorance, and abuse.[16] Yet there were instances when administrators became frustrated because some black women acknowledged their involvement in the sex trade but were reticent about conveying further details. For example, one twenty-year-old Virginia native was characterized as "pleasant" and "truthful," but she was also said to have provided officials with "little information about herself."[17] Thus, white female administrators (and one white male superintendent) also documented black women's sense of propriety when they, as inmates, refused to talk about their sexual experiences or indicated how they attended to traditional moral proscriptions by rejecting premarital sex.

Female offenders' responses to prison administrators might be seen as evidence of the state's continued intrusion into black women's lives as well as its attempt to construct and promote derogatory images.[18] No doubt, black women understood administrators' skepticism when what they recounted failed to coincide with long-standing racial and sexual stereotypes. Consider, for instance, the sexual history of one inmate who revealed the complex parameters of a life that included being raped, her revelation that she prostituted herself twice, and her adamant stance that she was not promiscuous. The administrator seemed to dismiss the woman's difficult circumstances by focusing solely on her interview demeanor. The official concluded, in part, that the woman's "better education [had given] . . . her [a] superior manner" so that she did not have an "attractive personality" because she seemed "distant and haughty."[19] Indeed, what administrators thought as well as how they documented what they observed and chose to hear from black women shaped the information within all case files.[20] Yet these partial transcripts also show how inmates challenged the public discourse that delineated all black women as pathologically promiscuous. These women's responses were also influenced by attempts to negotiate Bedford's indeterminate sentencing, which, based on how an administrator assessed an inmate's behavioral improvement, could include a minimum sentence of several months or a maximum sentence of three years.

While exploring offenders' responses to questions about sexual behavior, this study takes seriously the possibility that black women who felt compelled to silence may have seen the admission interview as an opportunity to document their incidences of desire as well as abuse. Some women described experiences that ranged from initial romance to participation in the sex trade. Others revealed the dangers found by young and independent women living in a large city. Understanding that society questioned most black women's complicity in their rapes, these inmates may have viewed administrators' direct question about whether their first "sexual offense" was consensual or rape as a chance to address their abuse in ways that may not have been possible among friends, family members, community leaders, or the police. Administrators' decision to label young women's first sexual encounters as criminal offenses reminds us of their moral position on premarital sex and makes clear their preconceived notions about all incoming and primarily working-class women.

Officials also documented "harmful intimacy," or, rather, the interracial relationships, they observed at Bedford. While acknowledging the prevalence of same-sex desire among white inmates, administrators seemed most concerned with developing attachments between black and white women. Evidence of such relationships stemmed largely from the various conduct violations (described variously as "fond of colored girls" or "seen passing notes to black inmates") noted within white women's files.[21] Black women also received conduct violations, which would indicate that they actively participated in interracial liaisons. Administrators, however, portrayed "harmful intimacy" as white women's heterosexual attraction to black women, whose dark skin color supposedly represented virility.[22] Dismissing their own notations, officials attempted to ignore black women's participation in "harmful intimacy" and same-sex desire among black women.

These same officials also overlooked their own evidence of black women's varied sexual experiences and instead based many of their inmate evaluations on powerful racial stereotypes. Centuries-old images that defined black women as immoral and pathological deeply influenced these officials' perceptions. As the scholars Jennifer Morgan and Deborah Gray White have shown, already in the seventeenth century, male European travelers depicted African women's bodies as savage, lewd, and unfeminine, and they unleashed Christian, moral condemnations of various cultural practices such as seminudity, polygamy, and dancing, narratives that eventually justified the slave trade.[23] Such observations of cultural differences shaped the development of enslavement and led to correlations between lasciviousness and Africans generally. As Sander Gilman has argued, Europeans eventually viewed black men's and women's bodies as "icon[s] for deviant sexuality."[24] In the context of American slavery, antebellum southerners accepted the image of the sexually insatiable enslaved woman, thereby characterizing all white men as victims of sepia temptresses.[25] The direct connections that southerners made between black women, immorality, and promiscuity remained vivid in popular culture long after slavery ended.[26] In 1904, when one southern white woman commented that she could not "imagine such a creation as a virtuous black woman," she captured the sentiments of many late-nineteenth- and early-twentieth-century white Americans.[27]

When black women were imprisoned for sex-related and other minor offenses, Bedford prison officials' knowledge of prevailing stereotypes affected their overall assessment of black women's culpability. It was not uncommon for administrators to conflate their ideas about an uncivilized Africa with their physical descriptions and overall behavioral assessments of incoming black women. In 1923, written comments such as "true African type . . . inclined to be somewhat vicious looking" and "a typical African cunning calculating eyes" indicated the depth of their prejudices in evaluating individual women's cases.[28] More positive appraisals such as "appears intelligent for one of her race and station" and "has little moral sense but appears more decent than the average colored girl" still revealed their beliefs in black people's inferiority.[29] Along with observations of black women that ranged from "refined looking pretty colored girl" to "very inferior looking colored girl," regional biases also influenced initial interviews.[30] Administrators making notations akin to the following description—"peculiar way of speaking, a drawl and a typically Southern way of pronouncing words"—often questioned southern migrants' level of intelligence, fitness for urban life, and susceptibility to crime based on their diction.[31] Thus, not only did these officials evaluate and categorize Bedford's working-class and poor women, but their notations also illustrate their specific beliefs in black women's criminality.

In 1924, Mabel Hampton, characterized by Bedford's superintendent, Amos Baker, as a "bright and good looking colored girl," simultaneously reinforced yet complicated Bedford officials' assumptions. Administrators never questioned the validity of her arrest but did acknowledge that Hampton seemed unique. Even though she fervently denied her solicitation charge, her comportment impressed prison administrators. They found her "alert" and "composed" with a "pleasant voice and manner of speaking"; in a separate interview, officials noted that Hampton's "attitude and manner seem[ed] truthful" as she talked "freely and frankly conceal[ing] nothing" about her everyday life and what she considered to be her false arrest.[32] While administrators found Hampton attractive, personable, and honest, they still imprisoned her. Ignoring their own observations regarding her credibility, officials judged Hampton based on their assumption that black women's sexual misconduct, when not a direct legal violation, could also be attributed to their innate susceptibility to unfortunate associations with "bad company."[33] Hampton, however, explained her police altercation quite differently, as she called her arrest a "put up job."[34]

The "ill-feeling" that Hampton expressed "toward her accuser" mirrored the sentiments of a number of black women and community members as they contended that police corruption rather than black women's behavior accounted for high numbers of prostitution arrests.[35] Caught in a house raid when her employer of two years took an extended European trip, Hampton was most likely arrested because she was "between jobs."[36] The fact that Hampton had access to her employer's home shows that she was trusted, but that same employer's absence from the court proceedings indicated that once in court, Hampton had no one to vouch for her reputation.[37]

Her arrest also illuminates how the courts expanded the legal definition of vagrancy to include prostitution. During this period, vagrancy laws were defined more broadly instead of the traditional perception of a person with no employment or a public drunkard. In 1919, the New York statute encompassed prostitution and included anyone who "in any way, aids and abets or participates" in the sex trade.[38] In Hampton's case, a plainclothes detective charged her with being an accessory to a sex crime by alleging that she permitted a female friend to use her employer's apartment for the "purposes of prostitution." According to Hampton, on the night of the arrest she and a friend waited for their dates, "who promised to take them to a cabaret." Shortly after the men's arrival, the police raided her employer's home and arrested both women.[39] Initially, the arrest may have puzzled Hampton, as she denied ever prostituting herself, contending that she had been seeing her date for a month. Although she seemed conflicted about his romantic pursuit, she also stated that he "wanted to marry her." Hampton's perception of her boyfriend and the incident changed when she surmised that her date worked as a "stool pigeon" or police accomplice who arranged her arrest.[40] Thus, Hampton's evening excursion led to her subsequent imprisonment because in court the police officer's word was deemed more legitimate than that of a young black domestic.

Hampton was not alone in her desire for entertainment and companionship, nor was she exempt from experiencing the dangers that such yearnings posed. Indeed, working women's longing to escape the everyday toil of personal service labor by attending cabarets and dance halls at night could result in arrest or what most women called a police set-up.[41] In 1923, Harriet Holmes, a laundress making fifteen dollars per week, argued that she was falsely arrested when leaving a popular dance hall. It is not clear if she arrived at the function with friends, but when she left at one thirty in the morning she was alone. The twenty-three-year-old said that when she was walking to her apartment on West 133rd Street, a car stopped at the curb, and four men, claiming that they were police, pulled her in and, according to her, "without any reason . . . declared that she was guilty of prostitution."[42] In a similar case, a twenty-two-year-old decided that she would leave a cabaret alone at one thirty in the morning.

In this instance, her girlfriend refused to leave with her, so she reportedly followed her sister's advice, which stressed that "after dark always take a taxi" home, to no avail. When she got in the cab, "two men stepped in with her." She fought them, thinking they were robbers. Instead, she was taken to the police station and arrested for prostitution.[43]

In addition to attending cabarets and dance halls, young black women found that the cheap and pleasurable practice of visiting friends' homes could also be a dangerous form of leisure.[44] A number of women discovered that the simple act of enjoying the company of friends in their tenement or boardinghouse rooms could result in a solicitation arrest. Twenty-four-year-old Millie Hodges had been in New York for a few weeks working in a coat factory before her arrest and Bedford sentence. Having recently separated from her husband of nine years, she decided to leave Chicago and come to New York so that she could make a fresh start. Without any relatives in the city, she sought a supportive community and was visiting on 132nd Street when her friend's boardinghouse was raided and its occupants charged with "being disorderly."[45] Her denials about solicitation and her claims that she had never been arrested failed to change her fate; she gained a criminal record by simply being in a seemingly appropriate residence at the wrong time. Incidences such as this one reinforced the dilemma young black women faced in Harlem: they had the freedom to participate in various commercial and informal amusements, but the stigmas attached to working-class and black communities meant that their behavior was regulated on a consistent and often discriminatory basis.

Some black women, however, made entertainment choices based on the short-term benefits of pleasure rather than thinking through the implications of associating with bad company or, rather, men and women with morally questionable backgrounds. Scenarios ranged from those instances when young women misjudged the character of their acquaintances to when they knowingly associated with bad company and were led into dubious and sometimes illegal activities.

Having lived in her furnished room for two weeks before her prostitution arrest, twenty-four-year-old southern migrant Sarah Woods claimed that she believed that her West 140th Street boardinghouse was run by a "respectable [colored] woman." Woods later discovered that the house had been raided; moreover, her landlady was described by the police as a white woman in an interracial marriage and with a previous arrest for running a disorderly household.[46] While Woods may have suspected her landlady's racial identity, she would have been less able to know of her arrest record, which illustrates how some women simply became caught up in unforeseeable circumstances. Alice Kent's case nevertheless illustrates how young women's associations with bad company could be fun but lamentable. Once she arrived in New York, the twenty-year-old Philadelphia native immediately made friends with people who shunned legitimate employment but devoured Harlem's nightlife. Kent's troubles began when she and a friend attended the Savoy Dance Hall on Lenox Avenue and there met two men with whom they eventually cohabitated and who partially supported them. While social workers contended that she prostituted herself during her New York tenure, Kent fervently denied her culpability and later wrote to a friend (in a letter that was confiscated by prison officials and never mailed), admitting her mistakes: "I was furious for a time, having the knowledge of my innocence. But I am now coming to the conclusion that it was more or less my fault for staying there, knowing what was going on. We are always judged by our companions. This has taught me a lesson. . . . I will always remember my (A.B.C.) that is to avoid bad company."[47]

Kent's reaction shows that she understood the precarious nature and consequences of Harlem's quick friendships and fast living. Twenty-two-year-old Wanda Harding, described as a native of the British West Indies, acknowledged her relationships with inappropriate acquaintances by referencing her Pentecostal background. When confronted about her misconduct, she responded that she recognized her "great weakness and craving for the attractions of this world." She also seemed to suggest that others should empathize with her slip-ups and noted that "everybody . . . [was] a born a sinner."[48] Harding's sentiments reveal a young woman's acute awareness of her personal mistakes and subsequent psychological struggles when forced to face the consequences of having disregarded proper decorum. Reinforcing the fact that "her father and mother were devout Christians" and concerned about her moral dilemma, Harding's minister concluded that "through bad company she went astray [and] through good company she will be brought back again to the narrow way."[49] His comment exemplifies how the negative consequences resulting from black women's associations with bad company only underscored reformers' and relatives' contentions that these women ought to socialize only with respectable people and under appropriate circumstances.

In this sense, black relatives and community members, while acknowledging rampant police corruption, simultaneously expressed myriad concerns about black women's naive or wayward personal behavior. They empathized with some of these young women's grievances regarding false arrests, but, emphasizing a woman's appropriate decorum, they also often questioned these women's decision to attend unsupervised dances, associate with questionable people, or walk unaccompanied late at night. Relatives were especially anxious. Consider, for instance, the mother of one eighteen-year-old Long Island native whose frustration with her daughter's behavior is clear: "Her going to the bad was going to dances and then being led by others older than herself."[50] While this mother accepted the fact that her daughter was "going to the bad fast," she also revealed how she worked diligently to safeguard and raise all of her children properly. "I have tried to bring my children up in a christian way [and] have done the best I knew of," she explained, "but you know the world has to[o] many charms for young people of today."[51] Similar to reformers' concerns, working-class parents believed in the need for suitable recreational facilities and activities for black youth because they agreed that the urban trappings of "silk and electric lights" and other "evil influences" such as dance halls and saloons caused young women to go astray.[52]

## Regulating Black Women, Regulating Harlem

During the 1920s, Harlem was part of a Renaissance in black cultural production that included the height of dance hall and nightclub gaiety, the popularity of rent parties, and a growing characterization that the neighborhood was accepting of various forms of sexual expression. Many black residents and leaders, as the previous discussion has shown, expressed grave and conservative concerns about the confluence of popular entertainment and nonmarital sex. It seems that they were also particularly concerned about the growing presence of same-sex relationships. Many would have heard about the openly lesbian references in blues singers' songs like Gertrude "Ma" Rainey's "Prove It on Me Blues" or even the much-noted, outrageously popular, and sexually decadent Harlem parties.[53] Yet outside of the music industry and within many working-class communities, publicly expressing one's sexuality and desire, whether single or married, was discouraged.[54]

Ironically, some black churches were discovering their own gay congregants during this time. The pulpit denouncement of such relationships, however, conflated two distinct issues: same-sex desire and ministers who preyed on young male congregants without condemnation from their parishioners. Rev. Adam Clayton Powell of the Abyssinian Baptist Church, a most vocal critic, briefly noted that young women were increasingly engaged in same-sex relationships, although he did not distinguish consensual from predatory relationships. "Homosexuality and sex-perversion among women," argued Powell, "has grown into one of the most horrible debasing, alarming and damning vices of present day civilization." Powell was not simply concerned that homosexuality was "prevalent to an unbelievable degree" but also that such relationships, according to him, were "increasing day by day." Powell's conflation of same-sex desire and sexual abuse of children gained strong support from his colleagues as well as his congregation, whose responses on the day of his sermon indicated that his "opinions were endorsed and approved without limitations."[55]

Mabel Hampton (mentioned at the start of this essay) was not a member of Powell's church, yet it is not difficult to believe that she would have understood the minister's sentiments as representing the views of most Harlem residents, since she actively sought to hide her sexual orientation in her Harlem neighborhood before acting on her desire for women at private rent parties. At the same time, while they may not have condoned such behavior, most Harlemites in Powell's congregation would not have found the fact that Hampton frequented rent parties all that unusual. Large numbers of working-class residents gladly paid fees to enjoy a night of food, Prohibition Era drinking, dancing, and music while also contributing financially to a fellow neighbor's rent. They, like Hampton, attended "pay parties" and "rent parties" in various people's homes, and, according to her, depending on the night and the residence, one could eat "chicken and potato salad," "pig feet, chittlins," and, "in the wintertime," black-eyed peas.[56] She recalled that, having paid the fee, one could just "dance and have fun" until the early hours of the morning. But Hampton partied exclusively with other women. Her reminiscences about those moments indicate that while black Harlemites may have acknowledged the existence of rent parties, they would not have as easily accepted a party of women desiring women. Explaining her predicament, Hampton revealed that, on the one hand, as a young Harlemite she experienced a "free life" where she "could do anything she wanted," yet, on the other hand, publicly expressing her developing and complex desires for women was out of the question.[57] "When I was coming along everything was hush-hush," she recalled. She and women like her felt safer meeting at house parties—"private things," she noted, "where you'd go with" a woman without fear of reprisals.[58]

Hampton's experience strongly suggests that black women who desired women usually disguised their feelings in public, negotiating not only the police but also black Harlem. She disclosed that when black women attended house parties, they made distinct choices about their public appearance that depended on whether they walked or drove to a particular function. In the privacy of an apartment, they openly expressed their same-sex desires, yet Hampton also emphasized how much more cautious they were about exposing their sexual desire when out and about in the larger Harlem community. According to her, when women attended various parties "very seldom did any of them [wear] . . . slacks . . . because they had to come through the streets." Instead, they played it safe and dressed in women's suits. She later confirmed that she always wore women's suits when attending parties. "You couldn't go out there with too many pants on because the men was ready to see . . . and that was no good." Instead, she explained that "you had to protect yourself and protect the woman that you was with."[59]

Hampton never revealed if she had ever experienced repercussions from having expressed her attraction to women, but she seemed to have managed her life by limiting her contact with men and those persons who were not "in the life." She told a personal friend later in her life that even during the height of the pleasure-seeking of the Harlem Renaissance, "you had to be very careful," which meant that Hampton and her friends "had fun behind closed doors."[60] For her, going out to bars was too much of a hassle because, as she put it, "too many men [were] taggled up with it; . . . they didn't know you [were] a lesbian . . . [and] they didn't care." "You was a woman . . . [so] you had the public [and] you had the men to tolerate," she recalled. She later contended that while she met a number of girlfriends as a dancer in Harlem cabarets such as the Garden of Joy, she eventually ended her dancing career because it created unwanted exchanges with men. "I gave up the stage," she explained, "because unless you go with men you don't eat."[61]

In hindsight and as a gay rights activist, Hampton spoke about herself as a young adult as having embraced lesbianism directly and publicly, yet when she was arrested for prostitution in 1924, she may not have been as forthcoming about her sexuality. Her arrest, after all, stemmed from a heterosexual double date gone awry. Her experience suggests that her later characterization of the solicitation arrest as absurd because she was considered a "woman's woman" might reveal more about her later life than how she worked to address her feelings and desires for women and men at that time.[62] Hampton's sentiments were shared by other women, black and white, but the general focus of urban reformers and criminal justice administrators as well as the federal government resulted from their attempts to regulate the behavior of those they believed to be dangerous, heterosexual, working-class women.

Alongside reformers' and relatives' concerns, young women's arrests during and after World War I also reflected the federal government's attempt to prevent the spread of venereal disease. In particular, a series of vagrancy and prostitution statutes landed primarily working-class women in state reformatories and detention houses. For instance, reformers' general anxieties about sexually active young women resulted in the federal government appropriating funds for at least forty-three reformatories and detention homes nationwide that housed, cared for, and treated "women and girls who, as actual and potential carriers of venereal diseases were a menace to the health of the Military Establishment of the United States."[63]

The increased scrutiny of all working women's sexuality directly influenced black women's treatment in social welfare reform and the criminal justice system. Originally, seventeen-year-old Amanda B. was arrested for incorrigibility when her parents "could no longer keep . . . her from attending dances and associating with bad company." Yet Amanda's harsh Bedford sentence stemmed from social workers' discovery that she had refused treatment for a venereal disease at the City Hospital even before considering her mother's initial court petition.[64] Because of the nation's and particularly New York City's heightened alert about the connection between working-class women and venereal disease, Amanda's family's concerns about her inappropriate behavior were virtually ignored. Their attempt to regulate her youthful waywardness led to her imprisonment in a state institution rather than in the local rehabilitative home as well as to her permanent arrest record. Caught in a moment when their experimentation with leisure and sexuality was perceived as a national security threat, working-class women found that their behavior was deemed suspect. Black women in particular discovered that the police's perception of their supposed innate promiscuity and criminality shaped their arrests.

Ruby Brooks's case shows how reformers' as well as the federal government's anxieties about working-class women's sexual behavior and venereal disease continued even after World War I. In 1924, the thirty-year-old domestic worker revealed that as she was walking home one evening she was approached by a man who asked if he could go home with her. When she responded, "No, I have no place to take you," another man appeared and arrested her for prostitution. Brooks, with no prior criminal record and a solid work history, believed that her arrest had been a frame-up and contended that she would not have been sent to Bedford if she had not been adamant about keeping "her arrest from her family," with whom she still lived. Other case file evidence, however, indicates that her imprisonment more than likely stemmed from the fact that she had tested positive for a venereal disease. Brooks's claim that she had only had intercourse with her fiancé was recorded but ignored, as he was investigated rather than clinically tested. For prison administrators, regardless of Brooks's verified background and upstanding fiancé, her medical condition posed a danger to society, thus justifying her yearlong imprisonment and multiple parole delays until she was cured with medical treatments.[65] For Brooks, the arrest and imprisonment were simply unjust and disregarded all of her personal attempts to live morally. "Being that I have worked all my life for 30 years," she explained, "I think it's pretty hard to be arrested."[66] Imprisoned in the same year as Mabel Hampton, Brooks believed that she understood the parameters of moral and legal behavior, but Bedford officials felt differently. Their objectives entailed rehabilitating and controlling the purported sexual deviancy of women as similar but distinct as these.

## Bedford and Racial Segregation

By the time of Brooks's and Hampton's arrests, Bedford had already long worked to fulfill its basic objective to reform young women. The opening of the institution in 1901 occurred simultaneously with changing perceptions of aberrant female behavior, from nineteenth-century fallen woman to twentieth-century sexual delinquent. During the 1870s, reformers addressing the growing number of young women in custodial prisons pushed for the institution because they believed it would play a major role in rehabilitating wayward women and primarily first offenders between the ages of sixteen and thirty; they believed that young female offenders had the capacity to be reformed.[67] Thus, during Bedford's initial years, administrators believed that working-class women's delinquent behavior could be redressed and even eliminated through proper training. The institution's first superintendent, Katharine Bement Davis, noted that Bedford received "women capable of such education and industrial training" that "would restore them to society, self-respecting and self-supporting."[68] City magistrates and some state legislators, however, found the practical application of the reformatory's objective too expensive, and it was consistently underfunded. Reformers protested, arguing that expenses related to rehabilitation far outweighed the consequences of being apathetic about urban crime and that the institution's three-year sentence was an insufficient training period for certain women. Bedford administrators contended that "the cost to the State of allowing [young women] to lead dishonorable, and perhaps criminal lives, . . . [perpetuating] their kind in succeeding generations in an ever-increasing propensity to evil [was] so very great that the State [should consider these women's] reformation . . . as the cheapest means of securing the public welfare."[69]

Reformers instituted a number of practical initiatives with varying degrees of success. Over the years, the institution maintained administrative policies whereby inmates were constantly occupied through industrial classes, religious services, and extracurricular activities. Instead of prison cells, women resided in individual cottages with designated matrons who encouraged a family-style structure. Some inmates seemed to enjoy this arrangement, as a number of paroled women wrote Bedford for permission to come back to visit their friends.[70] Specific buildings separated inmates by age in 1901, but by 1924, the year that Ruby Brooks and Mabel Hampton were admitted, Bedford had become segregated according to an inmate's psychological diagnosis and race, with cottages designated for a range of inmates from feebleminded white girls to newly admitted colored girls.[71] Some women found interacting with fellow inmates frustrating and even detrimental to their eventual discharge. Brooks, for instance, was so anxiety-ridden about how other black inmates' behavior would affect her release that she wrote prison administrators: "I was not brought up to fight and curse and I am willing to take any kind of [parole] job . . . as long as I get away from here."[72] Brooks's trouble with unruly cottagemates and her location in segregated housing reflected some of the major changes and problems Bedford experienced in implementing reform.

Although administrators insisted that inadequate funding affected Bedford's upkeep, hiring practices, and expansion, they also agreed that probation (supervision of a woman within her community without imprisonment) changed the type of inmate they received.[73] Introduced in 1901, probation slowly parceled out the most redeemable female offenders, according to Bedford administrators, and left the institution with an incoming population of probation violators, recidivists, and uncontrollable women.[74] Superintendent Davis identified such inmates as the major impediment to Bedford's rehabilitation process. As early as 1906, Davis argued that if Bedford was to "receive so large a proportion of 'difficult' young women, whom probation and private institutions . . . [had] failed to help, the public must recognize the task" Bedford had before it.[75] Probation did not significantly decrease black women's presence, as they had difficulty obtaining it; however, their numbers increased as the institution's reputation as a model reformatory declined. Thus, most black women who were first-time offenders, like Brooks and Hampton, were admitted along with those white women whose behavior failed to warrant probation or who had violated probation. These problems were exacerbated by the fact that more young women overall were being committed to Bedford, which led to subsequent overcrowding.[76]

Bedford's problems with funding, increasing numbers of problematic inmates, and overcrowding led to a scathing 1914 State Commission of Prisons inspection report that culminated in several public hearings a year later.[77] While the commission report noted myriad problems with Bedford, from its location to how it should be more self-sustaining because it held "several hundred able-bodied young women delinquents whose labors should suffice for their maintenance," Inspector Rudolph Diedling focused on the institution's inability to properly address its disciplinary problems.[78] In 1915, during public hearings, Diedling's criticisms

were addressed, but investigators added an issue to the investigator's list by noting that the most troubling issue involved same-sex romances between black and
white inmates. Bedford's administrators publicly disclosed that the institution's
primary disciplinary dilemma stemmed from interracial sex, which it designated
as "harmful intimacy."[79]

When the State Board of Charities' special investigative committee addressed
Bedford's "harmful intimacy," it focused on the fact that, unlike most women's
prisons in the North as well as in the South, Bedford was integrated. When questioned about this policy, former superintendent Katharine Davis explained that
she did "not believe in segregation by color in principle and [had] not found it to
work well in practice."[80] The committee strongly recommended otherwise. With
Davis no longer the superintendent, Bedford's board of managers agreed with the
committee's final recommendations, which cited segregation as the most viable
solution to inappropriate interracial relationships.[81] Denying that its concerns
were based on racism, the board argued that it made no objection to the housing
of black and white inmates because of race. Its members' decision stemmed from
the fact that they found "undoubtedly true that most undesirable sex relations
[grew] out of [the] . . . mingling of the two races."[82] As such, the board defended
its right to segregate inmates against the protest of those who argued that racial
segregation was "contrary to the equal rights of all citizens under the Constitution."[83] Explaining the discretionary power given to them by the State Charities
Law, the board argued that "individual [inmate] rights [were] not disturbed by
the separation of delinquents into groups when such segregation [was] likely to
promote reformation and prevent undesirable relations."[84] In 1917, Bedford institutionalized racial segregation, with two cottages "set apart" for black women.[85]
Superintendent Helen Cobb also explained that in addition to disciplinary concerns, the separate cottages were established as a result of written requests by
black inmates.[86] During Mabel Hampton's and Ruth Brooks's imprisonments at
Bedford, designated cottages housed black women who were characterized as
"recently admitted," "younger," "more unruly," and "quiet."[87] Ironically, even after
racial segregation was established, administrators failed to acknowledge publicly
that "harmful intimacy" persisted as inmates continued to pursue relationships
with one another.[88]

## "Harmful Intimacy": Interracial Sex within and outside of Bedford

The actions of Bedford administrators and state officials coincided with the
concerns of most early-twentieth-century women's prison administrators, psy-
chiatrists, and reformers. Generally, they addressed the issue of female homo-

sexuality by emphasizing, to the virtual exclusion of other romantic and/or sexual attachments, the problem of developing relationships between white and black inmates.[89] They portrayed white women's desires in same-sex, interracial relationships within the confines of the prison as a longing for masculinity.[90] The body of scientific observers argued, as did the psychologist Margaret Otis in 1913, that whether viewed as "an affair simply for fun and . . . lack of anything more interesting to take up their attention" or a relationship of "serious fascination and . . . intensely sexual nature," the racial and gendered identities of such affairs were clear.[91] "The difference in color," Otis explained, "takes the place of difference in sex."[92] Otis's explanation of same-sex desire equated black women's darker skin color with virility; moreover, such relationships could be described as "racialized gender inversion."[93] In fact, she revealed that one white woman "admitted that the colored girl she loved seemed the man."[94] Similarly, in 1921, a Bedford official explained that black women's supposed "abandon and virility . . . offered" white women "the nearest substitute" for the opposite sex.[95] According to her, black women functioned as masculine substitutes who fulfilled white women's heterosexual desire. Observations of white women's attraction for one another were categorized as nothing more than crushes (young women's courtship of one another during which, according to one report, they "vow that they will be friends forever, dream and plan together, confide their deepest secrets"), with no serious connection to homosexuality.[96] Thus, white inmates, whether aggressors in the affairs or not, maintained a normative and heterosexual status. In this sense, administrators failed to address directly same-sex desire but rather constructed their explanations so that, as Regina Kunzel notes, "homosexuality was heterosexuality; the unnatural was natural."[97] In contrast to white inmates, black women at Bedford were rarely portrayed as initiating relationships, although they may have done so.[98] They also were not characterized as responding in like manner to the attention of white women.[99] Black women's sexuality on its own terms, as a crush, heterosexual or homosexual, was ignored.[100]

Even though officials noted numerous instances of intense and sometimes even violent romantic relationships among white women, they continually focused on the impact of interracial sex. Accordingly, they consistently agreed with the assessment of assistant superintendent Julia Jessie Taft, who defined the disciplinary problem as stemming from "colored girls [who were] extremely attractive to certain white girls" and who also noted the fact that "the feeling [was] apt to be more intense than between white girls alone."[101] Taft emphasized that black women had an "unfortunate psychological influence" on white inmates.[102] One white woman's attraction for black women, for instance, was noted as being so "extreme" that she was described as staring at her "temporary object of . . .

affection as an animal might watch its prey, oblivious to all that was going on about her."[103] Yet such cases never diminished the number of similar incidents among white women. What, then, did officials find so damaging about "harmful intimacy"? Siobhan Somerville's work suggests that interracial relationships in reformatories highlighted "two tabooed sexualities—miscegenation and homosexuality."[104] During the 1915 State Board of Charities inquiry, investigators certainly raised concerns about both "harmful intimacy" continuing beyond the women's release from Bedford and the concomitant possibility of white women living in black neighborhoods.[105] With no likelihood of creating a separate state institution for black inmates (as some administrators suggested), Bedford officials' solution to this dilemma entailed imposing racial segregation. Ironically, this decision failed to address how "harmful intimacy" thrived among women living in different buildings. Indeed, administrators ignored Taft, who testified that she dealt with same-sex relationships "all the time" and stressed that these romantic attachments usually occurred between women "in separate houses."[106]

Racial segregation, as a result, would not solve the problem of same-sex relationships, but it would address institutional and national anxieties about interracial sex.

Between 1916 and 1918, the psychiatrist Edith Spaulding of Bedford's Laboratory of Social Hygiene conducted the most extensive and documented study into "harmful intimacy." Examining those women who were deemed psychopathic, Spaulding concentrated primarily on white inmate behavior. Although she diagnosed some black inmates, a number of the black women whom she referenced worked in the hospital as laundresses, housecleaners, and cooks. Bedford's accounts were distinct from those of most institutions in that they argued that black inmates were passive recipients rather than aggressive participants in homoerotic relationships. Spaulding's findings reinforced administrators' premise that the attraction white women felt toward black women stemmed from the fact that black inmates seemed more masculine. One example may be found in her analysis of Amanda B., the seventeen-year-old noted earlier who was charged with incorrigibility but imprisoned because she had contracted a venereal disease. When writing about Amanda's experience as an employee, Spaulding described the teenager as a problem because white inmates desired her. Eventually, she was removed from the hospital because of the "infatuation which two white girls showed for her and the resulting disturbance caused by their jealousy."[107] For Spaulding, Amanda's appearance as a "young colored woman with thick lips and very dark skin" made her seem virile and thus accounted for her popularity among white inmates.[108] She further explained that Amanda was "not unattractive in personality and always ready for fun, [but] she readily supplied through

her racial characteristics a feminine substitute for the masculine companionship [white women] were temporarily denied."[109] Spaulding's analysis implicitly
contended that Amanda became a possible partner for white women because of
specific "racial characteristics." She rejected the possibility of genuine and mutual
interracial, same-sex desire because only "feebleminded" white inmates became
"attached to" Amanda. Interestingly enough, Spaulding also portrayed Amanda as
an unwitting and thoroughly desexualized object of desire who was "fairly passive
in the affair," although "she enjoy[ed] the situation keenly."[110]

The attraction that white inmates expressed for black women like Amanda
was usually diagnosed by administrators as mental deficiency (in ways that ranged
from feeblemindedness to psychopathy) as well as being symptomatic of their
working-class backgrounds. When defending Bedford from charges that the institution fomented interracial, same-sex relationships, the president of Bedford's
board of managers, James Woods, argued that these associations were initiated
before the women entered the reformatory. His brief discussion conflated inmates' working-class status with deviant sexual behavior. Addressing the overall
problem without direct reference to black women, Woods in fact suggested that
white women desired women outside of the prison, concluding that this behavior
was "not uncommon among the people of this class and character in the outside
world, and when inmates addicted to these practices [came] into the institution
it [was] practically impossible to prevent them finding an opportunity in some
way or other to continue them."[111] Woods's assessment provides an example of
how administrators attempted to deflect responsibility for an increasing disciplinary problem but also raised the idea that these relationships should not be solely
defined as "situational homosexuality" or rather the consequence of a commitment in a women's reformatory.[112] Instead, Woods's perspective highlighted what
administrators had already discovered, that these homoerotic relationships, as the
earlier discussion of Mabel Hampton's experience reveals, were a part of developing sex practices in the larger society, black and white.

While officials writing about Bedford's "harmful intimacy" framed these relationships as aggressive white women pursuing passive black women, the reality of
their observations suggests more complex evidence of black women's individual
sexual agency and desire. From their records, black women seemed to be active
participants in interracial romances. Spaulding, for instance, observed but failed
to reassess her conclusions about "harmful intimacy" in light of a black inmate's
pursuit of a white inmate: "While the girls were at chapel, a popular colored girl
was reprimanded for talking to the white girl of her affections. When asked to
change her seat the colored girl became defiant and there ensued an unpleasant
episode in the midst of the service, in which she had to be taken from the room

for striking the matron who had spoken to her."[113] Conduct infractions in black women's files—such as "passing a note" or "2 girls in room with door closed. In room indefinitely"—indicate the possibility of same-sex relationships, but the fact that these reports were written in race-neutral language also strongly suggests the existence of intraracial romances.[114] Spaulding's observation of a disturbance caused by the "deep affection" that one black inmate held for another black woman mirrored the problems that she observed with white inmates, in that the two black women created a disturbance when one admired the other. Apparently more concerned with whether these women finished their jobs as hospital laundresses, Spaulding seemed to dismiss the sexual implications behind their actions and finally explained the altercation by linking their conduct as "two tigresses" to racial violence, noting that "primitive fires of that kind do not die down."[115] Like other administrators' observations of black women's involvement in "harmful intimacy," Spaulding's provided no sustained analysis of the detrimental moral effects of such attachments. Her and other officials' lack of concern might represent what they saw as general knowledge rather than their ignoring aberrant reformatory conduct. In this sense, black inmates' behavior seemed to confirm prevailing beliefs about black women's innate promiscuity and resulting sexual deviancy.

While not contradicting general sexual stereotypes regarding black women, the case of Lynette Moore does show how a black woman's behavior and appearance disrupted prison administrators' questionable premise regarding "harmful intimacy." According to one Bedford superintendent, seventeen-year-old Moore did "fairly well" while imprisoned but had a "great attraction for . . . white girls," making her a "troublemaker."[116] Initially, Moore's physical appearance—she was described as a "colored girl with . . . light skin and rather pretty, wavy hair"—garnered just as much attention from officials as her incorrigibility.[117] "I have an idea," one physician concluded, that "she has been rather good looking and considered clever by her set and has managed to get off with a good many things."[118] In light of their apathetic stance toward black inmates' active involvement with other women, administrators seemingly could not ignore Moore's appearance or behavior. Moore's actions even prevented her from corresponding with her parents, as the superintendent wrote her mother that Moore was in "punishment for improper actions with another girl."[119] A black woman whom even officials found physically attractive, she consistently pursued "undesirable" relationships with other, primarily white, inmates while at Bedford as well as when she was paroled.

After being discharged, Moore married but still maintained contact with the same white inmate, Connie Carlson, with whom she had developed an "undesirable friendship" in Bedford. In fact, after problems in Moore's marriage, the two women began living together while Moore was still pregnant with her estranged husband's child. Prison administrators gained access to this information when an anonymous letter was sent to a charitable agency noting that Moore had become a beggar and that Carlson was "usually with her."[120] While the interracial relationship caused problems at Bedford, such a friendship was also problematic once both women were released. Unlike Mabel Hampton's attempts to keep her relationships private, Moore's case shows how her public display of interracial romance prompted a neighbor to write a letter regarding the possibility of "harmful intimacy" outside of prison.

Moore's story did not end here. Five years later she was arrested for gun possession and again sent to Bedford. Although Bedford officials refused to keep her, they did interview her. While working as a nightclub hostess, Moore explained, she had continued to experience relationship problems, as she wanted to marry her boyfriend but had not divorced her first husband. Her second case file shows one documented instance of how women charged with "harmful intimacy" struggled to maintain these relationships once released from Bedford. Moore and Carlson learned tough lessons about the possibilities for their love. As evidenced by the fact that Moore was reduced to asking for charity, neither woman could support the other or Moore's infant. Yet it seems that they dealt with those outside forces that challenged their intimate bond in distinct ways. Moore clearly established a life for herself in Harlem, and when rearrested she acknowledged her continued connection with Carlson by listing her, along with family members, as a friend who lived in Long Island.[121]

Mabel Hampton's experience also complicated officials' essentialized portraits of homoerotic relationships. The story of her lesbianism, which was never directly mentioned in her case file but revealed through her subsequent social activism, challenged Bedford administrators' constructed premise about "harmful intimacy" and highlights many of the institution's evaluative discrepancies. In Hampton's brief account of her Bedford experience, she openly acknowledged the prevalence of as well as her participation in same-sex relationships (she did not indicate whether they were interracial or intraracial).[122] She remembered such Bedford relationships as being comforting. After she and another prisoner revealed their attraction to one another, Hampton noted that her fellow inmate "took me in her bed and held me in her arms and I went to sleep."[123] Although she desired women and dated men before her imprisonment, her Bedford experience may have provided Hampton with an opportunity to embrace fully her same-sex desire. For instance, another inmate claimed that she learned about sex from "Bedford girls."[124] Hampton's looks also failed to fit administrators' characterizations of a black woman involved in "harmful intimacy." Instead of being portrayed as masculine, she was described in the most feminine manner by

Bedford's superintendent, Amos Baker, as a "small rather bright and good looking colored girl."[125] Because of her dissembling, Hampton never received any conduct violations. Her family members, however, may have sensed that she was not only being influenced by "bad company" but also expressing a troubling affection for women. During her parole, her aunt wrote to Bedford officials, noting that Hampton was "very much infatuated with a middle-aged colored woman, with whom she became acquainted a short time before her arrest, and whom she [her aunt] thought was not a good influence on the girl."[126] Hampton's case strongly suggests administrators' indifference to black women's sexuality within the prison and underscores why some black women might have chosen to hide their same-sex relationships.[127]

Like Hampton, other black women made attempts to maintain intimate liaisons, especially during their parole. Ironically, Bedford sought to create a family-like atmosphere when young women were imprisoned but penalized parolees for interacting too closely with one another once they left the institution. Twenty-one-year-old Addie King reportedly experienced some difficulty keeping her distance from other Bedford women. Social workers discovered that she lived with another black parolee as well as a "masculine sort of woman known as 'Alec.'" King was also found in a cooperative living arrangement, more than likely a reflection of her dire financial situation. When social workers decided to rearrest her as a parole violator, they discovered not only that she lived intermittently with another Bedford parolee and three other women but also that these women shared an apartment with ten men.[128]

The nature of King's associations with the black women and men with whom she lived is not clear, but there is evidence that she attempted to maintain at least one interracial sexual relationship. When she worked as a live-in domestic, King's different employers often complained that she disregarded her curfew, sometimes arriving home late or never returning home until the next morning. In one instance, King brought a white Bedford parolee to her employer's house and "tried to keep her there all night unknown to the family." When family members discovered her there, King's companion was asked to "get up and leave." The white employer believed that the interracial friendship was inappropriate but became increasingly disturbed when evidence indicated that the two women's relationship was not platonic. Reportedly, the employer contended that the affection between the women was "disgusting."[129]

It would be impossible to gauge how many of these relationships continued after a stint at Bedford, but evidence clearly shows that same-sex desire was not simply a situational condition for white or black women created by their imprisonment.[130] Whether Bedford women gave up on same-sex desire or became more adept at masking these relationships from their employers and social workers, examples show that homoerotic relationships existed outside the prison, however difficult. More importantly, these examples reflect how some women managed multiple relationships with men and women. Not surprisingly, social workers noted, primarily through violation reports, that black parolees were still in contact with their mates just as they were during their imprisonment. Sometimes their relationships were discovered when former inmates obtained permission to visit Bedford. A confiscated letter in one black parolee's file, for instance, explained how the former inmate "walked up to the Nursery" and picked up the child of her white girlfriend, asking "her if she didn't know her own daddy." Reportedly, "all the girls [in the nursery] laughed."[131] While some inmates began these relationships as a sign of temporary rebellion that rejected the controlling influences of Bedford administrators, other inmates saw these relationships as more than a crush or temporary desire.[132] Most importantly, these inmates strove to maintain relationships developed in Bedford; moreover, these inmates, as Mabel Hampton's case indicates, may have also desired women before their imprisonment.

MABEL HAMPTON'S EXPERIENCES in early-twentieth-century New York as understood through prison administrators' notations and her subsequent reflections upon her life provide a unique lens through which we might view black women's sexuality. She was not a reformer advocating the "politics of respectability," nor was she a blues singer expressing sexual desire through performance. Rather, her life represents the complex ways that young women acknowledged the relevance of proper decorum but also participated in the growing consumer culture of commercial amusements. Women like her faced enormous challenges as they sought to embrace their independence in a society that simultaneously offered carefree and uninhibited opportunities for pleasure while at the same time feeling threatened by working-class women's sexual behavior. As a result, relatives, community members, and law officers monitored young women's sexual expression and generally supported the rehabilitative objectives of state institutions like Bedford.

By studying the case files of black women like Hampton, we get a sense of the language that ordinary black women used to express heterosexual and same-sex desire. Acknowledging that such evidence has been mediated through prison administrators' biases, we still can discern the stories that black women chose to impart behind official responses to those narratives.

Although administrators' actions reflected prevailing racial and sexual stereotypes, the experiences that they documented offer complex perspectives on how working-class and poor black women dealt with chastity, premarital sex, rape, prostitution, and same-sex desire. Black women revealed not only certain aspects of their conduct but also how the concerns of relatives and other community members regarding their behavior often conflicted with what they wanted for themselves. Frequently, their interactions with the community's representatives were as heavily regulated as those with state representatives. Indeed, Mabel Hampton's reflections about Harlem highlighted how she often dissembled in her neighborhood. As a black woman who desired women she explained her caution about publicizing those relationships because "you had to be careful" and "you had [to have] fun behind closed doors."[133]

Although Hampton seems to have hidden her relationships with women when she was incarcerated, other women, black and white, flaunted these attachments. Bedford administrators claimed that the majority of their disciplinary problems stemmed not simply from same-sex relationships but rather from "harmful intimacy," or interracial sex. Their anxieties about such relationships mirrored the concerns of a nation that generally discouraged interracial social and sexual relationships in law and practice. Attempting to solve their dilemma by instituting racial segregation served only to temporarily assuage their racial anxieties more than it addressed the crux of the issue. When some officials argued that young women brought same-sex romance into the institution rather than those relationships being a consequence of imprisonment, they illuminated the fact that sexual expression varied both within and outside of Bedford. Emphasizing the latter point, this study offers a perspective from which to understand the complexity of black women's experiences in early-twentieth-century New York by exploring how they addressed the myriad pleasures and dangers of urban sexuality.

## Notes

1. James Weldon Johnson, *Black Manhattan* (1930; New York: Da Capo, 1991), 160–61.

2. Jervis Anderson, *This Was Harlem: A Cultural Portrait, 1900–1950* (New York: Farrar, Straus, Giroux, 1981), 139.

3. Johnson, *Black Manhattan*, 160–61.

4. See Allan M. Brandt, *No Magic Bullet: A Social History of Venereal Disease in the United States since 1880* (New York: Oxford University Press, 1987); and Elizabeth Clement, *Love for Sale: Courting, Treating, and Prostitution in New York City, 1900–1945* (Chapel Hill: University of North Carolina Press, 2006), esp. chap. 4.

5. See Estelle Freedman, *Their Sister's Keepers: Women's Prison Reform in America, 1830–1930* (Ann Arbor: University of Michigan Press, 1984), 109–42; Mary Odem, *Delinquent Daughters: Protecting and Policing Adolescent Female Sexuality in the United States, 1885–1920* (Chapel Hill: University of North Carolina Press, 1995), 1–7, 95–127; and Ruth Alexander, *The "Girl Problem": Female Sexual Delinquency in New York, 1900–1930* (Ithaca, N.Y.: Cornell University Press, 1995), 1–7, 33–66.

6. Many women were also incarcerated for public order crimes such as drunkenness, petty larceny, and incorrigibility.

7. Danielle L. McGuire's work provides another example of black women's testimony when she addresses their experiences of rape and sexual violence during the post–World War II era ("'It Was Like All of Us Had Been Raped': Sexual Violence, Community Mobilization, and the African American Freedom Struggle," *Journal of American History* 91, no. 3 [2004]: 906–31). I want to thank Nancy Hewitt for encouraging me to think about these connections.

8. Evelyn Brooks Higginbotham, "African-American Women's History and the Metalanguage of Race," *Signs* 17, no. 2 (1992): 262–66. Higginbotham contends that the "metalanguage of race signifies . . . the imbrications of race within the representation of sexuality" (262). For background on the practice of treating, see Kathy Peiss, *Cheap Amusements: Working Women and Leisure in Turn-of-the-Century New York* (Philadelphia: Temple University Press, 1986), 108–14; and Clement, *Love for Sale,* 45–75.

9. My thinking about working-class women's sexuality has been influenced by Kathy Peiss, "'Charity Girls' and City Pleasures: Historical Notes on Working-Class Sexuality, 1880–1920," in *Passion and Power: Sexuality in History,* ed. Peiss and Christina Simmons (Philadelphia: Temple University Press, 1989), 57–69; Peiss, *Cheap Amusements*; Odem, *Delinquent Daughters;* Alexander, *The "Girl Problem"*; and Christine Stansell, City *of Women: Sex and Class in New York, 1789–1860* (Urbana: University of Illinois Press, 1987). Some examples of black working-class women expressing same-sex desire are found in Karen V. Hansen, "'No Kisses Is Like Youres': An Erotic Friendship between Two African-American Women during the Mid-Nineteenth Century," *Gender and History* 7, no. 2 (1995): 153–82; Farah Jasmine Griffin, ed., *Beloved Sisters and Loving Friends: Letters from Rebecca Primus of Royal Oak, Maryland, and Addie Brown of Hartford, Connecticut, 1854–1868* (New York: Knopf, 1999); and Elizabeth Lapovsky Kennedy and Madeline D. Davis, *Boots of Leather, Slippers of Gold: The History of a Lesbian Community* (New York: Routledge, 1993).

10. My thinking about the complexity of the black working class has been influenced by the work of Nell Irvin Painter, *The Narrative of Hosea Hudson: The Life and Times of a Black Radical* (New York: Norton, 1994); Nell Painter, *Sojourner Truth: A Life, a Symbol* (New York: Norton, 1996); Tera Hunter, *To 'Joy My Freedom: Southern Black Women's Lives and Labors after the Civil War* (Cambridge: Harvard University Press, 1997); Tera Hunter, "'The Brotherly Love for Which This City Is Proverbial Should Extend to All': The Everyday Lives of Working-Class Women in Philadelphia and Atlanta in the 1890s," in *W. E. B. Du Bois, Race, and the City,* ed. Michael B. Katz and Thomas Sugrue (Philadelphia: University of Pennsylvania Press, 1998), 127–51; Robin D. G. Kelley, *Race Rebels: Culture, Politics, and the Black Working-Class* (New York: Free Press, 1994); Robin D. G. Kelley, "'We Are Not What We Seem': Rethinking Black Working-Class Opposition in the Jim Crow South," *Journal of American History* 80, no. 1 (1993): 75–112; and Elsa Barkley Brown, "Negotiating and Transforming the Public Sphere: African American Political life in the Transition from Slavery to Freedom," *Public Culture* 7, no. 1 (1994): 107–46.

11. Evelynn Hammonds, "Black (W)holes and the Geometry of Black Female Sexuality," *differences: A Journal of Feminist Cultural Studies* 6, nos. 2–3 (1994): 138. For discussions of black women's sexuality in literature, see Carol Batker, "'Love Me Like I Like to Be': The Sexual Politics of Hurston's *Their Eyes Were Watching God,* the Classic Blues, and the

Black Women's Club Movement," *African American Review* 32, no. 2 (1998): 199–213; Farah Jasmine Griffin, "Textual Healing: Claiming Black Women's Bodies, the Erotic and Resistance in Contemporary Novels of Slavery," *Callaloo* 19, no. 2 (1996): 519–36; Deborah E. McDowell, "'It's Not Safe. Not Safe at All': Sexuality in Nella Larsen's *Passing*," in *The Lesbian and Gay Studies Reader*, ed. Henry Abelove, Michele Aina Barale, and David M. Halperin (New York: Routledge, 1993), 616–25; and Hazel V. Carby, *Reconstructing Womanhood: The Emergence of the Afro-American Woman Novelist* (New York: Oxford University Press, 1987); see also Deborah E. McDowell's introduction to Nella Larsen, *Quicksand and Passing* (New Brunswick, N.J.: Rutgers University Press, 1986), ix–xxxv.

12. Evelyn Brooks Higginbotham, *Righteous Discontent: The Women's Movement in the Black Baptist Church, 1880–1920* (Cambridge: Harvard University Press, 1993), 185–229. Elsa Barkley Brown raises a critical point regarding the problems associated with the entire community following a politics of respectability when she notes that "the struggle to present Black women and the Black community as 'respectable' eventually led to repression within the community" ("Imaging Lynching: African American Women, Communities of Struggle, and Collective Memory," in *African American Women Speak out on Anita Hill–Clarence Thomas*, ed. Geneva Smitherman [Detroit: Wayne State University Press, 1995], 108).

13. Darlene Clark Hine, "Rape and the Inner Lives of Black Women in the Middle West: Preliminary Thoughts on the Culture of Dissemblance," in *Unequal Sisters: A Multicultural Reader in U.S. Women's History*, ed. Ellen Carole DuBois and Vicki L. Ruiz, 2nd ed. (New York: Routledge, 1994), 342–47. See also Hazel V. Carby, "Policing the Black Woman's Body in an Urban Context," *Critical Inquiry* 18, no. 4 (1992): 738–55; and Beverly Guy-Sheftall, *Daughters of Sorrow: Attitudes toward Black Women, 1880–1920* (New York: Carlson, 1990). For scholarly work that explores black women's responses to negative stereotypes, see Hine, "Rape and the Inner Lives"; Dorothy Salem, *To Better Our World* (New York: Carlson, 1990); Higginbotham, *Righteous Discontent;* Deborah Gray White, *Too Heavy a Load: Black Women in Defense of Themselves* (New York: Norton, 1999); Michele Mitchell, *Righteous Propagation: African Americans and the Politics of Racial Destiny after Reconstruction* (Chapel Hill: University of North Carolina Press, 2004); and Kevin Gaines, *Uplifting the Race: Black Leadership, Politics, and Culture in the Twentieth Century* (Chapel Hill: University of North Carolina Press, 1996).

14. Evelynn Hammonds, "Toward a Genealogy of Black Female Sexuality: The Problematic of Silence," in *Feminist Genealogies, Colonial Legacies, Democratic Futures*, ed. M. Jacqui Alexander and Chandra Talpade Mohanty (New York: Routledge, 1997), 175. Hazel V. Carby addresses the heroine in Harlem Renaissance literary texts: "The duty of the black heroine toward the black community was made coterminous with her desire as a woman, a desire which was expressed as a dedication to uplift the race. This displacement from female desire to female duty enabled the negotiation of racist constructions of black female sexuality but denied sensuality and in this denial lies the class character of its cultural politics" ("'It Jus Be's Dat Way Sometime': The Sexual Politics of Black Women's Blues," in DuBois and Ruiz, *Unequal Sisters*, 332). See also Michele Mitchell's discussion of this issue in her "Silences Broken, Silences Kept: Gender and Sexuality in African-American History," *Gender and History* 11, no. 3 (1999): 440.

15. For a discussion of black women's sexuality and its relationship to blues, see Carby,

"It Jus Be's Dat Way Sometime," 330–41; and Angela Davis, *Blues Legacies and Black Feminism: Gertrude "Ma" Rainey, Bessie Smith and Billie Holiday* (New York: Vintage, 1998). Davis argues that the "blues songs recorded by Gertrude Rainey and Bessie Smith offer us a privileged glimpse of the prevailing perceptions of love and sexuality in postslavery black communities in the United States. . . . The blues women openly challenged the gender politics implicit in traditional cultural representations of marriage and heterosexual love relationships" (41). See also Ann Ducille, "Blue Notes on Black Sexuality: Sex and the Texts of Jessie Fauset and Nella Larsen," *Journal of the History of Sexuality* 3, no. 3 (1993): 418–44; and Hortense J. Spillers, "Interstices: A Small Drama of Words," in *Pleasure and Danger: Exploring Female Sexuality,* ed. Carole S. Vance (Boston: Routledge and Kegan Paul, 1984), 74.

16. On a practical level, all women who entered Bedford were queried about who told them about sex, when and at what age they had their first sexual encounter, and if that encounter was consensual. Finally, they were asked whether they practiced prostitution, and if they did, at what age they entered the trade as well as how much money they accrued.

17. Inmate #3724, Admission Record, August 1924, Series 14610–77B, Bedford Hills Correctional Facility, 1915–30, 1955–65, Records of the Department of Correctional Services, New York State Archives and Records Administration, State Education Department, Albany (hereafter BH). I have used pseudonyms for inmates' names but have retained their original inmate case numbers.

18. Hammonds, "Toward a Genealogy," 176.

19. Inmate #3706, History Blank, 8 July 1924, BH.

20. Regina Kunzel addresses how historians need to understand that "case records often reveal as much, if not more, about those conducting the interview as they do about those interviewed." See her "Pulp Fictions and Problem Girls: Reading and Rewriting Single Pregnancy in the Postwar United States," *American Historical Review* 100, no. 5 (1995): 1468–69. See also how Timothy Gilfoyle discusses the difficult questions that historians of sexuality must pose regarding their evidence. See his "Prostitutes in History: From Parables of Pornography to Metaphors of Modernity," *American Historical Review* 104, no. 1 (1999): 139–40.

21. See Inmate #2475, Conduct Record, October-December 1918, and Inmate #4044, Conduct Record, 13 June 1926, BH.

22. Margaret Otis, "A Perversion Not Commonly Noted," *Journal of Abnormal Psychology* 8, no. 2 (1913): 113.

23. Jennifer L. Morgan, "'Some Could Suckle over Their Shoulder': Male Travelers, Female Bodies, and the Gendering of Racial Ideology, 1500–1770," *William and Mary Quarterly* 54, no. 1 (1997): 167–92; see also Higginbotham, "African-American Women's History," 263–64. My interpretation in this section has also been influenced by Deborah Gray White, *Ar'n't I a Woman?: Female Slaves in the Plantation South,* rev. ed. (New York: Norton, 1999), esp. 27–61.

24. Sander L. Gilman, "Black Bodies, White Bodies: Toward an Iconography of Female Sexuality in Late-Nineteenth-Century Art, Medicine, and Literature," *Critical Inquiry* 12, no. 1 (1985): 209.

25. White, *Ar'n't I a Woman?,* 30.

26. Higginbotham, "African-American Women's History," 263.

27. "Experiences of the Race Problem: By a Southern White Woman," *Independent*, March 1904, 46.

28. Inmate #3533, History Blank, 24 October 1923, and Inmate #3521, History Blank, 20 September 1923, BH. Scholars have shown how physical descriptions of black women were used to construct and later fulfill stereotypes that played major roles in American enslavement as well as to define black femininity and criminality. Subjective comments by Bedford officials (both male and female) about black women's appearance seem to reiterate and even perpetuate the earlier assessments of European male travelers in Africa who, in a different context, "grappled with the character of the female African body—a body both desirable and repulsive, available and untouchable, productive and reproductive, beautiful and black" (Morgan, "Some Could Suckle," 170). See also Kathleen Brown, *Good Wives, Nasty Wenches, and Anxious Patriarchs: Gender, Race, and Power in Colonial Virginia* (Chapel Hill: University of North Carolina Press, 1996), 107–36; Walter Johnson, *Soul by Soul: Life inside the Antebellum Slave Market* (Cambridge: Harvard University Press, 1999), 135–61; White, *Ar'n't I a Woman?*, 27–61; and Gilman, "Black Bodies, White Bodies."

29. Inmate #3699, Admission Record, 10 July 1924, and Inmate #3502, History Blank, 22 August 1923, BH.

30. Inmate #3333, History Blank, 26 December 1922, and Inmate #3728, Admission Record, 19 August 1924, BH.

31. Inmate #4477, Escape Description Record, 19 July 1928, BH.

32. Inmate #3696, History Blank, 10 July 1924, BH. I have revealed this inmate's name and case file in accordance with the Freedom of Information Act of 1966, U.S. Code, sec. 552, pt. 1, subchap. 2.

33. Inmate #3696, Recommendation for Parole, n.d. (ca. January 1925), BH.

34. Inmate #3696, History Blank, 10 July 1924, BH.

35. Inmate #3696, History Blank, 10 July 1924, BH.

36. Joan Nestle, "Lesbians and Prostitutes: An Historical Sisterhood," in *A Restricted Country* (New York: Firebrand, 1987), 169.

37. After returning from Europe, Hampton's employer was apparently so "indignant at the idea of her apartment having been used for purposes of prostitution that she refused to appear" in court to vouch for Hampton's character. Although Hampton had been in "faithful service" for at least two years, her employer disregarded various friends' advice and chose not to support Hampton's court case (see Inmate #3696, letter from Amy M. Prevost to Dr. Amos T. Baker, 13 November 1924, BH).

38. Arthur Spingarn, *Laws Relating to Sex Morality in New York City* (New York: Century, 1926), 32–33; see there Crim. P. 887, subdivisions 1–4, especially 4e, "permitting premises to be used for a purpose forbidden thereby is valid where testimony is sufficient to show that such use was with the guilty knowledge of [the] defendant" (33).

39. Joan Nestle, "'I Lift My Eyes to the Hill': The Life of Mabel Hampton as Told by a White Woman," in *A Fragile Union* (San Francisco: Cleis, 1998), 34.

40. Inmate #3696, Recommendation for Parole, 13 January 1925, BH.

41. For discussion of the problems associated with working-class black women and leisure in Atlanta, see Hunter, *To 'Joy My Freedom*, 168–86.

42. Inmate #3474, History Blank, July 1923, BH.

43. Inmate #3489, History Blank, 1 August 1923, and Preliminary Investigation, ca. June 1923, BH.

44. William Fielding Ogburn, "The Richmond Negro in New York City: His Social Mind as Seen in His Pleasures" (master's thesis, Columbia University, 1909), 60–61.

45. Inmate #3535, History Blank, 18 October 1923, BH.

46. Inmate #2480, Statement of Girl, 23 June 1917, BH.

47. Inmate #4501, letter (more than likely confiscated) from Inmate to Friend, 19 January 1928, BH, emphasis added.

48. Inmate #3377, History Blank, 16 February 1923, BH.

49. Inmate #3377, letter from Minister to Bedford Reformatory, 13 August 1923, BH.

50. Inmate #4058, letter of Inmate's Mother to Superintendent Baker, 26 April 1926, BH.

51. Inmate #4058, letter of Inmate's Mother to Superintendent Baker, 17 April 1926, BH.

52. "Silk and Lights Blamed for Harlem Girls' Delinquency," *Baltimore Afro-American*, 19 May 1928, Reel 31, Tuskegee News Clipping File.

53. For analysis of the song, see Davis, *Blues Legacies*, 39–40; and Carby, "It Jus Be's Dat Way Sometime," 337.

54. See, for example, Evelyn Brooks Higginbotham, "Rethinking Vernacular Culture: Black Religion and Race Records in the 1920s and 1930s," in *The House That Race Built: Original Essays by Toni Morrison, Angela Y. Davis, Cornel West, and Others on Black Americans and Politics in America Today,* ed. Wahneema Lubiano (New York: Vintage, 1998), 157–77. In the context of religion and the black working class, Higginbotham notes that the "storefront Baptist, Pentecostal, and Holiness churches along with a variety of urban sects and cults . . . were doubtless more effective than middle-class reformers in policing the black woman's body and demanding conformity to strict guidelines of gender roles and sexual conduct" (171).

55. Eric Garber, "A Spectacle in Color: The Lesbian and Gay Subculture of Jazz Age Harlem," in *Hidden from History: Reclaiming the Gay and Lesbian Past,* ed. Martin Bauml Duberman, Martha Vicinus, and George Chauncey Jr. (New York: Meridian, 1989), 318–31. See also "Dr. A. C. Powell Scores Pulpit Evils," *New York Age,* 16 November 1929, 1; "Dr. Powell's Crusade against Abnormal Vice Is Approved," *New York Age,* 23 November 1929; and "Corruption in the Pulpit," *New York Amsterdam News,* 11 December 1929, 20. George Chauncey also discusses this issue in his *Gay New York: Gender, Urban Culture, and the Making of the Gay Male World, 1890–1940* (New York: Basic, 1994), 254–57.

56. Nestle, *A Fragile Union,* 36. David Levering Lewis notes that "for a quarter, you would see all kinds of people making the party scene; formally dressed society folks from downtown, policemen, painters, carpenters, mechanics, truckmen in their workingmen's clothes, gamblers, lesbians, and entertainers of all kinds." He stressed that "rent parties were a function . . . of economics, whatever their overlay of camaraderie, sex, and music" (*When Harlem Was in Vogue* [New York: Oxford University Press, 1979], 107–8); see also Katrina Hazzard-Gordon, *Jookin': The Rise of Social Dance Formations in African-American Culture* (Philadelphia: Temple University Press, 1990), 94–116.

57. Hampton, interview by Nestle, 10.

58. Ibid., 11.

59. Mabel Hampton, interview by Joan Nestle, "LFL Coming Out Stories," 21 June 1981, 8, Box 3, MHC. Another version of this interview is also in Nestle, *A Fragile Union*, 36.

60. Hampton, interview by Nestle, 9. The material cited in the text refers to Hampton's response to Nestle's questions: "How would you describe the twenties? Was it a good period to be gay?"

61. "LFL Coming Out Stories," 9.

62. Hammonds argues that "rather than assuming that black female sexualities are structured along an axis of normal and perverse paralleling that of white women we might find that for black women a different geometry operates." She refers to Alice Walker's *The Color Purple* in raising the possibility of "desire between women and desire between women and men simultaneously, in dynamic relationship rather than in opposition" ("Black (W)holes," 139); I want to thank Doreen Drury for her critical questions regarding this issue. See also Nestle, "Lesbians and Prostitutes," 169.

63. Mary Macey Dietzler, *Detention Houses and Reformatories as Protective Social Agencies in the Campaign of the United States Government against Venereal Diseases* (Washington, D.C.: Government Printing Office, 1922), 27. See also Brandt, *No Magic Bullet*, 52–121; and Clement, *Love for Sale*, 114–43.

64. Edith R. Spaulding, *An Experimental Study of Psychopathic Delinquent Women* (New York: Patterson Smith, 1923), 271–72.

65. Inmate #3715, Recommendation for Parole, ca. 1925, BH. This inmate was considered for parole from February until August 1925 but was not released because of her venereal disease.

66. Inmate #3715, History Blank, 12 August 1924, BH.

67. See Barbara Brenzel, *Daughters of the State: A Social Portrait of the First Reform School for Girls in North America, 1856–1905* (Cambridge: MIT Press, 1983); Freedman, *Their Sister's Keepers*; and Alexander, *The "Girl Problem."*

68. Katharine Bement Davis, "A Plan for the Conversion of the Laboratory of Social Hygiene at Bedford Hills in to a State Clearing House . . . ," Bureau of Social Hygiene General Material 1911–16, Box 6, Record Group 2, Rockefeller Boards, Rockefeller Archive Center, Tarrytown, New York.

69. *New York State Reformatory for Women at Bedford Hills, Second Annual Report for the New York State Reformatory for Women at Bedford* (Albany, N.Y.: J. B. Lyon, 1902), 7. Almost twenty-four years later, Bedford still assessed its mission based on young women's need to be rehabilitated because, as administrators believed, young women were either "unfit to make the fight alone" or represented women whose lives were "wrecked by chance misfortune" (see *New York State, Salient Facts about the New York State Reformatory for Women, Bedford Hills* [Bedford Hills, N.Y.: Reformatory, 1926], 3).

70. See, for example, Inmate #2507, letter from Inmate to Superintendent Cobb, 1 March 1920, BH.

71. *New York State Reformatory for Women at Bedford, Annual Report of the New York State Reformatory for Women at Bedford for the Year Ending September 30, 1901* (Albany, N.Y.: J. B. Lyon, 1902), 17–18. Expectant mothers and inmates with children no more than two years old were also housed in a separate cottage. See Isabel Barrows, "Reformatory Treatment of Women in the United States," in *Penal and Reformatory Institutions*, ed. Charles Richmond Henderson (New York: Charities Publication Committee, 1910), 156.

72. See Inmate #3715, letter from Inmate to Superintendent Baker (Harriman Cottage), 7 August 1925, BH. According to a State Commission of Prisons report, Harriman Cottage was designated for "more unruly colored girls" (*State of New York, State Commission of Prisons, Thirty-First Annual Report* [Albany, N.Y.: Commission, 1925], 172).

73. Freedman, *Their Sister's Keepers*, 138–39.

74. Charles L. Chute, "Probation and Suspended Sentence," *Journal of Criminal Law and Criminology* 12, no. 4 (1922): 559.

75. *State of New York, New York State Reformatory for Women at Bedford, Sixth Annual Report of the New York State Reformatory Women at Bedford* (Albany, N.Y.: J. B. Lyon, 1906), 17. Davis revealed that the change in the type of inmate committed to Bedford was noticed in 1905.

76. Freedman, *Their Sister's Keepers*, 138–39.

77. For the report, see *State of New York, State Commission of Prisons, Twentieth Annual Report of the State Commission of Prisons* (Albany, N.Y.: Commission, 1914), 116–19. For the hearings, see *State of New York, State Board of Charities, Report of the Special Committee Consisting of Commissioners Kevin, Smith, and Mulry, Appointed to Investigate the Charges Made against the New York State Reformatory for Women at Bedford Hills, N.Y.* (Albany, N.Y.: J. B. Lyon, 1915), 3–29.

78. *State Commission of Prisons, Twentieth Annual Report*, 116–19, at 117.

79. For the administrators' reference to harmful intimacy, see *Report of the Special Committee*, 7.

80. "Miss Davis Stands by Bedford Home," *New York Herald*, 24 December 1914, 8.

81. *Report of the Special Committee*, 26–27.

82. Ibid., 26.

83. *State of New York, State Board of Charities, Annual Report for the Year 1915* (Albany, N.Y., 1915), 96. Although Bedford's board of managers described its response to critics, the report did not specify who had opposed its decision.

84. Ibid.

85. *State of New York, New York State Reformatory for Women at Bedford, Seventeenth Annual Report of the New York State Reformatory for Women at Bedford Hills, N.Y.* (Albany, N.Y.: J. B. Lyon, 1918), 8.

86. Ibid., 8, 16.

87. *State of New York, State Commission of Prisons, Thirty-First Annual Report of the State Commission of Prisons* (Albany, N.Y.: Commission, 1925), 172.

88. See, for example, Inmate #4044, Conduct Record, 13 June 1926, BH. One white inmate was cited in this record as having aided a black inmate who "passed a note from one of the Gibbons girls [black inmates]" to a white inmate during an institutional baseball game.

89. Estelle Freedman, "The Prison Lesbian: Race, Class, and the Construction of the Aggressive Female Homosexual, 1915–1965," *Feminist Studies* 22, no. 2 (1996): 400–401.

90. Freedman notes that "at the same time, assigning the male aggressor role to Black women and preserving a semblance of femininity for their white partners racialized the sexual pathology of inversion. In this interpretation, white women were not really lesbians, for they were attracted to men, for whom Black women temporarily substituted. Thus the prison literature racialized both lesbianism and butch/femme roles, implicitly blam-

ing Black women for aggression and, indeed, homosexuality, by associating them with a male role" (Freedman, "The Prison Lesbian," 400–401). See also Anne Meis Knupfer, "'To Become Good, Self-Supporting Women': The State Industrial School for Delinquent Girls at Geneva, Illinois, 1900–1935," *Journal of the History of Sexuality* 9, no. 4 (2000): 437–41; and Sarah Potter, "'Undesirable Relations': Same-Sex Relationships and the Meaning of Sexual Desire at a Women's Reformatory during the Progressive Era," *Feminist Studies* 30, no. 2 (2004): 394–415.

91. Otis, "A Perversion," 113–14.

92. Ibid., 113.

93. Regina G. Kunzel, "Situating Sex: Prison Sexual Culture in the Mid-Twentieth-Century United States," *GLQ: A Journal of Lesbian and Gay Studies* 8, no. 3 (2002): 262.

94. Otis, "A Perversion," 114.

95. Edith Spaulding, "Emotional Episodes among Psychopathic Delinquent Women," *Journal of Nervous and Mental Disease* 54, no. 4 (1921): 305. As Hazel V. Carby argues in her study of black female writers' response to ideologies of white and black womanhood, "the figurations of black women existed in an antithetical relationship with the values embodied in the cult of true womanhood, an absence of the qualities of piety and purity being a crucial signifier. Black womanhood was polarized against white womanhood in the structure of the metaphoric system of female sexuality, particularly through the association of black women with overt sexuality and taboo sexual practices" (Carby, *Reconstructing Womanhood*, 32).

96. J. L. Moreno, *Who Shall Survive?: A New Approach to the Problems of Human Interrelations* (Washington, D.C.: Nervous and Mental Disease Publishing, 1934), 229; see also Elizabeth Lunbeck, *Psychiatric Persuasion: Knowledge, Gender, and Power in Modern America* (Princeton, N.J.: Princeton University Press, 1994), 295–96.

97. Kunzel, "Situating Sex," 262.

98. Otis, "A Perversion," 114.

99. Moreno noted that black women were "the subject adored and rarely the wooer. . . . While overtly she responds with affection, she almost invariably ridicules the courtship" (*Who Shall Survive?*, 230).

100. Alexander, The *"Girl Problem,"* 92; Nicole Hahn Rafter, *Creating Born Criminals* (Urbana: University of Illinois Press, 1997), 181–82. White working-class women's arrest and imprisonment for sexual delinquency departed from the traditional script of the virtuous white woman needing protection from the black male rapist, yet administrators' concerns and responses to interracial same-sex romantic relationships showed how they were influenced still by society's long-standing anxieties about white female and black male unions, even to the point of perceiving black women as men. See Freedman, "The Prison Lesbian," 399–400; and Kunzel, "Situating Sex," 261–62. For more on the protection of white women from black men, see Jacquelyn Dowd Hall's cogent analysis of the rape-lynch narrative in her "'The Mind That Burns in Each Body': Women, Rape and Racial Violence," in *Powers of Desire: The Politics of Sexuality*, ed. Ann Snitow, Christine Stansell, and Sharon Thompson (New York: New American Library, 1983), 328–49. Bedford's accounts were distinct from those of most institutions in that they argued that black inmates were passive recipients rather than aggressive participants in homoerotic relationships.

101. *Report of the Special Committee*, 18.

102. Ibid.

103. Spaulding, *An Experimental Study,* 329.

104. Siobhan Somerville, "Scientific Racism and the Emergence of the Homosexual Body," *Journal of the History of Sexuality* 5, no. 2 (1994): 260. Somerville poses the cogent question: "Did the girls' intimacy trouble the authorities because it was homosexual or because it was interracial?" (261). See also Lisa Duggan's discussion in *Sapphic Slashers: Sex, Violence, and American Modernity* (Durham, N.C.: Duke University Press, 2000).

105. *Report of the Special Committee,* 18. Committee investigators asked Taft, "Do you think the relations between the white girls and the colored girls may be continued after the white girls leave the institution so that they may take up with living in colored neighborhoods?" (ibid.).

106. Ibid., 17–18.

107. Spaulding, *An Experimental Study,* 270.

108. Ibid., 272. In another case, white inmates were equally attracted to Emily J., a black inmate who in Spaulding's assessment had "thick lips, [and] deeply pigmented skin" (306). The presence of the seventeen-year-old, who had been charged with solicitation, reportedly elicited an "emotional disturbance" because, in Spaulding's estimation, "unstable white girls were uncontrollably attracted to [Emily] . . . because of her color" (308).

109. Ibid., 273; see also Edith Spaulding, "An Emotional Crisis," *Mental Hygiene* 5 (1921): 279. Nicole Hahn Rafter contends that although Spaulding "racializes lesbianism from a white, heterosexual perspective" and makes no attempt to "pathologize it," her lack of interest in a more sustained analysis stems from her study's timing (*Creating Born Criminals,* 181); see also Julian Carter, "Normality, Whiteness, Authorship: Evolutionary Sexology and the Primitive Pervert," in *Science and Homosexualities,* ed. Vernon A. Rosario (New York: Routledge, 1997), 168–69.

110. Spaulding, *An Experimental Study,* 273.

111. *Report of the Special Committee,* 8. See also Potter, "Undesirable Relations," 400.

112. Kunzel, "Situating Sex," 253–70, esp. 253–56.

113. Spaulding, "Emotional Episodes," 305.

114. Inmate #2466, Conduct Report, 12 May 1919, 27 October 1919, BH. See also conduct infractions such as "writing notes" and "receiving a note." Inmate #2496, Conduct Report, 9 May 1918, 23 July 1918, BH.

115. Edith Spaulding, "The Problem of a Psychopathic Hospital Connected with a Reformatory Institution," *Medical Record* 99, no. 20 (1921): 818. Yet the issue of interracial attraction and the developing romantic relationships in women's prisons was more complex than Spaulding's observations suggested. For instance, one study completely disagreed with Spaulding and in fact completely reversed her assessment by noting that white women were not attracted to dark-complexioned black women but to those black women with a lighter hue. Offering a distinct perspective, this study was still laden with racist stereotyping. It rejected the premise that "some administrators of women's prisons [thought] it [was] because white women associate masculine strength and virility with dark color"; instead, the study noted that "usually it is not the very dark negro women who [were] sought after for such liaisons, but the lighter colored ones; and those who [were] most personable, the cleanest and the best groomed" (ibid.). See also Joshua Fishman, *Sex in Prison: Revealing Sex Conditions in American Prisons* (New York: National Library Press, 1934), 28.

116. Inmate #2503, letter from Superintendent Helen Cobb to Department of Child Welfare, Westchester County, 28 May 1918, BH.

117. Inmate #2503, Information Concerning Patient, 8 August 1917, BH.

118. Inmate #2503, Staff Meeting, 29 September 1917, BH.

119. Inmate #2503, letter from Superintendent Helen Cobb to Inmate's Mother, 29 October 1918, BH.

120. Inmate #2503; see letter from Church Mission of Help to Bedford, 9 June 1921, and letter from Church Mission of Help to Superintendent Baker, ca. June 1921, BH.

121. Inmate #4092, Family History, ca. 1926, BH.

122. Nestle, "Lesbians and Prostitutes," 169. Although from a later period, Billie Holiday noted the prevalence of same-sex relations when she was an inmate in the Federal Women's Reformatory at Alderson, Virginia (see Billie Holiday, *Lady Sings the Blues,* with William Dufty [New York: Lancer, 1969], 132).

123. Nestle, *A Fragile Union,* 34–35.

124. Inmate #4092, History Blank, ca. May 1926, BH.

125. Inmate #3696, Admission Record, 9 July 1923, BH.

126. Inmate #3696, letter from Amy M. Prevost to Dr. Amos T. Baker, 13 November 1924, BH.

127. Nestle, *A Fragile Union,* 34. For more of Hampton's observations regarding 1920s Harlem, see Lillian Faderman, *Odd Girls and Twilight Lovers: A History of Lesbian Life in Twentieth-Century America* (New York: Columbia University Press, 1991), 76.

128. Inmate #4501, Parole Report, 1–2 March 1929, BH.

129. Inmate #4501, Parole Report, ca. 27 February 1929, BH.

130. See Kunzel, "Situating Sex."

131. Inmate #2380, Conduct Report and Confiscated Letter, n.d., BH.

132. See Alexander, *The "Girl Problem,"* 96–97.

133. Hampton, interview by Nestle, 9.

# Abject Correction and Penal Medical Photography in the Early Twentieth Century

These are some pictures taken at San Quentin in the early days 1913–1920. Many defects were corrected. Our aim was to turn a man out of prison in better condition than he was on entrance.

—L. L. STANLEY, *Album 17*

For without question the cultural treasures [the historian] surveys have an origin which he cannot contemplate without horror. . . . There is no document of civilization which is not at the same time a document of barbarism. And just as such a document is not free of barbarism, barbarism taints also the manner in which it was transmitted from one owner to another.

—WALTER BENJAMIN, *Theses on the Philosophy of History*, VII, 1940

On the morning of March 14, 1913—the first of many such times, Dr. Leo L. Stanley, the resident physician at San Quentin State Prison, took part in a man's execution. While Stanley waited anxiously under the scaffold in the prison's death chamber, above him, Poolos Prantikos, a forty-five-year-old Greek immigrant convicted of killing two police officers, awaited the moment of death. As Prantikos murmured prayers, Stanley noted the details around him—the scaffold's thirteen steps painted "robin's egg blue," the gray walls of the gallows room. Guards bound Prantikos's legs, pulled a black hood over his head, and tightened the noose's large knot behind his left ear.

As the prison's physician, Stanley's job was to count Prantikos's final heartbeats and pronounce the time of death. The trap opened and Prantikos's body whirled downward and jerked to a stop; the force of the fall whipped the black cap loose and yanked the slippers from his feet. Stanley—just inches away, his hand on

Prantikos's chest—"could not take [his] eyes from that awful head driven over to the right shoulder by the hangman's knot."[1] As Stanley went on to write:

> I have often wished that I could blot Prantiko's [sic] dying look from my memory. It was the most excruciating look of torture I have ever seen upon a human countenance. The black cap that covers the head of the condemned man hides a series of facial contortions that are uncannily awful to behold. Even when the cap hides the face, the suffering is expressed in the jerking of the dangling body.[2]

Stanley was "thoroughly shaken" by the sight of Prantikos's death. Few could participate in so barbaric an ordeal without suffering, Stanley ventured, and "those who can are strange in their mental make-up."[3] "Some," he noted, "reach the point where they like the spectacle, and are actually disappointed if the condemned man wins a reprieve."[4] In his meditations on the spectacle of execution, Stanley echoed a long tradition of liberal penal thinkers who believed that witnessing a hanging was demeaning. He would "come to regard with horror certain people who pester me before executions for tickets to 'the show.'"[5] Punishment was too important an exercise, too noble an ideal, he felt, to be sensationalized by a leering crowd. Like other administrative procedures designed for the social good during the Progressive Era, punishment was best left to experts, conducted out of the public eye. Despite Stanley's expressed discomfort at witnessing executions, he was hardly averse to seeing pain or suffering, or indeed of photographing, collecting, and intimately studying imagery of the same.

One week after Poolos Prantikos's execution and clear across the country, a black man named Johnson Grenson was lynched in Union City, Tennessee, before a crowd of one thousand people.[6] It is unknown whether or not photographers captured this particular spectacle, but they were commonly on hand at other lynchings. The pictures they took were frequently converted into mementos and souvenir postcards that were then put to various uses. Some were mailed to friends; others were kept in family albums or displayed on gas station walls, thereby publicizing the racially terrorizing effects of lynchings far beyond the original scenes.[7]

Of all the tortures available, lynch mobs often chose sexual mutilation, expressing culturally manufactured fears of black sexuality, particularly of black male sexuality. Such fears crystallized around the figure of the black male rapist, and perhaps largely for this reason, white mobs commonly fixated on the penises of lynching victims. While numerous scholars have examined the erotics of lynching, William F. Pinar has perhaps gone the furthest in interpreting lynching as a "mangled form of queer sex," as "interracial homosexual rape."[8] Sexual violence, whether against black men in the act of lynching or against black women in everyday life, was central to the exercise of southern white male rule.[9] Occasionally photographers who documented lynchings were more modest. For example, before John Richards was lynched in North Carolina in 1916, he was stripped naked from the waist down, like so many lynching victims, but when the photographer took a picture of Richards, a piece of canvas was draped over his legs.[10] It seems that according to some twisted southern etiquette, torturing and murdering a black man—and even displaying the results of these acts—was allowable, but showing his genitalia violated regional assumptions of visual decorum. When Leo Stanley took photos of inmates under his care in the name of modern prison medicine rather than southern rough justice, he had no such compunctions.

In this article, I examine a photo album that Leo Stanley kept between 1913 and 1920, a visual record of his early work on prisoners.[11] Despite the many available insights from existing discourses on visual culture that might help to explain Stanley's album, it can still be hard to read. The haphazard collection is something between a menagerie of medical curiosities and a collection of medical pornography.[12] Stanley provides no names, save for an occasional identifying convict number, and no dates, save the range from 1913 to 1920. Like other medical photographers of his day, he annotated only some of his photos, assuming that the images spoke for themselves.[13] That said, however, it is not clear that Stanley ever intended these images to be widely shown. And even if he did, for whom were they intended? What were viewers expected to see, to think? And what are we, in the twenty-first century, to think about the pictures Stanley made of these San Quentin inmates?

It is conceivable that these images were entirely for Stanley's personal use, providing him a means to study and reflect upon his medical practices, or perhaps to keep track of this growing collection of strange prisoners, much as other collectors of the day did with their own interests, in their own scrapbooks.[14] Or perhaps they were meant to be used as a teaching tool. We know that Stanley occasionally hosted medical students at San Quentin, perhaps using the prisoners to show students a range of human maladies, so it is also conceivable that the album had some instructional use.[15] More than fifty years after he took these photographs, Stanley left perhaps the best indication of his motives. Using a gray felt-tipped pen, he noted in his aged hand that these were "some pictures taken at San Quentin in the early days 1913–1920. Many defects were corrected. Our aim was to turn a man out of prison in better condition than he was on entrance."[16]

Whatever his reasons—and we must suppose they were complex and not entirely clear, not even to himself—Stanley made these images in the midst of a radical expansion of visual knowledge-power systems across social fields, at a moment in the development of "the determinative power of vision" in the modern world.[17] At one end of this radical expansion in the power of visual knowledge and practice stood portraiture, which offered the elite and middle classes a means of constructing themselves as privileged subjects and presenting the corresponding accoutrements of respectability, self-control, and bourgeois domesticity. At the other end stood photographic depictions of the various subordinate classes—the poor, the criminal, the sick and disabled, the racially marked, the immigrant— each category representing multiple points of contact with the state and the often stigmatizing media.[18]

Photographs, of course, can be read in countless ways; their multiple meanings circulate in various interpretive domains, and Stanley's are no different. My interest here, however, is in the place of Stanley's album in the visual archive of both legal and extralegal penality. In addition to mug shots and criminal anthropometry, this archive must also include the photographs of southern lynch mobs.[19] This is *not* to assert that the prisoners he photographed or otherwise dealt with were subjected to the equivalent of lynching. Lynch photos of the period showed the destruction of black men's bodies; I will argue that penal photography in California showed the abject correction of predominantly (but not exclusively) white men, men whose whiteness had been marred by criminal conviction. To put it in more theoretical terms, the relationship between these punitive practices and their attendant modes of seeing reveal the slippage between what Michel Foucault called biopolitics and Achielle Mbembe called necropolitics.[20] I attempt to interrogate Stanley's scrapbook for insight into the modes of state and racial-gender formation in the United States in the early twentieth century by reading images of these bodies, alternatively corrected and destroyed, in the name of social protection. Stanley would have rejected any such associations, particularly given his skepticism regarding the merits of even legal execution. But more important, Stanley considered himself a modern man, a scientist at the very vanguard of rational civilization. He believed in the processes of law and the power of the state, especially when working in conjunction with medical science, to correct rather than destroy. While lynchers might dismember black men to harvest souvenirs, Stanley's motives were different. When Stanley removed the testicles of an executed man—and he did this on many occasions—he did so for loftier purposes: to advance the cause of medical progress and scientific research.

Stanley's work at San Quentin must clearly be distinguished from the violent, virulent racism of lynch mobs, but his practices possessed their own raw power to control. Stanley clearly recognized and relished this fact, believing that medicine held a key disciplinary function in society in general, and in prison in particular. An enthusiastic eugenicist, he believed euthanasia was appropriate for some criminals. Medicine also had other appeals, both prosaic and profound.

First of all, prison medicine was a means of institutional discipline and labor control. With a thorough medical examination, Stanley believed that he could ferret out malingerers and others who might pretend to be ill in order to avoid the labor that was a part of their punishment. But Stanley knew that medicine's control penetrated deeper still, that it affected not just the body, but also inmates' very conceptions of themselves. According to Stanley, he had "seldom seen one whose ego does not diminish under the preliminary medical examination. . . . The doglike shaving, bathing, medical testings [sic], robs the most defiant law-breaker of bravado as it strips him of his clothes." He assured readers that the entrance examination was "not a grueling ordeal," nothing like an execution. "But it makes the dullest criminal realize how firmly he is trapped, and, perhaps for the first time in his life, he quails."[21] From the moment of their intake, prisoners were subjected to numerous degradation rituals, but being forced to strip naked compounded the insult.

As a prison physician, Stanley occupied a threshold space in which the lines separating punishment, healing, and research—commonly held to be distinct—were blurred. He understood his charge to be physiological, anatomical, and so-ciological: to forcibly correct men whose putative moral and physical ailments were presumed to be infectious to the body politic. It would not exaggerate the matter to suggest that San Quentin became a laboratory where Stanley honed biomedical, and indeed, biopolitical techniques meant to "perfect" the bodies of men he deemed defective, all in the name of protecting society from their ills. In other words, Stanley brought to San Quentin a physical image of proper white manhood, an image circulating broadly in the America of the early twentieth century, which he then forcibly, if paradoxically, attempted to inscribe on prison-ers' bodies, through scalpel, suture, and saw.[22] We must add the camera to this set of technological tools.

Stanley was very much invested in an image of himself as a firm but sympa-thetic healer. In truth, he was engaged in a violent project of shaping a civilized white masculinity—presumed to constitute the model of normality—and of "correcting" anything that lay outside this model. While Stanley's project would not likely be interpreted as conforming to the grotesque genocidal practices of Nazis and necropolitical southern lynch mobs, it helps to be reminded of Wal-ter Benjamin's suggestion that we are inclined to feel shame and horror at such practices and to distance them from our own. But the expansion of the modern penal state retained the logic that underlay Stanley's work. Even when seemingly sympathetic, corrective, scientific, far removed from the world of lynching, mod-ern modes of discipline were (and remain) based on similar modes of sexualized violence. Seeing the photographic evidence of that "sympathy," troubling as it is, forces us to confront its ongoing legacy.[23]

Photographs of prisoners' bodies considered here document one of the modern state's efforts to create—even under forcible conditions—a model of the healthy heterosexual white male citizen.[24] If we read Stanley's images against the larger, but parallel, archive of American lynching photography, California's supposedly more "modern" criminal justice system—along with its correspondingly more progressive and humane modes of punishment—comes to resemble its antimodern southern counterpart. In other words, California's legal system exhibited broader respect for the rule of law, while the avowedly antimodern southern system of punishment favored "community justice" and rejected formal due process, especially for African Americans. But, at least based on Stanley's practice, we might suggest that California justice, like its southern counterpart, was founded upon an oddly queer, sexualized white supremacy. Like the lynch mob, this most modern of prisons confirmed and captured the objects of white heterosexual male fear. It also offered a salve. The people whose deviant sexualities or threatening bodies haunted white fantasies would be either corrected or destroyed. Perversely, Stanley's photos showed that in some respects, and in the privacy of the prison, he could go further than public lynch mobs would dare.

STANLEY BEGAN HIS thirty-eight-year career at San Quentin with almost no surgical experience, undoubtedly thrilled at the variety of human bodies that would serve as the raw material for his working life.[25] "The experience was a great one in every way. Every opportunity for work was in the prison hospital. With the enthusiasm of youth," he waxed, "I plunged in."[26] More than just opportunities to hone his surgical skills beckoned for Stanley, who "saw at once chances for research that would have been impossible in private practice. My forty thousand clients, unable to break my diets or my orders, have yielded wonderful chances for medical experiment."[27]

And experiment he did. Stanley devised, refined, and discarded treatments and surgical procedures to rework inmates, from rhinoplasty to bunion repair—literally from nose to toes.[28] Many such images are captured in his album. He also granted access to visiting physicians to conduct experiments, and encouraged his assistants to do so as well. The most striking of his experimental procedures included implanting testicular material from goats and recently executed prisoners into his subjects. The experiments investigated how this raw form of testosterone might revitalize what he understood to be a manhood flagging under the multiple male crises of the early twentieth century.[29] An avowed eugenicist, Stanley also favored forcibly sterilizing "feebleminded" prisoners who constituted, by his estimates, 20 percent of San Quentin inmates. By 1940, he had sterilized some six hundred "volunteers." While Stanley may have been invested in "correcting" the physical ailments of his inmate wards, he hardly sought to improve their reproductive capacities. For Stanley, these men were mere specimens, an expendable population on whose bodies he might experiment so as to better treat law-abiding men on the outside. In other words, Stanley combined the "negative" aspects of the eugenics movement—sterilization—with its "positive" research practices—for purposes of evaluating the possibilities of "organotherapy" for reviving manhood-in-crisis.[30] The focus on what *made* a man deviant or normal (by his definitions) would remain Stanley's central preoccupation, a preoccupation which would ultimately lead to his most deeply disturbing photographs.

### Penal Scopophilia

Stanley's images are disturbing not least because they reveal his *scientific scopophilia,* a term Jennifer Terry uses to describe the pleasure of viewing that links visual positivism to sexual bodies.[31] His framing of the images also reveals the care that he put into this work: depth of field calculated, aperture set, backdrop hung and lighting arranged, negatives developed and positives rendered in the dark room.

As do most photographs, Stanley's urge us to consider the world beyond the frame, to attempt a reconstruction of the social and political dynamics implied in the photographic act. Such a process would logically begin with reconstructing the power asymmetries of the prison itself. The prisoner was called from his cell, his work assignment, or the hospital into whatever served as the doctor's "studio." He was instructed to undress while the doctor remained clothed. His intimate parts were then delicately or roughly shaven—perhaps as a medical procedure, but also to provide maximum visibility for the camera.[32] After the photos were made, the inmate would dress and return to his cell, work, or bed, into the everyday tumult of the Walled City of San Quentin. Stanley could arrange for prisoners under his care to eat better food than was available to most prisoners. I have argued elsewhere about the compulsions inherent in inmates' medical voluntarism, but one can imagine that prisoners might accept a good meal in exchange for participating in Stanley's photo shoots, if they were offered anything at all.[33]

Many of Stanley's photos focused on men's genitalia. Of these, images of penises—of different shapes and sizes, pointing this way and that, circumcised or not—stood out. The medical reason for many of these penis shots is not altogether clear. In another group of images, anuses predominated, but at least these showed evidence of some ailment. While some of these photos featured generic conventions of medical photography, I would suggest that the subject choice, as well as the visual proximity of penis to anus on many (though not all) of his pages, mark the images as much pornographic as medical.[34] Even as Stanley's images

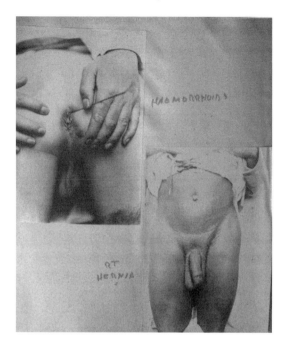

**Figure 1.**
Courtesy Anne T. Kent California
Room, Marin County Free Library

seemed cloaked in the guise of science, they can be understood nonetheless, to borrow from Pinar, as a queer form of photographic rape.

Here, the work of the nineteenth-century English feminist Josephine Butler is instructive. Butler lobbied against the Contagious Disease Acts, which tried to reduce venereal disease in the military through forcible vaginal inspections of women accused of prostitution. Butler, and the women she interviewed, identified this medical inspection as an explicit degradation, a form of instrumental rape.[35] More recently, the activist-lawyer Amanda George argued that the only difference between a prison body-cavity search and digital rape is that the perpetrator wears a state-issued uniform.[36] The same might be said of the prison doctor.

The preponderance of inmates' penises in the album indicates something of the nature of Stanley's scopophilia, especially when they need not have been depicted. A man with a swollen knee in an image captioned "Water in Left Knee" presumably might have been permitted to wear short underwear, or at least to have his shirtfront lowered rather than raised, as it is in the album. The man's injured knee—the subject of ostensible medical interest—would have remained visible. Another image shows the doctor's hands spreading apart a white inmate's buttocks. The caption "haemorrhoids" suggests that this ailment is what viewers are supposed to visually know, much as we are presumably supposed to learn something from the growths on the men's anuses and the overexposed, curiously taped penises and testicles in other images. In the top left image of figure 1, the two thin prods the doctor holds serve as prosthetic extensions of his fingers. They bear down on the shaven skin and are nearly inserted into the anus. The near-penetration of the prods into the prisoner and, moreover, the arrangement of this photo on the page—diagonally from an image of a black man's penis (he has a hernia)—suggest something of the doctor's conscious or subconscious visual desires. While the juxtaposition of penis and anus was common in the album, my intent here is not to suggest anything about Stanley's sexuality, whatever that may have been. Rather, I want to stress that, much as antisodomy and antiperversion laws in the early twentieth century reproduced the language that legislators claimed to find abhorrent, Stanley's visual focus on men's genitalia was simultaneously queer and, as we will see, virulently heteronormative.[37]

## Alternative Sexualities, Ambiguous Bodies

Stanley saw a profound danger in non-normative male sex, be it behavioral or anatomical. Indeed, California authorities struggled to repress the range of working-class men's alternative sexual practices, often racialized and attacked as "degenerate" at the same moment.[38]

Shortly before Stanley arrived at San Quentin, the San Francisco physician Alfred J. Zobel had treated three "white American" boys for rectal gonorrhea, claiming that the disease was caused in part by "the influx of foreigners from those countries where unnatural practices are common."[39] In one captionless photo, a pair of white hands stretch wide a black man's buttocks, showing tissue discolored from what appear to be genital warts. Another depicted a young, fair-skinned inmate from behind, naked from waist to thighs. Set with the caption *condyloma*, sexually transmitted genital warts spread across the prisoner's buttocks. The presentation of the ailment was surely medically fascinating to Stanley, but there was an indictment in the photo, too, as in related photos in the album. Stanley believed that these men and their maladies threatened society, not just because they were potential carriers of sexually transmitted disease, but also because Stanley assumed that homosexuals showed greater propensities for crime than "normal" men.[40] He shared with others a popular notion that homosexuality derived from depraved, nonwhite (or "not-fully-white" foreigners), as well as local, "degenerate" white homosexuals.[41] Regardless of their race, ethnicity, or origins, Stanley felt that men who had sex with men posed considerable threat to the normative order.

His description of inmate Gordon Northcott, but also others, made this quite clear. Northcott was one of San Quentin's most famous killers. Stanley noted "the queerness of his mind," and called Northcott "a sex-deviate, a pathological liar, a sadist, and a killer."[42] The subtle slippage here implied an equation between sexual "deviance" and criminality. In his memoirs, Stanley referred to Maurice, a "pretty boy" of twenty-six years, as especially dangerous. Identifying Maurice as a "prison queen"—that is, an imprisoned man who flaunted his sexual effeminacy—Stanley believed that Maurice was "more schooled in crime than many of his sin-scarred elders."[43] In portraying the effects of sexually transmitted diseases, Stanley may have been trying to document the racialized practices of these supposedly immoral, working-class men, whose sexual impropriety was just one element of their dangerousness.[44] But it was not just the evidence of their behavior (that is, signs of disease transmitted through anal sex) that drew his gaze, but also the anomalies of their bodies.

At the turn of the twentieth century, the state, fortified by the biomedical and sexological sciences, accrued knowledge-power systems over increasingly differentiated concepts of homosexuality and heterosexuality. Scientific concepts of normal male and female bodies—that is, clear sexual dimorphism—solidified at the same time.[45] Immigration inspectors at Ellis Island tried to prevent people with unusual genitalia from entering the nation, and Stanley's practice was very much related to these efforts.[46] As a part in this broader movement, men who displayed signs of anatomical sexual ambiguity featured prominently among Stanley's photos and in his writings. Indeed, he took special interest in men with what he considered anomalous genitalia, and who thus defied strict binary sexual categorization. One image depicts a man with what would today be known as gynecomastia, a male with an ostensibly feminine breast. Stanley also photographed an inmate whom he labeled a eunuch.

Stanley's work indicates a tendency to understand such bodies not as something between or in addition to normative male and female bodies, but rather as inhabiting the very edge of the human. He saw intersex prisoners as dangerous, pitiable, and therefore demanding of study. "Amazing is the percentage of the poor creatures—I hesitate to brand them with the medical term of monsters—who have committed strange and savage crimes."[47] While the word *monster* appeared to be a "technical" and therefore prescribed usage, Stanley's choice of the word *savage* was more deliberate, imputing as it did (and does) racial atavism. It demonstrated a persistent medical conceptualization of intersex people or hermaphrodites as an anatomically primitive class of being, lower on the scale of evolutionary development: as akin to nonwhite subjects, indicative of intrinsic barbarism and degeneracy.[48]

In this line, Stanley noted in his memoirs that San Quentin's most brutal serial killer was "strangely and secretly malformed." Perhaps he felt it unbecoming to give more detail in his public writings, but prurient hints were surely meant to allure:

> One of our strangest and most sinister killers is so peculiarly malformed that he might belong more in the animal than the human category. It is difficult to imagine the shock he must have received when, as a boy, he discovered himself to be shamefully different from all other men. That burning humiliation may have served to turn his self-hatred upon some victim. . . . [S]ince physically he is unlike the rest of us, mentally as well he is a creature apart.[49]

Sexologists of the day might seek the causes of homosexuality in intersex people, but Stanley was less interested in the roots of sexual practice than he was in the etiology of dangerousness. Anatomical and sexual difference led directly, in Stanley's formulation, to mass murder. Though his investigations lacked a control group, he saw a causal link between intersex bodies and gruesome violence. "The most notorious mass-murderer we have ever had in San Quentin was close to being a hermaphrodite" and "swayed between the mental processes of male and female."[50] Stanley may have been referring here to James "Bluebeard" Watson. Stanley opined that Watson appeared "effeminate" and as the type that does "not ordinarily care for the opposite sex." Yet, strangely, Stanley mused, he did. But Watson's anatomy revealed what Stanley believed to be the truth of his threat. "Biologically speaking, the queer little fellow was a monster. . . . The true hermaphrodite is rare in medical history, but Bluebeard Watson came close to being a bisexual monster." In 1928, the California writer and sometime prisoner Jim Tully referred to rumors of Watson's hermaphroditism, while two University of California "Special Lecturers in Criminology and Mental Hygiene" identified Watson as suffering from sexual perversion and hypospadius—a condition in which the urethra exits not at the tip of the penis, but rather underneath, more like a vagina.[51] This ambivalent anatomy, Stanley suggested, coupled with the alternating gendered "mental processes," led to Watson's killing at least seven women. Stanley's investigations were part of an "effort to find an explanation for such men."[52] He gazed closely at their genitals for answers.

Stanley's album contained numerous images of hypospadius among San Quentin inmates, though it is unknown if the genitalia in figure 2 belonged to Watson or someone else. Stanley appears to have arranged the images on the page to be read roughly top to bottom and left to right. If this is the case, one gets the sense that in this series, Stanley was initially hesitant to touch the prisoner's penis, or to have the prisoner hold it for the camera. Instead, and strangely, the man's penis is held aloft by a loop of knotted string—which one imagines can hardly have been comfortable. One hopes that the prisoner held the other end of the string, rather than a doctor's assistant or the doctor himself, for the thought of having someone hold a knotted string around another's penis is indeed terrifying.

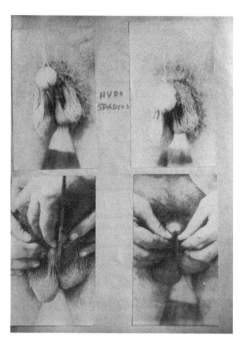

**Figure 2.**
Courtesy Anne T. Kent California Room,
Marin County Free Library

Regardless, it seems that neither of the top images satisfied the doctor's visual objectives. The bottom left image is a jumble of fingers, scrotum, and a somewhat tarnished metal instrument. Judging by the angles of the flexed fingers and the position of the thumbs, the inmate's two hands enter the frame at either side to lift and spread his scrotum. One of the doctor's hands comes into the frame from above, apparently cupping the prisoner's penis while inserting a probe into the urethra, demonstrating to the camera this unusual opening. Perhaps the doctor works the camera with his other hand. Again, one imagines that none of this was comfortable for the prisoner. The bottom right image—judging from the angle of the hands and fingers—depicts only the inmate, without the doctor's hand intruding into the visual field. It may show how the prisoner urinates, how he has accommodated the functions of kidney and the passing of fluid to his particular body. Perhaps because it shows what he might do "naturally"—that is, without the doctor's hand, a steel probe, or that terrifying piece of string, and beyond the implicit invasion of such an image—the aura of discomfort that infuses the others is marginally diminished.

In Stanley's formulation, sexual difference, whether it took the form of same-sex sex, or non-normative genitalia, exacerbated social dangerousness. If Stanley attempted some surgical correction for this man, no photographic evidence remains. Intersex prisoners could not yet be surgically "cured," as some others in his album could have been. A range of fixes would be proposed for intersexuals later in the century, though such cures would be undertaken less to prevent social danger than to avert the supposed tragedy of the intersexual's life.[53] In Stanley's studio, on the other hand, they could be photographed and studied. While locked behind tall walls, their bodies and lives could be manipulated. The doctor's diverse curiosities would be satisfied in the name and process of corrective study.

Despite accumulating compulsions to obedience at San Quentin in the early twentieth century—from batons to machine guns, from recreational activities and honor camps to medical controls—prisoners opposed the terms of their confinement and their medicalization in numerous ways. Ridiculing Stanley as the "chief croaker," inmates physically attacked him, and even publicly accused him of cruelty before a gubernatorial investigating committee.[54] Overall, there was relatively little room for resistance in the tightly controlled medical and visual field of Stanley's camera, but defiance flickers in the album nonetheless. A man in before-and-after images only identified by the diagnosis *fibroma molluscum*—nonmalignant tumors in the connective tissue of the skin—looks directly at the camera. His look is unabashed; it is strikingly similar to how Frank Embree, lynched July 22, 1899, in Fayette, Missouri, defiantly stared down at the photographer who would soon take part in his killing.[55] Stanley presumably wanted to document this man's surgical improvement, yet even after many of the tumors were removed and months later, his shorn hair now grown back, the man's eyes hardly appear grateful. The consistency of his demeanor—arms folded as if he has already had enough of this, in both sets of photos—suggests ongoing disdain. A similar look comes from the young man in figure 3, suffering from a hernia. He seems to have had little choice but to take down his trousers, but he has not doffed his cap. With his glare, the tilt of his head, and his narrowed eyes, he confronts the camera and the doctor's gaze.

The way these images were made and the strange combination of grim subordination and documentation bespeak the process that Julia Kristeva has called abjection. Kristeva famously argued that "the corpse, seen without God and outside of science, is the utmost of abjection," and Ken Gonzales-Day argued that such abjection played a considerable part in the lynch mob's fearsome display of white supremacy.[56] I would add that still-living bodies, depicted in much of Stanley's album—that is, precisely *within* penal scientific examination—were abjected differently through correctional medicine. It was part of inmates' formation through

**Figure 3.**
Courtesy Anne T. Kent California Room, Marin
County Free Library

their relationship with the modernizing state, because the prisoner-patient remained alive to both torment and release. Let me reiterate: this is not to assert
that these prisoners were lynched, in any metaphorical or literal sense. Lynching
was a horrific and destructive violence almost wholly aimed at black men in the
interest of securing a particular sort of white male rule in the transition from
slavery to a southern regional variant of capitalist modernity. In contrast, most
of Stanley's patients were of uncertain whiteness—many of whom he felt should
be denied the right to reproduce—but relatively few of them were black. The
biopolitical healing that Stanley offered, grim as it may have been, was obviously
and dramatically different from lynching's necropolitical destruction. His fixation
on intersex prisoners as intrinsically murderous, and his literal and conceptual
focus on homosexual prisoners made clear that the new regime shared lynching's
queerly sexual fixation. In contrast, California's more aesthetically modern system
was understood as marking a point of progress within a broader "corrections" system. It was represented as the arrival of a newer, better form of punishment, one
dramatically different from the violence of the lynch mob. Southern boosters and
legislators would come to see the California system as modern and thus less likely
to offend the sensibilities of the northern investors they so desperately courted.

Nevertheless, the inmates at San Quentin and elsewhere, who suffered from various infirmities, were multiply damned and multiply abjected by this emergent regime. Marked as criminal, they were tainted by the accusation of immorality as well as by the reality of criminal conviction. Unwell prisoners at San Quentin depended on Leo Stanley, who ostensibly held the key to their health, their comfort, and their bodies. Stanley's abject correction was a far cry from the crushing, wanton destruction of the lynch mob. His "corrections" promised his prisoners a better life, including the benefits of productive citizenship. In truth, however, citizenship was just as often withheld, as prisoners toiled at the limits of social being. Convicts suffered from civil death, but they *might* be reborn under a "progressive" regime, should they be seen—by prison officials from doctors to parole boards—to have become self-regulating, well-behaved men.

All of these images, the events they depicted (and in which they participated), and the people they represented (and whom they helped constitute in the process), worked to consolidate new kinds of social power and sovereignty based on bodily manipulation. In lynching, it was the power of an oddly queer, heteromasculinist white supremacy through the physical destruction of black men and the possibilities of black political participation. In Stanley's penal medical practice, the power consolidated was of a modern, expert-driven state, to normalize and correct when possible, but which would kill or crush when it deemed necessary, as when a Greek immigrant killed police officers. Regardless of Stanley's personal/medical fixations, his was a newfound mode of state power, a power trained not on the prisoner's soul, but on the health and normality of his body. Certainly not every prison physician made this sort of album, but the point is that the opportunities to do so were abundant. And while it might be satisfying to suggest that Stanley's practice was gruesome domination—which it clearly was—biopolitics were more supple. The inmate writer Jim Tully remembered Stanley as a warm and sympathetic man. Many of the prisoners he dealt with were indeed impaired. Prison was a dangerous place, after all, with countless threats to health and well-being, from disease to work injuries, attacks from guards or other prisoners. Many would have been in pain, many would have been dying, and Stanley's treatment offered one, albeit problematic, route to life, even if it were "bare life." Some of the prisoners he treated must surely have appreciated the tumors excised, the injuries treated, bullet fragments removed, and the bones set straight. But many also accused Stanley of sadism, and with cause. Medical care was denied to prisoners for punitive reasons. Inmates "volunteered" to be sterilized because Stanley convinced them they would benefit from the operation, because he deemed them feebleminded. He subjected others to countless experiments. All this and more reveal his sympathy's foundation.[57]

If Leo Stanley's album suggests a history of gendered violence that haunts and horrifies even as its memory was hidden, the traditions of medical neglect, medical violence, and sexual violence remain strong in American punishment. Engagement with the assaulted dignity of the men in these photos, as I have attempted here, cannot redress historical injustices of past treatment.[58] But as Walter Benjamin suggested in another thesis on history, historical work becomes significant when we seize hold of the flashes of memory that erupt in a moment of danger.[59] We live in one such moment; the issues at hand are hardly behind us. In 2006, the California Department of Corrections was put under federal oversight for the medical care it denied prisoners, but also for the dangers that sometimes accompanied such treatment.[60] Moreover, we can harbor few illusions about the rehabilitative value of contemporary incarceration. Across the twentieth century, the valuation of violently hierarchical masculinity, based on the subordination of women and effeminate men, has been among the most important lessons inmates learn.[61] The former prison guards who worked with their superiors at Abu Ghraib understood well that stripping and photographing a naked captive is an act of colonial dominance.[62] When rape is a feature of prison life—and keepers, it seems, are common perpetrators—and when prison rape becomes a means of entertainment on television beyond prison walls, even if it is intended to scare people "straight," rape becomes a tool of state control.[63] When prisoners and their families are routinely forced to undergo invasive and insulting searches, they learn once more about the state's overwhelming power to lay claim to their bodies, to search—indeed, to penetrate—them at will. Regardless of whether the search is in the name of medicine, of security, or in no name at all, the power of vision becomes one of subjection and degradation. Moreover, it has metastasized, from prisons to schools and airports. In the historical crisis of mass incarceration, we must not avert our eyes. It is our historical responsibility to look back.

## Notes

Many thanks to Miguel Farias, Ross Gibson, Scott Saul, David Serlin, Clarissa Ball, Frances Clarke, Stephen Berry, Karen Soldatic, Ben Harkin, and especially Deborah McDowell and Mary Bosworth for advice and criticism. Marin County librarians Laurie Thompson and Carol Acquaviva provided great help.

1. Leo L. Stanley, *Men at Their Worst*, with Evelyn Wells (New York: D. Appleton-Century, 1940), 44; see also Sheila O'Hare, Irene Berry, and Jesse Silva, *Legal Executions in California: A Comprehensive Registry, 1851–2005* (Jefferson, N.C.: McFarland, 2005), 229–30.

2. Stanley, *Men at Their Worst*, 44.

3. Ibid.

4. Ibid, 43.

5. Ibid, 44. There is a long literature on elite concerns over disorderly crowds at executions, but see Michel Foucault, *Discipline and Punish: The Birth of the Prison,* trans. Alan Sheridan (New York: Vintage, 1979); Louis P. Masur, *Rites of Execution: Capital Punishment and the Transformation of American Culture, 1776–1865* (New York: Oxford University Press, 1989); Peter Linebaugh, *The London Hanged: Crime and Civil Society in the Eighteenth Century* (Cambridge: Cambridge University Press, 1992); Michael Meranze, *Laboratories of Virtue: Punishment, Revolution, and Authority in Philadelphia, 1760–1835* (Chapel Hill: University of North Carolina Press, 1996); Stuart Banner, *The Death Penalty: An American History* (Cambridge: Harvard University Press, 2002); Annulla Linders, "The Execution Spectacle and State Legitimacy: The Changing Nature of the American Execution Audience, 1833–1937," *Law & Society Review* 36, no. 3 (2002): 607–55.

6. "Lynched in City Street: Negro Victim of Tennessee Mob Killed White Man for Revenge," *New York Times,* March 22, 1913, New York Times online, http://query.nytimes.com/mem/archive-free/pdf?res=9807E7DD173FE633A25751C2A9659C946296D6CF.

7. There is a substantial literature on lynching. On lynching and the circulation of its imagery, see *Without Sanctuary: Lynch Photography in America* (Santa Fe: Twin Palms, 2000); Ken Gonzales-Day, *Lynching in the West, 1850–1935* (Durham: Duke University Press); Grace Elizabeth Hale, *Making Whiteness: The Culture of Segregation in the South, 1890–1940* (New York: Vintage, 1998); Dora Apel, "On Looking: Lynching Photographs and the Legacies of Lynching after 9/11," *American Quarterly* 55, no. 3 (2003); David Garland, "Penal Excess and Surplus Meaning: Public Torture Lynchings in Twentieth-Century America," *Law and Society Review* 39, no. 4 (December 2005); and Michael J. Pfeifer, *Rough Justice: Lynching and American Society, 1874–1947* (Urbana: University of Illinois Press, 2004).

8. William F. Pinar, *The Gender of Racial Politics and Violence in America: Lynching, Prison Rape, and the Crisis of Masculinity* (New York: Peter Lang, 2001), esp. 11, 14; Jacquelyn Dowd Hall, *Revolt Against Chivalry: Jessie Daniel Ames and the Women's Campaign Against Lynching* (New York: Columbia University Press, 1997); W. Fitzhugh Brundage, *Lynching in the New South: Georgia and Virginia, 1880–1930* (Urbana: University of Illinois Press, 1993); Robyn Weigman, *American Anatomies: Theorizing Race and Gender* (Durham: Duke University Press, 1995), esp. 81–114.

9. Danielle L. McGuire, "'It Was like All of Us Had Been Raped': Sexual Violence, Community Mobilization, and the African American Freedom Struggle," *Journal of American History* 91, no. 3 (2004): 906–31.

10. Consider the lynching of John Richards in North Carolina in 1916, among others. See James Allen, *Without Sanctuary: Lynching Photography in America* (Santa Fe, N.M.: Twin Palms, 2000).

11. The album is archived as Album 17 in the Leo Stanley Collection, Kent California Room, Marin County Free Library. Stanley archived a handful of his records in this library. All images that follow draw from this album.

12. I use the term "pornography" in the second-wave feminist sense. As Angela Y. Davis recently put it, pornography entails the "objectification of the body, the privileging of the dismembered body" (Angela Y. Davis and Eduardo Mendieta, *Abolition Democracy: Beyond Empire, Prisons, and Torture* [New York: Seven Stories Press, 2005], 37). On post-second-

wave reevaluations of pornography, see Linda Williams, *Hard Core: Power, Pleasure, and "the Frenzy of the Visible"* (Berkeley and Los Angeles: University of California Press, 1999); and Linda Williams, *Screening Sex* (Durham: Duke University Press, 2008).

13. Daniel M. Fox and James Terry, "Photography and the Self-Image of American Physicians, 1880–1920," *Bulletin of the History of Medicine* 53 no. 3 (Fall 1978): 435–57, esp. 437, 442; Erin O'Connor, "Camera Medica: Towards a Morbid History of Photography," *History of Photography* 23, no. 3 (Autumn 1999): 232–44, esp. 241.

14. For a collection that shares much with Leo Stanley's (and published by the same press as *Without Sanctuary*), see Stanley B. Burns, M.D., *A Morning's Work: Medical Photographs from The Burns Archive & Collection, 1843—1939* (Santa Fe: Twin Palms, 1998). More broadly, see Susan Tucker, Katherine Ott, Patricia Buckler, eds., *The Scrapbook in American Life* (Philadelphia: Temple University Press, 2006); Donna Haraway, "Teddy Bear Patriarchy: Taxidermy in the Garden of Eden, New York City, 1908–1936," in *Culture/Power/History: A Reader in Contemporary Social Theory*, ed. Nicholas B. Dirks, Geoff Eley, and Sherry B. Ortner, 49–95 (Princeton: Princeton University Press.

15. In addition to the welcome he gave outside researchers, the album contains an image of Stanley, guards, and twenty-odd young men, labeled "Stanford Medical Students Tour San Quentin, 1920" (Album 17, Marin County Free Library, n.p.).

16. Album 17, Marin County Free Library, n.p.

17. James W. Cook, "Seeing the Visual in U.S. History," *Journal of American History* 95, no. 2 (2008): esp. 441.

18. If the family portrait and the criminal mug shot were foundational visual documents constructing two poles of modern subjectivity, as Allan Sekula and Shawn Michelle Smith have argued, prison medical photos represent a point even further from the position of privilege (Allan Sekula, "The Body and the Archive," in *The Contest of Meaning: Critical Histories of Photography*, ed. Richard Bolton [1986; Cambridge: MIT Press, 1989], 342–88; Shawn Michelle Smith, *Photography on the Color Line: W. E. B. Du Bois, Race, and Visual Culture* [Durham: Duke University Press, 2004], 8–9). On immigration and photography, see Anna Pegler-Gordon, "Chinese Exclusion, Photography, and the Development of U.S. Immigration Policy," *American Quarterly* 58, no. 1 (2006): 51–77.

19. On race and middle-class portraiture, see Smith, *Photography on the Color Line*, 8–9; and for a conceptualization of race, gender, and vision, see Weigman, *American Anatomies*, esp. 21–80. Analyses of the images of the criminal, the mad, and the ill tend to overlap. Nevertheless, on images of criminals, see especially Foucault, *Discipline and Punish;* Simon A. Cole, *Suspect Identities: A History of Fingerprinting and Criminal Identification* (Cambridge: Harvard University Press, 2001); Christian Parenti, *The Soft Cage: Surveillance in America, from Slave Passes to the War on Terror* (New York: Basic, 2003); John Tagg, *The Burden of Representation: Essays on Photographies and Histories* (Minneapolis: University of Minnesota Press, 1993); Sekula, "The Body and the Archive"; Cesare Lombroso, *Criminal Man*, trans. Mary Gibson and Nicole Hahn Rafter (Durham: Duke University Press, 2006); Marie-Christine Leps, *Apprehending the Criminal: The Production of Deviance in Nineteenth-Century Discourse* (Durham: Duke University Press, 1992); and David G. Horn, *The Criminal Body: Lombroso and the Anatomy of Deviance* (New York: Routledge, 2003). On images of the insane or the sick, see Sander L. Gilman, *Disease and Representation: Images of Illness from Madness to AIDS* (Ithaca: Cornell University Press, 1988);

Sander L. Gilman, *Health and Illness: Images of Difference* (London: Reaktion, 1995); Lisa Cartwright, *Screening the Body: Tracing Medicine's Visual Culture* (Minneapolis: University of Minnesota Press, 1995); and Marita Sturken and Lisa Cartwright, *Practices of Looking: An Introduction to Visual Culture* (Oxford: Oxford University Press, 2001), esp. 279–314. On medical photography, see Fox and Terry, "Photography and the Self Image of American Physicians, 1880–1920"; Erin O'Connor, "Camera Medica: Towards a Morbid History of Photography"; Kathy Newman, "Wounds and Wounding in the American Civil War: A (Visual) History," *Yale Journal of Criticism* 6, no. 2, (1993): 63–86; J. T. H. Connor and Michael G. Rhode, "Shooting Soldiers: Civil War Medical Images, Memory, and Identity in America," *Invisible Culture: An Electronic Journal of Visual Culture* 5 (2003), www.rochester.edu/in_visible_culture/Issue_5/ConnorRhode/ConnorRhode.html. On photography and disability, see David Hevey, *The Creatures Time Forgot: Photography and Disability Imagery* (London: Routledge, 1992). On "normal" and especially white raced and gendered bodies in the early twentieth century, see Gail Bederman, *Manliness and Civilization: A Cultural History of Gender and Race in the United States, 1880–1917* (Chicago: University of Chicago Press, 1995); John F. Kasson, *Houdini, Tarzan, and the Perfect Man: The White Male Body and the Challenge of Modernity in America* (New York: Hill and Wang, 2001); Julian B. Carter, *The Heart of Whiteness: Normal Sexuality and Race in America, 1880–1940* (Durham: Duke University Press, 2007); and David Serlin, *Replaceable You: Engineering the Body in Postwar America* (Chicago: University of Chicago Press, 2004).

20. Foucault, *The History of Sexuality, Volume 1: An Introduction*, trans. Robert Hurley (New York: Vintage, 1990); Foucault, *"Society Must Be Defended": Lectures at the Collège de France, 1975–1976*, trans. David Macey (New York: Picador, 2003); Mbembe, "Necropolitics," trans. Libby Meintjes, *Public Culture* 15 (2003): 11–40; as well as Georgio Agamben, *Homo Sacer: Sovereign Power and Bare Life*, trans. Daniel Heller-Roazen (Stanford: Stanford University Press, 1998); and Ruth Wilson Gilmore, "Race and Globalization," in *Geographies of Global Change: Remapping the World*, ed. R. J. Johnson, Peter J. Taylor, and Michael J. Watts, 2nd ed. (Malden, Ma.: Blackwell, 2002), esp. 261.

21. Stanley, *Men at Their Worst*, 2. The sociologist Erving Goffman evocatively identified the process of entering an institution as *mortification*. Yet Goffman focused on the disciplinary function of the examination, without addressing the medical components (for good, ill, or both), which were of key importance (Erving Goffman, *Asylums: Essays on the Social Situation of Mental Patients and Other Inmates* [New York: Penguin, 1961], 16).

22. Ethan Blue, "The Strange Career of Leo Stanley: Remaking Manhood and Medicine at San Quentin State Penitentiary, 1913–1951," *Pacific Historical Review* 78, no. 2 (2009): 210–41; Bederman, *Manliness and Civilization*; Kasson, *Houdini, Tarzan, and the Perfect Man*; Carter, *The Heart of Whiteness*. For the postwar period, see Serlin, *Replaceable You.*

23. If Stanley's photos must be examined in their historical context, some of them must also be seen. Since I first found his album in the Marin County Library, I have grappled with the ethical issues of reproducing the images it contains. I have taken into account the debates surrounding images from Nazi concentration camps, as well as those concerning American lynch mobs. Some critics have argued that to reproduce such images of human suffering is to perpetuate representational violence. While there is merit to such

arguments, there are perhaps more troubling consequences associated with not showing those images. Showing them can open a discussion of violent practices otherwise hidden from view, while simultaneously exposing the horror and barbarism that often attend, à la Benjamin, "documents of civilization." Having spent much of the past decade researching American prisons, I am convinced that violently sexualized degradation—a key aspect of the images under discussion—is a central tactic of modern penal statecraft, from its most therapeutic to its most brutal manifestations. That history must be seen and understood so that the forms of dominance it engenders might be challenged. Moreover, the images' awful intimacy collapses the distance between outside and inside, and may provocatively discomfit those of us who remain free from the abject subjection punishment entails, forcing a change from what Michelle Brown calls complicit "penal spectatorship" to radical engagement (Michelle Brown, *The Culture of Punishment: Prison, Society, Spectacle* [New York: New York University Press, 2009], esp. 21–49, 191–93, 200–201). A similar debate was raised by the *Without Sanctuary* book and exhibit of American lynching. Dora Apel has argued that lynching images *are* inherently violent, but that the cost of forgetting the racial terror may be higher than the clearly problematic memorialization. From a disability rights rather than racial justice perspective, David Hevey argued against what he calls a "tragic" portrayal of disability in photography, but argued for a "mobilized"—that is, a political—portrayal. Hilton Als argued and Victoria Ann Lewis showed more recently that there are no guarantees that such uses will not reproduce dominance (Dora Apel, "Looking at Lynching"; Ken Gonzales-Day, *Lynching in the West, 1850–1935* [Durham: Duke University Press, 2006]; David Hevey, *The Creatures That Time Forgot: Photography and Disability Imagery* [London: Routledge, 1992], 6); Als, in *Without Sanctuary;* and Lewis, "Radical Wallflowers: Disability and People's Theater," in "Disability and History," special issue, *Radical History Review* 94 [2006]: 84–110). Consider also Molly Rogers's fine treatment of similar issues of photographed slaves in *Delia's Tears: Race, Science, and Photography in Nineteenth-Century America* (New Haven: Yale University Press, 2010).

24. Stanley's eugenic practices signaled a sense of differentiated whiteness among Californians. Much of the whiteness literature has addresses issues of race, immigration, and labor, but in the case of California's eugenics movement, it also focused on "feeblemindedness" and insanity. For a brief sample of whiteness literature, see Matthew Frye Jacobson, *Whiteness of a Different Color: European Immigrants and the Alchemy of Race* (Cambridge: Harvard University Press, 1998); David R. Roediger, *Wages of Whiteness: Race and the Making of the American Working Class* (New York: Verso, 1991); Alexander Saxton, *The Rise and Fall of the White Republic: Class Politics and Mass Culture in Nineteenth-Century America* (New York: Verso, 1990); and on eugenics in California, see Alexandra Minna Stern, *Eugenic Nation: Faults and Frontiers of Better Breeding in Modern America* (Berkeley: University of California Press, 2006); Wendy Kline, *Building a Better Race: Gender, Sexuality, and Eugenics from the Turn of the Century to the Baby Boom* (Berkeley: University of California Press, 2002).

25. Curiously, he pointed out that the only exception to this was circumcision (Stanley, *Men at Their Worst*, 18).

26. Ibid, 23.

27. Ibid. A host of other American physicians have seen fertile ground for experimenting on prisoners. On medical experimentation in American prisons, see Allan M.

Hornblum, *Acres of Skin: Human Experiments at Holmsburg Prison* (New York: Routledge, 1998); Jon M. Harkness, "Research behind Bars: A History of Nontherapeutic Experimentation on American Prisoners" (Ph.D. diss., University of Wisconsin, Madison, 1996); David Oshinsky, *Worse Than Slavery: Parchman Farm and the Ordeal of Jim Crow Justice* (New York: Free Press, 1996); Susan E. Lederer, *Subjected to Science: Human Experimentation in America before the Second World War* (Baltimore: Johns Hopkins University Press, 1995); Harriet A. Washington, *Medical Apartheid: The Dark History of Medical Experimentation on Black Americans from Colonial Times to the Present* (New York: Anchor, 2006).

28. Leo L. Stanley and Louis W. Breck, "Bunions," *Journal of Bone and Joint Surgery* 17, no. 4 (October 1935): 961–64.

29. The threats to middle-class white manhood came from a range of sources: industrialization undercut traditional male economic roles and income, along with the patriarchal privilege it entailed; urbanization provoked new opportunities and fears of "overcivilization" and neurasthenia; women's suffrage movements challenged the foundation of male political citizenship; immigrants from the southern United States, as well as from southern and eastern Europe, reconfigured the urban, economic, and political landscape; war in Europe, using new technologies, revealed the fragility of men's bodies in the face of industrial war waged by nations that cared little for them.

30. Blue, "The Strange Career of Leo Stanley"; Kevin J. Mumford, "'Lost Manhood' Found: Male Sexual Impotence and Victorian Culture in the United States," *Journal of the History of Sexuality* 9, no. 3 (1992); Bederman, *Manliness and Civilization;* Laura Davidow Hirshbein, "The Glandular Solution: Sex, Masculinity, and Aging in the 1920s," *Journal of the History of Sexuality* 9, no. 3 (2000); Stern, *Eugenic Nation;* Kline, *Building a Better Race.*

31. Jennifer Terry, "Anxious Slippages between 'Us' and 'Them': A Brief History of the Scientific Search for Homosexual Bodies," in *Deviant Bodies: Critical Perspectives on Difference in Science and Popular Culture,* ed. Terry and Jacqueline Urla (Bloomington: Indiana University Press, 1995), esp. 140.

32. Williams, *Screening Sex,* 4.

33. Blue, "The Strange Career of Leo Stanley."

34. This statement extends to all of the photos in his album—not just the ones that show genitalia. Anne Fausto-Sterling has noted the similarities in medical works and explicitly pornographic texts like *Hustler,* and apparent erotic uses of medical photos. Many images of intersex genitals had been cut out of the texts she examined (*Sexing the Body: Gender Politics and the Construction of Sexuality* [New York: Basic, 2000], 277 n. 9).

35. Judith R. Walkowitz, *Prostitution and Victorian Society: Women, Class, and the State* (Cambridge: Cambridge University Press, 1980), esp. 109, 202; Anne Summers, "'The Constitution Violated': The Female Body and the Female Subject in the Campaigns of Josephine Butler," *History Workshop Journal* 48 (1999): 2, 8.

36. In Angela Y. Davis, *Are Prisons Obsolete?* (New York: Seven Stories Press, 2003), 81–83.

37. Peter Boag, *Same-Sex Affairs: Constructing and Controlling Homosexuality in the Pacific Northwest* (Berkeley and Los Angeles: University of California Press, 2003), 193–200.

38. See especially Nayan Shah, "Between 'Oriental Depravity' and 'Natural Degenerates': Spatial Borderlands and the Making of Ordinary Americans," *American Quarterly* 57, no. 5 (2005): 703–25.

39. Alfred J. Zobel, "Primary Gonorrhea of the Rectum in the Male," *American Journal of Urology* 5, no. 1 (November 1909), 451, quoted in Boag, *Same-Sex Affairs,* 59.

40. Margot Canaday, *The Straight State: Sexuality and Citizenship in Twentieth-Century America* (Princeton: Princeton University Press, 2009), 39.

41. Shah, "Between 'Oriental Depravity' and 'Natural Degenerates.'"

42. Stanley, *Men at Their Worst,* 208.

43. Ibid, 159–60.

44. Boag, *Same-Sex Affairs,* 79. See also Shah, "Between 'Oriental Depravity' and 'Natural Degenerates.'"

45. Gilbert Herdt, "Introduction: Third Sexes and Third Genders," in *Third Sex, Third Gender: Beyond Sexual Dimorphism in Culture and History,* ed. Herdt (New York: Zone, 1994), 28. Yet, as Regina Kunzel has shown, inmates' sexualities consistently queered and confounded these divisions (*Criminal Intimacy: Prison and the Uneven History of Modern American Sexuality* [Chicago: University of Chicago Press, 2008]).

46. Canaday, *The Straight State,* 44–45.

47. Stanley, *Men at Their Worst,* 66.

48. Terry, "Anxious Slippages," 132, 136.

49. Stanley, *Men at Their Worst,* 66.

50. Ibid.

51. Jim Tully, "A California Holiday" [1928], in *Prison Writing in 20th-Century America,* ed. H. Bruce Franklin (New York: Penguin, 1998), esp. 94; Ernest Bryant Hoag and Edward Huntington Williams, "The Case of J. P. Watson, the Modern Bluebeard," *Journal of the American Institute of Criminal Law and Criminology* 12, no. 3 (November 1921): 348–59, esp. 354, 57–58.

52. Stanley, *Men at Their Worst,* 166. Stanley also referred to a prisoner named Artie, who appeared to have had a sex change. Stanley called him a "moronic monster" who only "jabbered filth" and made "obscene replies"—clear indication of resistance—to the doctor's queries of sexual origins and true sexual identity (*Men at Their Worst,* 202, 203).

53. Fausto-Sterling, *Sexing the Body,* 47, 48.

54. On being attacked, see Leo Leonidas Stanley, M.D., "Twenty Years at San Quentin," *Centaur of Alpha Kappa Kappa* 39, no. 2 (January 1934): 398 (California State Library, California History Room, Call Number 365 S7). On accusations of maltreatment, see the testimony of Dominic Stanza, inmate #20733, vol. II: Witnesses before the Governor's Committee on Investigation of Folsom Prison, 370, California State Archives, Earl Warren Papers—Governor's Committee on Penal Affairs—1943–44. F3640:957. On Stanley as the "Chief Croaker," see John S. Baggerly, "Picture from the Past," *Los Gatos Times,* November 27, 1996, accessed online.

55. See Plate 42 in *Without Sanctuary,* 104.

56. Julia Kristeva, *The Powers of Horror: An Essay on Abjection,* trans. Louis-Ferdinand Céline (New York: Columbia University Press, 1982), 4; also in Gonzales-Day, *Lynching in the West,* 60.

57. Jim Tully, "A California Holiday" [1928], 94; Blue, "The Strange Career of Leo Stanley." On accusations of sadism, see Stanley, *Men at Their Worst,* 17. On malpractice, see the testimony of Dominic Stanza, Inmate #20733, vol. II: Witnesses Before the Governor's

Committee on Investigation of Folsom Prison, 370, California State Archives, Earl Warren Papers—Governor's Committee on Penal Affairs—1943–44. F3640·957.

58. Rogers, *Delia's Tears*, xxiii.

59. Walter Benjamin, Theses on the Philosophy of History, VI, in *Illuminations*, trans. Harry Zohn (1940; New York: Schocken, 1969), 255.

60. "New Prison Health Czar Tours San Quentin," April 23, 2006, KCBS, http://cbs5 .com/topstories/local_story_113165215.html. On the long-term negative health consequences of today's mass incarceration, see Ernest Drucker, *A Plague of Prisons: The Epidemiology of Mass Incarceration* (New York: New Press, 2011).

61. Davis, *Are Prisons Obsolete?*, esp. 191; Ethan Blue, *Doing Time in the Depression: Everyday Life in Texas and California Prisons* (New York: New York University Press, 2012).

62. Dylan Rodríguez, "(Non)Scenes of Captivity: The Common Sense of Punishment and Death," *Radical History Review* 96 (2006): 9–32.

63. Both male and female prisoners are subject to rape by keepers. Human Rights Watch Women's Rights Project, *All Too Familiar: Sexual Abuse of Women in U.S. State Prisons* (New York: Human Rights Watch, 1996); David Kaiser and Lovisa Stannow, "The Rape of American Prisoners," *New York Review of Books,* March 11, 2010, www.nybooks.com /articles/archives/2010/mar/11/the-rape-of-american-prisoners/?pagination=false.

# Mass Incarceration, Prisoner Rights, and the Legacy of the Radical Prison Movement

ANOOP MIRPURI

> In recent years, prison revolts have occurred throughout the world. . . . One
> may, if one is so disposed, see them as no more than blind demands or suspect
> the existence behind them of alien strategies. In fact, they were revolts, at the
> level of the body, against the very body of the prison. What was at issue was not
> whether the prison environment was too harsh or too aseptic, too primitive or
> too efficient, but its very materiality as an instrument and vector of power.
>
> —MICHEL FOUCAULT, *Discipline and Punish: The Birth of the Prison*

On the morning of September 13, 1971, state troopers stormed the Attica Correctional Facility in Upstate New York and opened fire indiscriminately, killing at least forty-three people.[1] The attack was a militarized police response to the takeover of the facility by prisoners four days earlier. Disillusioned by the reformist promises of the state corrections administration, under pressure from hostile guards, and seething at the violence fostered by the application of "correctional" techniques, prisoners overturned the authority structures of the prison and for a brief period demanded the attention of the entire nation. More than 1,200 of Attica's 2,243 inmates occupied one of the four prison yards, took forty-five hostages (mostly prison guards), and organized a leadership cadre and security force. Almost immediately, they began to call for meaningful action on a list of grievances and demands drafted weeks prior by the self-proclaimed Attica Liberation Faction.[2] During the next four days, a group of community leaders, attorneys, legal scholars, and journalists were called in to arbitrate the tenuous standoff between prisoners and the state corrections administration. After a critical impasse during which prisoners were given an ultimatum to surrender unconditionally, New York governor Nelson Rockefeller halted negotiations and gave the green light for law enforcement to retake the prison using deadly force.

From our contemporary vantage point—given the normalization of human rights violations from Guantanamo to Pelican Bay—it may seem unsurprising that in 1971 police killed thirty-three prisoners and ten prison guards without incurring legal sanction.[3] Indeed, the legal justification for the massacre was neatly cast in the language of "security."[4] More pressing at that time was its legitimation in the eyes of an American public that had My Lai and Kent State fresh in its memory. Faced with this problem, state actors chose to rationalize the massacre by circulating a fabricated story that would reveal the barbarous and grisly character of those whom society is forced to imprison. According to the story, rebel inmates had castrated white prison guards, after which they slashed their throats and stuffed the genitals of each guard into his own mouth. Upon learning what was happening in the prison, infuriated police initiated a mad assault on the prison yard. By the time the truth emerged—that state troopers had in fact killed the prison guards during the assault, and other than gunshot wounds, there was no evidence of bodily mutilation on the prison guards—it was too late to counter such a bizarre fiction, the cultural mobility of which was based in its capacity to confirm widely held assumptions about urban criminals and their supposedly violent and predatory tendencies.[5] The state had successfully constructed a narrative that was particularly appealing to the constituents of a populist law-and-order discourse, according to which a recalibrated white masculinity was charged with defending society against threats by whatever means necessary.

The state's narrative deftly combined racialized concerns over "crime in the streets" with expansionist Cold War antiradicalism. One might call this a generic hybrid of film noir and the classic Western. Invoking the narrative contours deeply embedded in U.S. histories of territorial conquest and military globalism, it cast the inmates as primitive guerrilla rebels, engaging in barbarous and uncivilized warfare, resisting the United States' role as guarantor of freedom and the rule of law. If the sanctity of the law was to be upheld, such resistance demanded swift and equally brutal reprisal by the state, even if this required the revocation of rights and suspension of law.[6] In any case, it was still an open question whether or not prisoners who rebelled—against the prison warden? against the corrections administration? against the state itself?—could even claim such rights. In other words, in explaining the Attica massacre, the state drew on the conceptual repertoire of U.S. mythmaking—particularly that which was used to frame Indian removal on the Western frontier—in which prisoners, like the Apache, were defined in opposition to civil society, for they were the savages who raped, tortured, maimed, scalped, and mutilated.[7]

According to *The Official Report of the New York State Special Commission on Attica*, "with the exception of Indian massacres in the late 19th century, the State

Police assault which ended the four-day prison uprising was the bloodiest one-day encounter between Americans since the Civil War."[8] This special commission was a key post-Attica voice proclaiming the scandal of American punishment and a proponent of implementing prison reforms according to liberal penology's imperative of convict rehabilitation. It is telling, then, that even as the commission professed a fundamental faith in the progressively inclusive nature of liberal governance, it evoked the Indian wars and the Civil War as reference points for historicizing the significance of the Attica massacre. In doing so, perhaps unwittingly, the commission located Attica within the tortuous history of state and civilian efforts to manage those who have been viewed as exceptions to the norms of liberal governance: the Indian and the slave.[9] In other words, the commission implicitly ratified the very claim being made by the radical prison movement: that prisoners, like Indians, slaves, and the colonized, have been cast outside the law's imperative to protect the integrity of the human body. In 1971, this argument cut to the heart of a prison system that came to be seen by many as lacking legitimacy.

For this reason, interpreting Attica and the larger prison movement of which it was a part would become crucial to contesting efforts to reconstitute the legitimacy and effectiveness of punishment during the last quarter of the twentieth century. And yet, even while Attica remains the most notorious prison rebellion in U.S. history, its cultural and political consequence to the recalibration of American punishment at the end of the twentieth century has been largely underexamined. Like contemporary U.S. prisons, Attica is both invisible and yet omnipresent, silently shaping the spatial, cultural, legal, and political terrain of the world we inhabit. On one hand, just as the prison's pervasiveness in contemporary cultural discourse belies the darkness that reigns in so-called "security housing units" (SHUs), the geographical remoteness of large penal institutions and detention centers conceals their relative ubiquity on the American landscape.[10] Similarly, the obscure history of Attica has shaped its capacity to operate as a conceptual reservoir for thinking about punishment, its legitimacy and its scandal.[11]

For many observers, the "prison riots" which spread from California to New York, erupting at Folsom, Auburn, San Quentin, Soledad, and the Tombs, should be viewed as a general outcry over prison conditions and a call for reform.[12] Others have largely interpreted these revolts according to the ideological imperatives of Cold War national security, which suggested that prisoner activism was part of a black radical and communist conspiracy to overthrow the state.[13] Despite what may seem like a divergence between these views, what they have in common is a basic unwillingness to reckon with the complexity or target of the prisoners' claims. As I examine below, it was in the course of a series of revolts sweeping the country that prisoners began to argue that the ideological division between "rcform" and "security" was a ruse, the power of which inhered in the modern penal theory that prisons should "rehabilitate" criminals. Anticipating the interpretive strategies of their enemies and would-be advocates, prisoners in revolt argued that the long-held belief that punishment should be "corrective" in fact served a bellicose American desire to protect the nation from perceived threats to the social order. In opposition to liberal democratic theories of punishment, they represented the prison as an institution on the margins of the law. The prison, they argued, was instrumental in producing a population that could be subject to the exercise of legitimate violence—and more, to the denial of their very claims to political subjectivity.

Indeed, at stake for the prisoners in revolt at Attica was a fundamental problem: would the state recognize such claims, or would they be relegated to what Hannah Arendt called "the abstract nakedness of being human"—and thereby stripped of the political integument necessary to ensure their protection as political subjects?[14] It is crucial to emphasize, however, that this claim to personhood was not so much an appeal to the state as a moment of insistent truth. In the process of demanding that the state respond to their grievances, the prisoners were immanently contributing to a critical theory of the relation between the prison and society. At the heart of this theory lay two critical questions: (1) Are prisoners worthy of the protections and rights accorded to U.S. citizens under the Constitution?; and (2) Would their status be recognized in accordance with the Standard Minimum Rules for the Treatment of Prisoners, adopted by the United Nations in 1957, and to which the United States is a signatory?[15] Clearly, the answer was "no." But the answer was not given in the textual language of judicial reasoning. On the contrary, the state recoded the status of prisoners as civilly "dead" in an act of performative violence.[16]

Borrowing from Frantz Fanon, we might say that the prisoners' claims were rejected—and their legal abjection reconstituted—in the "language of pure force."[17] In this sense, the state's response to the Attica rebellion was not just a legal refusal to recognize prisoners as political subjects. Rather, the very attempt by prisoners to aspire to political existence was seen as an imminent threat to state sovereignty necessitating the invocation of emergency conditions: a "state of exception" in which prisoner claims to political subjectivity represented an existential threat to state power. According to this reasoning, the emergency demanded that prisoners be forcibly extinguished without regard to the procedural imperatives of legal protection; a reasoning that exposes the liberal distinction between law and violence as contingent rather than categorical. What I am suggesting is that it was these prison revolts that posed the very questions that would come to be taken up by late modern theorists of sovereignty and the "state of exception." How do

we make sense of the fact that the symbolic reinforcement of the rule of law demanded that prisoners' lives be made vulnerable to violence and death? In what
sense is the *political existence* of prisoners a threat to state and society?[18]

I want to suggest that taking the political claims of the radical prison movement seriously demands not just reconsideration of the relation between the state
and civil society, but also of the state's and society's relationship to its captives.
In other words, rather than viewing incarcerated offenders as individual *objects
of legal exclusion* from civil society, it is worth asking to what extent practices of
American punishment create an image of the prisoner as a deserving *object of
violence*—that is, outside a theoretical sovereign community governed by a rule
of law.[19] In this sense, the condition of prisoners might be likened to that of the
slave or the Indian—not because the contemporary prison is a historical mutation
of the plantation or the reservation, but insofar as prisoners have also facilitated
the constitution of free citizen-subjects who enjoy the protections afforded by the
law. At the same time, this essay should be understood not so much as posing a
formalist question about whether prisoners can be liquidated with impunity, but
rather as exploring the conditions under which such liquidation and bodily disintegration might proceed. Perhaps more urgently, it poses a question about how
we choose to understand and define violence, its relation to punishment, and the
role of the prison in constructing the imagined boundaries between civilization
and barbarism.

Taking up the perspective of legal violence rather than legal exclusion requires
that we situate the 1971 uprising within a much broader history of conceptual
tactics used to conceal the "civilized" atrocities of colonial power. In this case,
such dissimulation required that the Attica rebels be transformed into insurgents
whose very existence threatened the foundations of state and society. Put differently, Attica is a historical flashpoint at which we might forge an epistemological
link between the scandalized history of American punishment and the singular
history of U.S. attempts to expand its territory, to open markets, to commodify
enslaved bodies, to extract natural resources, to devalue forms of human labor, to
fight terror and export liberty across the globe—in short, the long history of U.S.
imperial warfare.

As historians and legal scholars have demonstrated, it has never been a simple
matter to distinguish between *punishment* and *preemptive action* against perceived
security threats.[20] Indeed, populations construed as threats to the state and civil
society are more than likely to experience the "protections" afforded by police
power as expressions of a quasi-permanent state of emergency—one in which
the prison looms large. During the last thirty years, the use of incarceration to
manage extralegal crises generated by the need for resource extraction, capital

accumulation, and the regulation of surplus labor has once again muddled normative distinctions between *crime* and *warfare,* and between *prisoners* and *enemy combatants.* The problem is that these legal and conceptual distinctions are theoretically foundational to how liberal society construes the aims of punishment and the rights of various types of prisoners. Rather than understanding these as clear distinctions being undermined—or temporarily suspended—by strategic or cynical invocations of emergency conditions, my contention is that we have been witnessing the simultaneous positing and dissolution of the boundaries between fighting crime, punishing, and waging war. The distinctions between these categories "apply" insofar as they become inapplicable in accounting for late-modern developments such as the militarization of municipal police forces, the transfer of carceral expertise between supermax prisons and military "black sites." The state of exception is neither an abstract model of power that simply needs to be applied nor a tactic of sovereignty that proves the rule. Rather, it is something that is always with us—structuring the terms of political universalism in the United States—the operations, objects, and geography of which are always shifting. Whether or not there is a formal logic at work here, what is clear is that its consequences have placed in serious peril the effective potential of rights-based struggles to address today's crisis of mass-incarceration.

### Crisis and the Radical Prison Movement

Of course, the world is a different place today than it was forty years ago. One thing we do share with that earlier period, however, is a sense of crisis. Indeed, from this perspective, the early 1970s was in some respects oddly similar to our own moment. Although many have recognized the economic, ecological, and human rights catastrophes we face today as nothing less than dire (and rightly so), the points of convergence between now and then are worth thinking about, if only because today's crises of capital and state legitimacy are largely the outcome of how we worked through that previous conjuncture. The conditions are familiar: economic recession; sustained unemployment; fiscal insolvency; an economy of surplus; populist resentment of government liberalism long taken for granted; and anxieties over the decline of American global hegemony spurred by the costs and scandals of a decade-old military occupation.[21]

Even though we have witnessed an extraordinary contraction of the discursive space for progressive politics since the 1970s, the familiar conditions then precipitated concerns that were similar to our own as well. One widely accepted comparison is that, like the current occupations of Iraq and Afghanistan, the war in Vietnam sparked widespread outrage over suspected human rights violations hy the U.S. military.[22] But perhaps the strangest similarity between now and then is one that is almost never publicly acknowledged, and even more seldom recognized: the emergent debate over prisons and punishment. Difficult as it is to imagine, given that the United States has since become the world's most prolific incarcerator, the early 1970s saw a growing number of people beginning to seriously question the sustainability and effectiveness of American prisons. By 1973, a federal task force appointed to investigate U.S. correctional practices concluded that "the prison, the reformatory, and the jail have achieved a shocking record of failure. There is overwhelming evidence that these institutions create crime rather than prevent it."[23] Coupled with a more general erosion of trust in state power that characterized the decline of postwar liberalism, this suspicion of American punishment generated polarized divisions in a far-reaching debate over what rights should be accorded to prisoners.[24] But despite the differences in how (and how much) we punish, one could argue that the recurrence of the prison question today is not as remarkable as it first seems. After all, it is fairly customary that when state legitimacy is in crisis, attention turns to our prisoners.[25]

Perhaps this begins to explain why over the last few years there has been increased scrutiny directed toward the prison and criminal justice system from across the political spectrum. This concern has been placed on the agenda by a diverse array of cultural workers, including artists, prison abolitionists, legal scholars, human rights activists, and public health specialists. Indeed, it is safe to say that mass incarceration has again become a glaring crisis in American political and social life. For those of us who view mass incarceration as a problem, surely these tendencies in public and scholarly awareness represent an important development—and their potential impact should not be underestimated. Many initiatives on the part of social justice workers—which include the California-based abolitionist group Critical Resistance, the Sentencing Project, the Prison Moratorium Project, and Architects, Designers, and Planners for Social Responsibility (ADPSR)—have been influenced by the efforts of critical scholars to contest the claims made by politicians, criminologists, and conservative political scientists that U.S. prison growth has been both a logical response to rising crime rates and an effective deterrent of crime.[26]

At the same time, reformists since at least the early nineteenth century have viewed the prison as a failure of liberalism and an affront to the human rights tradition. These were often the very same reformers who argued that more stringent application of correctional punishment techniques was the most effective way to secure a prisoner's human rights. As Michel Foucault warned in 1975 on the heels of the last prison crisis in the wake of Attica, "for a century and a half the prison had always been offered as its own remedy: the reactivation of the penitentiary techniques as the only means of overcoming their perpetual failure; the realization of the corrective project as the only method of overcoming the impossibility of implementing it."[27] And yet, since Foucault's observation, we have witnessed neither a deliberate scaling back of the use of prisons nor the implementation of alternative modes of administering justice, but rather thirty years of arguably the most massive prison-building project in the history of the world.

This raises a series of difficult questions. That is, why have critical discourses surrounding the prison so permeated our intellectual and cultural landscape even as we have been unable to reverse the seemingly relentless growth of the prison itself? And why has the broad acknowledgment of mass incarceration as a crisis done relatively little to challenge its legitimacy? Perhaps even more disquieting is that even as the prison has come to represent the dark side of American practices of liberty and equality, the figure of the prisoner has retained an abject status outside the acceptable boundaries of human sociability.

Any attempt to answer these questions must engage with the critique of the modern history of captivity and punishment offered by prisoners in revolt in the late 1960s and early 1970s at places like Attica, Folsom, Auburn, San Quentin, Soledad, and the Tombs. This critique was partly inspired by the pressing vocabularies of freedom, struggle, and justice circulating in various radical social movements of the period. This vocabulary collided with the experiences of prisoners, who described themselves in manifestos as "domesticated animals," "slave labor[ers]" selected to "do [the] bidding" of "vile and vicious slave masters."[28] My goal here is not to romanticize the movement, but rather to seriously assess its contribution to a then emerging prison knowledge formation. Indeed, it was the impetus of this movement that provided the language for the critique of the prison as a central institution of liberalism and racial capitalism. At the same time, this movement has animated the political imagination of liberal scholars and intellectuals as part of a "what not to do" list in struggles for progressive change—scholars and intellectuals who have often been far more interested in the "moderate" and seemingly "realistic" goals of prison reform. Of course, it was the radical prison movement, personified most iconically by George Jackson and Angela Y. Davis, that launched the most thoroughgoing critique of liberal reformism as the primary means of extending the prison's coercive hold on society in the absence of a more radical pursuit of economic justice. The insidious implications of this process could only be seen, Jackson and Davis argued, by closely examining the function of black captivity as the basis of capitalist property relations.[29]

By 1964, after years of experiencing the criminalization of resistance to racial violence and segregation, crime, warfare, and captivity began to take on new valences and definitions within the black freedom movement. For example, Jackson and the Black Panther Party proclaimed that crime could function as a political act, and that all black prisoners could be considered "prisoners of war." In the midst of a deep political crisis generated by the collapse of Keynesian liberalism, and manifest in nationwide urban rebellions and violent police crackdowns between 1964 and 1968, these redefinitions of crime presented a real challenge to the legitimacy of government. A historically dense signifier with the capacity to index all kinds of crises and threats to the state, the meaning of "crime" was for a brief moment exploded, and radically contested by prisoners themselves. In these competing narratives, both ordinary prisoners and luminaries such as Jackson, Davis, and Malcolm X undermined the assumptions that had driven efforts at prison reform for two centuries.[30] Rather than the prison shaping the ideal citizen-subject through discipline, they saw the prison as a factory for producing groups that could be excluded from the privileges of personhood and citizenship. Rather than viewing the prison as a space that *failed* to live up to its real promise of rehabilitation, these authors represented the prison as a *successful* institution in a long line of American captive spaces, whose purpose was to divide the working classes and preserve the wealth and power of the richest members of society. These captive spaces—the plantation, the reservation, the internment camp, the ghetto, and the prison—were not viewed as exceptions to the rule of law. Rather, their endurance in American history suggested that they played a *constitutive* role in American social and political life. In other words, spaces of captivity helped underwrite the very legitimacy of the rule of law. They did so insofar as they came to be seen as necessary for protecting the life, health, and inviolable humanity of those so-called "law-abiding" citizens on the outside.

As a number of scholars and activists have argued, viewing the prison as a legacy of the plantation and the reservation has dramatic implications for how we understand the role of captivity in American life. It is important to remember, however, that if mass incarceration today stands out as a contemporary form of a deep historical problem, this is because the prison actually first emerged contemporaneously with plantation slavery and frontier warfare. In fact, even as the penitentiary, the plantation, and the reservation functioned as overlapping systems of forced labor extraction in the nineteenth century, legal theorists and reformers sought to make conceptual distinctions between them. In these theories, the penitentiary was seen as an enlightened modern institution that could correct and shape citizen-subjects without violating the body. By contrast, the plantation and reservation were seen as illiberal institutions meant to contain populations on the boundaries of the nation whose access to the privileges and protections of the law was always in question, if not in radical doubt. As the lawyer Thomas R. R. Cobb wrote in his *Inquiry into the History of Negro Slavery* (1858), "The condition of the slave renders it impossible to inflict on him the ordinary punishments, by pecuniary fine, by imprisonment, or by banishment." The slave, Cobb argued, "can be reached only through his body."[31]

The view that the penitentiary was developed in opposition to the violence of slavery was the very foundation of early prison reform discourse.[32] This distinction, between the slave's vulnerable body and the prisoner's penitent soul, has proven to be so productive that it continues to animate correctional ideology and punishment practices today. Indeed, it is precisely this ideology that has enabled a broad disavowal of the violence endemic to American punishment, most notably in the reemergence of traditional forms of bodily disintegration, such as solitary confinement. This practice of segregating prisoners in a small cell for from twenty-three to twenty-four hours a day, without any physical contact, unequivocally violates international standards governing the treatment of prisoners.[33] The ostensible goal of solitary confinement is, oddly enough, to minimize violence behind bars by immobilizing those considered to be the most hardened inmates. According to this calculus, solitary confinement is not really punishment, but rather a security measure; its technique of confinement without "touching the body" is considered humane treatment with a scientific precision.

These distinctions—violence/punishment, body/soul—have enabled the elaboration of a conceptual schema in which punishment is understood to be a tool of the law, the target of which is an individual's soul; while seemingly opposed to this, we have conditions of what Dylan Rodriguez calls "(undeclared) warfare," during which we suspend certain laws and exert bodily violence on enemies, or those we consider beyond the pale of humanity.[34] However, even this violence, according to international law, should be exercised only in cases of "necessity." More than forty years ago, the radical prison movement formulated the critique of this conceptual schema that has been so central to the history of American punishment. Those at the forefront of the radical prison movement effectively challenged the broad perception that the brutalized ontology of incarceration disqualified the political intelligibility of their critical visions—their capacities to understand and critique the social formation that locked them in cages.[35] The question asked by many activists and intellectuals circulating through American prisons was no longer the question of the prison reformist: that is, "Why do you violate my body when you say you are reforming my soul?" Instead, they began to ask, "What is the nature of a punishment directed at the captive's soul that leaves the body exposed to violence?" Put differently, inmate rebels from Folsom to Attica were fighting precisely to expose that it was the prison's theoretical commitment to "rehabilitation" which rendered prisoners exceptions to the norms of liberal governance. Looking back from our present vantage, as labor and hunger strikes begin to spread across U.S. prisons once again, it is becoming increasingly difficult to contest the veracity of their critique.

## "The Folsom Prisoners Manifesto"

One of the most important examples of how the radical prison movement recast the distinction between punishment and warfare emerges in a signal and pivotal text of the movement itself, "The Folsom Prisoners Manifesto of Demands and Anti-Oppression Platform."[36] Composed and printed inside California's Folsom State Prison in 1970, the manifesto emerged at the very apex of the movement's influence. Tensions between prisoners and the state increased between 1969 and 1970, resulting in key developments that dramatically shaped the movement's trajectory. First, Jonathan Jackson's courthouse uprising in San Rafael, California, for which Angela Davis was imprisoned and tried for murder; second, the indictment of the Soledad Brothers on charges of murdering a prison guard, a charge that carried the death penalty for George Jackson; third, a wave of strikes, revolts, and rebellions throughout the New York City jail system that would shake its very foundations; and fourth, the publication of Jackson's book of prison letters, *Soledad Brother*, which catapulted him and the prison movement to international fame and made them an object of national anxiety.

Just weeks after Jackson's book hit the shelves, the fledgling California Prisoners Union called a labor strike throughout the state's correctional facilities. Folsom emerged as the epicenter of this movement, and on October 29, 1970, prisoners mailed their manifesto of demands to the prison warden and the head of the California Department of Corrections, in which they announced plans for a November 3 strike. Although the figure has been disputed by prison authorities, as many as 2,100 out of 2,400 prisoners refused to emerge from their cells as part of an attempt to form and generate support for a prisoner union that would protect the labor of inmates from exploitation at paltry wages, while allying it with workers' struggles on the outside.[37] Not surprisingly, particularly in light of the discourse on racialized labor, slavery, and plantation life permeating the emerging prison knowledge formation, the Folsom prisoners' strike was animated by the identification of prisoners with convicts working on prison farms in the post-Reconstruction South. In turn, the scandal generated by carceral plantations such as Parchman and Angola in the early twentieth century was replicated in the large-scale public concern exhibited by labor organizations and civil rights activists for the California prisoners. Garnering the support of groups as diverse as the National Lawyers Guild, the American Federation of Teachers, and the Medical Committee for Human Rights, the Folsom rebellion became the longest prisoner strike in U.S. history, lasting nineteen days. On November 22, the strike was broken by prison guards at the command of Folsom warden Walter Craven. Prisoners were beaten, tortured, threatened with administrative punishment, and forced back to work. As many as fifty were placed in solitary confinement, and four strike leaders were transferred out of Folsom altogether.[38]

Despite the scale of the rebellion and the severity with which it was crushed, scholars of prison movements have paid very little attention to the Folsom prisoners' strike. Such neglect is curious given the fact that the strike occurred on the heels of Jonathan Jackson's August 7 rebellion in Marin County, the New York City jail riots (October 1970), and incidents of internecine violence taking place at nearby San Quentin and Soledad throughout the previous two years. It should be further noted that the prisoners' strike also emerged in the wake of other well-known feminist and black liberation manifestos of the period, and yet literary and cultural critics who study post-1965 radical liberation movements have neglected to read the "Folsom Manifesto" as a critical text of the archive.[39] This is all the more surprising in view of the fact that the "Manifesto" served as the inspirational template for the list of demands, as well as the "Manifesto" composed by the Attica Liberation Faction the following summer, just weeks prior to the breakout of the Attica revolt.

The few studies that have considered either the Folsom or Attica manifestos have read these texts as documents whose meanings are transparent and unambiguous. In doing so, they have focused solely on the *content* and *viability* of prisoners' demands, while abstracting them from both the political history of the manifesto form and the new theoretical innovations being made by prison movement intellectuals and activists. This interpretive tendency has facilitated the incorporation of prison manifestos firmly within the tradition of progressive appeals to the ideal of prison reform. Still others have read these manifestos as the distorted expression of unrealistic revolutionary aspirations by prisoners deluded as to their own position within wider social and political struggles.[40] However, the total dismissal of the possibility that prisoners could offer an expansive and incisive vision—a vision neither clouded by their day-to-day experience of isolation and brutality nor an expression of naïve political cynicism—has obscured precisely what the state found so threatening about the prison movement: its wide appeal as a challenge to the legitimacy of liberal punishment and the reason of state power that supported it.

The absence of serious attention to the Folsom and Attica manifestos has elided the enduring intellectual impact the prison movement has had on philosophical, activist, and cultural representations of incarceration since the 1970s. But critical attention to these dynamics requires approaching the "Folsom Manifesto" as something much more than simply a transparent historical document. Rather, it needs to be read as a text whose capacity to generate meaning is shaped not only by its political context and the complex substance of the arguments the prisoners decided to advance, but also by its stylistic attributes and *formal status as a manifesto*. As the literary critic Janet Lyon argues in her book *Manifestoes: Provocations of the Modern:* "It would be a mistake to see the form simply as a vehicle for complaints . . . the manifesto's formal contours actually produce and intensify the urgency of its particular imperatives." Given its symbolic force, as well as its "role in earlier political confrontations . . . the [manifesto] must be understood therefore as more than 'plain talk': [it] is a complex, convention-laden, ideologically inflected genre."[41]

So what does the manifesto do? In brief, it heralds the emergence of a movement and gives it substance by announcing its demands. In doing so, the manifesto's raison d'être is to performatively articulate the movement's words with its deeds. The text's production, circulation, and its embeddedness in a historically specific political struggle endow it with the functional qualities of what Martin Puchner, following J. L. Austin, calls a "speech act."[42] In other words, the manifesto as a textual form becomes a strategic maneuver, the mission of which is to have real-world effects, by representing the unity of language and the condition of embodiment. While its composition does not guarantee that the authorities and supporters to whom it is addressed will agree on how to read it, the form signals a desire for social transformation that at the very least renders a reformist reading disingenuous. In composing a text that is given shape and meaning by formal attributes demonstrating the unity of language and action—of subjectivity and embodiment—the Folsom prisoners were engaged in an act of literary and political creation that has yet to be entirely reckoned with. Put differently, the manifesto did far more than simply provide a set of formal conventions with which prisoners could express a series of grievances and demands. Rather, the genre itself takes on a rhetorical function that animates its critical edge. One might call it a formal subversion of the humanist binary that founds correctional ideology: the empirical division between body and soul—more specifically, between the slave's violated body and the prisoner's penitent soul. For the "Folsom Manifesto," what reformers, correctional administrators, and criminologists call the "soul" is not only something that is impossible to isolate and contain as an object of treatment: the "soul" is ineluctably embodied.

From this perspective, what allows liberal penology to make the distinction between "ordinary punishments" and efforts to "reach" an offender "through his body"?[43] If the slave is the unacknowledged figure enabling a certain dissembling around the distinction between violence and punishment, then perhaps the figure of the prisoner—as object of punishment—simultaneously shapes how we understand violence and the spaces in which (and the bodies upon which) we tolerate it. As a formal enunciation of a critique embedded in its analysis of the prison, the "Folsom Manifesto" resists attempts to read it as an invitation for a better application of correctional techniques. Indeed, it suggests that the separation of body from soul, of cruelty from correction, is precisely the ideological trap that enables a disavowal of the quotidian violence of American prisons.

This formal rhetorical structure functions as a base for a nuanced set of arguments, establishing twenty-nine demands, the principles of which would be canonized a year later at Attica. The substance of these demands effectively challenge the bodily domination inherent in key aspects of the prison's everyday functioning: ideological repression, solitary confinement, indefinite detention, and the withholding of adequate medical care. Summarizing the demands, the "Manifesto" argues:

> We the men of Folsom Prison have been committed to the State Correctional Authorities by the people of this society for the purpose of correcting what has been deemed as social errors in behavior, errors which have classified us as socially unacceptable until re-programmed with new values and a more thorough understanding of our roles and responsibilities as members of the outside community. The structure and conditions of the Folsom Prison program have been engraved on the pages of this manifesto of demands with the blood, sweat, and tears of the inmates of this prison.
>
> The program we are committed to under the ridiculous title of rehabilitation is likened to the ancient stupidity of pouring water on a drowning man, in as much as our program administrators respond to our hostilities with their own.[44]

I want to suggest that in describing the purpose of corrections as "re-programm[ing]" inmates "with new values," the "Folsom Manifesto" does not indict the prison's failure at accomplishing this task. Rather, the text contrasts this neutral description of correctional ideology with the image of the prison's operation "engraved" on the manifesto "with the blood, sweat, and tears" of the prisoners. In counterintuitive fashion, this juxtaposition conjures the pain and injury provoked by a regime whose purported goal is the reshaping and normalization of subjectivity. Because of this, it makes a point of enacting the understanding that the source of the manifesto resides in the molecules of the prisoner's body. The architects of the "Folsom Manifesto" understood that it is precisely the design of the prison in its utilitarian framework, "under the ridiculous title of rehabilitation," that constitutes the prisoner as a threat to the outside community. At issue for the Folsom prisoners is the conception of the prison's purpose: as the "correction" of the very people whose containment authorizes the state to represent its sovereign power and function as social protector. This process leads inevitably to violence, which goes largely unrecognized—this is what, for the Folsom prisoners, collapses the distinction between the liberal correctional ideal and the illiberal "concentration camp." In likening the state's effort at "rehabilitation" to "pouring water on a drowning man," these prisoners render the state's correctional regime (carried out in the name of protecting society) a practical absurdity. "Pouring water on a drowning man" may seem like an odd way to allegorize the violence of corrections, but given the allusive capacity of the "Manifesto," and the efforts of prisoners to situate their experiences in historical perspective, it is hardly out of the question to suspect that they would have knowledge of the relationship between captivity, punishment, and water torture.

It might thus be useful here to consider an anecdotal history of the United States' use of water torture. In 1858, *Harper's Weekly* published an exposé on what was then euphemistically called the "shower bath," which was, according to *Harper's*, "used as a means of coercing criminals into submission to the orders of prison authorities." The article described a convict at the Auburn State Prison who was "showered to death by prison officials. All the water that was in the tank was showered upon him in spite of his piteous cries; a few minutes after his release from the bath he fell prostrate, was carried to his cell, and died in five minutes."[45] It is unsurprising that, given the contemporary struggles over punishment, slavery, and abolition, this issue of *Harper's* was published the same year as Thomas Cobb's *Inquiry*, which attempted to establish the legal basis for corporal punishment inflicted on slaves on the grounds that they were legally different from prisoners.

Today, as the quasi-permanent state of exception in which we reside has led us to become increasingly familiar with the category of the "enemy combatant," we are more apt to recognize the term "waterboarding" than the "shower bath." But contrary to outraged pundits and spectators who argue that the current enmeshing of torture and empire is a radical departure in U.S. foreign policy, as the historian Paul Kramer has shown, the public contest over what was called "the water cure" during the U.S. occupation of the Philippines uncannily mirrored the contemporary debate over "enhanced interrogation techniques." One returning soldier described "the water cure" in a letter to the *Omaha World Herald* in May 1900: "Now, this is the way we give them the water cure. . . . Lay them on their backs, a man standing on each hand and each foot, then put a round stick in the mouth and pour a pail of water in the mouth and nose, and if they don't give up, pour in another pail. They swell up like toads. I'll tell you it is a terrible torture."[46] Indeed, as recent as January 1968, the *Washington Post* printed a front-page photo of a U.S. soldier supervising the waterboarding of a North Vietnamese soldier. The caption noted specifically that the technique induced "a flooding sense of suffocation and drowning meant to make him talk." These specific flashpoints, to which one might add the public record of the use of water torture by the French in colonial Algeria and the recent images of civil rights activists being hosed by police forces in the U.S. South, suggest that this is a history of which many prisoners in Folsom and other prisons would no doubt have been aware.

To be more precise, the Folsom prisoners' invocation of a relationship between corrections and torture, as part of a history of imperial warfare, constituted neither accidental nor reductive hyperbole. It was grounded in the experience of an anticolonial segment of the black freedom movement, upon which the federal government and urban police forces had unofficially declared war. Street-level assassinations, frame-ups, infiltration, and mass imprisonment were all manifestations of this state of war. In other words, if imperial warfare was the lens through which many prisoners interpreted their experience, then the prison could not be viewed as a place to reform captives; rather, it was a place to break them.

In contrast to previous efforts of prisoners to exploit the disjuncture between liberal penal rhetoric and the violence of prison practices by appealing to the discourse of reform, the "Folsom Manifesto" represents the discursive practices of corrections as themselves instruments of violence. If liberal penology was grounded in the ideological distinction between "violence" and "treatment," Folsom prisoners engaged the practices of "treatment" in order to expose the cruel rationalities behind their implementation and the corporeal violence that their practice facilitated.

Unpacking the dense referential field and formal conventions of the "Folsom Manifesto" reveals that it was neither simply about the improvement of conditions behind bars nor part of a foolish attempt to crack the edifice of state power. Rather, if we want to understand its political resonance and the danger it posed to state power, the "Folsom Manifesto" needs to be understood as an attempt to expose the humanist claims of correctional ideology as a kind of weaponry—indeed, as part of an entire cache of arms that could (and would) be mobilized to neutralize the movement with no accountability to the law. This unaccountability was rooted in a practice of punishment that functioned as a means of differentiating prisoners from the wider human community that deserved to be protected from violence.

### Violence in American Legal Practice

How is such violence calculated in American legal practice? The primary recourse for determining the constitutionality of punishment in the United States, of course, is the Eighth Amendment, which prohibits the use of cruel and unusual punishment. This is perhaps the single-most fundamental right meant to signify a liberal society's adherence to the Enlightenment norms of humane treatment and corporeal integrity. But as Colin (Joan) Dayan argues, the actual history of Eighth Amendment judicial reasoning has had little to do with protecting the body from violence and suffering. In fact, as Dayan argues, the language of "cruel and un-usual" first emerged as part of efforts to distinguish between "excessive" versus "legitimate" or "necessary" violence within the New World slave codes. As a result of these peculiar historical circumstances, and the tortuous efforts to conceptu-ally distinguish between slaves and prisoners, at issue in the Eighth Amendment was actually the *method of punishment,* rather than the prohibition of pain and cruelty. Prohibited were treatments such as the pillory, drawing and quartering, cutting off the hands and ears, branding, slitting the nostrils, and disemboweling, while other forms of violence—whipping, beating, hanging—were to be expected as matters of course. Legal precedent for Eighth Amendment decisions, then, has not tended to enforce restrictions on cruel and unusual punishment, but has rather established and defined the forms of violence necessary—and lawful—in a society founded on a central imperative: the subjugation of a population of slaves.[47]

In 1986, in accordance with the persistent efforts to delimit a more capacious understanding of "cruel and unusual" in American jurisprudence, the U.S. Su-preme Court undid the legal victories of the Warren Court's focus on prisoners' rights. Reversing legal precedent established decades earlier, and launching the prison back in time to the nineteenth and early twentieth centuries, the majority in *Whitley v. Albers* effectively ruled that prison conditions could no longer be challenged in court as violations of the Eighth Amendment. According to Chief Justice William Rehnquist's formalist logic, violence behind bars could not be deemed to constitute punishment. Rather, the punishment was the legal condi-tion of being imprisoned, while everything constituting the human experience of imprisonment was at the dispensation of the expertise and "good faith" of prison guards and administrators. As Dayan argues, *Whitley v. Albers* is critical to under-standing how the hard-won rights of prisoners in revolt in the early 1970s have been legally extinguished in favor of the increased reliance on the human rights catastrophes that we call supermax prisons.

*Whitley* also helps throw into relief the widening gap between U.S. punish-ment practices and international norms. This process has seen the United States increasingly draw upon its own legal history to establish the fundamental weak-nesses of postwar international conventions on human rights, and the aberrance of any supranational legal system that would seek to constrain the constituent power of the United States to continuously remake the globe.[48] It is from this perspective that we must view the recent Bush administration's decision to define prisoners held in military detention centers, such as Guantanamo Bay, as enemy combatants. The main goal of this designation was to exempt detainees from the more stringent standards governing the treatment of "prisoners of war" under the Geneva Conventions. Accordingly, this exemption thus put the onus on the administration's lawyers to prove they were in compliance with the U.S. Constitution, as opposed to international law. Based on the domestic legal precedents governing the treatment of American prisoners, this hardly proved difficult. Could solitary confinement and "enhanced interrogation techniques" constitute "cruel and unusual punishment"? The answer was no, because the detainees were not really being "punished." In fact, none of them had yet been charged with crimes, much less convicted. For those who might eventually be convicted, what happened behind prison walls could not constitute punishment so long as it was deemed "necessary" or "in good faith." The effect was to define the infliction of pain as an incidental outcome of interrogation, or the imperative to establish "security," rather than the basic means through which prisoners are administered.

As a result of these decisions, practices of incarceration that unequivocally violate international protocol, and which, in our geopolitical imagination, tend to be associated with autocratic regimes in the "non-Western" world, are normalized as the everyday lot of thousands of captives in U.S. prisons. Perhaps these facts compel us to tell an entirely different story about the emerging postwar hegemony of human rights discourse. The central dilemma that has consistently plagued liberal internationalism, of course, is American exceptionalism: the fact that the United States continually declares its sovereign right to wage war for humanitarian purposes while exempting itself from the bonds of international law at home and abroad. Inhabiting the perspective of the radical prison movement—where it meets the legacy of anticolonialism and black freedom struggles—perhaps we should view the international standards for humane treatment that were gradually defined in the wake of World War II genocide as *the exception,* which would prove a much more discomfiting rule. This is not a story of progress. One might argue that the postmodern critique of modern narratives of progress is not simply a response to the ruins of a genocidal twentieth century, but is rooted in the material conditions of late-modern geopolitics, which have seen the extension of capitalist market relations under American supervision effectively become the only possible guarantor of human rights. Indeed, the antistatist tendency in American politics that has increasingly replicated at home the growing economic inequalities of the structurally adjusted third world is central to today's prison crisis—though not solely, as some would have it, because of struggles over fiscal policy.[49] If the past is a guide to the future, there is hardly a limit (legal or otherwise) to the fortifications and zones of abandonment that may be built to contain the human and ecological fallout of a new era of capital accumulation.[50]

Keeping both these longer and recent histories in mind, how do we confront the phenomenal growth of mass incarceration since the very period in which the radical prison movement trenchantly exposed the inhuman conditions of U.S. prisons to the entire nation? I want to suggest that how we explain this extraordinary transformation over the last forty years is critical to addressing the crisis of imprisonment today. Moreover, explaining this transformation has much to do with how we remember and assess the radical prison movement and its legacy.

Despite the fact that many of the discursive practices of prisoners in revolt have been forgotten in contemporary scholarship, they paradoxically loom large, even if only as a spectral presence, in current debates about prisons. One tendency, evident in the language of governmental commissions on prison overcrowding to the progressive legalism of appeals courts, has been the truly well-meaning and often admirable attempts to incorporate the demands of rebellious prisoners within the very tradition of prison reform that they resisted. In the process, however, prison reform is reestablished as the only answer to the failure of prison reform.[51] The ironies of this incorporation mirror yet another tendency in current debates about prisons: to dismiss the entire prison movement, as well as its association with black radicalism, as the cause of the state's crackdown on crime and progressive politics in the late twentieth century. Those who subscribe to this narrative choose not to view mass incarceration today as a result of the recapturing of the levers of state power by corporations after the demise of postwar liberalism. Instead, many view the prison movement's espousal of supposedly extremist political views as derailing truly progressive efforts at prison reform.[52] In turn, they argue, the so-called excesses of black radicalism have led to a conservative backlash that has overseen a crisis-level increase in prison growth, and the normalizing of extreme forms of dehumanization, such as SHUs and supermax prisons. But this view relies on profoundly selective and impoverished readings of the prison movement and the broader history of captivity and warfare that it attempted to illuminate. If we have learned anything from the thousands of prisoners in revolt in places like Folsom and Attica, it is that the frontier-style law-and-order discourse that has called for smaller government, privatizing public resources, and the construction of massive war-making and punishment apparatuses since the 1980s is not really a backlash. It is rather a vigorous regeneration of political and economic practices developed in the nineteenth century, and which today places in jeopardy even the narrowest interpretations of "humanity" and the "public good."

Why, then, has the broad recognition of mass incarceration as a crisis done so little to reverse the process of U.S. prison growth? Perhaps the answer lies in the fact that most of us still expect that appeals to modern notions of humanity and human rights can be progressive in themselves. But as critics of neoliberal global-ization and U.S. imperialism have argued, rights become little more than a phrase when uncoupled from questions of material inequality and our modern legacy of colonial dispossession that passes for a market economy.[53] In the expectation that human rights discourse can be progressively and essentially transformative, we tend to ignore the fact that violence and suffering have been as much a part of the promise of modernity as the sanctity of human rights.[54] Indeed, it may be that genocide and warfare constitute the dark side of our most cherished notions of humane conduct, as Michel Foucault began to famously suggest not long after his own visit to Attica in the wake of the 1971 prison revolt.[55] From this perspective, it remains a serious question whether we should continue to resist prison growth through appeals to rights and moral notions of shared human identity. For despite the centuries-old claim by reformers that the rights of prisoners—as humans—should be respected, what we learn from prisoners in revolt is that it is precisely the boundaries of the human that prisons have functioned to protect.

## Notes

1. Thirty-nine people, including ten hostages, were killed during the initial attack, with at least four more prisoners being killed in the "disciplinary" period that followed.

2. The Attica Liberation Faction consisted of Attica prisoners Donald Noble, Peter Butler, Frank Lott, Carl Jones-El, and Herbert Blyden X.

3. Pelican Bay is a supermax prison in northern California. In July of 2011, prisoners in Pelican Bay organized a massive hunger strike in protest of the normalization of violence and suffering behind bars. After three weeks, prisoners decided to end the strike once the California Department of Corrections and Rehabilitation (CDCR) made public its intention to review the gang validation policy it used to decide which prisoners to place in SHUs. After continued dissimulation by the CDCR, prisoners went on another hunger strike in September 2011. The CDCR eventually released a new gang validation policy in March 2012. On the question of human rights violations in U.S. prisons and in the so-called "War on Terror," see Dylan Rodriguez, *Forced Passages: Imprisoned Radical Intel-lectuals and the U.S. Prison Regime* (Minneapolis: University of Minnesota Press, 2006); and Nikhil Pal Singh, "The Afterlife of Fascism," *South Atlantic Quarterly* 105, no. 1 (Winter 2006): 71–93.

4. "State Police Regulations Governing Use of Firearms," in New York State, Special Commission on Attica, *Attica: The Official Report of the New York State Special Commission on Attica* (New York: Praeger, 1972), 494–95.

5. Fred Ferretti, "Autopsies Show Shots Killed 9 Attica Hostages, Not Knives; State Official Admits Mistake," *New York Times,* 15 September 1971, 1; see also Herman Badillo and Milton Haynes, *A Bill of No Rights: Attica and the American Prison System* (New York:

Outerbridge and Lazard, 1972); Malcolm Bell, *The Turkey Shoot: Tracking the Attica Cover-Up* (New York: Grove Press, 1985).

6. William E. Farrell, "Governor Defends Order to Quell Attica Uprising," *New York Times*, 16 September 1971, 1, 48; Michael T. Kaufman, "Oswald Seeking Facility to House Hostile Convicts," *New York Times*, 29 September 1971, 1, 43.

7. Thomas Hietala, *Manifest Design: American Exceptionalism and Empire* (Ithaca: Cornell University Press, 2003); Paul Kramer, *The Blood of Government: Race, Empire, the United States, and the Philippines* (Chapel Hill: University of North Carolina Press, 2006); and Singh, "The Afterlife of Fascism."

8. New York State, *Attica*, xi.

9. See Frank B. Wilderson III, *Red, White & Black: Cinema and the Structure of U.S. Antagonisms* (Durham: Duke University Press, 2010); Jared Sexton, "People-of-Color-Blindness: Notes on the Afterlife of Slavery," *Social Text* 28, no. 103 (2010): 31–56.

10. Mike Davis, *City of Quartz: Excavating the Future in Los Angeles* (London: Verso, 1990); Ruth Wilson Gilmore, *Golden Gulag: Prisons, Surplus, Crisis, and Opposition in Globalizing California* (Berkeley and Los Angeles: University of California Press, 2007); Lorna Rhodes, *Total Confinement: Madness and Reason in the Maximum Security Prison* (Berkeley and Los Angeles: University of California Press, 2004).

11. It is important to recognize, however, that this relation between Attica and the contemporary prison is not merely analogical. Indeed, inquiries into the late-modern explosion of incarceration rates and prison construction have begun to increasingly refer to Attica as a watershed moment that precipitated the current prison crisis. The total statistical divergence between the technical use of incarceration in 1971 and today alone has been enough to spur this reference. According to statistics provided by the U.S. Bureau of Justice, the number of people locked up has risen dramatically only in the last thirty years, after holding constant for decades. Around the time of Attica, when the legitimacy of prisons was in severe doubt, there were fewer than 350,000 persons incarcerated in the United States. Today, there are more than 2.3 million persons behind bars (see Joy James, ed., *The New Abolitionists: (Neo)Slave Narratives and Contemporary Prison Writings* [Albany: State University of New York Press, 2005]; Frank Schmalleger and John Ortiz Smykla, *Corrections in the 21st Century* [New York: McGraw-Hill, 2006]; Heather Ann Thompson, *Attica: Race, Rebellion and the Rise of Law and Order America* [forthcoming]; and Loïc Wacquant, *Punishing the Poor: The Neoliberal Government of Social Insecurity* [Durham: Duke University Press, 2009], 113).

12. Badillo and Haynes, *A Bill of No Rights*; Eric Cummins, *The Rise and Fall of California's Radical Prison Movement* (Stanford: Stanford University Press, 1994); New York State, *Attica;* Larry E. Sullivan, *The Prison Reform Movement: Forlorn Hope* (Boston: Twayne, 1990); Bert Useem and Peter Kimball, *States of Siege: U.S. Prison Riots, 1971–1986* (New York: Oxford University Press, 1989).

13. Spiro Agnew, "The 'Root Causes' of Attica," *New York Times*, 17 September 1971, 43; William E. Farrell, "Rockefeller Sees Plot at Prison," *New York Times*, 14 September 1971, 1, 30; Russell Oswald, "Statement by Commissioner Oswald," *New York Times*, 14 September 1971, 28. For recent examples of scholarship that translates the earlier focus on conspiracy into a discourse on pathology, see Theodore Dalrymple, "The Cult of Insincerity," *New English Review* (October 2009); and Heather MacDonald, "The Jail Inferno," *City Journal* 19, no. 3 (Summer 2009).

14. Hannah Arendt, *The Origins of Totalitarianism* (1951; New York: Harcourt, 1968), 299.

15. While the Attica prisoners' demands did not explicitly refer to the U.S. Constitution or the United Nations conventions on the treatment of prisoners, this was largely because the list of demands was intended not as a rhetorical appeal but as a basis for substantive negotiations under a tense threat of violence. It was clear to all sides that the U.S. Constitution was the legal reference for their demands. Indeed, "The Attica Liberation Faction Manifesto," which was sent to New York Corrections Commissioner Russell Oswald weeks prior to the revolt—and to which Oswald mailed a response—did explicitly appeal to the U.S. Constitution. The "Folsom Prisoners Manifesto," upon which the Attica "Manifesto" and demands were modeled, appealed directly to the United Nations 1954 Geneva Convention (see New York State, *Attica*, 251–57; "The Attica Liberation Faction Manifesto of Demands and Anti-Depression Platform," *The New Abolitionists*, 303–9; and "The Folsom Prisoners Manifesto of Demands and Anti-Oppression Platform," in *If They Come in the Morning: Voices of Resistance*, by Angela Davis et al. [New York: Signet, 1971], 65–74). See also United Nations, *Standard Minimum Rules for the Treatment of Prisoners* (New York, 1957).

16. Walter Benjamin, "Critique of Violence," in *Reflections*, trans. Edmund Jephcott (New York: Schocken, 1986); Judith Butler, *Precarious Life: The Powers of Mourning and Violence* (London: Verso, 2004), 61–65; Jacques Derrida, "Force of Law: The 'Mystical Foundation of Authority,'" in *Deconstruction and the Possibility of Justice*, ed. Drucilla Cornell et al. (New York: Routledge, 1992).

17. Frantz Fanon, *Wretched of the Earth*, trans. Constance Farrington (New York: Grove Press, 1963), 38.

18. Giorgio Agamben, *Homo Sacer: Sovereign Power and Bare Life*, trans. Daniel Heller-Roazen (Stanford: Stanford University Press, 1998); Butler, *Precarious Life*; Colin Dayan, *The Story of Cruel and Unusual* (Cambridge: MIT Press, 2007); Rodriguez, *Forced Passages*; Singh, "The Afterlife of Fascism."

19. For examples of legal and moral critiques of mass incarceration, see Michelle Alexander, *The New Jim Crow: Mass Incarceration in the Age of Colorblindness* (New York: New Press, 2010); Glenn C. Loury, "Why Are So Many Americans in Prison? Race and the Transformation of Criminal Justice," *Boston Review* 32, no. 4 (2007); and Michael Tonry, *Malign Neglect: Race, Crime, and Punishment in America* (New York: Oxford University Press, 1995).

20. Kimberlé Crenshaw and Gary Peller, "Reel Time/Real Justice," *Denver University Law Review* 70, no. 2 (1993): 283–96; Bryan Wagner, *Disturbing the Peace: Black Culture and the Police Power After Slavery* (Cambridge: Harvard University Press, 2009), 18.

21. Some critics have even argued persuasively that we are at a decisive phase of a long conjuncture that began forty years ago. See Gilmore, *Golden Gulag*; David Harvey, *The Enigma of Capital: And the Crises of Capitalism* (New York: Oxford University Press, 2010); and Nikhil Pal Singh, "Beyond the 'Empire of Jim Crow': Race and War in Contemporary U.S. Globalism," *Japanese Journal of American Studies* 20 (2009): 89–111.

22. Mark Danner, *America, Abu Ghraib, and the War on Terror* (New York: New York Review of Books, 2004); Seymour M. Hersch, *Chain of Command: The Road from 9/11 to Abu Ghraib* (New York: HarperCollins, 2004).

23. National Advisory Commission on Criminal Justice Standards and Goals, *Task Force Report on Corrections* (Washington, D.C.: U.S. Government Printing Office, 1973), 597. Two years later, Michel Foucault characterized "prison failure" as the foundational and animating discourse of the expanding use and increasing self-evidence of prisons in liberal Western societies—particularly in the United States and France (see Michel Foucault, *Discipline and Punish: The Birth of the Prison,* trans. Alan Sheridan [New York: Vintage, 1997], 264–72). See also Ramsey Clark, *Crime in America: Observations on Its Nature, Causes, Prevention and Control* (New York: Simon and Schuster, 1970).

24. American Friends Service Committee, *Struggle for Justice: A Report on Crime and Punishment in America* (New York: Hill and Wang, 1971); Angela Davis et al., *If They Come in the Morning: Voices of Resistance* (New York: Signet, 1971); Robert Martison, "What Works? Questions and Answers about Prison Reform," *Public Interest* 35 (Spring 1974): 22–54.

25. Rebecca M. McLennan, *The Crisis of Imprisonment: Protest, Politics, and the Making of the American Penal State, 1776–1941* (New York: Cambridge University Press, 2008).

26. Elliott Currie, *Crime and Punishment in America* (New York: Metropolitan Books, 1998); Angela Y. Davis, *Are Prisons Obsolete?* (New York: Seven Stories Press, 2003); M. Davis, *City of Quartz;* Gilmore, *Golden Gulag;* Marie Gottschalk, *The Prison and the Gallows: The Politics of Mass Incarceration in America* (New York: Cambridge University Press, 2006); Joy James, ed., *States of Confinement: Policing, Detention, and Prisons* (New York: St. Martin's Press, 2000); Joy James, ed., *Warfare in the American Homeland: Policing and Prisons in a Penal Democracy* (Durham: Duke University Press, 2007); Jerome G. Miller, *Search and Destroy: African-American Males in the Criminal Justice System* (New York: Cambridge University Press, 1996); Michael Parenti, *Lockdown America: Police and Prisons in the Age of Crisis* (London: Verso, 1999); Loïc Wacquant, "From Slavery to Mass Incarceration: Rethinking the Race Question in the US," *New Left Review* 13 (2002): 41–60.

27. Foucault, *Discipline and Punish,* 268.

28. "The Attica Liberation Faction Manifesto of Demands and Anti-Depression Platform," in *The New Abolitionists,* 303.

29. Angela Y. Davis, "Political Prisoners, Prisons and Black Liberation," in *If They Come in the Morning,* by Davis et al.; George Jackson, *Soledad Brother: The Prison Letters of George Jackson* (New York: Coward-McCann, 1970).

30. George Jackson, *Blood in My Eye* (New York: Random House, 1972); Huey P. Newton and J. Herman Blake, *Revolutionary Suicide* (New York: Writers and Readers Publishing, 1995).

31. Quoted in Caleb Smith, *The Prison and the American Imagination* (New Haven: Yale University Press, 2009), 147.

32. Dayan, *The Story of Cruel and Unusual.*

33. Atul Gawande, "Hellhole," *New Yorker,* 30 March 2009, 36–45. Today there are more than sixty supermax prisons in the United States that use solitary confinement as their primary method of disciplinary control, with at least one hundred thousand inmates locked up in SHUs on any given day.

34. Rodriguez, *Forced Passages.*

35. This is a point on which conservatives and liberals responding to the contemporary prison crisis generally converge, and what I contend is the sociological legacy of the "racial

pathology" and "culture of poverty" debates of the 1960s (see Heather MacDonald, "The Jail Inferno").

36. "The Folsom Prisoners Manifesto of Demands and Anti-Oppression Platform," in *If They Come in the Morning*, by Davis et al.

37. While prison activists claimed the revolt involved more than two thousand inmates, state authorities put the number closer to five hundred. Neither of these figures has been accurately verified.

38. "Prisoners in Rebellion," in *If They Come in the Morning*, by Davis et al., 65–67.

39. Particularly notable here are Valerie Solanas's *S.C.U.M. Manifesto* and the Black Panther Party's "Ten Point Program."

40. Cummins, *California's Radical Prison Movement*; New York State, *Attica*; Useem and Kimball, *States of Siege*; Sullivan, *The Prison Reform Movement*. While different in many respects, these studies converge in their unwillingness to engage the relationship between race and state power, and in their tendency to view the claims of prisoners as always already compromised by their status as prisoners.

41. Janet Lyon, *Manifestoes: Provocations of the Modern* (Ithaca: Cornell University Press, 1999), 10.

42. Martin Puchner, *Poetry of the Revolution: Marx, Manifestos, and the Avant-Gardes* (Princeton: Princeton University Press, 2005).

43. Quoted in Smith, *The Prison and the American Imagination*, 147.

44. "The Folsom Prisoners Manifesto," 73–74.

45. "Torture and Homicide in an American State Prison," *Harper's Weekly*, 18 December 1858.

46. Quoted in Paul Kramer, "The Water Cure," *New Yorker*, 28 February 2008; Kramer, *The Blood of Government*.

47. Dayan, *The Story of Cruel and Unusual*.

48. Robert Kagan, "Power and Weakness," *Policy Review* 113 (June-July 2002); Charles Krauthammer, *Democratic Realism: An American Foreign Policy for a Unipolar World* (Washington, D.C.: American Enterprise Institute Press, 2004).

49. Ruth Gilmore provides perhaps the most useful analysis of U.S. prison growth and what she calls the "anti-state state" (see Ruth Gilmore, *Golden Gulag*). See also Loïc Wacquant, *Punishing the Poor*.

50. Mike Davis, *Planet of Slums* (London: Verso, 2007); David Harvey, *A Brief History of Neoliberalism* (New York: Oxford University Press, 2005); Naomi Klein, *The Shock Doctrine: The Rise of Disaster Capitalism* (New York: Henry Holt, 2007).

51. Brown, Government of California, et al. v. Plata et al., 563 U.S. __ (2011); Craig Haney, *Reforming Punishment: Psychological Limits to the Pains of Imprisonment* (Washington, D.C.: American Psychological Association, 2006).

52. This tendency has been most prominent in liberal lamentations of the (particularly "racial") excesses of the 1960s (that is, "how class-based progressive movements went awry") (see Cummins, *California's Radical Prison Movement*). A version of this has been effectively taken up more recently by the neoconservative heirs of the 1960s "culture of poverty" thesis, particularly in the work of think-tank intellectuals in the Manhattan Institute. For examples of the neoconservative approach to mass incarceration, see Myron Magnet, "In the Heart of Freedom, in Chains: Elite Hypocrisy, Gangsta Culture, and Fail-

ure in Black America," *City Journal* 17, no. 3 (Summer 2007); and Heather MacDonald, "Is the Criminal Justice System Racist?" *City Journal* 18, no. 2 (Spring 2008).

53. Angela Y. Davis, *Abolition Democracy: Beyond Prisons, Torture, and Empire* (New York: Seven Stories Press, 2005); Michael Hardt and Antonio Negri, *Multitude: War and Democracy in an Age of Empire* (New York: Penguin, 2004); Gayatri Chakravorty Spivak, "Righting Wrongs," *South Atlantic Quarterly* 103, no. 2–3 (2004): 523–84.

54. Smith, *The Prison and the American Imagination*, 208.

55. Michel Foucault, "Michel Foucault on Attica: An Interview," *Telos* 19 (1974): 154–61; Michel Foucault, *The History of Sexuality, Volume 1: An Introduction*, trans. Robert Hurley (New York: Random House, 1978).

# 2 Social and Economic Consequences of Punishment

Rather than assuming family structure is the core contributor to the growth in crime and incarceration, policy makers must consider the sobering fact that these families and communities are being devastated because of the mass incarceration of over a million black men and women. Rather than the overarching assumption that family structure leads to crime and incarceration, the question must be how have deeply rooted systemic racial, class, and gender inequalities led to the racialization of crime and the lock-up in the United States of the largest number of people in the world? The toll such incarceration has placed on families is chilling. At base is the punitive state, the state that locks away men, women, boys and girls far too often for the most minimal of crimes.

—Rose M. Brewer

The repercussions of prison policy extend to the labor market, the stability of neighborhoods, and the workings of democracy. Among the most serious effects of mass imprisonment are the negative consequences for children with parents in prison. Given the huge racial disparity in the prison population, most of this harm befalls Black families.

—Dorothy Roberts

# Economic and Relational Penalties of Incarceration

CHARLES E. LEWIS JR.

The election of Barack Obama as the forty-fourth president of the United States and the first person of African heritage to ascend to this nation's highest office gives us much to celebrate. However, enormous challenges still confront our nation and African Americans specifically. Many of the issues facing African Americans—health disparities, poor education and economic outcomes, and limited family formation—either lead to, stem from, or are in some way connected to the fact that so many African Americans are involved with the criminal justice system. Disproportionate involvement in the criminal justice system is arguably the most vexing civil rights issue confronting African Americans today.

As the experience of getting arrested and locked behind bars has become so common among young African American males, we have become inured to the enormous and ongoing loss of human capital this represents. About one in nine black males aged twenty to thirty-four is incarcerated in federal and state prisons and local jails on any given day, more than five times the rate of their white male counterparts (Warren 2008). African American males represent less than 7 percent of the U.S. population but account for more than 35 percent of those incarcerated. Researchers estimate that approximately 27 percent of African American males will spend some time of their lives behind bars, and many of these men will suffer profoundly negative consequences.

With so many Americans being caught up in the criminal justice system and spending time behind bars, policy makers must be concerned about the damage that incarceration may inflict on individuals and on society in general. More than 2.2 million Americans were incarcerated in federal, state, and local facilities in the United States on a given day in 2011 and nearly 7 million were under the jurisdiction of federal and state criminal justice systems (Glaze and Parks 2008). This represents a substantial loss in human capital—particularly for African Americans.

While it seems intuitive that being incarcerated would damage an individual's labor-market prospects, researchers have not been able to establish causal links because suitable data connecting incarceration and labor-market outcomes are not readily available. Two factors in the data's unavailability have been the difficulty of collecting data in criminal justice settings and the lack of pre-post data on earnings and employment. Nevertheless, researchers have used existing administrative and other data to document strong associations between incarceration and poor labor-market outcomes to present compelling evidence that individuals who are incarcerated suffer economic and relational penalties.

Should there be truth in the evidence, what implications does this have for society? One implication is that the weakened labor-market prospects of incarcerated individuals may cause them to be less desirable as employees and potential mates, which would impede the formation of healthy families. This is a significant concern for African Americans as African American males comprise the greatest proportion of individuals involved in the criminal justice system, offering a possible explanation for the woeful marriage rates in the African American community. At midyear 2008, 4,777 black male inmates were held in state and federal prisons and local jails per 100,000 black males, compared to 1,760 Hispanic male inmates per 100,000 Hispanic males and 727 white male inmates per 100,000 white males (West and Sabol 2009).

We begin our exploration of these troubling statistics and the questions they raise by looking at efforts to document the association between incarceration and poor labor-market outcomes, including my own research using data from the Fragile Families Study. We will then explore the nexus between incarceration and family formation, which I also explored in my dissertation using data from the Fragile Families Study.

## Incarceration and Labor-Market Outcomes

Researchers have sought to understand incarceration's effects on labor-market outcomes (e.g., Freeman 1991; Waldfogel 1993; Nagin and Waldfogel 1998; Western 2002; and Kling 2006). One of the primary challenges in much of this research has been the inability to account for the unobserved characteristics of incarcerated individuals that might help explain poor labor-market outcomes in the absence of incarceration. What innate characteristics might explain why these individuals wind up behind bars? What made them self-select themselves into jails and prisons? Would these same characteristics lead to lower labor-market productivity? If so, how do we know what effect, if any, incarceration may have on their labor-market prospects? Without controls for these unobserved characteristics, it is impossible to isolate the incarceration effect.

Conventional economic and sociological theories suggest that incarceration reduces labor-market earnings. The mechanisms through which incarceration exacts its harmful effects are fairly obvious. Incarceration generally results in gaps in one's employment history. Having been incarcerated is a negative reflection on one's character and trustworthiness. A substantial time behind bars—particularly during the early stages of one's life—deprives a person of labor-market capital that would be gained by on-the-job training and work experience.

Labor-market economists beginning with Jacob Mincer (1962) and Gary S. Becker (1964) found positive relationships between human-capital investments through education and on-the-job training and earnings over the lifetime. Mincer estimated that as much as half of a worker's human capital is attributable to on-the-job training. Since antisocial behaviors and criminal histories tend to begin in adolescence (Sampson and Laub 1993; Pager 2003), many individuals who are ultimately incarcerated would lose valuable educational and job-training opportunities. To the extent that incarceration retards or impedes the development and accumulation of human capital, being incarcerated is expected to be associated with lower earnings and diminished labor-market opportunities.

Research in criminology and economics on the relationship between crime and the labor market has focused on the effects of economic disadvantage on criminal activity (e.g., Freeman 1991; and Hagan and Peterson 1995). However, a few studies reverse the causal sequence to examine how involvement with the criminal justice system impacts employment opportunities. With one exception, all of these studies find large negative effects.

Bruce Western used a nationally representative sample of young men—the National Longitudinal Survey of Youth (NLSY)—in his 2002 study and found that after controlling for individual-level fixed effects and period effects to account for declining wages among low-educated men, incarceration reduced wage rates by 16 percent. Freeman's earlier study in 1991, also using the NLSY (but limiting the sample to high school dropouts), found that after controlling for preincarceration employment and other demographic differences, incarceration reduced work probability by 25 to 30 percent.

Other research has used data generated by the criminal justice system. Because the data are limited to those arrested and/or convicted, estimates of the effects of incarceration are produced by use of comparison groups, before-after comparisons, and instrumental variables techniques. Waldfogel's 1993 study found that conviction of offenders who committed fraud or committed a breach of trust on the job reduced their employment opportunities by 5 percent and depressed their income by as much as 30 percent. His sample was primarily white (83.3 percent) and better educated than the general population. Using the same data for their 1998 study, Nagin and Waldfogel found that first-time conviction effects vary significantly by age while subsequent convictions reduced income at all ages.

In a 1995 study, Jeffrey Grogger found large incarceration effects on annual earnings, quarterly earnings, wage rates, and employment for both jail and prison experiences over time. Because his data do not contain information on length of prison sentence, he had no way of distinguishing declines in earnings during incarceration from declines in postincarceration earnings. On the other hand, Kling (2006), using data from the Florida state system and California federal system, did not find any negative effects of incarceration length on employment and earnings seven years after incarceration after controlling for a battery of individual characteristics and adding instrumental variables for sentence length based on random judge assignments. In fact, he found that longer incarceration sentences were associated with more positive labor-market performance.

## Incarceration and the Fragile Families Study

In an effort to further isolate the incarceration effect, I sought to address the issue of inherent human-capital deficits associated with poor labor-market outcomes— poor schooling, mental health issues, and substance abuse problems—by using a relatively new national data set, the Fragile Families Study, to find new measures to control for these factors. The Fragile Families and Child Wellbeing Study— a joint effort by Princeton University's Center for Research on Child Wellbeing (CRCW) and the Center for Health and Wellbeing, and Columbia University's Social Indicators Survey Center and the National Center for Children and Families (NCCF)—is tracking a cohort of children born between 1998 and 2000 in twenty large cities in the United States.[1]

All mothers who gave birth during the data-collection period were approached in the hospital and asked to participate in the study. Approximately 93 percent of the mothers agreed to participate and provided locating information about the fathers, who were contacted at the hospital or shortly after the birth of the child. Approximately 75 percent of unmarried fathers and 90 percent of married fathers agreed to participate. The baseline dataset includes 4,898 completed mother interviews (1,186 marital births and 3,712 nonmarital births) and 3,830 completed father interviews. One-year follow-up interviews were conducted between June 1999 and March 2002. The one-year data set includes 4,365 completed mother interviews and 3,367 completed father interviews. The full twenty-city sample was used for our study because the nationally representative sample is substantially smaller (1,300 fewer observations), and more important, the differences between descriptive statistics in the two samples are minimal (generally 0–1 percent and maximum 3 percent).

Unmarried births were oversampled, and the analysis was restricted to unmarried fathers to increase homogeneity between fathers who were incarcerated and those who were not. Fragile Families data contain not only self-reports of incarceration from the ex-offenders but also reports from the child's mother. For some analyses, self-reported data on fathers were supplanted with information obtained from the mothers in place of fathers who could not be located.

The measure of incarceration is a self-reported retrospective measure. Fathers and mothers were asked to report information about the father's incarceration history. If either the mother or father reported that the father had been incarcerated, he was classified as "ever incarcerated"; if both reported that the father had never been incarcerated or one reported no prior incarceration and the other's report was missing, he was coded as "never incarcerated"; if reports from both mother and father were missing, he was coded as "incarceration status unknown." The combined measure was used for multivariate analyses. Fathers who were incarcerated at the time of the interview were omitted from the analyses.

Given that our principal concern is the relationship between incarceration and postincarceration labor-market experience, a second advantage of the Fragile Families data is that they provide control variables other than age, education, and ethnicity—all included in previous studies on incarceration. Fragile Families data also include measures on the subject's physical and mental health, drug and alcohol use, and relationship with his biological father or another significant male figure.

Because slightly more than a quarter of the fathers were not interviewed, we use mother-reported data about the father's incarceration history and labor-market experience to analyze the full sample ($N = 3,293$), allowing for the largest possible number of cases and eliminating the selection bias that might occur if we limited the sample to interviewed fathers. However, the mothers' surveys allow us to analyze only one employment outcome—whether or not the father worked for pay the previous week. The subsample of fathers ($N = 2,406$)—though smaller than the full mother-interview sample—allows for evaluation of a richer array of dependent variables for employment and earnings.

Using the smaller father sample raises questions of selection bias because it is likely that fathers who made themselves available for interview are more attached to their children or to the mothers of their children. We expect the men in the fathers' subsample to work more and to have experienced less incarceration. Thus, limiting the study to these fathers may lessen the expected negative effects of incarceration on outcome variables. However, we found little or no variation in the statistics reported in both the father-reported and mother-reported data.

**Table 1.   Descriptive statistics among unmarried fathers**

| | Father sample (N = 2,406) | | | | | | Mother sample (N = 3,293) | |
| | All fathers | | Ever incarcerated | | Never incarcerated | | | |
| | Mean | S.D. | Mean | S.D. | Mean | S.D. | Mean | S.D. |
|---|---|---|---|---|---|---|---|---|
| REGULAR SECTOR | | | | | | | | |
| Worked last week? (mother report) | 0.73 | 0.44 | 0.58 | 0.49 | 0.83 | 0.38 | 0.72 | 0.45 |
| Worked last week? | 0.73 | 0.44 | 0.60 | 0.49 | 0.81 | 0.39 | X | X |
| Annual earnings | 21,315 | 57,270 | 15,939 | 18,353 | 24,525 | 70,791 | X | X |
| Weeks worked past 12 months | 37.85 | 19.48 | 31.59 | 21.34 | 41.66 | 17.19 | X | X |
| Hours worked per week | 43.78 | 19.40 | 40.87 | 21.76 | 45.56 | 17.59 | X | X |
| Hourly wage rate | 12.83 | 37.15 | 12.18 | 38.12 | 13.19 | 36.63 | X | X |
| Underground work | | | | | | | | |
| Participated? | 0.35 | 0.48 | 0.43 | 0.49 | 0.31 | 0.46 | X | X |
| Annual earnings | 2,546 | 13,013 | 3,277 | 14,922 | 2,173 | 11,695 | X | X |
| CONTROL VARIABLES | | | | | | | | |
| Age | 27.8 | 7.1 | 27.8 | 7.0 | 27.8 | 7.1 | 27.8 | 7.2 |
| Non-Hispanic white | .13 | .34 | .14 | .34 | .13 | .33 | .12 | .32 |
| Non-Hispanic black | .56 | .50 | .62 | .49 | .53 | .50 | .58 | .49 |
| Hispanic | .28 | .45 | .22 | .42 | .31 | .46 | .28 | .45 |
| Other race | .03 | .17 | .02 | .15 | .03 | .17 | .03 | .16 |
| Less than high school | .39 | .49 | .45 | .50 | .35 | .48 | .39 | .49 |
| High school graduate | .36 | .48 | .37 | .48 | .36 | .48 | .38 | .48 |
| Some college | .21 | .41 | .16 | .37 | .24 | .43 | .20 | .40 |
| College graduate | .04 | .18 | .01 | .11 | .05 | .22 | .03 | .18 |
| Had drug/alcohol problem | .17 | .37 | .22 | .42 | .17 | .37 | X | X |
| Depressed 2 weeks | .16 | .37 | .20 | .40 | .14 | .35 | X | X |
| Poor health | .17 | .38 | .21 | .41 | .15 | .35 | X | X |
| Not involved with father | .33 | .47 | .38 | .48 | .30 | .46 | X | X |

Descriptive statistics on the dependent and independent variables are presented in table 1. The first column in the table shows data for all fathers in the subsample. The next two columns compare fathers who were incarcerated to fathers who were never incarcerated. The fourth column presents data for the full mother sample.

Just over 10 percent of our sample of unwed fathers was white; nearly 60 percent of the sample was non-Hispanic black; and slightly less than 30 percent was Hispanic. Nearly 40 percent of the fathers did not complete high school; another 40 percent had only a high school diploma; and less than 5 percent earned a college degree. Seventeen percent of fathers reported drug or alcohol problems that interfered with their work or family; 16 percent reported some symptoms of depression; 17 reported poor or bad health; and 33 percent grew up without fathers. These statistics are consistent in both the full sample and the smaller sample of fathers.

Almost three-quarters of the fathers in both samples reported that they were employed the week prior to their interview. That the proportion in the subsample is nearly identical to the proportion in the full sample of mothers' reports suggests that the subsample may suffer minimally from bias. Fathers reported an average of $21,315 in annual salary; worked about thirty-eight weeks in the year on average; and worked about forty-four hours per week. These fathers reported average hourly earnings of $12.83. About a third of the fathers indicated that they had unreported income; this group earned slightly less than $2,600 off the books on average annually.

There is a large gap in work and earnings between fathers who had been incarcerated and those who were never incarcerated. Previously incarcerated fathers were only three-quarters as likely to have been working the week prior to their interviews; worked ten fewer weeks per year; worked five fewer hours per week; earned about one dollar per hour less; and earned ten thousand dollars less annually. Previously incarcerated fathers also worked and earned more in the underground economy. (The underground economy refers to market activity that is unreported either to evade taxes or because it involves criminal activities. This can be as benign as unreported tips or fees for services but may include illegal activities such as drug sales.)

Previously incarcerated fathers in our study are more disadvantaged—more likely to be black and Hispanic; to have grown up without a father; to be a high school dropout; and to have poor physical and mental health. Some of these disadvantages such as physical and mental health may be a result of incarceration. But others, such as race/ethnicity and growing up without a father, clearly precede incarceration and are likely to contribute to differences in labor-market outcomes.

Descriptive statistics indicated that fathers who had been incarcerated differed from those who had not in ways that would lead them to have lower earnings even if they had not been incarcerated. Therefore, we use logistic regression to control for the differences, using a dichotomous dependent variable indicating whether the father was working during the previous week and employing ordinary least squares (OLS) regression to analyze outcomes using the smaller father-reported sample.

Table 2.    Odds ratios for the effects of incarceration on fathers' employment in the week prior to interview

|  | Model 1 (full sample) | Model 2 (father sample) | Model 3 (father sample) |
|---|---|---|---|
| Ever incarcerated | **0.34 (10.85) | **0.53 (5.91) | **0.57 (4.98) |
| Incarceration unknown | *0.49 (1.87) | — | — |
| Never incarcerated (omitted) |  |  |  |
| Age | **1.02 (2.71) | 1.00 (0.47) | 1.01 (0.72) |
| Non-Hispanic black | **0.33 (5.68) | **0.40 (4.60) | **0.41 (4.20) |
| Hispanic | .69 (1.64) | 1.11 (.46) | 1.13 (.51) |
| Other race | **.30 (3.51) | **.34 (3.14) | **.35 (2.98) |
| Non-Hispanic white (omitted) |  |  |  |
| High school graduate | **1.67 (4.64) | **1.68 (4.31) | **1.49 (3.18) |
| Some college | **2.21 (5.53) | **2.58 (6.07) | **2.05 (4.45) |
| College graduate | *2.23 (2.40) | **4.30 (3.68) | **3.39 (3.05) |
| Less than high school (omitted) |  |  |  |
| Had drug/alcohol problem |  |  | 0.78 (1.71) |
| Depressed 2 weeks |  |  | **0.61 (3.49) |
| Poor health |  |  | **0.41 (6.61) |
| Not involved with father |  |  | 0.95 (.45) |
| Constant |  |  |  |
| Observations | 2,573 | 2,261 | 2,212 |

*Note:* Standard deviations are in parentheses.
*$p \le .05$
**$p \le .01$
***$p \le .001$

Odds ratios for the effects of incarceration on whether fathers were employed during the week prior to being interviewed are presented in table 2. Model 1 reports coefficients using the full sample of mother-reported data. As expected, there is a significant association between incarceration and employment, with fathers who had been incarcerated being 34 percent as likely to be working the previous week compared with fathers who had not been incarcerated. Using father-reported data, the association is weaker, but still highly significant, with fathers who had been incarcerated being 57 percent as likely to be working in model 3 with all controls added.

While our primary focus is the association between incarceration and employment, there are other factors that are interesting although predictable. Race and education are significant factors in our models, as are the additional control variables. In model 3, with all controls added, black fathers were 41 percent as likely to be working compared with white fathers. Fathers of other races were also significantly less likely to be working than white fathers. Also in model 3—as expected—as the father's education level increased, so did the likelihood that he would be working compared with those who had dropped out of high school.

Fathers who reported being depressed were 61 percent as likely to be working, and fathers who reported less than good health were 41 percent as likely to be working. These results were expected. Fathers who reported that they had problems with drugs and alcohol were 78 percent as likely to be working, although this was significant only at the $p < .10$ level. The results of the OLS regressions on father-reported data on earnings are presented in table 3. Fathers who were incarcerated during the year were excluded from the analyses because including such fathers would confound an incapacitation effect with a postincarceration effect on earnings. In model 2—with all control variables included—previously incarcerated fathers reported 28 percent less earning than fathers who had never been incarcerated, significant at the $p < .05$ level. Previously incarcerated fathers also worked 3.6 fewer weeks per year (highly significant at the $p < .001$ level) and worked a half hour less per week, although this result was not significant. We found that previously incarcerated fathers earned a slightly smaller (but not significant) hourly wage rate than those who were never imprisoned.

Logistic regression analysis found that previously incarcerated fathers were significantly more likely to participate in underground or off-the-books employment. Previously incarcerated fathers would be 1.5 times as likely to be involved in work in the underground economy. These fathers who had been incarcerated earned 66 percent more in the underground economy than fathers who had never been incarcerated.

The results of our analysis provide strong evidence that, even after controlling for a substantial number of demographic and behavioral differences between offenders and nonoffenders, ex-offenders work and earn substantially less in the legitimate market. Still, the possibility remains that some or most of the difference is due to unmeasured differences between offenders and nonoffenders. We use instrumental variables to address the causation issue.

The state incarceration rates are taken from the Bureau of Justice Statistics. State incarceration rates are a significant predictor of differences in individual incarceration rates, indicating they are good instrumental variables. The third column in table 3 presents second-stage IV coefficients and standard errors for earnings and labor-market variables. First, note that all IV coefficients for the legitimate labor-market variables are negative and that all, except for the hours worked, are statistically significant.

Second, the IV coefficients are quite large, especially when compared to the

**Table 3.   OLS and logistic regression results for regular earnings, weeks worked, hours worked per week, hourly wage rate, and underground employment and earnings**

|  | Model 1 | Model 2 | IV Results |
|---|---|---|---|
| REGULAR SECTOR EMPLOYMENT | | | |
| Log of annual earnings | **−0.40 (.12) | *−0.28 (.12) | *−2.73 (2.02) |
| Weeks worked | ***−4.53 (.85) | ***−3.60 (.84) | *−26.02 (2.37) |
| Hours worked per week | −1.04 (.86) | −0.56 (.87) | −12.96 (1.25) |
| Log of hourly wage rate | *−.06 (2.08) | −.04 (1.26) | **−1.13 (2.75) |
| UNDERGROUND EMPLOYMENT | | | |
| Participated† | ***1.53 (4.26) | **1.43 (3.46) | −0.54 (.76) |
| Log of underground earnings | **0.78 (4.58) | **0.66 (3.81) | −3.74 (1.67) |

*Note:* Standard deviations are in parentheses; *t* scores are listed below.
*$p \leq .05$
**$p \leq .01$
***$p \leq .001$
† The coefficients are the results of logistic regression and not OLS.

OLS coefficients. However, the range of variation in the aggregate incarceration rates underlying the IV estimates—.30 to .44—is much lower than the individual range of variation, zero to one. Indeed, when the IV coefficients are multiplied by the difference between the highest and lowest incarceration rates—.14—the implied reductions in earnings closely resemble those from the OLS coefficients in magnitude. The reductions in earnings due to incarceration are respectively 28 percent versus 42 percent. In short, the OLS and IV legitimate-earnings results are within a reasonable range of consistency. Both indicate that the effects of incarceration on earnings are quite large. The IV results for underground work and earnings were not significant.

## Incarceration and Family Formation

Limited research has been conducted on the effects of incarceration on marital or cohabiting relationships. Although a substantial body of literature examines the impact of incarceration on families, few empirical studies have been published. Few, if any, studies have examined the effects of incarceration on family formation. Although logic would suggest that incarceration negatively impacts family formation, researchers caution that the marriage prospects of criminal offenders are weak even without incarceration. They warn that criminal offenders "may be egocentric, have little self-control, and have weak social connections to stable family and economic life" (Western, Lopoo, and McLanahan 2002, 4).

In a 2004 study, the sociologist Bruce Western found that incarcerated men were only about half as likely to be married as noninstitutionalized men of the same age. Western cautioned about the difficulty of studying the links between incarceration and marriage that—unlike economic factors—have tangled correlations among marriage, economic disadvantage, criminal behavior, and incarceration. Using data from the Fragile Families Study, Western and McLanahan (2000) examined the links between incarceration and cohabitation or marriage, using logistic regression analysis to determine the probability of a couple living together one year after the birth of their child. Based on the reports of mothers, they found that if the father had been incarcerated, he was 19 percent less likely to be cohabiting and 37 percent less likely to be married than fathers who were never incarcerated. They found that black couples were half as likely to be living together as white couples and that Latinos had outcomes similar to whites.

Incarceration's impact on marriage and family formation may be linked to the evidence that incarcerated individuals' labor-market prospects are reduced and render them less desirable for potential partners (Edin 2000). Gary S. Becker (1981) first proposed a link between family formation and the labor market, suggesting that marriage and marital stability depended on couples having greater utility in marriage than as single persons. He linked the rise in divorce and decline in fertility to the increase in female labor-market participation. A 1994 study by T. Paul Schultz found that men's market wages were significantly associated with more frequent marriage and higher fertility, and that higher wage opportunities for women substantially reduced marriage and fertility.

In a 1995 study, Jessie M. Tzeng and Robert D. Mare used a probability sample of 12,686 men and women in the National Longitudinal Survey of Youth for 1979–87, the National Longitudinal Survey of Young Men, and the National Longitudinal Survey of Young Women to measure the effect of the labor-market and socioeconomic factors on marital stability. They found that couples who were better educated and had stronger attachment to the workforce enjoyed more stable marriages. They found that greater equality between husbands and wives in work experience had negative effects on marriage. They attributed the lower socioeconomic status of blacks to their high rates of marital dissolution.

Using 1970, 1980, and 1990 U.S. census data in a 2000 study, Francine D. Blau, Lawrence M. Kahn, and Jane Waldfogel found that better labor markets for women and a less favorable ratio of marriageable men reduced marriage rates for young white women (sixteen to twenty-four years old) in all education groups. They found that better male market prospects raised rates among these women. They also found similar effects among older white women (twenty-five to thirty-four years old) and stronger effects for older black women.

Christina M. Gibson-Davis, Kathryn Edin, and Sara McLanahan, using data from the Fragile Families Study and embedded qualitative interviews, found in their 2005 study that stable employment and financial responsibility were very important to young women's decision making about marriage. They found support for William Julius Wilson's theories about the decline in the marriageable pool of African American men in that women must be convinced that their potential spouse will be a good breadwinner. A few other studies supported the thesis of the sociologist William Julius Wilson that the declining economic prospects of black men were largely responsible for the worsening marriage rates among black women (see Lichter et al. 1992; Darity and Myers 1995; and Testa and Krogh 1995).

In a 1991 study, Robert D. Mare and Christopher W. Winship attributed 20 percent of the decline in marriage among young black men to declining job prospects, pointing out that marriage rates had declined among employed black males as well. However, in his 1989 study, Robert Lerman disputed Wilson's theory, noting that marriage rates among marriageable men declined almost as much as they did for less marriageable men. He found that between 1973 and 1986, the percentage of men married and living with their wives fell as much for college graduates as for less-educated groups suffering losses in earnings. In a 1995 study, Robert Wood supported Lerman's findings when he found that the dwindling pool of marriageable black men accounted for only 3 to 4 percent of the falling marriage rates of young black women during the 1970s.

Labor-market theory suggests that poor economic prospects among unmarried men would render them less likely to marry or have stable unions. However, the evidence is inconclusive. David T. Ellwood and Jonathan Crane (1990) suggest that economic models have not been successful in explaining changes in black or white families, which are the results of a "complex interaction of social, cultural, legal, and economic factors" that would be difficult to unweave.

## Family Formation in Fragile Families

Using data collected from Austin, Texas, and Oakland, California, for my dissertation, I examined the association between incarceration and whether parents in the study were married, cohabiting, or in no relationship at all. Data from the first two cities were the only available data at the time. Table 4 presents the results of cross-tabulations of the effects of incarceration on marriage and cohabitation. As expected, just 22 percent of the fathers who were incarcerated were married to their children's mothers compared to 42 percent of the never-incarcerated fathers. The difference in cohabitation rates was not significant. Of the fathers who were

**Table 4.   Marriage and cohabitation by incarceration status**

|  | Never Incarcerated | Incarcerated | Unknown |
|---|---|---|---|
| Married | .42 (.03) | ***.22 (.02)<br>7.94 | ***.13 (.03)<br>6.16 |
| Cohabiting | .45 (.03) | .47 (.04)<br>0.46 | ***.20 (.04)<br>4.80 |

*Note:* Standard deviations in parentheses; *t* scores are listed below.
***$p \leq$ .001.

**Table 5.   Multinomial logistic regression for marriage and cohabitation**

| Incarceration status<br>(omitted = never) | Model 1 | | Model 2 | |
|---|---|---|---|---|
|  | Married | Cohabiting | Married | Cohabiting |
| Incarcerated | *** .21<br>(−4.22) | *** .39<br>(−3.33) | ** .30<br>(−2.77) | * .53<br>(−1.98) |
| Incarceration unknown | *** .09<br>(−6.07) | *** .09<br>(−7.55) | * .24<br>(−2.39) | *** .21<br>(−3.71) |

*Note:* z scores are in parentheses.
*$p \leq$ .05
**$p \leq$ .01
***$p \leq$ .001

incarcerated, 47 percent were cohabiting with the mother compared to 45 percent of those never incarcerated.

A multinomial logit model was used to analyze the effects of incarceration on the probability that a mother would chose to marry, cohabit, or do neither. A multinomial logit model allows several discrete alternatives to be considered at the same time. One alternative is selected as the base, or omitted, category, and each possible choice is compared to the base alternative with a logit equation. The omitted category in this analysis is not married *and* not cohabiting. Table 5 presents the results of the multinomial regression. In model 1, all control variables for mothers (age; race; education; lived with both parents at fifteen years old; health; and substance use) were added with controls for father's age, race, and education. In model 2, additional controls were added for fathers' health, depression, substance use, and whether he lived with both biological parents at fifteen years old.

In model 2, with all controls included, fathers who had been incarcerated were 30 percent as likely to be married as fathers who had never been incarcerated and 53 percent as likely to be cohabiting with their child's mother as those who had never been incarcerated. Fathers with an unknown incarceration status were even more unlikely to be married or cohabiting as those who had never been incarcerated—perhaps an indication of a less trusting relationship as this important detail about the father remained undisclosed between the mother and father. These results are consistent with the 2000 findings of Bruce Western and Sara McLanahan, who found—using the full sample of Fragile Families data—that couples where the father had been incarcerated were significantly less likely to be living together one year after the birth of their children.

### Discussion and Implications

The evidence presented here supports the idea that incarceration negatively impacts an individual's employment and relational opportunities. However, because of our inability to control for all unobserved heterogeneity, we cannot conclude that the negative effects can be attributed to incarceration rather than to traits and characteristics among people who land behind bars. However, by controlling for many traits associated with poor labor-market outcomes—education, family background, substance abuse, and race—we present a strong case that incarceration significantly impacts one's labor-market outcomes.

We do know that far too many people with mental deficiencies are imprisoned in federal and state prisons and local jails. According to the Bureau of Justice Statistics, at midyear 2005, more than half of the inmates in prisons and jails had a mental-health problem: 705,600 in state prisons, 70,200 in federal prisons, and 479,900 in local jails (James and Glaze 2006). Female inmates had higher rates of mental problems than men, and the prevalence rates among juveniles in lockups are known to be higher than adult rates. Improved efforts to prevent and treat mental problems in the early stages of life may significantly reduce the number of people engaged with the criminal justice system.

A related issue that needs to be mentioned is the enormous price that children of incarcerated parents pay for their parents' reduced economic viability and their inability to form and maintain strong and healthy families. More than 1.7 million children in the United States have a parent incarcerated in prisons or jails, and African American children are more than 7.5 times as likely to have a parent incarcerated in state or federal prison (Glaze and Maruschak 2008). When the number of children with parents in jails is included, that number will easily exceed 2 million. More than 10 million children either have or have had a parent incarcerated (Women's Prison Association & Home, Inc. 2007).

When parents are incarcerated, the lives of their children are often disrupted by separation from fathers and mothers, severance from siblings, and displacement to different caregivers (Simmons 2000). Children with parents behind bars arc more likely to experience poverty and parental substance abuse and mental illness; they also face an increased risk for mental health problems, and higher rates of major depression and attention disorders, than the general population of youth (Dallaire 2007). Using data from the Fragile Families Study, Wildeman and Western (2010) identified a number of research studies that found strong associations between parental incarceration and negative outcomes for their children. For a more thorough discussion of this topic, see Wildeman's essay in this volume.

Children of incarcerated parents are for the most part undocumented. Children who can be identified are those who are already being served in some way by a social service agency. Children may not be identified at the time of a parent's arrest because parents withhold information about children or have no contact with them and the responsible agencies lose contact with children after services are terminated. No single government entity is responsible for identifying or recording the status of children of incarcerated parents. Few agencies or organizations keep reliable data on them, and the existing data come primarily from criminal justice or social service agencies and occasionally from academic research efforts.

Incarceration is punitive by nature, and its effects do much to harm individuals and families. Arguably, most incarcerated individuals have made personal choices that landed them in prison. But as the industry grows and becomes more profitable, pressures evolve that pull more people—particularly young black males—into our nation's jails and prisons. If the plan is to rescue and strengthen families, society must resist the urge to put more people in prison.

Families begin with children, who are future husbands, wives, mothers, and fathers. Incarceration damages family structure by removing a parent from the home and limiting the amount of time that parents spend with their children (Currence and Johnson 2003). The degree to which young people are allowed to develop human capital through education and on-the-job training without being scarred by the criminal justice system will affect their chances of living productive lives and forming stable families.

Obviously, more research is needed about incarceration's impacts on men and women in various correctional settings. States are beginning to collect more relevant data that will inform future studies. Research is needed on incarceration's impact on families and children. Children of different ages and genders vary in their reaction to parental incarceration.

With Barack Obama in the White House, the Justice Department may revisit some of the punitive policies of the "get tough on crime" approach of the conservative era. Fair access to legal services and drug treatment should be common practice. The federal government should do all it can to prevent young people from getting entangled in the criminal justice system—particularly young people born into dysfunctional environments—yet funds for juvenile delinquency prevention programs have all but disappeared during the last thirty years of conservative policies.

Federal and state governments should address the disproportional use of criminal sanctions by revisiting laws and policies that stimulate disproportionate arrests, convictions, and sentences; by treating drug use and abuse as a public health issue rather than only as criminal conduct; by providing adequate services and education for all its citizens; and by ensuring that an encounter with the criminal justice system does not become a life sentence.

Finding solutions will not be easy. Writing in the *Atlantic Monthly*, Eric Schlosser (1998) was among the first to use the phrase "prison-industrial complex" to describe the massive bureaucracy that has developed as a result of the spiraling incarceration rates. In light of their economic dependence on the status quo, corrections unions and rural communities in which prisons have replaced factories will not be easily persuaded about the need for reform. These groups exert significant lobbying influence on lawmakers as they seek to protect their economic interests.

The disproportionate minority involvement with the criminal justice system continues to wreak havoc in communities of color and arguably infringes on the civil rights of African Americans. For all of former president Bill Clinton's reputation as a friend to African Americans, he presided over the largest growth in incarceration in the nation's history. President Obama must do better. How we use prisons ranks high among the issues in need of urgent national attention.

### Note

1. Additional information on the Fragile Families Study can be obtained at http://crcw .princeton.edu.

### Bibliography

Becker, Gary. S. 1964. *Human capital: A theoretical and empirical analysis, with special reference to education.* 3rd ed. New York: National Bureau of Economic Research.

Blau, Francine D., Lawrence M. Kahn, and Jane Waldfogel. 2000. Understanding young women's marriage decisions: The role of labor and marriage market conditions. *Industrial and Labor Relations Review* 53, no. 4: 624–47.

Currence, P. L. J., and Waldo E. Johnson. 2003. *The negative implications of incarceration on black fathers.* www.rcgd.isr.umich.edu/prba/perspectives/winter2003/currence.pdf.

Dallaire, Danielle H. 2007. Incarcerated mothers and fathers: A comparison of risks for children and families. *Family Relations* 56: 440–53.

Darity, William A., Jr., and Samuel L. Myers Jr. 1995. Family structure and marginalization of black men: Policy implications. In *The decline in marriage among African Americans: Causes, consequences, and policy implications,* edited by M. Belinda Tucker and Claudia Mitchell-Kernan, 263–308. New York: Russell Sage Foundation.

Edin, Kathryn. 2000. What do low-income single mothers say about marriage? *Social Problems,* 47, no. 1: 112–33.

Ellwood, David T., and Jonathan Crane. 1990. Family change among black Americans: What do we know? *Journal of Economic Perspectives* 4, no. 4: 65–84.

Freeman, Richard B. 1991. *Crime and the employment of disadvantaged youth.* Working Paper No. 3875. National Bureau of Economic Research.

Gibson-Davis, Christina M., Kathryn Edin, and Sara McLanahan. 2005. High hopes but even higher expectations: The retreat from marriage among low-income couples. *Journal of Marriage and Family,* 67, no. 5: 1301–12.

Glaze, Lauren E., and Laura M. Maruschak. 2008. Parents in prison and their minor children. Washington, DC: Bureau of Justice Statistics.

Glaze, Lauren, E., and Erika Parks. 2012. *Correctional populations in the United States, 2011.* Washington, DC: Bureau of Justice Statistics.

Grogger, Jeffrey. 1995. The effect of arrests on the employment and earnings of young men. *Quarterly Journal of Economics* 110, no. 1: 51–71.

Hagan, John, and Ruth D. Peterson, eds. 1995. *Crime and inequality.* Stanford, CA: Stanford University Press.

James, Doris J., and Lauren E. Glaze. 2006. *Mental health problems of prison and jail inmates.* Washington, DC: Bureau of Justice Statistics.

Kling, Jeffrey R. 2006. Incarceration length, employment and earnings. *American Economic Review* 96, no. 3: 863–76.

Lerman, Robert I. 1989. Employment opportunities of young men and family formation. *American Economic Review* 79, no. 2: 62–66.

Lichter, Daniel T., George Kephart, Diane K. McLaughlin, and David J. Landry. 1992. Race and the retreat from marriage: A shortage of marriageable men? *American Sociological Review* 57, no. 6: 781–99.

Mare, Robert D., and Christopher W. Winship. 1991. Socioeconomic change and the decline of marriage for blacks and whites. In *The Urban Underclass,* edited by C. Jencks and P. E. Peterson, 175–95. Washington, D.C.: Brookings Institution.

Mincer, Jacob. 1962. On-the-job training: Costs, returns, and some implications. *Journal of Political Economy* 70: 50–79.

Nagin, Daniel, and Joel Waldfogel. 1998. The effect of conviction on income through the life cycle. *International Review of Law and Economics* 18: 25–40.

Pager, Devah. 2003. The mark of a criminal record. *American Journal of Sociology* 108: 937–75.

Sampson, Robert J., and John H. Laub. 1993. *Crime in the making: Pathways and turning points through life.* Cambridge: Harvard University Press.

Schlosser, Eric. 1998. The prison-industrial complex. *Atlantic Magazine.* www.theatlantic.com/magazine/archive/1998/12/the-prison-industrial-complex/4669/.

Schultz, T. Paul. 1994. Marital status and fertility in the United States: Welfare and labor market effects. *Journal of Human Resources* 29, no. 2: 636–69.

Simmons, Charlene Wear. 2002. Children of incarcerated parents. *California Research Bureau Note* 7, no. 2: 1–11.

Testa, Mark, and Marilyn Krogh. 1995. The effect of employment on marriage among black males in inner-city Chicago. In *The decline in marriage among African Americans: Causes, consequences, and policy implications,* edited by M. Belinda Tucker and Claudia Mitchell-Kernan, 59–95. New York: Russell Sage Foundation.

Waldfogel, Joel. 1993. The effect of criminal conviction on income and trust reposed in the workmen. *Journal of Human Resources* 29, no. 1: 62–81.

Warren, Jennifer. 2008. *One in one hundred: Behind bars in America 2008.* Washington, DC: Pew Charitable Trusts.

Western, Bruce. 2002. The impact of incarceration on wage mobility and inequality. *American Sociological Review* 67: 526–46.

———. 2004. *Incarceration, marriage, and family life.* Princeton, NJ: Russell Sage Foundation.

Western, Bruce, Leonard M. Lopoo, and Sara McLanahan. 2002. *Incarceration and the bonds among parents in fragile families.* Center for Research on Child Wellbeing Working Paper #02–22-FF. Princeton, NJ.

Western, Bruce and Sara McLanahan. 2000. *Fathers behind bars: The impact of incarceration on family formation.* Center for Research on Child Wellbeing Working Paper #00–08. Princeton, NJ.

Wildeman, Christopher, and Bruce Western. 2010. Incarceration and Fragile Families. *Future of Children* 20, no. 2: 157–77.

Women's Prison Association & Home, Inc. 2007. Partnerships between corrections and child welfare: Collaboration for change. Baltimore: Annie E. Casey Foundation.

Wood, Robert G. 1995. Marriage rates and marriageable men: A test of the Wilson hypothesis. *Journal of Human Resources* 30, no. 1: 163–93.

# Implications of Mass Imprisonment for Inequality among American Children

CHRISTOPHER WILDEMAN, ANNA R. HASKINS, AND CHRISTOPHER MULLER

In 1973, the American imprisonment rate began an ascent from which it has only recently deviated. In just over thirty-five years, the rate grew fivefold, from roughly 100 per 100,000 people to roughly 500 per 100,000 (figure 1). Although the incarceration rates of comparable nations have also grown over the same period, none approaches that of the United States. England, the nation with the second-highest incarceration rate among long-standing Western democracies, incarcerates its residents at a rate one-fifth as high as that of the United States (Western 2006: 14).

Imprisonment has long been a topic of penological and criminological inquiry, but in recent years it has gained the attention of scholars of social, political, and economic inequality as well. Studies of the relationship between imprisonment and inequality fall into two broad categories: those focusing on imprisonment as a reflection of inequality and those focusing on imprisonment as an engine of inequality. The first category of research examines racial and economic disparities in the chances of imprisonment—whether, in other words, some groups are more likely to experience imprisonment than others. The second asks whether imprisonment itself might exacerbate already existing racial or economic inequalities.

In the first strand of inequality research, two facts are glaringly clear. First, racial disparity in the risk of imprisonment is stark. African Americans have drastically higher lifetime risks of imprisonment than comparable white men at every level of educational attainment. Whereas about one in five African American men can expect to go to prison at some point in his lifetime, only about 3 percent of white men can expect the same (table 1; Western and Wildeman 2009: 231). Racial disparities in imprisonment mirror those in a host of other domains (table 2). Inequality in the incarceration rate is not new; racial disparity in imprisonment long preceded the prison boom (Muller 2012).

Second, racial inequality in contact with the penal system widens as one de-

**Figure 1**

U.S. imprisonment rates, 1925–2006

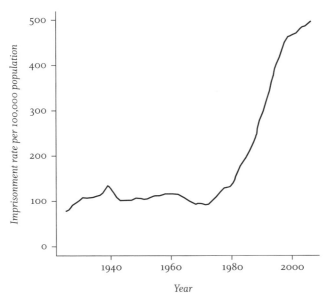

scends the hierarchy of educational attainment. This facet of inequality in an individual's chances of imprisonment is newer (Pettit 2012). By their mid-thirties, for example, African American male high school dropouts born in the late 1970s had nearly a 70 percent chance of having ever been imprisoned—a risk about five times that of comparable men born thirty years earlier. This fact leaves little doubt that widening economic inequality in American society at large finds expression in class disparities in imprisonment.

The second strand of research on imprisonment and inequality sets itself a more formidable challenge. It asks whether the experience of incarceration itself can generate inequality. Identifying the effect of imprisonment alone is especially difficult given the conclusions of the first strand of research reviewed above. If social inequalities so strongly determine the distribution of prison inmates, how can one distinguish the effects of going to prison from the effects of being the type of person likely to go to prison? Findings in this area are scanter, but offer suggestive evidence that imprisonment diminishes men's economic viability (e.g., Lewis, this volume; Western 2002; Western and Beckett 1999), increases their risk of marital dissolution (e.g., Lopoo and Western 2005), compromises their health (e.g., Johnson and Raphael 2009; Massoglia 2008a, 2008b; Schnittker and John 2007), and diminishes their political participation and civic engagement more broadly (e.g., Weaver and Lerman 2010).

Table 1.    Cumulative risk of imprisonment by age 30–34 by race and education for men born
1945–1949 to 1975–1979

| | Birth cohort | | | | | | |
|---|---|---|---|---|---|---|---|
| | 45–49 | 50–54 | 55–59 | 60–64 | 65–69 | 70–74 | 75–79 |
| WHITE MEN | | | | | | | |
| High school dropouts | 4.2 | 7.2 | 8.0 | 8.0 | 10.5 | 14.8 | 15.3 |
| High school only | 0.7 | 2.0 | 2.1 | 2.5 | 4.0 | 3.8 | 4.1 |
| All non-college | 1.8 | 2.9 | 3.2 | 3.7 | 5.1 | 5.1 | 6.3 |
| Some college | 0.7 | 0.7 | 0.6 | 0.8 | 0.7 | 0.9 | 1.2 |
| All men | 1.2 | 1.9 | 2.0 | 2.2 | 2.8 | 2.8 | 3.3 |
| BLACK MEN | | | | | | | |
| High school dropouts | 14.7 | 19.6 | 27.6 | 41.6 | 57.0 | 62.5 | 69.0 |
| High school only | 10.2 | 11.3 | 9.4 | 12.4 | 16.8 | 20.3 | 18.0 |
| All non-college | 12.1 | 14.1 | 14.7 | 19.9 | 26.7 | 30.9 | 35.7 |
| Some college | 4.9 | 3.5 | 4.3 | 5.5 | 6.8 | 8.5 | 7.6 |
| All men | 9.0 | 10.6 | 11.5 | 15.2 | 20.3 | 22.8 | 20.7 |

*Source:* Western and Wildeman (2009:231).

Table 2.    Percentage of non-Hispanic black and white men, born
1965–1969, surviving to 1999, by life events experienced

| Life event | White men (%) | Black men (%) |
|---|---|---|
| ALL MEN | | |
| Prison incarceration | 3.2 | 22.4 |
| Bachelor's degree | 31.6 | 12.5 |
| Military service | 14.0 | 17.4 |
| Marriage | 72.5 | 59.3 |
| NONCOLLEGE MEN | | |
| Prison incarceration | 6.0 | 31.9 |
| High school diploma/GED | 73.5 | 64.4 |
| Military service | 13.0 | 13.7 |
| Marriage | 72.8 | 55.9 |

*Source:* Pettit and Western (2004:164).

There is, however, a third strand of research at the nexus of inequality and imprisonment that has yet to receive much attention. It considers the intergenerational durability of inequality stemming from mass imprisonment. As striking as
the imprisonment rates discussed at the beginning of the chapter are, they mask
the fact that point-in-time measures of imprisonment take a snapshot of a prison

population that is reproduced day to day and year to year. With a median prison sentence of thirty-six months (Pastore and Maguire 2003: 451), many more individuals in the population have cycled in and out of prisons than are captured by the imprisonment rate. It follows that imprisonment has affected the lives of the children of many more individuals than are currently in prison.

Research on the reproduction of inequality through imprisonment examines outcomes similar to those studied in the research on imprisonment and inequality discussed above. Studies consider either inequality in a child's risk of having a parent go to prison, or the effects of parental imprisonment itself on childhood inequality and well-being. These are the strands of research we discuss in this chapter.

We proceed in two steps. First, we present estimates of racial and educational disparities in the risk of parental imprisonment for two birth cohorts. These estimates (first reported in Wildeman 2009) provide the first comprehensive picture of inequality in children's experience of parental imprisonment. Second, we discuss how imprisonment might disadvantage children and review research on the consequences of parental imprisonment for children's educational achievement, behavioral problems, and risk of experiencing severe forms of deprivation. We close by considering directions for future research on the question of whether mass imprisonment generates durable racial and economic inequality. Whereas other scholars consider the historical causes and contemporary consequences of mass imprisonment, we explore the intergenerational consequences of mass imprisonment for American inequality.

### Inequality in the Risk of Parental Imprisonment

For mass imprisonment to exacerbate racial and economic inequality among American children, it must both be increasingly unequally distributed by race and class and have demonstrable negative effects on children. In this section we consider the distribution of parental imprisonment, discussing recently constructed estimates of the risk of parental imprisonment for black and white children in two birth cohorts, by parental education.

Table 3 presents estimates of the risk of paternal, maternal, and parental imprisonment by age fourteen for black and white children born in 1978 and 1990. The risk of paternal imprisonment for white children was small regardless of their birth cohort. Only about 3.6 percent of white children born in 1990 experienced paternal imprisonment. Risks of maternal imprisonment were even smaller. White children born in 1990 had less than a 1 in 100 chance of experiencing maternal imprisonment.

**Table 3.** Cumulative risk of paternal, maternal, and parental imprisonment by exact age for children born in 1978 and 1990, by child's age and race

| Age (years) | Paternal (%) | Maternal (%) | Parental (%) |
|---|---|---|---|
| WHITE CHILDREN | | | |
| Born 1978 | | | |
| Age 2 | 0.4 | 0.0 | 0.4–0.4 |
| Age 6 | 0.9 | 0.1 | 0.9–1.0 |
| Age 10 | 1.5 | 0.1 | 1.5–1.6 |
| Age 14 | 2.2 | 0.2 | 2.2–2.4 |
| Born 1990 | | | |
| Age 2 | 0.7 | 0.1 | 0.7–0.8 |
| Age 6 | 1.5 | 0.2 | 1.5–1.7 |
| Age 10 | 2.8 | 0.4 | 2.8–3.2 |
| Age 14 | 3.6 | 0.6 | 3.6–4.2 |
| BLACK CHILDREN | | | |
| Born 1978 | | | |
| Age 2 | 2.6 | 0.2 | 2.6–2.8 |
| Age 6 | 6.8 | 0.5 | 6.8–7.3 |
| Age 10 | 9.9 | 0.8 | 9.9–10.7 |
| Age 14 | 13.8 | 1.4 | 13.8–15.2 |
| Born 1990 | | | |
| Age 2 | 6.3 | 0.4 | 6.3–6.7 |
| Age 6 | 14.9 | 1.4 | 14.9–16.3 |
| Age 10 | 20.2 | 2.5 | 20.2–22.7 |
| Age 14 | 25.1 | 3.3 | 25.1–28.4 |

Source: Wildeman (2009:271). For sources and methods, see Wildeman (2009).
Note: The high estimate for the cumulative risk of parental imprisonment assumes that no children have both parents imprisoned; the low estimate assumes that all children experiencing parental imprisonment have both parents imprisoned.

The risks of paternal, maternal, and parental imprisonment were much larger for African American children. African American children born as early as 1978 — when the American imprisonment rate had just begun to increase—had a 13.8 percent chance of experiencing paternal imprisonment. By 1990 that risk had grown to 25.1 percent. The risk of maternal imprisonment for black children is also notable—especially in comparison to the risk of paternal imprisonment for white children. Black children have nearly as high a risk of experiencing maternal imprisonment (3.3 percent) as white children have of experiencing paternal imprisonment (3.6 percent). This fact is especially striking given that men make up the vast majority of America's prisoners. For black children born in 1990, the risk of having a parent imprisoned at some point by age fourteen (28 percent) ex-

Table 4.    Cumulative risk of paternal and maternal imprisonment by exact age for children born in 1978 and 1990 by child's age, child's race, and parental education

| | White children | | | | Black children | | | |
|---|---|---|---|---|---|---|---|---|
| | Paternal (%) | | Maternal (%) | | Paternal (%) | | Maternal (%) | |
| Age (years) | 1978 | 1990 | 1978 | 1990 | 1978 | 1990 | 1978 | 1990 |
| ALL NONCOLLEGE | | | | | | | | |
| Age 2 | 0.6 | 1.0 | 0.0 | 0.1 | 3.1 | 7.8 | 0.2 | 0.5 |
| Age 6 | 1.4 | 2.7 | 0.1 | 0.3 | 7.9 | 18.5 | 0.5 | 1.6 |
| Age 10 | 2.1 | 4.3 | 0.1 | 0.5 | 11.4 | 24.6 | 0.9 | 2.8 |
| Age 14 | 2.9 | 5.6 | 0.2 | 0.8 | 15.6 | 30.2 | 1.5 | 3.6 |
| HIGH SCHOOL DROPOUT | | | | | | | | |
| Age 2 | 0.9 | 1.4 | 0.0 | 0.1 | 5.2 | 14.3 | 0.2 | 0.5 |
| Age 6 | 2.2 | 3.7 | 0.1 | 0.4 | 13.2 | 33.3 | 0.7 | 2.0 |
| Age 10 | 3.3 | 5.8 | 0.2 | 0.7 | 17.7 | 42.7 | 1.2 | 3.8 |
| Age 14 | 4.1 | 7.2 | 0.2 | 1.0 | 22.0 | 50.5 | 1.9 | 5.0 |
| HIGH SCHOOL ONLY | | | | | | | | |
| Age 2 | 0.4 | 0.9 | 0.0 | 0.1 | 1.2 | 4.6 | 0.1 | 0.4 |
| Age 6 | 0.9 | 2.3 | 0.1 | 0.3 | 3.7 | 11.3 | 0.3 | 1.3 |
| Age 10 | 1.3 | 3.6 | 0.1 | 0.4 | 6.4 | 15.8 | 0.5 | 2.0 |
| Age 14 | 2.0 | 4.8 | 0.2 | 0.7 | 10.2 | 20.4 | 0.9 | 2.6 |
| SOME COLLEGE | | | | | | | | |
| Age 2 | 0.1 | 0.2 | 0.0 | 0.0 | 0.8 | 2.4 | 0.1 | 0.3 |
| Age 6 | 0.4 | 0.7 | 0.1 | 0.1 | 2.2 | 6.9 | 0.3 | 1.1 |
| Age 10 | 0.8 | 1.2 | 0.1 | 0.2 | 3.6 | 10.6 | 0.5 | 1.9 |
| Age 14 | 1.4 | 1.7 | 0.2 | 0.3 | 7.1 | 13.4 | 1.2 | 2.6 |

*Source:* Wildeman (2009:273). For sources and methods, see Wildeman (2009).

ceeds the probability of having a college-educated father (27 percent). The figures reported in table 3 demonstrate that imprisonment is sufficiently differentially distributed by race to affect racial inequality in child well-being.

Table 4 presents estimates of the risk of paternal and maternal imprisonment for white and black children by parental education and birth cohort. The estimates suggest that economic inequality in the risk of parental incarceration among whites has grown. Whereas the risk of paternal imprisonment for white children of high school dropouts increased from 4.1 to 7.2 percent over the period, the risk of paternal and maternal imprisonment for white children of college-educated parents scarcely grew at all.

Economic inequality in the risk of parental imprisonment was also large for

African American children. But despite absolute increases in economic inequality in the risk of parental imprisonment among African American children, unlike white children, they did not experience relative increases. Among black children born in 1978 to fathers who did not complete high school, fully 22.0 percent could expect to experience paternal imprisonment. Even at the beginning of the prison boom, the risk of paternal imprisonment for African American children of low-education parents was relatively large.

Despite long-standing economic inequality in the risk of parental imprisonment among African American children, table 4 indicates that even black children of highly educated fathers were not insulated from the experience of paternal imprisonment. Although the 20.4 percent and 13.4 percent respective risks of paternal imprisonment for black children of high school graduate and college-educated fathers may appear small relative to the alarming 50.5 percent risk for black children of high school dropouts, these risks are roughly similar to those of the children of white high school dropouts.

Tables 3 and 4, in short, report stark racial and economic disparities in the risk of paternal, maternal, and parental imprisonment. Economic disparities in the risk of parental imprisonment grew for white but not black children. Parental imprisonment was commonly experienced even by black children born to college graduates. Among black children born to high school dropouts in 1990, parental imprisonment was modal. These estimates suggest that the risk of parental imprisonment for black children, and especially black children of high school dropouts, is sufficiently large to have important implications for population-level racial and economic inequality among children.

## Consequences of Parental Imprisonment for Children

If the negative consequences of imprisonment for adults are only beginning to be documented, research on the effects of parental imprisonment on children has barely begun. Sharp racial and economic disparities in imprisonment make it particularly important to ask whether the intergenerational effects of mass incarceration might contribute to durable patterns of social inequality. Accordingly, we now turn to the consequences of parental imprisonment for inequality in childhood wellbeing.

Previous studies point to three possible ways parental incarceration might affect children: by (1) conferring stigma, (2) inducing trauma, and (3) causing strain. The stigma associated with having a family member incarcerated can create a sense of social isolation and shame that may lead families to recoil from valuable social interactions (Foster and Hagan 2007; Goffman 1963; Murray and

Farrington 2008a). As Goffman (1963) demonstrated, stigma travels, attaching itself not only to individuals, but also to their friends and kin. The anticipation of judgment may impede the social integration of already marginal families and children, potentially worsening their health and diminishing their sources of communal, emotional, and economic support (Braman 2004; Schnittker and John 2007). Studies focused on trauma emphasize children's social and behavioral problems resulting from both parental separation and reunification following release (Braman 2004; Comfort 2007). Children express trauma in a variety of ways, from anxiety, confusion, and loneliness to anger, depression, sleep problems, and even developmental regression (Poehlmann 2005). Studies emphasizing strain, finally, consider the social, psychological, and economic challenges facing the children of the incarcerated due to decreased financial support or family disruption and dissolution (Geller, Garfinkel, Cooper, and Mincy 2009; Geller, Garfinkel, and Western 2011; Hagan and Dinovitzer 1999; McLanahan and Sandefur 1994; Western and Lopoo 2006). Despite the prominence of these mechanisms in the studies cited above, very few of them have been directly tested. To date, only the trauma thesis has found empirical support (Wildeman 2010).

Although most studies suggest that children suffer from parental imprisonment, some children may derive a short-term benefit from the removal—whether through imprisonment or by other means—of an addicted or abusive parent from the home (Wildeman 2010, 2012). Criminological theories of selection and self-control (Gottfredson and Hirschi 1990; Wilson and Hernstein 1985), meanwhile, hold that biosocial selection and genetic predisposition largely explain away correlations between parental incarceration and negative child outcomes. Research on the durable effects of mass imprisonment, therefore, must answer the challenges of those who expect heterogeneity in the effects of parental imprisonment on children and those arguing that the association between imprisonment and childhood inequality is driven by omitted variables.

Incarceration does not occur at random in the population. As the discussion above makes clear, the incarcerated are drawn disproportionally from the population of African Americans and the poorly educated (Uggen, Wakefield, and Western 2005; Western and Beckett 1999). Since the children of incarcerated parents are more likely to suffer from forms of socioeconomic disadvantage prior, or in addition to their parent's incarceration, researchers must contend with the possibility that these preexisting differences account for many of the disadvantages the children of incarcerated parents face. Yet most studies exploring the effects of parental imprisonment have been either qualitative or correlational.[1] While these studies provide the kind of useful descriptive statistics and rich portrait of the lives of those touched by incarceration necessary to generate hypotheses about the impact of incarceration on children, they cannot address issues of selection and omitted variable bias and therefore provide little empirical evidence about the causal effects of parental imprisonment.

Research to date considers three broad sets of outcomes for children: (1) educational achievement or attainment; (2) behavioral problems or mental health; and (3) the risk of experiencing severe forms of deprivation. At such an early stage of research, investigations into racial and economic differences in the effects of parental incarceration on children are almost entirely absent from the literature.[2] Still, given what we know about the racial and economic distribution of incarceration, studies attempting to show the average effects of paternal incarceration across all racial groups and classes shed light on some potential implications of mass imprisonment for racial and economic inequality.

A handful of studies explore the effects of parental incarceration on child educational outcomes. Since educational attainment is a major engine of stratification in the United States, this research has clear implications for our understanding of racial and class inequality. Using data from the National Longitudinal Study of Adolescent Health, Foster and Hagan (2007) examine the effects of paternal imprisonment on the social exclusion of children during their transition to adulthood. They hypothesize that a father's incarceration reduces his child's educational attainment and ultimately results in the child's adult social exclusion. In a subsequent analysis, Foster and Hagan (2009) attempt more carefully to correct their estimates for selection bias by using propensity score matching.[3] The authors conclude that paternal incarceration has negative effects on children's cumulative GPA as well as their educational attainment, findings that support their claim that paternal incarceration decreases the educational attainment of children in emerging adulthood.

In a similar study, Haskins (2009) uses the Fragile Families and Child Well-being dataset and propensity score matching to estimate the effect of paternal incarceration on school readiness. Studying the effect of having a father incarcerated between the ages of one and five, she finds that children who experience paternal incarceration have significantly lower school readiness than their matched controls. Provided that school readiness measures a developmental outcome necessary for successful entry into formal schooling, and that early developmental and cognitive abilities are central to children's later academic success, differences in school readiness may affect children's future academic and labor market trajectories.

Finally, in a set of studies looking at elementary-aged children in the Chicago public schools, Cho (2009a, 2009b) uses a variety of state administrative datasets from Illinois to examine the impact of maternal incarceration on two educational outcomes: a child's educational achievement and the probability of being held back in school. Given that grade retention implies a low level of, or decline in, school performance, Cho (2009a) proposes that if a child's likelihood of grade retention increases following the incarceration of his or her mother, maternal incarceration may lead to decreased school performance. She finds instead that having an incarcerated mother slightly reduces the possibility of retention. In a second study examining children's educational achievement and addressing selection and overestimation concerns by using a comparison group composed of children whose mothers spent three or fewer days in jail (as opposed to prison), Cho (2009b) finds that maternal imprisonment is not associated with a decline in academic achievement as measured by standardized math or reading test scores. Together, Cho's findings suggest that maternal incarceration has either no effect or even a potentially positive one for children. The conflicting results of the studies discussed here make it premature to conclude that parental imprisonment negatively affects childhood educational outcomes. Instead, they provide weak support for the hypothesis that there is heterogeneity in the effect of imprisonment on child outcomes.

Children's educational achievement, advancement, and subsequent attainment often depend on successful sociobehavioral development. The majority of studies on the behavioral effects of parental incarceration focus on child or adolescent outcomes such as aggression, delinquency, or depression. Scholarly emphasis on these areas stems mainly from criminological interest in the intergenerational transition of criminality. Using longitudinal data from the United Kingdom and a series of comparison groups, Murray and Farrington (2005) estimate the effect of parental imprisonment on boys' odds of exhibiting a variety of externalizing behaviors over their life course.[4] The authors conclude that compared to boys experiencing other forms of parental separation or no parental separation at all, boys who experience paternal incarceration score worse on measured antisocial and delinquency outcomes. It is unclear whether these results generalize to the children of the American prison boom.

Wildeman (2010), using Fragile Families data, and Wakefield and Wildeman (2011), using data from Chicago alongside multiple comparison groups, explore the associations between parental incarceration and children's physically aggressive behaviors and mental health, respectively. These studies draw upon data that better represent children affected by mass imprisonment in the United States. Wildeman (2010) finds that paternal incarceration increases physical aggression in young boys, but not in girls. Wakefield and Wildeman (2011), employing an expansive measure of behavioral problems, find that parental incarceration negatively affects children's mental health and behavior. In sum, the literature addressing the relationship between parental incarceration and children's behavioral outcomes points to consistent negative associations.

The final body of research on the consequences of parental imprisonment proposes that having an incarcerated parent increases children's risk of experiencing severe forms of disadvantage, such as homelessness or entrance into the foster care system. Homelessness is especially likely for children exiting the foster care system or living with a parent who has recently returned from prison (Bernstein 2005). Foster and Hagan (2007) find the paternal incarceration-homelessness tie to be especially strong among adolescent daughters due to their increased exposure to neglect or abuse in the absence of a birth father.

Other research indicates that maternal incarceration increases children's risk of foster care placement. In an investigation of what caused foster care caseloads to double between 1985 and 2000, Swann and Sylvester (2006) find that increases in female incarceration were more important than either the crack cocaine or AIDS epidemics—even more important than increases in paternal incarceration. Childhood risks of permanent parental separation due to maternal imprisonment are especially likely in the wake of the Adoption and Safe Families Act of 1997, which speeds the termination of parental rights for children who have been in foster care for fifteen of the last twenty-two months (Travis 2002).

Finally, Wildeman (2012) considers the effects of parental imprisonment on infant mortality. Using state-level data from 1990–2003 and individual-level data from 1990–2003, he finds that state-level infant mortality rates are positively associated with state-level incarceration rates. The recent incarceration of a parent, moreover, increases an infant's risk of early mortality. Providing evidence that the American infant mortality rate is higher than that of comparably developed democracies such as the United Kingdom, Germany, France, and Canada, Wildeman (2012) argues that the prison boom may be partially responsible for the United States' singularly high infant mortality rate.

In the aggregate, the evidence on the effects of parental imprisonment on children is suggestive but inconclusive. Most of the literature points to consistent negative associations. Some studies argue that parental incarceration not only exacerbates inequality during childhood, but potentially extends disadvantages into adulthood. Still, the identification strategies of all of the studies examined here could be called into question. Before making strong conclusions about the effects of parental imprisonment on children, we need better evidence, more studies, and especially studies able to make stronger causal claims.

The evidentiary basis of this program of research would be especially enhanced by studies of the race- and class-specific effects of parental incarceration. If the effects of parental incarceration are the same regardless of race and class, then mass imprisonment should have large effects on inequality because of the unequal distribution of the risk of parental incarceration. If the effects are larger for white children and children of more educated parents, then the implications of mass imprisonment would be less severe because fewer whites and highly educated individuals compared to blacks and individuals with lower levels of educational attainment experience incarceration. But if the effects are larger for black children and children of low-education parents, then the consequences of mass imprisonment for American inequality could be potentially more detrimental than the already disparate incarceration rate suggests.

Finally, although the results presented in this section suggest that parental incarceration probably disadvantages children, in some cases it may temporarily improve (or at least not harm) child well-being. Scholars have long pointed to the detrimental effects of exposure to violence or abuse on child well-being (see Murray and Farrington 2008a for a discussion). To the degree that incarcerated parents were violent or abusive toward their children before being confined, in some cases parental removal, whether through imprisonment or another means, might provide these children temporary respite. Research considering this possibility is still in its infancy, but two studies indicate that whether a father is incarcerated for a violent offense or was abusive toward a family member alters the relationship between paternal incarceration and child well-being (Wildeman 2010, 2012). This finding is especially noteworthy in light of Jonathan Simon's (this volume) observation that absent changes in the sentences meted out for violent offenders, the American imprisonment rate will not decline dramatically. Above all, it pushes scholars and advocates to consider separately the many facets of a prison sentence. The effects of temporarily removing an individual from a community may differ considerably from the effects of subjecting him or her to the regular surveillance, isolation, and coercion that characterize the prison experience.

THIS ESSAY ASKS whether mass imprisonment might generate durable inequality by restricting the life chances of the children of the incarcerated. Noting that to do so, mass imprisonment would need to be increasingly unequally distributed by race and class, and to affect children negatively, we considered, first, inequalities in a child's risk of having a parent go to prison and, second, how parental imprisonment might affect childhood well-being.

The results of the first inquiry are clear and striking. The risk of parental imprisonment is so large for African American children—especially African American children of high school dropouts—that mass imprisonment could have important population-level implications for inequality in child well-being. Racial disparity in parental imprisonment, moreover, is severe. While 1 in 25 white children born in 1990 are at risk of experiencing parental imprisonment, the rate for black children in the same cohort is 1 in 4.

The results of the second inquiry are suggestive, but require additional research. Studies of the effects of parental imprisonment on behavioral problems and mental health, as well as the risk of experiencing severe forms of deprivation, suggest that parental imprisonment may compromise child well-being. To be able to make stronger causal claims, however, we need more and better-identified studies. Recent evidence of heterogeneity in the effect of imprisonment should encourage researchers to compare the consequences for children of incarceration versus other types of parental removal.

## Notes

1. See Hagan and Dinovitzer (1999) or Murray and Farrington (2008a) for comprehensive reviews.

2. But see Roettger and Swisher (2011) for an early exploration of this question.

3. While propensity score matching on observable characteristics most likely reduces bias in their estimates, it cannot solve any potential omitted variable problems (Imai, King, and Stuart 2008).

4. See Murray and Farrington (2008b) for estimates of the effect of imprisonment on internalizing behaviors.

## References

Bernstein, Nell. 2005. *All Alone in the World: Children of the Incarcerated.* New York: New Press.

Braman, Donald. 2004. *Doing Time on the Outside: Incarceration and Family Life in Urban America.* Ann Arbor: University of Michigan Press.

Cho, Rosa. 2009a. "Impact of Maternal Imprisonment on Children's Probability of Grade Retention." *Journal of Urban Economics* 65:11–23.

———. 2009b. "The Impact of Maternal Imprisonment on Children's Educational Achievement: Results from Children in Chicago Public Schools." *Journal of Human Resources* 44:772–97.

Comfort, Megan. 2007. "Punishment beyond the Legal Offender." *Annual Review of Law and Social Science* 3:271–96.

Foster, Holly, and John Hagan. 2007. "Incarceration and Intergenerational Social Exclusion." *Social Problems* 54:399–433.

———. 2009. "The Mass Incarceration of Parents in America: Issues of Race/Ethnicity, Collateral Damage to Children, and Prisoner Reentry." *Annals of the American Academy of Political and Social Science* 623:179–94.

Geller, Amanda, Irwin Garfinkel, Carey Cooper, and Ronald Mincy. 2009. "Parental

Incarceration and Child Wellbeing: Implications for Urban Families." *Social Science Quarterly* 90:1186–202.

Geller, Amanda, Irwin Garfinkel, and Bruce Western. 2011. "Parental Incarceration and Support for Children in Fragile Families." *Demography* 48:25–47.

Goffman, Erving. 1963. *Stigma: Notes on the Management of Spoiled Identity.* Englewood Cliffs, N.J.: Prentice-Hall.

Gottfredson, Michael, and Travis Hirschi. 1990. *A General Theory of Crime.* Stanford, Calif.: Stanford University Press.

Hagan, John, and Ronit Dinovitzer. 1999. "Collateral Consequences of Imprisonment for Children, Communities, and Prisoners." *Crime and Justice* 26:121–62.

Haskins, Anna R. 2009. "The Effects of Paternal Incarceration on Child School Readiness." Presented at the Annual Meeting for the Population Association of America, April 30–May 2, in Detroit, Michigan.

Imai, Kosuke, Gary King, and Elizabeth A. Stuart. 2008. "Misunderstandings between Experimentalists and Observationalists about Causal Inference." *Journal of the Royal Statistical Society* 171:481–502.

Johnson, Rucker C., and Steven Raphael. 2009. "The Effects of Male Incarceration Dynamics on Acquired Immune Deficiency Syndrome Infection Rates among African American Women and Men." *Journal of Law & Economics* 52:251–93.

Lopoo, Leonard, and Bruce Western. 2005. "Incarceration and the Formation and Stability of Martial Unions." *Journal of Marriage and the Family* 67:721–34.

Massoglia, Michael. 2008a. "Incarceration as Exposure: The Prison, Infectious Disease, and Other Stress-Related Illnesses." *Journal of Health and Social Behavior* 49:56–71.

———. 2008b. "Incarceration, Health, and Racial Disparities in Health." *Law & Society Review* 42:275–306.

McLanahan, Sara, and Gary Sandefur. 1994. *Growing Up with a Single Parent: What Hurts, What Helps?* Cambridge: Harvard University Press.

Muller, Christopher. 2012. "Northward Migration and the Rise of Racial Disparity in American Incarceration, 1880—1950." *American Journal of Sociology* 118:281—326.

Murray, Joseph, and David Farrington. 2005. "Parental Imprisonment: Effects on Boys' Antisocial Behavior and Delinquency through the Life-Course." *Journal of Child Psychology and Psychiatry* 46:1269–78.

———. 2008a. "Effects of Parental Imprisonment on Children." *Crime and Justice* 37: 133–206.

———. 2008b. "Parental Imprisonment: Long-lasting Effects on Boys' Internalizing Problems through the Life Course." *Development and Psychopathology* 20:273–90.

Pastore, Ann L., and Kathleen Maguire, eds. 2003. *Sourcebook of Criminal Justice Statistics.* www.albany.edu/sourcebook.

Pettit, Becky. 2012. *Invisible Men: Mass Incarceration and the Myth of Black Progress.* New York: Russell Sage Foundation.

Pettit, Becky, and Bruce Western. 2004. "Mass Imprisonment and the Life Course: Race and Class Inequality in U.S. Incarceration." *American Sociological Review* 69:151–69.

Poehlmann, Julie. 2005. "Representations of Attachment Relationships in Children of Incarcerated Mothers." *Child Development* 76:679–96.

Roettger, Michael E., and Raymond R. Swisher. 2009. "Associations of Fathers' History of

Incarceration with Sons' Delinquency and Arrest among Black, White, and Hispanic Males in the United States." *Criminology* 49:1009–47.

Schnittker, Jason, and Andrea John. 2007. "Enduring Stigma: The Long-term Effects of Incarceration on Health." *Journal of Health and Social Behavior* 48:115–30.

Swann, Christopher, and Michelle Sheran Sylvester. 2006. "The Foster Care Crisis: What Caused Caseloads to Grow?" *Demography* 43:309–35.

Travis, Jeremy. 2002. Invisible Punishment: An Instrument of Social Exclusion. In *Invisible Punishment: The Collateral Consequences of Mass Imprisonment,* edited by Marc Mauer and Meda Chesney-Lind, 15–36. New York: New Press.

Uggen, Christopher, Sara Wakefield, and Bruce Western. 2005. "Work and Family Perspectives on Reentry." In *Prisoner Reentry and Crime in America,* edited by Jeremy Travis and Christy Visher, 209–43. Cambridge: Cambridge University Press.

Wakefield, Sara, and Christopher Wildeman. 2011. "Mass Imprisonment and Racial Disparities in Childhood Behavioral Problems." *Criminology and Public Policy* 10:793–817.

Weaver, Vesla M., and Amy E. Lerman. 2010. "Political Consequences of the Carceral State." *American Political Science Review* 104:817–33.

Western, Bruce. 2002. "The Impact of Incarceration on Wage Mobility and Inequality." *American Sociological Review* 67:526–46.

———. 2006. *Punishment and Inequality in America.* New York: Russell Sage Foundation.

Western, Bruce, and Katherine Beckett. 1999. "How Unregulated Is the US Labor Market? The Penal System as a Labor Market Institution." *American Journal of Sociology* 104:1030–60.

Western, Bruce, and Leonard Lopoo. 2006. "Incarceration, Marriage and Family Life." In *Punishment and Inequality in America,* by Western, 131–67. New York: Russell Sage Foundation.

Western, Bruce, and Christopher Wildeman. 2009. "The Black Family and Mass Incarceration." *Annals of the American Academy of Political and Social Science* 621:221–42.

Wildeman, Christopher. 2009. "Parental Imprisonment, the Prison Boom, and the Concentration of Childhood Disadvantage." *Demography* 46:265–80.

———. 2010. "Paternal Incarceration and Children's Physically Aggressive Behaviors: Evidence from the Fragile Families and Child Wellbeing Study." *Social Forces* 89:285–10.

———. 2012. "Imprisonment and Infant Mortality." *Social Problems* 59:228–57.

Wilson, James Q., and Richard Hernstein. 1985. *Crime and Human Nature.* New York: Simon and Schuster.

# The "Hard Back" of Mass Incarceration

*Fear, Structural Racism, and the Overpunishment of Violent Crime*

Jonathan Simon

ecent efforts to limit mass incarceration have focused on moving persons convicted of drug or property crimes into drug treatment through diversion or enhanced probation programs as an alternative to imprisonment. These measures have much merit, and the political risks of pursuing them seem minimal. The public does not perceive drug users and drug addicts who commit property crimes as inherently dangerous; and the policy case for improving future outcomes at less cost through treatment has achieved compelling force in our political culture at the present juncture.[1] Moreover, many blame the "War on Drugs" for targeting minorities and reinforcing structural barriers to racial equality in the United States by damaging the human capital of the incarcerated and depriving minority communities of the net gains to social capital provided by many who use illegal drugs or are in the illegal markets associated with the buying and selling of them.

In this essay, I explore an important limit of this strategy of focusing on what we might think of metaphorically[2] as the "soft underbelly" of mass imprisonment: those imprisoned for drug or property crimes. To extend the metaphor, this strategy leaves intact the "hard back" of mass imprisonment: those imprisoned for crimes of violence. The public's fear of violence, inflamed since the 1960s and 1970s (and renewed episodically since), has driven prison sentences for violent crime to extraordinary lengths compared with other societies and with our past. These longer sentences, especially "life" sentences, constitute an unexamined and important source of mass imprisonment. The overincarceration for violent crime highlights different dimensions of America's racist past than does the "War on Drugs," and it plays an equally important role in reinforcing structural racial inequality. In other words, despite the political attractiveness of focusing on the perpetrators of drug-related offenses and nonviolent crime—the "soft underbelly"—I want to argue that the underbelly and the hard back cannot be neatly separated as factors in the production of mass incarceration. The fear of violent crime operates as a constant pressure to expand incarceration for more minor offenses such as drug-related and nonviolent crime.

Moreover, even if we could limit prison sentences to violent crime, we would continue to have a prison population many times our historic norms, and just as highly racialized.[3] This essay makes the case for a new strategy focused on weaning the public from overly harsh sentences for violent crime, one that simultaneously softens the "hard" back and shrinks the "soft" underbelly of mass incarceration.

## Structural Racism and the Emerging Critique of Mass Incarceration

The heavy racial disproportionality of our prison population has come to seem an increasing problem for the nation, one encompassing much more than civil rights. Indeed, this nation's record of mass incarceration has become an embarrassment in light of the world's interest in our penal practices generally. For much of American history, the routine racism of American society was reproduced in the penal system. For example, the residential segregation of African Americans and their relegation to the least desirable positions in the labor market were reproduced in most American prisons until at least the 1960s, when African American prisoners, like their counterparts in the community, began to resist such practices. Today, perhaps for the first time in our history, our penal system is clearly a good deal more racist than the society it purports to represent. Thus in California, decades after housing discrimination was made illegal under federal law, the state was found to be routinely segregating cell assignments by race.[4] Further, certain recent events that recall the overt racism of the pre–civil rights era society have emerged from the racial imperatives of the penal system. For example, the 1998 murder of a forty-nine-year-old African American man, James Byrd, by three younger white men near the town of Jasper, Texas, had all the features of the sort of racist lynching once common in the American South. Byrd was chained alive to a pickup truck by the three white men and dragged behind the truck. He died when his head and right arm were severed after hitting a culvert. Byrd's body was later dumped outside an African American cemetery. Public reaction to the grotesque and unprovoked killing was justifiably significant, and helped prompt both Texas and the federal government to adopt new "hate crime" legislation. Far less discussed was the fact that the two white men most involved in Byrd's killing had served time in Texas prisons, where they had joined a white racist prison gang for protection.[5] In short, Byrd's murder had less to do with the racism of Jasper, Texas, and more to do with the racial climate in Texas prisons.

Likewise, research on employment discrimination suggests that a criminal record reduces the employment prospects of a person just as much as does being African American (Pager 2007).[6]

Much of the racial critique of mass incarceration has focused on the "War on Drugs." Perhaps no penal law has more infamously symbolized the discriminatory logic of mass incarceration than the 1986 law that made possession of more than five grams of crack cocaine subject to a mandatory minimum sentence of five years of imprisonment,[7] the same sentence applicable to possession of more than 500 grams of powder cocaine. Research suggests that the selection of those intoxicating substances proscribed as illegal drugs is primarily linked to racist narratives regarding drug use associated with specific minorities within the United States: opium and the Chinese, marijuana and Mexicans, cocaine and African Americans (Musto 1973; Beckett et al. 2005; Beckett, Nyrop, and Pfingst 2006).[8]

This racial critique of the drug war has found common cause with renewed interest in clinical and treatment solutions to drug abuse, as well as harm reduction strategies such as needle exchange. For a growing portion of the public, treatment appears to be a more humane and effective approach than incarceration. In 2000, for example, California voters passed Proposition 36, the Substance Abuse and Crime Prevention Act, which permits persons convicted for a first or second time on simple drug possession charges to receive treatment instead of incarceration. There is also growing support for a regulatory framework that would allow adults to legally purchase marijuana while maintaining laws against providing the drug to underage users.[9]

This treatment-focused movement has been largely aided by the fact that the public does not greatly fear drug crime itself, but tends to support drug prohibition policies. Their support is based on the assumption that drugs are associated either with violence supposedly inherent in the drug trade or the violent actions of drug-addicted users. Support for treatment as an alternative to incarceration reflects the common view that drug users are not themselves a serious danger to public safety. Much of the same logic applies to recent efforts to reduce the use of incarceration for parole violators, young offenders, and women. These groups, who form the soft underbelly of incarceration, are most likely to benefit from well-designed public education and reform campaigns.

Reforms that tend to favor treatment can certainly help reduce incarceration rates, but alone they will neither reverse the historic growth of incarceration since the 1970s nor arrest its racial disproportionality. Most importantly, these reforms have proven to be ineffectual at reducing the public fear of violent crime. It is precisely this fear that facilitates the politics of criminalization and incarceration, and thus poses the greatest threat of increased incarceration.

## Fear of Violent Crime

Despite the attractions of a reform strategy that aims primarily at the soft under belly of mass incarceration, we must never forget that it is fear of violent crime that animates the larger cultural project of the "War on Crime" and the "War on Drugs." And thus we cannot extricate ourselves from mass imprisonment with a strategy focused exclusively on moving drug offenders out of prison. Indeed, unless self-consciously directed, the campaign to reduce the soft underbelly of incarceration can paradoxically reinforce the hard back of mass incarceration. As Marie Gottschalk has argued:

> While the drug and sentencing ballot initiatives vary greatly, they share some com-
> mon features. They risk reinforcing a disturbing distinction between deserving and
> undeserving offenders. Many of these initiatives sanction throwing the book at drug
> dealers, recidivists, and violent offenders, thus reinforcing powerful stereotypes
> about crime and criminals that may help bolster the fundamental legitimacy of the
> carceral state. (Gottschalk 2006, 258)

At its best, the drug reduction strategy will produce an incarceration rate in America that is 25 to 45 percent lower than it is now, but that remains two or three times the norm for the twentieth century. This prison population will be just as overpopulated with people of color who come from neighborhoods (now often rural as well as urban) where they face multiple disadvantages. At worst, given our current practices of excess punishment for violent crime, a reduction strategy focused on the soft underbelly may only anchor a sensibility that will lock us into mass imprisonment and distort the way America rebuilds its urban landscape over the coming decades. We must confront our fears rather than avoid them. One way to do that is to situate them historically. The politics of fear that have reshaped penal policies toward both violent crime and drug crimes has its origin in the "War on Crime" that began in the late 1960s and built momentum during the 1970s.

Fear of "black crime" and violent crime by African Americans against whites was not new in the 1960s; rather, it dates to the time of slavery. Indeed, the 1960s and 1970s were characterized by violence in the form of a series of tragic spec-tacles that captivated the cultural imagination of the nation, from the 1963 assas-sination of President John Kennedy in Dallas, to the violent urban disorders that began in 1965 in Los Angeles and spread to other cities during the remainder of the decade, to the 1968 assassination of the Reverend Dr. Martin Luther King Jr. in Memphis, to the serial killers who haunted the 1970s (from Zodiac to Ted Bundy). That many of the perpetrators were white did little to alter the fear, ingrained in American culture since the nineteenth century, that crime wore a black face.

The political response to the turmoil of this period was a "War on Crime" that would have as its unstated target the reduction of violence through the suppression of young African American men. The first wave of this "war," and the crime policies it spawned in the late 1960s and 1970s, focused on increasing the resources and legal powers of the police. The turn toward long prison sentences for "violent crime" began to take shape in the 1980s. While that decade's "War on Drugs" would see increasing numbers of nonviolent drug and property offenders (many of the latter driven by drug use) being sent to prison rather than being sentenced to jail or probation sentences as they might have been before, the difference between nonviolent and violent crime was being redrawn by the formation of extremely long sentences for violent crime, especially murder.

## The Example of Murder: Life Means Life in California

Few crimes generate the kind of popular fear and anxiety that homicides do. People can insure against theft and reject the temptations of addictive drugs. They cannot, however, erase the possibility that another person with force or stealth can attack them.[10] The dramatic increase in the U.S. homicide rate that began in the mid-1960s was a crucial catalyst for the "War on Crime" that developed by the end of that decade (Simon 2007). While the targets of this war would spread well beyond homicide to include many nonviolent crimes, it is the fear of homicide that provided the continuing moral support for that war. While the rise of the homicide rate would halt in the second half of the 1970s, it remained well above its post–World War II lows throughout the next two decades, with periodic escalations, and only began to return to its 1960 levels in the late 1990s.[11]

Historically the structure of the law of homicide was well suited to mediate the relationship between public fear of crime and the demand for harsh punishment (Simon 2011). The death penalty was available (and widely used in the first half of the twentieth century) to address those killings that most alarmed the public (Banner 2002). For the vast majority of others convicted of murder, either a very long term of years in a prison or, often, a life sentence was formally imposed. Few served such lengthy sentences, and a less visible, though strong presumption grew in favor of an eventual release date for prisoners serving life sentences, particularly if they avoided trouble and actively sought rehabilitative programming.

To a large extent, the expectation that prisoners should be eventually released has long divided along racial lines. Black violence against whites has historically met with harsh punishment, lynching, execution, or decades at hard labor. Black violence against black victims, or white violence against black victims, was met very differently, with far less severe punishment. For example, the famous blues singer Huddie Ledbetter, or Lead Belly, as he was best known, served seven years of a seven- to thirty-five-year sentence for killing an African American victim. By contrast, a relative of his was later convicted of attempted murder and sentenced to four years for having a knife fight with a white man. Likewise, certain kinds of homicides were punished more harshly because their victim was an intimate partner, generally a woman, rather than a stranger.

Significantly, the grading of homicides was organized variously throughout the twentieth century, as well as from state to state. For most of the century, however, discretion operated at both ends of the system. At the front end, prosecutors and ultimately juries decided who should face execution or very harsh prison sentences. At the back end, the power to grant clemency and to release prisoners much earlier than their stated sentences had been exercised by governors. In the case of early release, administrative authorities often known as parole boards adjudicated. The role of racial, class, and gender bias at both ends of this continuum has been documented by a great deal of sociolegal work over the past half century.

The front end of the system has remained remarkably stable. Despite enormous changes in the structure of the death penalty, and of parole systems, prosecutors continue to wield enormous discretion over who faces the harshest punishment, and juries continue to have an ultimate veto over these choices through acquittal. The major change here has been the reduction of discretion over the death penalty. The Supreme Court decisions in the 1970s that first struck down all existing death sentences and then permitted some death sentences handed down under new statutes to go forward seemed to place limits on which murders could be punished with death, although some experts now believe these limits are in practice quite modest (Steiker and Steiker 1995).

At the rear end of the system, the past century has seen significant changes. With the "War on Crime" and the politicization of all decisions that could benefit convicted criminals and especially prisoners, back-end release through the parole system has been greatly reduced and in some cases halted altogether. People sentenced to prison are now very likely to serve the vast majority of their sentences, and for life sentences that can mean literally life. For murder, the mean time served is close to twenty-five years.[12] In contrast, time served for murder in the 1970s was probably fewer than fifteen years nationally.[13] In California, which has seen an extreme combination of all these trends, a combination of longer minimum sentences, a parole board dominated by law enforcement and victim representatives, and a requirement of approval by the governor for each parole of a murderer has produced a parole rate so low that it is likely that most murderers will die in prison (Irwin 2009). This is an astoundingly severe punishment for murder by global standards.

## Nonlethal Violence

Homicide is not the only crime punished with extraordinary severity. Consider a recent case from the streets not a twenty-five-minute bus ride from my desk.

Jared Adams, twenty-six, of Oakland was convicted in 2009 of a string of serious violent felonies committed in late December 2007 and early January 2008. In the most serious incident, Adams's wild gunshots during an armed robbery of a service station paralyzed Christopher Rodgers (now twelve) as he was taking a piano lesson in Oakland. A few weeks earlier, Adams attempted to carjack an automobile on the streets of downtown Oakland by pointing his gun in the face of the driver (who turned out coincidentally to be Senator Don Perata of Oakland, at that time the president pro tem of the California Senate).

Adams is a good example of why state prison remains a valuable option for community safety. He is as clear and present a danger to his community as a person's behavior can indicate. Few would question the need to isolate Adams from the general community, and for longer than jails are currently permitted to hold people (one or two years at the most). But how long should a violent twenty-six-year-old spend in prison?

Judge Larry Goodman of Alameda County Superior Court sentenced Adams to seventy years to life in prison, meaning Adams, now twenty-six, will not be even eligible for parole until he is eighty-six. While California's sentencing law gave Judge Goodman little actual discretion to shorten this sentence, the judge took the occasion to forcefully express his frustration with violent crime in Oakland: "In Mr. Adams' world, there are simply victims and predators, and when they see something they want, they take it," Goodman said in sentencing Adams in Alameda County Superior Court. He called Adams a parasite in a city where residents are frustrated with violence. Then he read out all of Adams's convictions and their corresponding sentences, a process that took more than fifteen minutes.

Even with much more in-depth knowledge about his background and record, few would want to predict with precision how many years in prison it would take to substantially eliminate the threat that Adams would return to his previous reckless lethality. What will he be like at forty (in fourteen years)? Or at fifty (in twenty-four years)? Criminologists have known for decades that aging diminishes even the most potent criminal motivation. Much would depend on what prison conditions were like and what use Adams made of programming opportunities in prison to work on himself. Administrative boards, like California's Board of Parole

Hearings, possessing the power to regularly review Adams's time in prison and condition are undeniably far better suited than trial courts sitting in the present. Yet under California law, it will take until Adams is fifty-seven (after thirty-one years in prison) before the parole authorities can even consider whether he is safe to be released under supervision in the community. This is not just a California phenomenon. Violent offenders in the United States spend five to ten times as long in prison as those in France (Gottschalk 2006, 21).

The extraordinarily long sentence handed down in the case of Jared Adams suggests that even if reformers succeeded beyond current expectations in promoting alternatives to prison for nonviolent crime, the overpunishment of violence would continue to create a system of mass incarceration far larger than the total U.S. prison population historically, far larger than prison populations in other democratic societies. Further, inmates in U.S. prisons would continue to be disproportionately African American and Latino, convicted of drug and property crimes. Such predictions largely reflect underlying patterns of violent crime itself (approximately half of all murders involve an African American victim and perpetrator). But they also reflect the fact that prosecutors have great discretion over charges (for example, assault versus attempted murder can mean a difference of decades in prison). It is fairly axiomatic that communities of color are particularly vulnerable to receiving the harsh edge of prosecutorial discretion because most prosecutors are elected in white majority counties but control charging decisions over largely minority populations in central cities.

So long as fear of violent crime drives penal policy, even the seemingly realizable goal of reducing the use of imprisonment for nonviolent crimes is vulnerable to reversal because the overpunishment of violence bleeds back into our penal appetite for punishing the nonviolent.

## Violent Crime Sentences as a Price Signal

Behavioral economists have long noted the power of influential price signals in anchoring expectations about reasonable choices for decisions under uncertainty (Kahneman 1992). The so-called reference price establishes a level below which consumers will feel that they are getting a good deal, and above which consumers feel they are experiencing a loss. So the forty-dollar surf-and-turf special on the menu at your local "nice" restaurant probably makes it more likely you will spend twenty-nine dollars on a steak rather than nineteen dollars on a pasta dish.

Prison sentences for violent crimes—especially murder, which receives the most popular attention—are likely to have an outsized influence on our overall scale of penal justice. The trend toward very long prison sentences for violent crime, including whole-life sentences for even nonaggravated murder, sets a reference price for crime that makes extreme but less severe punishments for other crimes seem appropriate. In other words, decades spent in prison for crimes like robbery, burglary, and drug dealing may not seem disproportionate when compared to the severity of execution, or life in prison without parole.[14]

## Violence and Net Widening

In America, the intense fear of violence—a legacy of slavery and the ethnic cleansing of the Native Americans—has long been married to great confidence in the ability of science and technology to provide solutions for violence and other social problems. The birth of the penitentiary in the Jacksonian era (Rothman 1971); the burst of penal innovation during the Progressive Era (1890s); and mass incarceration since the 1970s have exemplified this marriage in one form or another, while reflecting an optimism that violence can be prevented by arresting criminal deviance early in the path toward antisocial behavior (Simon 2006). While murder is the enigma that has fueled popular interest in criminology, criminology has always pushed crime policy in the direction of early intervention. If this historic alliance had a slogan, it might be "nip it in the bud," or "an ounce of prevention is worth a pound of cure."

In the Progressive Era, intervention took the form of juvenile justice and probation, practices designed to reach wayward youth before they became committed to lives of crime. In the era of mass imprisonment, intervention has come to mean imprisonment for drug and property offenders as a way of preventing murder.

## Violence and the Origins of the 1960s "War on Crime"

Nixon's "War on Crime" campaign in 1968 made violent crime a recurring theme. As Rick Perlstein recalls in *Nixonland*, the campaign issued a lengthy position paper, *Towards Freedom from Fear*, which invoked Roosevelt's Four Freedoms to cast violent crime as the equivalent of the fascist threat identified by FDR twenty-seven years earlier in 1941: "If the present rate of new crime continues, the number of rapes and robberies and assaults and thefts in the United States will double by the end of 1972. This is a prospect America cannot accept. If we allow it to happen, the city jungle will cease to be a metaphor, it will become a barbaric reality" (Perlstein 2008, 268).

As Nixon's "jungle" metaphor suggests, the law-and-order campaign was laden with barely disguised invocations of racial stereotypes (that is, African Americans as primitive and predatory) designed to appeal to antiblack sentiments among not only white southerners who were still trying to defend segregation, but also among northern whites. George Wallace, like Nixon, sought to establish a connection between antiblack and anticrime politics. Even in the 1960s, however, these "backlash" elements of governing through crime (efforts to reverse elements of civil rights law like busing schoolchildren to integrate schools, or open housing laws) were combined with what Vesla Weaver (2007) has called a "frontlash" (efforts by groups defeated on civil rights to prioritize new issue fields in which they have an advantage and in which supporters of civil rights laws were disadvantaged). In turning to a new topic—in this case, crime control—frontlash need not take its core values from the earlier struggle over race. Fear of crime and the desire to be secure from crime had independent moral value that could appeal to many Americans unmoved by segregation. No doubt "black crime" was in the news in the late 1960s and had alarming extensions in the big-city riots, and some of the foco-terrorism of the black power movement (Cummins 1994), but it was not black crime that was truly new to the "fear of crime" discourse of the late 1960s and early 1970s. Black crime had long been a focus of both popular and criminological writing about homicide. Indeed, the pioneering criminologist Cesare Lombroso, writing at the end of the nineteenth century, identified "the Negro" as a major component of America's homicide problem: "[The Negro] is still too often indifferent to and careless of the lives of others, and he betrays the lack of the sentiment of pity, commonly observed among savage races, which causes him to regard homicide as a mere incident, and as glorious, especially in cases where it is the outcome of revenge" (quoted in Simon 2006, 2155).

The assassinations of both Kennedys and King were blamed on two white men and one man of Palestinian Arab nationality. Mass murderers like Charles Whitman (1966, Austin, Texas) and Richard Speck (1968, Chicago) were white. White protesters, not just black rioters, were framed as the enemies of law and order. Drugs and gruesome murders like those committed by the Manson family in August 1969 (the same summer that "yippies" fought with police and the SDS splinter group the Weathermen came into the public eye as a potential terrorist wing of the antiwar movement). This generalized threat of crime that seemed new to many people in the 1960s extended beyond the low-income neighborhoods and specific social networks in which it had been largely framed. When, in his convention acceptance speech in 1968, Richard Nixon focused heavily on crime, he could presume a widespread fear that any citizen could potentially fall victim to violence. "The first civil right of every American is to be free from domestic violence" (Perlstein 2009, 306). Earlier that summer, President Lyndon Johnson's signing statement for the Omnibus Crime Control and Safe Streets Act uf 1968 spoke ominously of needing to try something that could "lift the shadow fear and the stain of crime from the streets of America's cities" (Simon 2007).

The centrality and generality of violence is also testified to on both sides of *Furman v. Georgia* (1972), the pivotal Supreme Court decision striking down the death penalty as then practiced in America. In his dissent, Justice (and Virginian) Lewis Powell pointed to this history of murder in the 1960s as forming a powerful influence on public attitudes:

> [B]rutish and revolting murders continue to occur with disquieting frequency. Indeed, murders are so commonplace in our society that only the most sensational receive significant and sustained publicity. It could hardly be suggested that any of these highly publicized murder cases—the several senseless assassinations or the too numerous shocking multiple murders that have stained this country's recent history—the public has exhibited any signs of "revulsion" at the thought of executing the convicted murderers. The public outcry, as we all know, has been quite the contrary. (quoted in Simon 2007, 119)

In his concurrence that formed part of the fragmented majority in *Furman*, Justice Marshall, who would have preferred to find capital punishment unconstitutional under any circumstances, pointedly referenced the climate of violence: "At a time in our history when the streets of the nation's cities inspire fear and despair, rather than pride and hope, it is difficult to maintain objectivity and concern for our fellow citizens. But, the measure of a country's greatness is its ability to retain compassion in time of crisis" (quoted in Gottschalk 2006, 216).

One need not conclude that the "War on Crime" was a simple response to violent crime; indeed, there is good evidence to support the argument that the political rhetoric of the era preceded and helped to define the fear well before the crime rise was truly pronounced (Beckett 1999). But the fear of violent crime, and especially murder, forms the emotional core, the sense of grievance, required for fueling the massive reordering of governmental priorities. The "War on Crime" represented precisely such a reordering. While partisan differences surround the execution of the "War on Crime" (capital punishment, racial profiling, etc.), a commitment to protecting the public from the threat of violent crime became a bipartisan consensus in American public affairs. This may well be part of a broader "civilizing process" (Elias 2000, 1939) that has made violence of all kinds less publicly acceptable over time (consider domestic violence), and made violent crime into a consensus issue on which conservatives and liberals can join. Along with this alliance came a commitment to something like a "precautionary principle," the idea that against certain especially grave risks, government must take preemptive action, even when the likelihood of the risk coming to pass is indeterminable. Against violence crime, such preemptive action takes the form of extended sentences, supposedly designed to preempt possible violence in the community. Increasingly, prisoners sentenced to life for murder have to convince parole authorities that they pose essentially zero risk of crime in order to have any chance of being released. Because such authorities are not easily convinced, a life sentence extends to the duration of a prisoner's life. Only by reassessing our commitment to zero-risk policies toward violence can we begin to recover a capacity for judgment on punishment.

## Race and Violence

Critics of the "War on Drugs" point out that persons of color, especially African Americans, are far more likely than whites to be in prison for a drug crime. Indeed, good evidence suggests that police tend to target those drug markets, especially crack cocaine, which are primarily patronized and serviced by African Americans (Beckett, Nyrop, and Pfingst 2006; Beckett et al. 2005). But when we look at incarceration rates for those convicted of violent crime, especially murder, we also find considerable racial disproportionality. Life prisoners (overwhelmingly convicted of murder) are more likely to be African American than prisoners under a sentence of a term of years. The disparities here, however, hew more closely, in the view of most criminologists, to underlying differences in violent crime risks between whites and African Americans (with Latinos falling between). While, when it comes to drug crimes, police tactics account largely for the excess in incarceration rates of African Americans and Latinos (relative to whites), by comparison, police investigation of violent crime is often hampered by the trust deficit they face in many minority communities.

From this perspective, we can see why the defenders of southern Jim Crow segregation welcomed the issue of violent crime, even if many of the most publicized perpetrators were white. The underlying base rates of the activities made African American violence a prime target.[15] Moreover, by the 1960s African American violent crime was primarily a northern rather than a southern problem. Racial liberals followed a different path to a war on violent crime. If homicide was a special scourge in areas of urban poverty—primarily African American and Latino areas by the 1960s—liberals could see stronger law enforcement and stricter punishment as a way to save the lives of minority citizens and repudiate a racist tradition of underpunishing black-on-black crime.

To return to my original premise, rather than contradicting the centrality of violence, the "War on Drugs" reflected a logical path for a "War on Violence." While both liberals and conservatives had good reasons for being wary of a "War on Drugs" (and drug punishments became more lenient for a while), the role that drugs were alleged to play in the genesis of violent crime and the widespread organized nature of drug markets made a war on drugs an ideal focus for a governmental campaign to repress violence. The police focus on young black men may well be driven by fear of guns and pressure to drive down homicide rates, but the immediate result of such policing tactics are generally more drug arrests and convictions.[16]

THE PROJECT OF mass incarceration stands at a moment of vulnerability for the first time in decades. Mass incarceration has become problematized not because there is any agreement that it has failed. As with most massive governmental projects, outcomes are complicated to interpret. Further, they are likely to be read with one's ideological glasses on. The status of social policies tends to depend on how they are framed and contextualized rather than on the accumulated weight of empirical evidence. Just as cash assistance for the poor in the United States (the usual and highly racialized meaning of "welfare" in American politics) began to be delegitimized in the 1980s despite a far from settled empirical picture of its success in fighting poverty (Gilens 1999), today mass incarceration is in the process of being reframed as a source of new social problems of great significance including potentially unconstitutional prison conditions, the aggravation of racial inequality, and the production of an underclass of the formerly incarcerated who are largely locked out of the economy and the democratic process (Western 2006; Clear 2008).

These new social problems have allowed critics of mass imprisonment to move beyond the largely unanswerable question of whether mass imprisonment lowers crime and instead to define mass incarceration as a threat to America's market economy, as well as to its democratic polity. Such observations coincide favorably with the emergence of a new environmental meta-problem facing not only the United States, but the world, that is, human-induced climate change and the potentially catastrophic risks it poses to our habitats and food chains.

Historians may observe that the hold of mass incarceration on American government from 1980 to 2005 emerged at a time when efforts to mobilize government against environmental concerns were stymied. The major environmental laws of the 1970s might have required far-reaching changes in the production and cost of energy, but by the early 1980s they were hopelessly bogged down in costly court battles and in a federal court system destined to become substantially more pro-business under Presidents Ronald Reagan and George H. W. Bush. The emergence of climate change as a significant risk to human populations may be reversing that process. While effective national action against that threat has yet to take shape in the United States, concerns about the consequences of unregulated carbon production are clearly growing.

The primary mediating structure between mass incarceration at the policy level and the renewed urgency of environmental threats is the pattern of urban development and, perhaps even more profoundly, energy consumption. Broadly speaking, mass imprisonment thrived alongside a pattern of development emphasizing centrifugal movement to the outer edges of the metropolitan area (Davis 1991). Both developments shared a commitment to security through a combination of incarcerating the dangerous and hardening a protective shell around the middle-class family (Davis 1998). Whether the lonely suburbs helped generate mass imprisonment by sparking a greater degree of crime-specific insecurity (Garland 2001) or whether fear of crime drove the middle class out of cities is debatable. Undoubtedly there is some truth to both theories. That this dual pattern also produced a higher degree of racial segregation than any other period in American history is indisputable.

The emergence of climate change as a global meta-social problem marks a fundamental transformation in this pattern of fear-based sprawl and segregation. The endless expansion of the boundaries of metropolitan areas has relied on automobility, which in turn has been a function of relatively cheap energy and relatively diminished concern with the environmental consequences of commuting. That is almost certainly over, which means that development will almost certainly become centripetal.

But if the city is going to be reborn, what kind of city will it be? This is where the relationship between mass imprisonment and structural racism is at its most salient. For the rebirth of the great American cities opens the door to the creation of a racially integrated society for the first time in nearly thirty years (since the collapse of the probably futile school-based effort to forge such a society). Fear of crime, especially violent crime, is the greatest obstacle to realizing this vision. In the short term, these fears are likely to drive the middle class to accept higher economic costs to sustain their suburban lifestyle. This resistance will prove futile in the long run, but if the middle classes come back to the cities with their current prioritization of security from "stranger danger" intact, they will likely choose highly segmented and segregated residential developments, creating gated-community-type enclaves within a tighter geographic frame.

It is in relationship to this fear of violent crime that we must challenge mass imprisonment today. If mass imprisonment has supposedly operated significantly to reduce this fear, there is at least a case to be made that it is worth all its other noxious externalities. But if the new problematization of mass incarceration has taught us anything, it is that such incarceration encourages fear of violent crime (and the larger risk paradigm I call "stranger danger") by producing an underclass of seemingly ungovernable people (the strangers) who cannot be integrated into society. Further, this fear of violent crime has served to prevent (financially and in the blockage of the imagination) new and innovative strategies for preventing violence within and without American homes.

The fear of violence at the heart of the political project of mass incarceration cannot be arrested and reduced by strategies that aim at decarcerating drug users and other nonviolent offenders. There are good reasons for adopting such strategies, but we must not allow them to distract us from the hard work of creating not only a new public conception of violence, but also a new image of the violent offender. Unless we cease to demonize these populations, we risk expanding the hard back of mass incarceration, further entrenching it in our polity and society.

## Notes

1. This is not to say, of course, that these initiatives do not face fierce resistance from law enforcement and other prison interests.

2. Following George Lakoff and Mark Johnson (1980) and Steven Winter (2001), I take the metaphor here quite seriously as a way of knowing and acting on a problem.

3. African Americans and Latinos are also extremely overrepresented in the population of those incarcerated for violent crimes. For example, as of 2003, African Americans made up 53 percent of all state prisoners imprisoned for drug crimes, and 46 percent of all state prisoners imprisoned for violent crimes (Sourcebook of Criminal Justice Statistics Online, table 6.0001.2003, www.albany.edu/sourcebook/pdf/t600012003.pdf).

4. See Johnson v. California, 543 U.S. 499 (2005) (holding that California's unwritten [but admitted] policy of racially segregating prisoners placed in double cells after arrival in prison reception centers should be evaluated under the "strict scrutiny" test of the Equal Protection Clause).

5. A jailhouse letter from one of the two, intercepted by law enforcement, made clear that the killing was intended as a gesture within the racist prison gang system (see "Closing Arguments Today in Texas Dragging-Death Trial," CNN, February 22, 1999, http://articles.cnn.com/1999–02–22/us/9902_22_dragging.death.03_1_judge-joe-bob-golden-john-william-king-draggingdeath?_s=PM:US).

6. Race and criminal conviction appear to be additive, meaning the disproportionate impact of criminal convictions on African Americans and other minorities is roughly doubling the residual discrimination they already face in the labor market.

7. Federal Anti-Drug Abuse Act of 1986. The law was amended by the Fair Sentencing Act of 2010, which reduced, but did not eliminate, the disparity.

8. The current concern with methamphetamine may reflect the cultural downgrading of rural and urban whites from the relative insulation of white populations from harsh

drug enforcement. Very harsh drug laws against marijuana users were reformed in the 1970s as a result of the large numbers of white middle-class youth threatened with prison under then-existing statutes.

9. In November 2010, California voters narrowly rejected a proposition that would have legalized sale and possession of marijuana by adults (see Marc Lacey, "California Rejects Marijuana Legalization," *New York Times*, November 3, 2010). But California already has an existing medical marijuana law that permits tens of thousands of users to obtain the drug legally with a doctor's recommendation. Some sixteen states now permit marijuana to be sold and consumed for medical purposes.

10. Indeed, the political theorist Thomas Hobbes argued that the threat of murder was the great equalizer among human beings, and a threat that no individual alone could relieve. Instead, the fear of homicide leads humans to enter the compact that forms the sovereign state as the only mechanism for reducing the risk of violent attack (Thomas Hobbes, *Leviathan* [Oxford: Basil Blackwell, 1960], 80).

11. See U.S. Bureau of Justice Statistics, Homicide Trends in the United States, http://bjs.ojp.usdoj.gov/content/homicide/homtrnd.cfm

12. The mean sentence for murder in a sample of violent felons sentenced between 1990 and 2002 was more than three hundred months (Reaves 2002, 8).

13. In their assessment of prison population growth since the 1970s, Blumstein and Beck note that "murder is the offense with the strongest upward trend in time served, a 4.8 percent annual rate of increase" (1999, 41).

14. David Garland, in discussion, usefully raises the question of whether it is not escalation in the punishment of these serious but nonhomicidal crimes that drives increases in the severity of punishment for murder. It is true that some of the first extreme sentences arise in antinarcotics crimes. For example, the infamous Rockefeller drug law of 1973 made the sale of two ounces or more of a controlled substance (including marijuana) punishable by fifteen years to life in prison. The Rockefeller laws permitted parole. Even more severe antidrug laws have been adopted in Michigan and many other states, resulting in, under the federal sentencing guidelines, decades of imprisonment for those convicted of possessing sufficiently large quantities of drugs. The sequencing of homicide penalties and drug laws in the various states should be carefully examined. As a whole, during the 1970s and 1980s, drugs—at least "hard drugs"—came to be linked to the possibility, or even the likelihood, of death. Selling large quantities of drugs in this respect might be seen as a kind of murder. Indeed, the Rockefeller laws explicitly linked the penalties for drugs to the penalties for second-degree murder.

15. As noted above, African Americans are involved (as both victim and perpetrator) in about half of all homicides. Sociologists have long recognized that this results from the concentration of violence promoting social pathologies in communities of economic disadvantage and discrimination. However, it underscores the fact that harsh penalties for violent crime can be seen by some as a good-faith effort to bring relief to African American victims.

16. Recent empirical research by Katherine Beckett and her colleagues provides some support for the theory that racialized policing of drugs in Seattle is driven by a police emphasis on crack cocaine. More than any other recent drug, crack and its distribution have been associated with gun violence and homicides (see Beckett et al. 2005).

## References

Banner, Stuart. 2002. *The Death Penalty: An American History.* Cambridge: Harvard University Press.

Blumstein, Alfred, and Allen J. Beck. 1999. "Population Growth in US Prisons, 1980 to 1996, *Crime & Justice* 26:17–62.

Beckett, Katherine. 1999. *Making Crime Pay: Law and Order in Contemporary American Politics.* New York: Oxford University Press.

Beckett, Katherine, Kris Nyrop, and Lori Pfingst. 2006. "Race, Drugs and Policing: Understanding Disparities in Drug Delivery Arrests." *Criminology* 44:105–38.

Beckett, Katherine, Kris Nyrop, Lori Pfingst, and Melissa Bowen. 2005. "Drug Use, Drug Possession Arrests, and the Question of Race: Lessons from Seattle." *Social Problems* 52:419–41.

Clear, Todd. 2008. *Imprisoning Communities: How Mass Incarceration Makes Disadvantage Neighborhoods Worse.* New York: Oxford University Press.

Cummins, Eric. 1994. *The Rise and Fall of California's Radical Prison Movement.* Stanford: Stanford University Press.

Davis, Mike. 1991. *City of Quartz: Excavating the Future in Los Angeles.* London: Verso.

———. 1998. *The Ecology of Fear: Los Angeles and the Imagination of Disaster.* New York: Metropolitan Books.

Elias, Norbert. 2000. *The Civilizing Process: Sociogenetic and Psychogenetic Investigations.* Oxford: Blackwell.

*Furman v. Georgia* (1972) 408 U.S. 238.

Garland, David. 2001. *The Culture of Control: Crime and Social Order in Contemporary Society.* Chicago: University of Chicago Press.

Gilens, Martin, 1999. *Why Americans Hate Welfare: Race, Media, and the Politics of Antipoverty Policy.* Chicago: University of Chicago Press.

Gottschalk, Marie. 2006. *The Prison and the Gallows: The Politics of Mass Incarceration in America.* Cambridge: Cambridge University Press.

Irwin, John. 2009. *Lifers: Seeking Redemption in Prison.* London: Routledge.

Kahneman, Daniel. 1992. "Reference Points, Anchors, Norms, and Mixed Feelings." *Org. Behav. & Hum. Decision Processes* 51: 296–300.

Lakoff, George, and Mark Johnson. 1980. *Metaphors We Live By.* Chicago: University of Chicago Press.

Musto, David. 1973. *The American Disease: The Origins of Narcotics Control.* New York: Oxford University Press.

Pager, Devah. 2007. *Marked: Race, Crime and Finding Work in an Era of Mass Incarceration.* Chicago: University of Chicago Press.

Perlstein, Rick. 2008. *Nixonland: The Rise of a President and the Fracturing of America.* New York: Scribner.

Reaves, Brian A. 2002. *State Court Processing Statistics, 1990–2002: Violent Felons in Large Urban Counties.* Washington, D.C.: Bureau of Justice Statistics Special Reports.

Rothman, David. 1971. *Discovery of the Asylum.* Boston: Little, Brown.

Simon, Jonathan. 2006. "Positively Punitive: How the Inventor of Scientific Criminology Who Died at the Beginning of the Twentieth Century Continues to Haunt American Crime Control at the Beginning of the Twenty-First." *Texas Law Review* 84: 2135–72.

————. 2007. *Governing through Crime: How the War on Crime Transformed American Democracy and Created a Culture of Fear.* New York: Oxford University Press.

————. 2011. "How Should we Punish Murder? Excessive Punishment and the Structure of the Law of Murder." *Marquette Law Review* 94:101–69

Steiker, Carole, and Jordan Steiker. 1995. "Sober Second Thoughts: Reflections on Two Decades of Constitutional Regulation of Capital Punishment." *Harvard Law Review* 109:355–438

Weaver, Vesla. 2007. "Frontlash: Race and the Development of Punitive Crime Policy." *Studies in American Political Development* 21:230–65

Western, Bruce. 2006. *Punishment and Inequality in America.* New York: Russell Sage Foundation.

Winter, Steven. 2001. *A Clearing in the Forest: Law, Life, and Mind.* Chicago: University of Chicago Press.

# 3 Race, Prison, and the Aesthetic Imagination

It's around midnight. The lights are out and the T.V.'s off. For the past hour some young bloods, huddled in the back of the cage, have been do/wopping some old songs. This is my best time; I just lie/back on my bunk and space out. Right now a dude in the cage behind me is singing, "I've seen fire, I've seen rain—I've seen sunny days. . . ." This is the first time I've really listened to the lyrics; it's a heavy song. And the dude has a good solid voice—you can hear it leaving his throat. For some reason—perhaps it's the steel and the corridors— the acoustics in jail are extraordinary. Sounds carom down the corridors, reverberating and magnifying. You can lie in your cell and dig the whole joint with your ears: a man urinating, the toilet flushing, a man screaming in his sleep, another coughing and snoring and always—keys jingling and bells ringing steel doors slamming. Jail sounds, sounds of ice.

—ETHERIDGE KNIGHT

Sometimes I think this whole world is one big prison yard
Some of us are prisoners, the rest of us are guards.

—BOB DYLAN, *"George Jackson"*

In a universe of cells—who is not in jail?

—BOB KAUFMAN, *"Jail Poems"*

# Rage against the Machine

*African American Music and the Evolution*
*of the Penitentiary Blues, 1961–2000*

Claudrena N. Harold

Late in the afternoon of April 4, 2003, an eclectic crowd of two thousand crammed into Treme Community Center in New Orleans, Louisiana, for the opening session of the conference "Critical Resistance South: Beyond the Prison Industrial Complex." Commencing on the thirty-fifth anniversary of Dr. Martin Luther King Jr.'s assassination, the three-day conference featured several prominent intellectuals, prison abolitionists, and penal reform advocates, including Angela Davis, Jason Zeidenberg of the Justice Policy Institute, former Black Panther Robert Wilkerson, and Dan Horowitz de Garcia, program director of Project South in Atlanta, Georgia. Over the course of the historic gathering, attendees listened to moving lectures and testimonials on how the nation's penal system imperiled rather than protected communities of color. To their credit, conference organizers not only included the perspectives of academics, policy experts, and veteran activists, but they also allocated time to younger African Americans interested in articulating their own concerns about what it means to live in a carceral state. Taking advantage of that opportunity, Tambourine and Fan, a local youth ensemble based in the Ninth Ward of New Orleans, took the stage on the conference's second day.[1] The group wasted no time in situating their generation's struggle against the prison industrial complex within a broader historical context. To the audience's delight, Tambourine and Fan performed a moving rendition of Billie Holiday's 1939 classic "Strange Fruit." Twelve-year-old Tarik Smith mesmerized conference attendees with his syncopated drum patterns while his peers recited the lyrics of the antilynching song. Tambourine and Fan's performance was hugely important and symbolic for the group not only because it countered myopic portrayals of young people as politically disengaged, but it also reminded the audience of how music continues to function as a critical site of political memory and social protest against legal and extralegal forms of racial punishment.

It requires no great leap of imagination to acknowledge music's political significance as an important discursive arena in which African Americans have confronted many of the issues raised in this volume. In fact, one of the most persistent political themes in African American music, from the blues songs of the first half of the twentieth century to the protest lyrics of the hip-hop era, has been the "hyper- and excessive policing" of the African American body politic.[2] Especially within the popular music industry, African American performers have long been concerned with the white-supremacist thought and practice undergirding the U.S. criminal justice system.[3] Looking back at the period between the collapse of Reconstruction and the Great Migration, the historian Leon Litwack identifies the discriminatory policies of the criminal justice system as the political issue attracting the greatest amount of attention from blues singers:

> When blues singers emerged in the late nineteenth and early twentieth centuries, they focused on subjects that were part of the day-to-day lives of black Southerners. If most of them avoided disfranchisement and segregation, if few of them addressed directly the issue of lynching, they commented in a variety of ways on an experience they could share with everyone in the audience, and that was the blatant unfairness of the judicial and law enforcement systems.[4]

Today, this long-standing tradition of engaging the undemocratic practices of the U.S. penal system continues in the work of musicians like Meshell Ndegeocello, the Roots, Immortal Technique, and dead prez. On their studio recordings and in their live performances, these artists, among others, vividly recount the devastating effects of police brutality, draconian sentencing laws, and the corporatization of the American prison system on African American communities throughout the nation. Across a broad artistic spectrum, ranging from avant-garde jazz to mainstream pop, a critical mass of African American musicians have registered their discontent with the entrenched racism of dominant criminological discourses and their damaging discursive work in the representational fields of television, cinema, and the World Wide Web. At the same time, black cultural performers have also cast a critical eye on the carceral characteristics, techniques, and logics of everyday space and cultural practices.[5] With painstaking detail, they illustrate the place of public housing, recreational parks, and public schools on the "carceral continuum." As a result, the "prison narratives" of many contemporary black musicians offer not just a portrait of their communities' encounters with the criminal justice system but also critical insight into the complex ways in which carcerally inflected landscapes contribute to the formation of prison subjectivities among certain segments of the "free population."

In discussing the brutal realities of living in a carceral society, many politically engaged musicians have spared neither themselves nor their peers from serious critique when confronting the cultural forms and conditions that help inform popular understandings of race, criminality, and legal punishment. Typical of this self-reflective approach is the political work of the hip-hop band the Roots. On their critically acclaimed 2008 release *Rising Down,* the Roots detail how many of the marketing strategies and mass-mediated images mobilized by the popular culture industry reify the idea of African Americans as the predatory other. As band member Dice Raw bemoans in his analysis of the mass media's treatment of African American men, "They act like I'm something to fear."[6] To situate their critique of commercial popular culture within a larger historical context, the Roots used an adaptation of the racist 1898 campaign poster *The Vampire That Hovers over North Carolina (Negro Rule)* as the cover art for their recording. The cover's message is unequivocally clear: in the popular white imagination, every African American male represents an actual or potential predator, ready to wreak havoc on the white citizenry. Notably, the Roots also draw attention to how many of their hip-hop peers have been complicit in the global marketing of African Americans as the criminal other. In songs such as "I Will Not Apologize," the group condemns certain members of the hip-hop community, along with black-owned media, particularly Black Entertainment Television (BET), for circulating narratives that serve the interests of the ruling elite. The strength of the Roots' critique lies in its contextualization of black self-commodification within the larger reality of the corporatization of hip-hop culture. If the group's call for hip-hop artists to "stop the lies" provides a much-needed internal critique of the genre for trafficking in racist stereotypes, their commentary on the insatiable appetite of many white consumers for hardened, criminalized representations of black masculinity partially explains why some artists willingly perform what Andrea Queeley refers to as "the Blackness of the white imagination."[7]

Frustrated by the representational landscape of blackness within the entertainment industry and the larger society, the Roots embraced the opportunity to challenge cultural images and representations detrimental to the life chances and experiences of African Americans, especially inner-city black youth. In doing so, the group added its name to a long list of artists who have relied on their musical talents to enrich an important aspect of the black protest tradition in American music.

Combining theoretical insights from the fields of African American studies, history, and ethnomusicology, this essay considers music's political importance as both a pedagogical tool and mobilizing force in African Americans' perennial struggle to radically transform (or abolish) the U.S. penal system. It proceeds from the epistemological premise that penological discourses emanating from the vibrant world of black music deserve serious attention not just from cultural theorists but from social scientists as well. Admittedly, space does not permit an exhaustive analysis of the varied ways in which African American music has functioned as a critical source of counterknowledge to mainstream discourses on the policing and punishing of African American communities. Thus, my analysis focuses primarily, though not exclusively, on six recordings released between 1961 and 2000: Harry Oster's *Angola Prisoners' Blues* and *Prison Worksongs;* Gil Scott-Heron's *Free Will* and *The Mind of Gil Scott-Heron;* Archie Shepp's *Attica Blues;* and dead prez's *Let's Get Free.* All of these recordings provide useful case studies for assessing how conversations on race and punishment have shifted during critical junctures in U.S. history. Moreover, they all give voice to political communities—black youth, prisoners, and the working poor—that are frequently rendered voiceless in scholarly discussions of the racial politics of punishment.

Organized chronologically, this essay encompasses three historical stages: the civil rights era, the Black Power period, and our current age of mass incarceration. The broad temporal space covered here should not be read as a reflection of this essay's all-inclusiveness; rather, my historical overview of penalogical discourses within African American music should be seen as a modest attempt to introduce the general reader to critical texts in the prison blues genre, as well as to provide a skeletal framework for further interrogations into African American musicians' complex and ever-evolving discourses on the racial dimensions of crime and punishment in American society. It is my hope that the following pages will provoke greater discussion of popular music's mobilizing potential, as well as its political limitations.

## Race, Punishment, and the Aesthetic Imagination

As previously mentioned, songs about the racial politics of crime, deviancy, and punishment have long been a part of the black music tradition. The vast catalogue of classic blues material dealing with police harassment and brutality, racial profiling, unfair trials, and inhumane prison conditions includes such standards as Bessie Smith's "Jail House Blues," Texas Alexander's "Levee Camp Moan Blues," Leroy Carr's "Prison Bound," and Blind Lemon Jefferson's "Penitentiary Blues."[8] A common theme in all of these songs is how the constitutional guarantee of equal protection under the law rarely extends to African Americans, particularly those living below the Mason-Dixon Line. Well into the electric blues era (1945–60), musicians persisted in their critiques of the criminal justice system, its blatantly racist policies, and its negative impact on African American family life. Classic numbers like Lightnin' Hopkins's "Prison Blues Come Down on Me," along with

John Lee Hooker's "I'm Prison Bound," reminded record buyers that despite the demographic, political, and social changes taking place in post–World War II America, the problem of race and punishment remained a matter of serious concern for African American communities and the nation at large.[9] Thus, even as African American music underwent monumental changes in the 1950s and 1960s, the penitentiary blues tradition remained an important part of the musical landscape of black America. On blues stations across the country, in "down home" juke joints stretching from Chicago to Memphis, and in notorious prisons like Mississippi's Parchman Farm, gripping narratives about crooked cops, shady district attorneys, and violent wardens found a receptive audience among many African American women and men.

To illustrate the enduring legacy of the penitentiary blues tradition, as well as to shed additional light on the criminal justice concerns of the civil rights generation, I now turn to Harry Oster's *Angola Prisoners' Blues* and *Prison Work-songs*. These 1961 recordings constitute invaluable resources for a wide range of scholars, including ethnomusicologists seeking to understand how political developments within the larger society informed the prison blues genre; literary and cultural critics interested in how the experience of confinement influences the artistic imagination; and historians committed to broadening our existing knowledge of prison culture during the 1950s.

## Angola Bound: Prison Blues Narratives in the Age of Freedom (1951–1964)

In *The Brothers*, Cyril Neville described the Angola prison as a constant "specter" in the minds of young black men in New Orleans: "Angola was the threat, the nightmare, the worst-case scenario." The "worst-case scenario" became a lived reality for the Neville family in 1964. Convicted of felony drug possession by a New Orleans jury, Charles Neville was sentenced to five years at the Louisiana State Penitentiary (LSP) in Angola, Louisiana. Though the twenty-five-year-old had already experienced his share of trials and tribulations, nothing prepared him for the brutal conditions and existential anguish of prison life. "Angola," Neville later recalled, "was a world so isolated, so brutal, so volatile that whatever survival skills I honed had to be seriously rehoned and sharpened. My aim was simple—to simply serve my time and get the fuck out with sanity and soul intact." Staying sane was no easy task, but Neville found strength in music. Shortly after his arrival in Angola, he joined an all-black prison band (the Knickknacks), a decision he later credited with saving his life: "Music protected me and saved my sanity. Without music, I'm not sure I would have gotten through Angola. Music made the difference."[10]

Eight years before Neville arrived in Angola, LSP inmates echoed similar sen
timents to the noted folklorist Harry Oster during his extended research visit to
the infamous penitentiary. Coming to Angola in 1958, Oster, an English professor
at Louisiana State University, was primarily concerned with archiving what he
viewed as two dying forms of black artistic expression—the worksong and the
spiritual. Nothing was explicitly political about Oster's visit, but the same cannot
be said about the prisoners' performances. Covering topics ranging from law enforcement officials' discriminatory application of vagrancy laws to the subjective
transformations engendered by their experience of incarceration, Angola inmates
seized the opportunity to vent their frustrations with the racial and class biases
embedded in the penal system. Their musical reflections were shaped by past
experiences, as well as the spatial politics, conditions, and history of the LSP.

Situated on 18,000 acres of farmland in Angola, Louisiana, the Louisiana State
Penitentiary claims a history steeped in class and racial domination. Named after
the African region from which Louisiana's slaveholding class imported a significant number of its slaves, Angola transitioned from slavery to convict leasing with
relative ease during the postemancipation period. Four years after Robert E. Lee's
surrender at Appomattox, a former Confederate officer, Samuel Lawrence, successfully consolidated several massive slave plantations into an expansive farm-
ing community. Convicts planted and harvested crops, picked cotton, repaired
railroad track, and constructed and maintained levees on the Mississippi River.
Subjected to various forms of physical, verbal, and psychological abuse, prison
inmates routinely endured fourteen- to eighteen-hour workdays, subsisted on a
diet devoid of key nutrients, and rarely received the proper medical attention.
Unfortunately, life for convicts remained deplorable after the state's takeover of
the "Angola farm" in 1901. Succinctly described by the historian Mark Carleton
as an "economic and sociological anachronism," the Louisiana State Penitentiary
operated under an inadequate budget and depended on an incompetent and un-
derpaid staff unafraid to use the most brutal force against "incorrigible" prisoners.[11] Flogging, sexual abuse, and murder ran rampant as prison officials relied
on the most extreme forms of discipline. Notwithstanding numerous complaints
from prisoners, the horrific conditions at the LSP did not receive widespread condemnation until 1951.

That year, on the morning of February 19, thirty-one white inmates in Camp E
slashed their Achilles tendons as a protest against abusive guards. State penitentiary officials sought to keep the incident out of newspapers, but an unidentified
inmate successfully leaked details of the protest to the *Shreveport Times*.[12] The
story moved with remarkable speed from Shreveport to the nation's capital. On
February 27, the *Washington Post* gave a step-by-step recounting of how inmates

"mutilated their tendons" and then proceeded hopping "about their barracks in a weird snake dance, trailing blood and singing 'Heel-String Boogie.'" Facing great pressure from the U.S. Congress and the larger public, Governor Earl Long appointed a thirty-four-member Citizens Committee to investigate conditions at Angola. Upon the completion of its investigation, the committee recommended the "creation of a comprehensive program of rehabilitation, abolition of corporal punishment, segregation of first time offenders, a merit system for employees, and the appointment of a certified penologist as warden."[13]

Few, if any, African Americans found cause to celebrate, since none of the reforms addressed the racially specific problems facing black inmates. Emblematic of conditions in the larger society, labor arrangements at the LSP remained structured along racial lines, with blacks performing the hardest and dirtiest work. African Americans worked primarily in the fields, on the levees, and as servants in the homes of LSP employees. Sunup-to-sundown work schedules taxed black bodies beyond the point of exhaustion, sending hundreds of African Americans to an early grave. On top of these harsh working conditions, blacks endured segregated and unequal living quarters and eating facilities, inadequate medical care, and abuse from convicts-turned-guardsmen.

Fed up with conditions at Angola, 120 black inmates went on strike on May 20, 1952. "Everybody decided," Roosevelt Charles later remembered, that "we wasn't gonna let nobody out. We locked the doors . . . and all us big stripped boys, we stayed inside." To the yard captain's demand that the men immediately report to work, the inmates responded: "Nobody coming out this morning. We looking for higher wages. . . . We tired of the food we're eating." Convinced that their requests were more than reasonable, the inmates demanded a meeting with Reed Cozart, who was responsible for determining work hours at the penitentiary. Instead of obliging the inmates' request, the yard captain dispatched Warden D. D. Bazer. "Now I wants to know," a condescending Bazer queried, "what is the matter with my old niggas?" To this question, a defiant inmate shot back: "You been shuckin us long enough. We don't wanna see you, we wanna see Mr. Reed Cozart. You been shuckin' us for a long time and we don't wanna hear nothing else you got to say." Meanwhile, LSP officials readied themselves for a violent showdown. Nearly five hours after the inmates began their strike, state troopers and police from Baton Rouge and New Orleans arrived at the penitentiary in dramatic fashion. "It was cars behind cars," Charles later recalled. "They fell out like it was the gang of gangsters in the yard. Machine guns, shot guns, sawed off shot guns, pistols and rifles too." To break the stalemate, troops shot off three tear gas bombs inside the prison. Choking inmates hurriedly vacated their cells while angry guards pounded them with baseball bats and sticks. "You'd thought they was having a ball game out there," one inmate remembered, "some was running and some was hollerin but that still didn't help them. . . . Because they was knockin homeruns on their head, back, just anywhere they could get a lick. . . . [T]hem guards wasn't havin' no mercy."[14]

Not an isolated incident, the Angola strike was part of a much larger political movement. In 1952 alone, twenty-three uprisings broke out in prisons and reformatories across the nation. The worst rebellion occurred at the state penitentiary in Jackson, Michigan, where six thousand prisoners staged what the *New York Times* described as "the worst prison riot in American history."[15]

It is within this context of political upheaval that listeners must engage the political fervor and poetic beauty of Harry Oster's *Angola Prisoners' Blues* and *Prison Worksongs*. On these two recordings, Angola inmates offer vivid and rather critical portraits of prison life at the LSP, as well as the circumstances responsible for their entanglement in the state's penal system. Capturing what the literary critic Houston Baker defines as "the poetry of impulse," they present "black articulateness and lyricism in the very face of violence, catastrophe, rejection, and exploitation."[16] Especially impressive in this regard is the *Angola Prisoners' Blues* collection, which provides a more comprehensive portrait of the inmates' encounter with the criminal justice system than the *Prison Worksongs*.

All of the songs on *Angola Prisoners' Blues* are deeply moving, but none matches the intensity of Robert Williams's "Some Got Six Months." Interweaving the personal with the political, Williams movingly details the many injustices of the judicial system, its adverse impact on the life chances and experiences of black working-class humanity, and the urgent need for penal reform. Four years had passed since Williams began serving a life sentence for a murder he claimed to have committed in self-defense, but his anger at his lack of legal counsel and the judge's unwillingness to consider his spotless record had not subsided. As Williams sings with great emotional affect:

> Some got six months, some got a solid year,
> But me and my buddy, we got lifetime here[17]

Unsatisfied with simply assailing the wrongs of the judicial system, Williams also added his voice to the chorus of inmates condemning the working conditions and disciplinary practices at Angola. The strenuous work routine that led some inmates to regard life at Angola as "worse than slavery" would be taken up in such moving numbers as "Early in the Mornin'," "I Got a Hurtin in My Right Side," and "Angola Bound." On "Early in the Mornin'," a song about sugarcane cutting, Johnny Butler groans, "Don't come to Angola, this is a murderer's home."[18] A similar lament echoes in "Angola Bound," which features the chilling verse, "oh these drivers on this 'Gola, tryna kill poor me."[19]

Striking similarities exist between Angola inmates' complaints about their working conditions and earlier blues numbers detailing the abuses of prison life. Yet, the historical distinctiveness of the *Angola* collection should not be overlooked. Far more explicit in their political commentary than their blues predecessors, the Angola inmates frequently coupled their critiques of daily life at the LSP with strong calls for prison reform. As Robert "Guitar" Welch exhorts in "This Old Hammer":

> All I want is my regular rights
> three hard meals and my rights at night
> three hard meals and my rights at night[20]

Obviously, Welch's call for decent meals and a reduction in working hours repeated demands put forth by the courageous inmates who went on strike in February 1952.[21]

If Welch and his colleagues expected their gripping accounts of Angola's horrific conditions to galvanize the outside world, they were in for a major disappointment. Initially released on Arhoolie Records in 1961, *Angola Prisoners' Blues* and *Prison Worksongs* generated no political response from the larger public. Writers for *Time* and *Downbeat* applauded the inmates for their musical gifts but said very little about the prisoners' riveting narratives on the abuses taking place in the nation's courtrooms and in its leading penal institutions.[22] No mention was made of how inmates' calls for justice corresponded with recent developments in civil rights hotbeds like Greensboro, North Carolina; Jackson, Mississippi; or even nearby New Orleans. Instead, music critics treated the Angola recordings as nothing more than an entertaining piece of folk history.

Fortunately, by the mid-1960s, music was one of many mediums through which African Americans could address the multitude of problems within the U.S. justice system. In the tumultuous decade following the passage of the Civil Rights Act of 1964, inmates at Angola and other state and federal prisons petitioned their wardens and their state legislators for penal reform, organized sit-ins and hunger strikes, and used the judicial arm of the state to challenge previous convictions.[23] Significantly, as the Black Power movement created spaces for unconventional political actors, many ex-offenders raised their voices against the brutal conditions of America's prisons. Writing to the *Louisiana Weekly* in 1972, Jabeel Abdul Abdullah challenged African Americans who had served time to devote more of their resources to transforming the nation's penal institutions:

> It's pathetic that so many ex-convicts could forget the "House of Shock" where they were forced to live under unbelievable conditions. I am told that when some persons experience a horrible act, they just might black it out of their minds. What's your

excuse "Brother convict?" Is it because you will return to the "House of Shock?" Please don't let this fear stop you from joining those who are struggling to bring about a change in the penal system. We, the ex-convicts, parolees and probationers should and must form an organization for our own protection and should support those who are still behind bars. Those who are still being oppressed need and will get our support.[24]

Over the course of the Black Power era, African Americans' commitment to transforming the American judicial and penal systems would be felt not only in the formal political arena but also in the world of arts and letters. As Howard Bruce Franklin explains, "The political movement of the 1960s and 1970s generated an unprecedented surge of prison literature and also created an audience for it."[25] Among the more popular prison narratives were Malcolm X's *The Autobiography of Malcolm X*, George Jackson's *Soledad Brother*, Eldridge Cleaver's *Soul on Ice*, Iceberg Slim's *The Naked Soul of Iceberg Slim*, and Etheridge Knight's "The Warden Said to Me the Other Day" and "Hard Rock Returns to Prison from the Hospital for the Criminally Insane." Several of these literary pieces became sources of inspiration for a younger generation of artists. For instance, on her 2004 classic *Cookie: Anthropological Mixtape*, Meshell Ndegeocello sampled Knight's "Hard Rock Returns to Prison" and "The Warden Said to Me the Other Day."

Similarly, Ndegeocello and other contemporary musicians have drawn inspiration from the music of the Black Power era. As many readers are well aware, the late 1960s and early 1970s witnessed a noticeable expansion in the number of African American musicians assailing the criminal justice system, the repressive policies of state and federal penitentiaries, and the transparent attempts by white conservatives to roll back the gains of the civil rights movement through law and order rhetoric and legislation. Songs like Curtis Mayfield's "(Don't Worry) If There's a Hell Below, We're All Gonna Go" and "Back against the Wall"; The Temptations' "Slave"; Billy Paul's "I'm Just a Prisoner"; and Stevie Wonder's "Living for the City" highlighted the suffering of incarcerated blacks serving sentences for crimes they did not commit, prisoners cut off from loved ones and friends, and ex-felons struggling to reintegrate into their communities and the larger society. The creators of these songs also sought to present narratives that reflected the new challenges of the times. No longer did Jim Crow judges or horrific southern prisons like Angola and Parchman function as metonyms for the nation's racist legal system, for similar abuses in the North commanded the attention of various artists. It bears notice, for example, that Stevie Wonder's choice of geographical setting in his 1973 classic "Living for the City" is New York, where the criminal justice system is on trial. In New York the male protagonist is hustled by a slick northerner, subjected to an unsympathetic jury, and given a ten-year sentence for drug trafficking. Near the end of the song, the combination of the warden's demanding, "come on, get in that cell nigger" with the protagonist's plaintive plea for assistance from a higher power ("God, Lord") sends a clear message: No safe space exists for the black working poor, since the racial inequities and class biases of the legal system transcend geographical boundaries.

Wonder was hardly alone in his concern about the repressive and ever-expanding power of the criminal justice system. If we dig deeper into the cultural history of the Black Power era, we will encounter clamorous critiques of law enforcement officials, newly passed criminal legislation, and racist judges emanating from various corners of the black music world. Indeed, a host of performers pushed their listeners to think critically about the old and new ways in which state-sponsored forms of policing and punishment circumscribed African Americans' civil and human rights. No two artists, however, were more radical in their assertions than Gil Scott-Heron and Archie Shepp.

## Gil Scott-Heron, Archie Shepp, and the Evolution of the Penitentiary Blues in the Black Power Era

An interdisciplinary artist whose influence transcends generational boundaries, Gil Scott-Heron stands out as much for his fiery political lyrics as his judicious fusion of spoken-word poetry, the blues, and jazz. His impressive discography includes political anthems like "The Revolution Will Not Be Televised," "Winter in America," "Johannesburg," and "We Almost Lost Detroit." Never confined to one segment of the black community, Scott-Heron achieved success among mainstream audiences enamored with the soulful sounds of Aretha Franklin, James Brown, and Curtis Mayfield, as well as African Americans who preferred the avant-garde offerings of John Coltrane, Albert Ayler, and Pharaoh Sanders. One reason for Scott-Heron's broad appeal was his focus on an issue many segments of the black population could agree upon: the ubiquity of racist practices within the law enforcement community and their damaging impact on America's most vulnerable citizens.

Especially disconcerting for Scott-Heron were the racist ideologies behind the construction and application of certain legislation proposed by President Richard Nixon. One law in particular, the District of Columbia Court Reform and Criminal Procedure Act of 1970, became the target of Scott-Heron's unrelenting criticism. Commonly referred to as the "no-knock" law, the Criminal Procedure Act granted law enforcement officials the authority to enter a person's residence without announcing their identity or purpose.[26] The political intentions of the law's principal backers, most notably Attorney General John Mitchell, would be taken up by Scott-Heron on "No Knock," a song from his 1972 album *Free Will.* Calling into question Mitchell's public statements that the new law was designed to protect the people, Scott-Heron poses a poignant question for Mitchell and other members of the law enforcement community: "who's gonna protect me from you?" The justification of such a query becomes apparent when the talented musician recalls state-sanctioned attacks on prominent black activists: "No knocked on brother Fred Hampton, bullet holes all over the place. No knocked on my brother Michael Harrison, and jammed a shotgun against his skull."

Two minutes of lyrical fury, "No Knock" serves three political purposes: (1) it alerts African Americans to the dangers of the Criminal Procedure Act and the political designs of the law's primary architects; (2) it illuminates the criminality of the justice system by drawing attention to the assassination of Fred Hampton; and (3) it connects President Nixon's "law-and-order" policies to his larger conservative agenda. Notably, Scott-Heron's cogent analysis of the Criminal Procedure Act anticipates arguments put forth by a later generation of musicians concerned with how certain drug legislation (that is, the Rockefeller Drug Laws) and sentencing policies buttress the racial order.

Time and again, Scott-Heron exposed the racist intent of various criminal laws, as well as the persistence of state-sponsored violence against black, brown, and poor communities throughout the country. The gifted songwriter also exposed the glaring hypocrisy and criminality of conservative politicians in classics like "Bicentennial Blues," "We Beg Your Pardon (Pardon Our Analysis)," and "H2O Gate Blues." Spiro Agnew, Richard Nixon, John Mitchell, Ronald Reagan, and Frank Rizzo—none of them escaped Scott-Heron's fierce condemnation. Nothing was equivocal about Scott-Heron's principal message: Anything but a protector of the people, the state was a criminal enterprise of the worst order. To substantiate his claims, Scott-Heron invoked the names of women and men dehumanized, brutalized, and terrorized by the U.S. justice system: the Wilmington Ten, Gary Tyler, and countless others. Perhaps none of his musical libations for the legal system's many victims proved as gripping as "A Poem for Jose Campos Torres," written in honor of a twenty-three-year-old Vietnam veteran bludgeoned to death by law enforcement officials in Houston, Texas. Identifying Torres as a "common, ancient bloodline brother," Scott-Heron not only mourns another victim of police brutality, but he also communicates the emotional fatigue engendered by producing protest art. He opens with the haunting confession, "I had said that I wasn't gonna' write no more poems like this," and then moves into a vivid description of the repressive activities of the state. "The dogs, rabid and foaming with the energy of their brutish ignorance," he notes, "stride the city streets like robot gunslingers and spread death as night-lamps flash crude reflections from gun butts and police shields." To his credit, Scott-Heron moves beyond the white-black binary in his recounting of the targets of state sanctioned violence.

> In Houston, maybe someone said Mexicans were the new niggers
>
> In LA, maybe someone said Chicanos were the new niggers
>
> In 'Frisco, maybe someone said Asians were the new niggers
>
> Maybe in Philadelphia and North Carolina, they decided they didn't need no new niggers[27]

Scott-Heron's political voice was singular, yet it was also shaped by the larger context of African Americans' collective struggles in both the political and cultural spheres. Heron drew inspiration from the seemingly countless stories of black women and men railroaded by the system, as well as fellow musicians willing to speak truth to power.

The same can be said about another musician whose contribution to the evolution of the penitentiary blues tradition during the Black Power era was immense: the tenor saxophonist Archie Shepp. One year after accepting a position as a professor of music in the Afro-American Studies department at the University of Massachusetts, Shepp created quite a buzz in the jazz world with the release of a record explicit in its support of the prisoners' rights movement. On the heels of the Attica Prison uprising in the fall of 1971, Shepp, a former protégé of the late jazz great John Coltrane and an active participant in the Black Arts movement, recorded a jaw-dropping tribute to the twenty-nine inmates murdered during the five-day Attica clash. "Attica Blues" and "A Blues for George Jackson" establish Shepp's political loyalties with unequivocal clarity. On the latter song, one of Shepp's background singers belts, "Some people think they're within their rights, when on command they take a black man's life."[28]

Everything about Attica Blues, from the artwork to the liner notes, to the music itself, was unabashedly political. Coming out at a time when the legal struggles of noted activists like Angela Davis routinely captured the headlines of the nation's major newspapers, Attica Blues underscored black radicals' growing commitment to building a culture of solidarity around the struggles of political prisoners. This brilliant recording also reflected the community's shifting views on the pivotal role of African American prisoners in the black freedom struggle. On Attica Blues, incarcerated African Americans function not as passive objects in need of political assistance, but as revolutionary agents of change whose political sacrifices and initiatives factor significantly in creating a more liberated existence for all of humanity.

Whereas Harry Oster's Angola collection received very little coverage following its release, *Attica Blues* was discussed at length in several major publications. Celebrating the recording on the pages of the *Rolling Stone*, music critic Stephen Davis praised *Attica Blues* for its artistic brilliance and political audacity. Never one to mince words, Davis demanded that

> the maddest, blackest and most visceral expression of musical rage ever produced be played by every radio station in the country, not only as some token, a sadly minuscule reparation for the massacre of over 40 prisoners and guards during last year's uprising at New York's Attica State Prison at the hands of a brutal state government, but also because this incredible lament is simply a hurricane of rock and roll that must be heard by people and understood for what it is. Archie Shepp, the disciple who has in time become the Master, has brought in the tide with this record.[29]

That a rock critic felt so passionately about an avant-garde jazz recording was hardly surprising given recent developments in mainstream pop. The same year *Attica Blues* hit record stores, the former Beatles legend John Lennon and his wife, Yoko Ono, released the agitprop classic *Some Time in New York City,* which included several songs protesting the murder of Attica inmates in particular and the American criminal justice system in general. Lennon and Ono were not the only music stars interested in Attica.[30] Only a few months before the arrival of *Some Time in New York City,* Bob Dylan released "George Jackson," a poignant tune that propped up Jackson as a real American hero victimized by the legal system.[31]

These developments, along with black America's increased focus on political prisoners, proved quite beneficial for Archie Shepp. Not only did *Attica Blues* boast impressive sales for a jazz record, but it also received positive reviews in several respected music periodicals, most notably *Rolling Stone, Billboard,* and *Downbeat.*[32] The critical tenor of *Attica Blues* struck a responsive chord with many who believed that the U.S. penal system had denied far too many African Americans their civil and human rights. As Lee Bernstein points out, "the cultural meaning of prisons was up for grabs during the period, with sharply contested ideas about their function."[33]

Unfortunately, the political activism and optimism that fueled the music of Shepp, Scott-Heron, and many other artists subsided as the Black Power movement entered its declining years. One of the consequences of the movement's decline was a noticeable decrease in the number of mainstream artists producing politically explicit music geared toward challenging the repressive politics of the state. Narratives about the injustices of the penal system had been a constant in black music since the classic blues era of Bessie Smith and Blind Lemon Jefferson, but from the mid-1970s through the mid-1980s, many artists turned their attention to other matters. Interestingly enough, this political retreat coincided with the expansion of the U.S. carceral state and the penal system's growing role as an "instrument for managing dispossessed and dishonored groups."[34]

## From Black Power to the Age of Mass Incarceration

Today, in a country that promotes itself as a beacon of democracy, more than 2 million people live behind bars while another 7 million are under some form of correctional supervision. To understand this current reality, one must consider the political forces and public policy decisions responsible for the emergence of what sociologist Loïc Wacquant calls a "hyperactive and hypertrophic penal state."[35] Starting with Barry Goldwater's presidential campaign of 1964, the Republican Party increasingly relied on the racially coded language of law and order, which in its cumulative impact and expansive reach continues to take an immense and disproportionate toll on communities of color.

One legislative example is the oft-discussed Rockefeller Drug Laws. Under the guidance of Governor Nelson Rockefeller, the 1972 New York State Assembly enacted legislation that imposed harsh minimum prison terms on first-time drug offenders. Anyone in possession of four ounces of narcotics was given a minimum sentence of fifteen years, the same amount of time meted out for second-degree murder. Five years later, tough mandatory sentencing laws passed in Michigan. There, the state legislature's infamous "650-lifer" law mandated life sentences for drug offenders convicted of selling or delivering more than 650 grams of narcotics. Other states followed suit in the 1980s as President Ronald Reagan's "War on Drugs" campaign came into full swing. To further cement the penal system's punitive turn, the U.S. Congress in 1986 enacted mandatory minimum sentencing laws, ordering judges to deliver fixed sentences to individuals convicted of a crime without considering mitigating factors. A person's sentence was to be based on the type and weight of the drug in their possession and the number of prior convictions. Much to the disdain of its critics, the new law stipulated that judges could not consider the offender's role, motivation, and the likelihood of recidivism in determining his or her sentence. In fact, only by assisting the government in prosecuting a separate case could an offender be eligible for a sentence reduction.

Stringent law-and-order legislation, passed at both the federal and state levels, hiked the country's prison population during the Reagan/Bush presidencies. Unfortunately, the situation would not improve after Democrats captured the White House in 1992. Under the guidance of President Bill Clinton, the U.S. Congress passed the largest crime bill in U.S. history, allocating billions of dollars to prison construction and the hiring of more law enforcement officials. Seemingly comfortable with living in a carceral state, millions accommodated themselves to mass imprisonment, the privatization of the prison industry, and the narrowing of democratic participation brought about by the disfranchisement of felons.

Conversely, a critical mass of African American musicians have spent the past quarter century assailing the rising rates of incarceration within communities of color and the undemocratic consequences of the prison industrial complex. Most notably within the genre of hip-hop, politically engaged artists have called attention to the deleterious effects of America's fixation on crime, highlighted the racist assumptions embedded within crime control rhetoric and institutions, and put forth their own views of retributive and restorative justice.[36] Without question, rap music has been more critical of the excessive policing and criminalization of black and brown bodies than any other musical genre. It has also been the most persistent in challenging the utility of the criminal justice system as well as broadcasting the antidemocratic consequences of a nation that governs through the "technologies, discourses, and metaphors of crime."[37]

## Prophets of Rage: Hip-Hop in the Age of Mass Incarceration

Starting in 1987 and continuing until 1993, an avalanche of rap recordings called attention to inner-city communities victimized by the country's prison industrial complex, the Reagan administration's "War on Drugs," and mass-mediated images that marked black male bodies as inherently and irredeemably criminal.[38] Standout protest anthems included but were not limited to NWA's "Fuck tha Police," Ice Cube's "Endangered Species," KRS-ONE's "Black Cop" and "The Sound of the Police," Sister Souljah's "The Final Solution: Slavery's Back in Effect," and Public Enemy's "Black Steel in the Hour of Chaos." Of the artists mentioned above, none were more impressive, hard-hitting, and influential than Public Enemy. Coming to the public's attention in 1987 with their debut release, *Yo! Bum Rush the Show*, Public Enemy possessed the rare ability to move bodies as well as provoke deep critical reflection. Their incendiary lyrics and provocative covers angered the establishment yet delighted younger African Americans, who loved their political intensity. One reason for their success on the political front was the booming voice of the group's leader, Chuck D, who attacked the repressive policies of the state with unparalleled precision. As the journalist Greg Tate notes:

> For sheer audacity and specificity, Chuck D's enemies list rivals anything produced
> by the black Liberation Army or punk—rallying for retribution against the Feds

for the Panthers' fall ("Party for Your Right to Fight"), slapping murder charges on the FBI and CIA for the assassinations of MLK and Malcolm X ("Louder Than a Bomb"), condoning cop-killing in the name of liberation ("Black Steel in the Hour of Chaos"), assailing copyright law and the court system ("Can We Get a Witness?").[39]

Not that Public Enemy and their peers need legitimacy from the academy, but it is interesting to note how their political content mirrored many perspectives within the field of radical criminology. One of the major tenets of radical criminology, according to Michael J. Lynch and W. Byron Groves, is the belief that the "criminal justice system is not in a position to solve the problems inherent in capitalist production, problems which create criminal behavior and the criminalization of certain forms of behavior." Another important tenet posited by many radical criminologists asserts that "punishing individuals will not affect rates of criminal behavior, nor will it correct the social conditions which caused criminal behavior in the first place."[40] Far from a deterrent, punishment "serves many ideological functions, reinforcing certain beliefs about the content of appropriate behavior patterns."[41]

Three important themes associated with the field of radical criminology pervade the music of many rappers: (1) the criminality of the state and the ruling elite; (2) the necessity of considering the social-structural features of capitalism when discussing crime and punishment; and (3) the inadequacy of any penal reform strategy not predicated on a thoroughgoing transformation of capitalist society. Rejecting the common portrayal of black and brown people as the criminalized other, rappers routinely present the state as the perpetrators of society's worst crimes. On many of their recordings, the idea of the state as a criminal entity finds its strongest expression in lyrics condemning the surveillance and punishment tactics of law enforcement officials. One case in point is KRS-ONE's 1993 classic "Sound of Da Police." Combined with its focus on how mass imprisonment promotes a racial caste system, "Sound of Da Police" puts forth an image of contemporary law enforcement officials as nothing more than modern-day overseers.[42]

Though much has changed in the world of hip-hop since KRS-ONE, N.W.A., and Public Enemy shocked the world with their "fuck the police" anthems, the deep-rooted racism of the criminal justice system remains a popular topic of conversation for many rappers. Infuriated by quotidian forms of police harassment rarely covered in the mainstream press, as well as high-profile police brutality cases such as the NYPD's vicious slaying of Amadou Diallo in 2000, rappers have remained quite critical of what they view as the justice system's open warfare on inner-city black communities.

Especially noteworthy in this regard has been the work of the highly acclaimed underground duo dead prez. As Joy James points out in her article, "F\*\*K the Police (State)," no contemporary group has been more aggressive in exposing the devastating consequences of mass imprisonment for black families and communities. Comprised of the Florida-born emcees stic.man and M-1, dead prez masterfully blends the anticop lyrics of KRS-ONE, Public Enemy, and Ice Cube with a staunch anticapitalist perspective based on the theoretical interventions of Angela Davis, Frantz Fanon, and Walter Rodney. Their critically acclaimed debut, *Let's Get Free*, garnered widespread attention for its razor-sharp analyses of the problem of mass incarceration, the ideological work that prisons perform in a capitalist society, and the need for a social justice movement focused not on prison reform but massive decarceration. On this brilliant recording, old blues narratives of corrupt cops and racist judges coexist with sophisticated dialogues on how the penal system interacts with other institutions of confinement (that is, the public school system and inner-city ghettos) to discipline and control the African American populace. That dead prez did not view the hyperincarceration of African Americans as an unfortunate anomaly in an otherwise perfectly functioning democracy was quite apparent in "Police State," an engrossing song in which incarcerated African Americans are presented not as social deviants trapped in the pathologies of the ghetto but as members of a much larger community oppressed by racism, capitalism, and sexism.

Though cognizant that the repressive powers of the police state reach far and wide, dead prez sympathized most deeply with the plight of black youth and their disproportionate contact with the U.S. justice system. The duo's concern was definitely warranted. On the eve of dead prez's debut release, the number of juveniles held in state prisons was 70 percent greater than in 1985. Even worse, the growth in "under-18 prison admissions" for black males outpaced the increase of white male juveniles by more than 30 percent.[43] Of course, these figures were the by-products of monumental changes in the nation's juvenile crime policies. As Elizabeth S. Scott and Laurence Steinberg note in *Rethinking Juvenile Justice*: "In less than a generation, a justice system that viewed most juvenile law breakers as youngsters whose crimes were the product of immaturity has been transformed into one that holds young offenders to the same standard of criminal accountability it imposes on adults. . . . Through legal reforms in almost every state, youths barely in their teenage years can be tried and punished as adults for a broad range of crimes."[44]

None of these developments escaped the notice of dead prez. In "Behind Enemy Lines," the group spoke of impoverished communities in which "most of the youth never escape the jail fate."[45] Instead of presenting young African Americans as criminal, dead prez insisted that the state had systematically failed black youth. One of their principal targets of criticism was the public school system, which in the duo's opinion played a vital role in criminalizing young blacks. "Man that school shit is a joke," dead prez rages at the beginning of "They School," "the same people who control the school system control the prison system, and the whole social system."[46] Countering narratives that posit formal education as a deterrent to a life of crime, dead prez treats public schools as "temporary holding cells" for future prison populations: "In the hallways, the popo [the police] was always present, search through niggas possessions, looking for dope and weapons. . . . [T]he principal is like a warden."[47] Unfortunately, the scene described by dead prez was far too real for many of their supporters. Far too often, excessive policing is the rule rather than the exception at schools dominated by black and brown children from working-class and working poor communities.

Self-proclaimed as the "Black Panthers of hip-hop," dead prez deemed it their responsibility to use their musical talents to expose the social forces contributing to the rising rates of imprisonment among African Americans, as well as mobilize their communities around the prison abolition movement. As the duo's primary spokesperson, stic explains: "What we are trying to do in those songs and our albums in general is use the commercial, which just means the medium of hip-hop business, to promote revolutionary ideas and revolutionary change and honest expression."[48] A major factor in stic's commitment to putting his artistic talents to political use was his awareness of how the cultural arena has and continues to shape public attitudes on race, crime, deviance, and incarceration.

Today, narratives of crime and punishment permeate every aspect of popular culture, from mainstream radio to the World Wide Web. Tremendously popular series such as *Law and Order, Oz,* and *The Wire* are promoted by their creators and the mass media as realistic portraits of both the ubiquity of criminal activity in contemporary society and the inner workings of the American penal system. More often than not, shows that revolve around issues of crime and control reinforce understandings of criminality, deviance, and punishment that pervade the dominant culture. Moreover, as Aaron Doyle demonstrates in *Arresting Images,* fictionalized and reality-based programming has also influenced criminal justice practice. "The emergence of informal rituals of punishment for the camera" and the "spectacularization of arbitrarily selected day-to-day instances of crime and punishment" provide strong evidence of the dangerous intersections and connections between the mass culture and punishment industries.[49]

Another development worthy of consideration in any discussion of the normalization of racialized mass incarceration is the prisonization of certain cultural styles, language, and sartorial choices. Chiseled black male bodies covered in tattoos and or adorned in sagging, oversized pants signified (for some) the rising influence of the carceral aesthetic during the 1990s and early 2000s. As the cultural geographer Rashad Shabazz notes in his analysis of the emergence of a postindustrial carceral masculinity, "an important element of the symbiosis between prison and Black masculinity is perhaps the most unassuming and yet most pervasive—aesthetics. Characterized by baggie [sic] pants, exposed boxer shorts, large t-shirts, and bandanas, this aesthetic formation, although it emerged from prison, has infused hip-hop culture."[50]

Voyeuristic forays into the world of the criminal justice system offered through the embrace of certain carceral aesthetics, along with the consumption of television programs and cinema centered on the "prison experience," seldom require serious meditation on the lives of those who have been negatively affected by the U.S. justice system. Thus, a deliberate blurring of fantasy and reality in most mass-mediated representations of our nation's punishment industry has rendered many Americans numb to the pain and suffering endured by millions of women, men, and children.

To their credit, many hip-hop artists have sought to disrupt this numbing process by challenging the criminalization of marginalized sectors of U.S. society, pointing out the dangers of the nation's punitive turn, and putting forth alternatives to prevailing regimes of punishment. As many readers are well aware, the hip-hop community has also made its presence felt at the political level. Not all but many of that community's political initiatives have been channeled through the Hip-Hop Summit Action Network (HSAN), founded by Russell Simmons in 2001. The HSAN's stated mission was broad, but foremost on its agenda was repealing New York's notorious Rockefeller Laws. Thanks to public support from Jay-Z, Sean "Puffy" Combs, Erykah Badu, M-1 from dead prez, and other artists, HSAN leaders drew more than sixty thousand people to its first "Anti–Rockefeller Law" rally, held in front of New York's City Hall on June 4, 2003. This spirited rally, along with other public demonstrations, would not be in vain. On March 4, 2009, the New York State Assembly "approved legislation, 96 to 46, that would restore judges' discretion in many lower-level drug-possession crimes that are felonies by eliminating laws that require a prosecutor's consent before judges can send certain felons to drug treatment instead of prison."[51] New York legislators also approved sentence reductions for more than two thousand prisoners convicted under the Rockefeller Laws.

Needless to say, much more work remains to be done at the grassroots level if we are to eliminate mass incarceration as a socially accepted form of control and punishment. Thus, it seems to me that one of the greatest challenges facing contemporary black musicians committed to creating new systems of justice in the United States will be mobilizing their communities in ways that produce substantive dialogue and meaningful change at the public policy level.

## Notes

1. *National Catholic Reporter,* May 16, 2003.
2. Joy James, *Warfare in the American Homeland* (Durham: Duke University Press), 19.
3. See Ted Gioia, *Work Songs* (Durham: Duke University Press, 2006), 200–224; Ted Gioia, *Delta Blues: The Life and Times of the Mississippi Masters Who Revolutionized American Music* (New York: Norton, 2008), 77–110; William Ferris, *Give My Poor Heart Ease: Voices of the Mississippi Blues* (Chapel Hill: University of North Carolina Press, 2009), 77–88; Mark Allan Jackson, "Angola Blues: The Prison Songs of Robert Pete Williams," in *Crossroads: A Southern Culture Annual,* ed. Ted Olson (Macon: Mercer University Press, 2007), 93–103; Ethan Blue, "Beating the System: Prison Music and the Politics of Penal Space," in *Isolation: Places and Practices of Exclusion,* ed. Carolyn Strange and Alison Bashford (London: Routledge, 2003), 56–71; Tricia Rose, *Black Noise: Rap Music and Black Culture in Contemporary America* (Middletown: Wesleyan University Press, 1994), 105–14, 126–29; Joy James, "'F**K the Police (State)': Rape Warfare, and the Leviathan," in *Hip Hop and Philosophy: Rhyme 2 Reason,* ed. Derrick Darby and Tommie Shelby (Chicago: Open Court, 2005), 65–76; Paul Butler, *Let's Get Free: A Hip-Hop Theory of Justice* (New York: New Press, 2009), 123–46.
4. Leon Litwack, *Trouble in Mind: Black Southerners in the Age of Jim Crow* (New York: Vintage, 1999), 260.
5. See G. Rashad Shabazz Sanders, "'They Imprison the Whole Population': U.S. and South African Prison Literature and the Emergence of Symbiotic Carcerality" (Ph.D. diss., University of California, Santa Cruz, 2008).
6. The Roots, "Criminal," *Rising Down,* Def Jam, 2008.
7. Andrea Queeley, "Hip Hop and the Aesthetics of Criminalization," *Souls: A Critical Journal of Black Politics, Culture, and Society* 5 (2003): 10.
8. Bessie Smith, "Jail House Blues," *The Complete Recordings, Vol. 1,* Sony Music, 1991; Texas Alexander, "Levee Camp Moan Blues," *Texas Alexander, Vol. 1,* Document Records, 1991; Leroy Carr, "Prison Bound," *Leroy Carr Vol. 1 (1928–1929),* Document Records, 1992; Blind Lemon Jefferson, "Penitentiary Blues," *Blind Lemon Jefferson Vol. 3,* Document Records, 2005.
9. John Lee Hooker, "I'm Prison Bound," *The Country Blues of John Lee Hooker,* Fantasy Records, 1991; Lightnin Hopkins, "Prison Blues Come Down on Me," *Country Blues,* Rykodisc, 1991.
10. Art Neville, Aaron Neville, Charles Neville, Cyril Neville, and David Ritz, *The Brothers: An Autobiography* (Cambridge: Da Capo, 2001)145.
11. Mark T. Carleton, *Politics and Punishment: The History of the Louisiana Penal System* (Baton Rouge: Louisiana State University Press, 1971), 139.
12. *Washington Post,* February 27, 1951.
13. Carleton, *Politics and Punishment,* 155.
14. Roosevelt Charles, "Strike at Camp I," *Angola Prisoners' Blues,* Arhoolie, 1996.

15. *New York Times,* January 25, 1953, May 30, 1954.

16. Houston Baker, *I Don't Hate the South: Reflections on Faulkner, Family and the South* (New York: Oxford University Press, 2007), 76.

17. Robert Williams, "Some Got Six Months," *Angola Prisoners' Blues.*

18. Johnny Butler, "Early in the Mornin'," *Prison Worksongs.*

19. A Capella Group, "Angola Bound," *Angola Prisoners' Blues.*

20. Robert "Guitar" Welch, "This Old Hammer," *Prison Worksongs.*

21. It should be noted that the inmates' strike in 1952 failed to secure better conditions.

22. *Downbeat,* January 19, 1961.

23. See *New York Times,* April 1, 1966; *Louisiana Weekly,* August 12, 1967.

24. *Louisiana Weekly,* March 4, 1972.

25. Howard Bruce Franklin, *Prison Writing in 20th-Century America* (New York: Penguin, 1998), 12.

26. See "No Knock" Search and Seizure and the District of Columbia Crime Act: A Constitutional Analysis," *Journal of Criminal Law, Criminology, and Police Science* 62, no. 3 (September 1971): 350–62.

27. Gil Scott Heron, "Jose Campos Torres," *The Mind of Gil Scott-Heron,* Arista, 1978.

28. Archie Shepp, "Attica Blues," *Attica Blues,* Impulse, 1972.

29. *Rolling Stone,* August 17, 1972.

30. John Lennon and Yoko Ono, *Sometime in New York City,* EMI, 1972.

31. Bob Dylan, "George Jackson," Ram's Hour Music, 1971.

32. *Rolling Stone,* August 17, 1972; *Billboard,* May 20, 1972; Fred Ho, "The Damned Don't Cry: The Life and Music of Calvin Massey," in *Wicked Theory, Naked Practice: A Fred Ho Reader,* ed. Diane C. Fujino (Minneapolis: University of Minnesota Press, 2009), 141.

33. Lee Bernstein, *America Is the Prison: Art and Politics in Prison in the 1970s* (Chapel Hill: University of North Carolina Press, 2010), 5.

34. Loïc Wacquant, "Deadly Symbiosis: When Ghetto and Prison Meet and Mesh," *Punishment and Society* 3, no. 1 (2001): 95.

35. Loïc Wacquant, *Prisons of Poverty* (Minneapolis: University of Minnesota Press, 2009), 159.

36. Erin I. Kelly, "Criminal-Justice Minded: Retribution, Punishment, and Authority," in *Hip Hop and Philosophy: Rhyme 2 Reason,* ed. Derrick Darby and Tommie Shelby (Chicago: Open Court, 2005), 183–92.

37. Jonathon Simon, *Governing through Crime: How the War on Crime Transformed American Democracy* (New York: Oxford University Press, 2007), 4.

38. As mentioned earlier, many critics, including some within the rap community, would argue that hip-hop has also contributed to the "archive" of images that portray African Americans as inherently and irredeemably criminal.

39. Greg Tate, *Flyboy in the Buttermilk: Essays on Contemporary America, An Eye-Opening Look at Race, Politics, Literature, and Music* (New York: Fireside, 1992), 125.

40. Lynch and Groves, *A Primer in Radical Criminology* (New York: Harrow and Heston, 1989), 99.

41. Ibid., 117.

42. KRS-ONE, "Sound of the Police," *Return of the Boom Bap,* Jive Records, 1993.

43. *Juvenile Offenders and Victims: National Report Service Bulletin,* July 2004.

44. Elizabeth S. Scott and Laurence Steinberg, *Rethinking Juvenile Justice* (Cambridge: Harvard University Press, 2008), 4.

45. dead prez, "Behind Enemy Lines," *Let's Get Free,* Loud Records, 2000.

46. dead prez, "They School," *Let's Get Free,* Loud Records, 2000.

47. Ibid.

48. Quoted in Ethan Blue, "Beating the System," 64.

49. Aaron Doyle, *Arresting Images: Crime and Policing in Front of the Television Camera* (Toronto: University of Toronto Press, 2003), 58.

50. Shabazz, "They Imprison the Whole Population," 67.

51. *New York Times,* March 4, 2009.

# Law and Dis/Order

## *The Banefully Alluring Arts of the Carceral Imaginary*

MARLON B. ROSS

I want to start with a self-humbling confession. I love the TV series *Law and Order*. I used to love the HBO series *Oz*. Even more insidious than these shows is the recent reality TV show *Inside American Jail* (Spike TV). Focused ostensibly on actual inmates behind bars, this new show is by the same team that gave us the reality show *Cops,* which captures police officers in various cities making arrests of suspects (faces often covered). These suspects are presumed guilty upon the filmed arrest, despite the disclaimer asserting the contrary at each episode's end. These shows are so exploitative of the punishment imagination that even I, a confessed TV junkie, cannot stomach them. Through the mediation of such imagery of "cops and robbers," "criminality" and its "enforcement" become at once monstrously exotic and familiarly banal. Together these shows eviscerate the viewer's capacity to imagine beyond or outside these highly scripted scenarios of law and disorder, crime and punishment. Even those of us "on the outside" with close kin or other personal ties to the incarcerated can find it hard to resist the seductive allure of watching the details of life "on the inside." In this shadowy space we innocuously label "behind bars," the violence that structures law enforcement at every level can play out its brutal logic without much check or recourse from the public.

I could easily try to rationalize my passion for the better-scripted carceral narratives based on aesthetic criteria—arguing that they are unusually well-written shows with fascinating developments of plot, character, setting, cinematography, and skilled acting performance—but that would be dishonest. Besides, I don't believe in the autonomous power of the aesthetic to determine what attracts and keeps my attention. As if being thrilled by these shows were not sin enough, I must also admit that I know while watching them that any and every episode may be terribly baneful to the cultural imagination, to my imaginative health, and indeed to my engagement with the larger national and global culture being mediated by such shows. I fear that, as a result of viewing these shows, any curiosity I might have about the welfare of actual prisoners might be sensationally satiated through my vicarious peek behind the fictive prison walls. I fear moreover that as a fan, any rage I may feel about the sorry state of incarceration in the United States has been diverted from, or at least has not been constructively channeled toward, productive action.

What kind of ideological work is this carceral imaginary doing? Why are these images of incarceration so powerful and so seductive? Why do they so disarm the intellect's resistance to their basic premises: that crime can be adjudicated by an extreme binary of guilt versus innocence; that the only outcome for the so-called guilty is state-inflicted punishment; that an appropriate punishment must be isolation and erasure from "outside" society; that the violence enforced and administered within prison fits the crime perpetrated on "innocent" society by the guilty; and that the hyperbolic and racialized fear that fuels a desire for law and order serves to protect the suburbanized white middle class from the consequences of crime and punishment? As is often noted, the effects of this nationalization (and naturalization) of incarceration are both obvious and subtle. They range from our complicit acceptance of "domestic" torture as a strategy for "domestic security" to the immeasurable psychological, emotional, and economic impacts of a securitized way of life, in which every moment of our "free" existence on the "outside" is monitored or videotaped. Whether on the street, in department stores, going through traffic lights in our cars, in airports, or in our homes—we are subject to a privatized security industry often subsidiary to the same companies marketing incarceration services for those "behind bars."[1] In other words, we on the "outside" live a much more innocuous, attenuated version of the brutal regime honed against those on the "inside."[2]

The televisual exhibition of the "inside" of incarceration is not a singular enterprise, for the business of exposing incarceration is highly profitable for movies, bookstores, newspapers, magazines, radio stations, popular music (especially hip-hop and country western), and the Internet—all of which are currently inundated with carceral narratives (fictional, documentary, and autobiographical stories about prisoners' lives). But the mass popularity of such arts and media seems not to reflect or encourage a reciprocal collective concern for the condition of actual prisoners.[3] I wonder, then, whether the easy availability of such fictional and "documentary" representations tends to assuage our individual anxieties over the expansion of incarceration while also numbing our collective will to protest either this exploding carceral nation or its far-flung deleterious effects. Ironically, as the population of prisoners has mushroomed and the number of prisons has proliferated across the U.S. landscape, prisons and prisoners have become more segregated, in fact invisible, to most of us not *blatantly* affected by the incarceration explosion. We might thus ask whether such media saturation masks how carceral segregation dictates social distance and interpersonal absence between prisoners and nonprisoners? This topical media saturation can also lead us to compartmentalize the actual impact of living ourselves in an increasingly policed state. We can be led to believe that our everyday lives "outside" of prison are not directly affected by the experiences of the imprisoned, except perhaps only insofar as we feel ourselves and our property to be endangered or our taxes to be unfairly eaten up by housing and feeding those "inside."

To the contrary, the incarceration nation has a *direct* impact on the quality of culture—indeed, the quality of life—for all of us. The imaginative contact with the imprisoned enabled by carceral media may come at another kind of cost—difficult to track or calculate—not only to social action but also to the personal and collective health of the national and global cultural imaginary.

The proliferation of carceral narratives may at least have the benefit of acknowledging, however problematically, the *fact* of incarceration as a national reality at a time when the carceral state seeks to block the imprisoned and their cultural experiences and expressions both from our body politic and our social conscience. Simultaneously, though, the mass mediation of imprisonment serves, however unintentionally, as a placebo for our actual human interaction with or obligations to the incarcerated. In this sense, any carceral representation must necessarily sugarcoat the realities of imprisonment because representation cannot place us inside the brutally monotonous experience of being encaged day in and day out, sometimes for years on end. Beholden primarily to the profit motive of mass entertainment, mass-media carceral narratives rarely display or enfold activist intentions as radical as prison abolition, or for that matter, display intentions even as moderate as prison reform.

Exploiting violent images of suffering to motivate the body politic toward a liberatory cause has a long history. Antislavery abolitionists come immediately to mind with their demands to see the welts on the backs of former slaves in order to authenticate the depth of slavery's brutality. But then as now, spectators are vulnerable to developing a form of visual overload, which desensitizes us to the call of mass imagery on behalf of the violently oppressed. Exploring the impact of what I'm calling carceral segregation on the efforts of nonprisoners to understand and intervene in the punishment establishment, Michelle Brown makes a similar point: "To conceive of ourselves as penal spectators asks us to consider a different set of aspects about the practice of punishment. First, it foregrounds the fact that for those of us without direct connections to formal institutions of punishment, a kind of experiential distance defines our relationship to its practice—its infliction of pain."[4] It is notoriously difficult to articulate the feeling of pain (as medical practitioners have long understood as patients and caregivers must resort to metaphorical formulae like "sharp," "dull," "throbbing," etc.), and all the more impossible to represent it with any degree of subtlety. It is thus no surprise that representations of imprisonment—whether mass media, popular, or elite, whether produced by nonprisoners or by prisoners—tend to focus on the most *sensational* dimensions of prison life: stories of aggression, despair, violence, social upheaval, and same-gender rape when negatively framed; stories of dramatic personal growth and transformation when framed positively.

Why are we so captivated by media constructions of captivity, crime and punishment, law and dis/order, even when we know the errancy of such constructions, even when we have good reason to suspect the cultural harm they do? This is not to suggest that I intend a determinist or economistic inquiry, for I do not see representations of imprisonment as either unidirectional or one-dimensional. "The cultural imaginary is not subject to simple cause and effect models," notes Michelle Brown; it is "a nebulous, playful arena where vicarious identities and moralities are picked up and later discarded" (57). That there is identifiable harm in mass-media representations does not equate with the notion that such representations can *only* produce social injury. As Brown continues, despite its nebulous play, the "cultural imaginary" reproduces "consistent patterns and attractions to particular disguises." Regarding punishment, "these processes render representations of imprisonment a particularly seductive site for the production of cultural scripts and classifications on the part of the spectator" (57). We might ask a deeper question here: Why we are so attracted to such imaginary representations in a body politic that has thus far accepted—and in many ways promoted—the inhumane warehousing of increasing numbers of actual prisoners farther and farther out of ken from "our" everyday lives.[5] The increasing fascination with media representations of prison life seems to mirror not only the increase in prisoners, but also the increasing separation between "them" and "us." If cultural media allow us, in some small way, to imagine ourselves behind prison walls, do they simultaneously encourage us to estrange ourselves further from actual prisoners?

The role of dominant media in sustaining a national culture of incarceration is only half the question. The other half, the impact of imprisonment and of prisoners on culture, particularly creative culture, is even less audible in the national discourse. Culture usually enters discussions of imprisonment in one of two ways, both based in a notion of culture as an observable pattern of social attitudes, behavior, and structures; both positioning the prisoner as a social *object* within that pattern. In his helpful essay "Concepts of Culture in the Sociology of

Punishment," David Garland delineates the use of culture in prison scholarship in quite a different way, proclaiming "the new prominence of the concept of culture in contemporary studies of punishment."[6] Garland departs from the Marxist and Foucault-inspired scholarship of the 1970s and 1980s in which culture tended to be neglected as scholars sought "to identify the social determinants and functions of penal institutions" (420). Garland goes on to schematize two ways in which culture is embraced in recent punishment literature: "In the first sense, the analysis asserts the importance of distinctly cultural factors as a causal force in shaping penal institutions (*culture* as opposed to *not culture*) while in the second, the analysis points to different cultures (*this* culture as opposed to *that* culture) and seeks to show that contrasting cultures produce different patterns of penality" (422). Significantly, neither of Garland's definitions of culture emphasizes prisoners as producers, creators, and interpreters of culture; neither indicates how their experiences have an impact on or within culture in its largest sense.

My interest in this essay concerns just this: the ineradicable will to create culture by those so ostracized in U.S. society that their cultural agency has often been disappeared, and along with it, consciousness of the palpable impact of this cultural creativity across the carceral divide. Mass-media representation gives us one flawed vantage point toward understanding this relation between creative culture and the carceral nation; another just as flawed vantage point seeks to hear the voices and visions of the imprisoned delivered from their own perspective. We enter such a double inquiry, however, with a caution: the voices of the imprisoned are themselves necessarily conditioned by mass-media structures and conventional artistic forms as well as by the logic of state "corrections," and thus no voice can be heard outside the very media—fiction, memoir, feature film, documentary film, photography, journalistic interview, musical composition, philosophical meditation, protest manifesto, social critique—already operative as arbiters of cultural experience and expression. How else can the imprisoned hope to be heard either among themselves or on the other side of the fortress walls except through the cultural forms and structures already carved out for the rest of us? This does not mean, of course, that such cultural forms and structures of expression cannot be altered, sometimes radically, by the conditions and occasions of their carceral rearticulation. Our need to double the inquiry—mass mediation from the outside versus prison culture from the inside—results from a belief in a carceral divide between us and them, acknowledging the literal barriers of the prison fortress and all other apparatuses erected to prevent communication, intellection, interaction, and touch across that divide. I want to suggest that belief in this divide, though materially as undeniable as the physical and social barriers of Jim Crow segregation (and serving a similar socioeconomic purpose), is largely erroneous where creative culture is concerned. When the object is culture, the will to create communicable expressions in the interest either of an oppressed group or of our common humanity, the carceral divide is a figment of our own imaginings. In this sense, it does not exist, or it exists at best and worst as fantasy.

## Mass-Mediated Incarceration

Mass-carceral narratives necessarily tend to *mis*represent incarceration as a pathology of the imprisoned, which supposedly works to normalize and thus exculpate the rest of us. The nature of cultural media partly explains such misrepresentation, but so does incarceration as an instrument of state "corrections." Mass media assumes its audience as nonprisoners, not ex-convicts, and certainly not the kind of people who commit ostensible crimes or who suffer the indignities of arrest and imprisonment. The sole reason for airing such narratives is to expose the "innocent" public—shut off in the privatized comforts of a "family room" or the darkness of a movie house—to the tainted exotica hidden behind impenetrable prison walls. This exposure produces the ironic fact of hiding the criminalized class so that our "access" to them can be managed and monitored through the voyeuristic and vicarious distance of mass-media reenactments. Loïc Wacquant identifies this collective psychodrama, labeling it "penal pornography," a peculiarly U.S. phenomenon that gets globalized with the emergence of neoliberal economics:

> First, the rampant gesticulation over law and order is conceived and carried out not so much for its own sake as *for the express purpose of being exhibited and seen*, scrutinized, ogled: the absolute priority is to put on spectacle, in the literal sense of the term. . . . This explains why, much like the staged carnal entanglements that fill pornographic movies, they are extraordinarily repetitive, mechanical, uniform, and therefore eminently *predictable*.[7]

Although mass-media carceral narratives do not result from the kind of orchestration identified by Wacquant in relation to the discourse of political elites, they imperfectly exhibit ritualistic, predictable, pornographic characteristics of scapegoating spectacle. Even if mass-media claims to report realistically the experiences of the imprisoned on behalf of the imprisoned, as a journalistic exposé or a show like Oz endeavors or pretends to do, the fact that the audience is presumed to be the nonimprisoned and the never-to-be-imprisoned shapes the kind of "reality" that can be portrayed. The scripts of prison dramas inevitably—loaded with a history of class, gender, and racial biases—insist on alien insiders (the imprisoned abnormal) versus familiar outsiders (we the normal). Thus is preserved a dichotomy between proven predators (them) and potential victims (us) across the carceral divide.

In the classic form of prison narratives, this carceral divide is a doubling dichotomy in that it also predicates within the prison cage a Manichean rivalry between routine predators (inmates by choice and thus no kin to us) versus exceptional victims (criminals by untoward circumstance and thus distant cousins to us). A touchstone of the inmate by choice is Truman Capote's characterization of the sociopath Perry Smith in the 1966 "nonfiction novel" *In Cold Blood,* and the 1967 Richard Brooks film of the same title (reprised in Bennett Miller's 2005 biopic *Capote*). The touchstone for the circumstantial inmate is the 1965 *Autobiography of Malcolm X,* coauthored with Alex Haley, and Spike Lee's 1992 film adaptation, *Malcolm X.* The predictable point of view of carceral narratives (stories about law and order, cops and criminals, guards and inmates), on those rare occasions when they do take a prisoner's frame of reference, is that of the circumstantial inmate, the one who, in his heart of hearts, suffers remorse and regret for breaking society's laws—the coerced criminal whose hardened chest buries a heart of gold. As such, even the most radical of these narratives tend to take the form of conversion narratives, whereby the inmate's transformation proffers hope for society's reform. These circumstantial inmates are our eyes within the cage, enabling us to imagine ourselves, in a moment of psychological or economic desperation, performing some deed that would land us in a cell alongside some outright villain trapped by choice. The inside/outside logic of the carceral divide thus echoes as a similar inside/outside narrative device in representing the prison as a bifurcated physical, social, and psychic space. The motives of a criminal/inmate by choice are indeterminate and perhaps indeterminable because we (outsiders) are not able to enter his mind, defined in popular imagery as sociopathology. The horror of Capote's Perry Smith, for example, is not only the monstrosity of his crimes but also the impossibility of our ever understanding them. Despite detailing Smith's life and experience (ostensibly from the inmate's point of view), Capote's investigation turns out to "expose" the inmate's lack of interiority.

If the inmate by choice is characterized by a lack of interiority, the inmate by circumstance exhibits an interiority accessible to outsiders which facilitates exchange, sharing, and a simulacrum of reciprocity across the segregating carceral divide. The writers of *Oz* very cleverly follow this script by providing a single narrator—a native informant—in the person of Augustus Hill, who is the only character in the vast cast with an interior life shared directly with the audience beyond the screen (as extradiegetic address, Greek chorus–like). Paralyzed from the waist down, Hill is not coincidentally in a wheelchair to maximize the burden of his circumstantial status as both perpetrator (as drug dealer) and victim (as drug user) introduced into the trade as a teenager by his godfather. When we get Hill's backstory, we realize just how much like us he might have been. In a narrative retrospect revealed in the show's second episode, we see the SWAT team burst into his apartment while Hill is making love to his wife (in a way that a paraplegic could never do); in the ensuing fray, he shoots and kills a SWAT team member and is thrown off the building in retaliation—the source of his paraplegia. It is also no coincidence that Hill is a slightly built African American man-boy, for his diminutive black physique channels what society has unfairly done to him in regard to his race, class, and gender. But at the same time, his physique channels that for which he cannot be forgiven: "doing back" to society (at least ostensibly) what society has done to him, which amounts to overcompensating for his racial predicament—a formula constitutive of liberal ideology.[8] (Circumstantial criminals are represented as preying not only upon us, largely unwittingly, but also upon themselves, either through self-destruction or remorseful self-regard.) Given the disproportion of people of color and the poor within U.S. prisons, as well as the ways in which alienated others are already racially objectified through the exoticizing voyeurism in U.S. discourse, it is no surprise that the media exploits carceral narratives to hype and intensify such objectification, while exoticizing the imprisoned as stigmatized others.[9]

Whatever small sympathy is garnered on behalf of an inmate-narrator like Hill is readily bartered at the expense of the larger prison population. Hill stands out not only as narrator with a conscience as well as the vocabulary of interiority to articulate it, but also as one in need of the camaraderie of other circumstantial inmates. The morally principled black Muslim leader Kareem Said (clearly modeled on Malcolm X) and the white old-timers Bob Rebadow and Agamemnon Busmalis meet this need. Each is incapable of understanding the new breed of hardened criminals, whose hardness is captured in the racial divisions maintained by the violence of the Aryan Brotherhood versus the Homeboys.[10] Such relatively "innocent" characters are rendered exceptional within the prison and thus distant cousins to spectators by a vast roster of irredeemable others: the white supremacists led by Vernon Schillinger (the chilling name says it all), the Homeboys led by Simon Adebisi (whose deviance is heightened by his Nigerian English accent and his penchant for raping new young prisoners), and a bevy of other ethnically based gangs and occasional evil loners.

Mass-carceral narratives tend to alienate outside spectators from the incarcerated mass, ironically by singling out such liminal figures as Hill, whose exceptional line-walking between inside and outside serves to cast the remainder of the prisoners as variously expendable. Incarceration is intended to depersonalize the prisoner's existence, to rob prisoners of their individuality, not least because the American rights of citizenship are so indebted to the myth of fierce individuality. Like *Oz*'s Augustus Hill, many liberal or reformist carceral narratives seek redress for such depersonalization by spotlighting an exceptional individual, in a way similar to slave narratives and Jim Crow autobiographies. This practice can underplay the brutal modes used to enforce institutional uniformity as an efficient and cost-effective means of social control.[11] The interplay between the impersonal criminal by choice versus the highly personalized inmate by circumstance is an attempt to embody this problem of the state's brutality against human subjectivity without giving up on individualism as the basis for extending liberal democratic citizenship. In *Oz*, racial division—Aryans versus Homeboys as the polar extremes enclosing other intermediating racial groups—emblematizes the threat of mass identity, and its attending seduction for those confronted with demands for institutional conformity.

In an astute and largely laudatory analysis of *Oz*, Brian Jarvis captures the show's uniqueness in trying to forestall the typical reliance on a romanticized script of the exceptional heroic outlaw. "Mainstream prison film is preoccupied with life on one side of the bars in its romanticized depiction of the prisoner-hero," he notes, "but *Oz* tracked a network of relations, of shifting alliances and antagonisms between inmates and prison staff over seven series."[12] Although I agree with Jarvis that the show fought hard not to romanticize prison life and exploited racialized factions to that end, the show is even a better barometer of mass media's difficulty at escaping one of two predominant approaches, either the romanticized hero-outlaw (exceptional individualism) or the criminally monstrous alien (the indeterminate mass). Against the backdrop of racialized factions whose leaders lack interiority, the audience is kept hopeful by figures like Hill, whose interiority is a hedge against the disorderly conformity represented in these mass identity groups. In the end, however, the show is overwhelmed by its own determination to exhibit the brutality of imprisonment through the often unmotivated savagery of the mass prisoners (and guards, to a lesser degree)—a brutality focused most on prisoners' violence against one another, rather than the punishment system as an unrelenting scene of state-sponsored violence. That even our prisoner-narrator Hill cannot be protected from such violence is indicated by his sacrificial death in the final season, stabbed while interceding on behalf of his godfather, the very man who had introduced him to criminality in the first place. Revealingly, in death, Hill is able to feel his legs even as he loses consciousness—a blackout of the narrative interior that puns on the relation between Hill's power to communicate with us versus his paraplegia as an emblem for his incapacity as a criminalized victim of circumstance.

*Oz* is among the most searching of the lot of mass-carceral narratives, but even it cannot manage to overcome the inside/outside logic that conventionally structures spectatorship across the carceral divide, and the show's devolution into a maelstrom of unpredictable violence (anyone can be killed off at any moment in the final episodes) pays homage to the fear of criminality that justifies the carceral nation while simultaneously diminishing any sense that cultural creativity among the imprisoned can survive such inchoately self-inflicted violence.[13]

As is so often the case with narrative sympathy—as with charity in general—the benefit accrues to the ones who extend it, not to the persons who are made its object—as August Hill's death poignantly reminds us. As the narrative's—and our—inside spokesman, Hill is thus the perfect liberal vehicle. He is also a liminal perpetrator/victim through whom we can emote our psychic and moral ambivalence. A key element of state "corrections" is to punish criminals by ostracizing "them" from "us," and yet we demand the right to experience guilt and pity for the rightful harshness of that punishment. For doesn't the penalty always fit the crime? James Baldwin repeatedly refers to the American psychology that demands to be held uncorrupted by a corrupt national history as "a state of innocence":

> I do not think, for example, that it is too much to suggest that the American vision of the world—which allows so little reality, generally speaking, for any of the darker forces in human life, which tends until today to paint moral issues in glaring black and white—owes a great deal to the battle waged by Americans to maintain between themselves and black men a human separation which could not be bridged. It is only now beginning to be borne in on us—very faintly, it must be admitted, very slowly, and very much against our will—that this vision of the world is dangerously inaccurate, and perfectly useless. For it protects our moral high-mindedness at the terrible expense of weakening our grasp of reality. People who shut their eyes to reality simply invite their own destruction, and anyone who insists on remaining in a state of innocence long after that innocence is dead turns himself into a monster.[14]

Baldwin's statement helps to clarify how the United States administers crime and punishment, law and order through a carceral complex that seeks to quarantine mass numbers of supposedly "corrupt" human beings, while protecting a largely white, middle-class identity as incorruptibly innocent.[15] Mass-media carceral narratives are devoted to this mission of stoking the myth of our national innocence ("innocent until proven guilty," indeed), even as our governance, jurisprudence, economy, and system of education are committed to the highest levels of incarceration recorded in human history. If those behind prison walls can be guilty alone of our vast national crimes, then we on the outside remain protected from our own accountability and thus our own collusive guilt. We are rarely pressed to ask in our mass national discourse why criminality is both so feared and so stoked in the American middle-class psyche, overseen by a sophisticatedly violent mass media, or why violence—in actuality and in the media—is so endemic to the American way of life.[16] In those crisis moments when violence is addressed as potentially endemic to the national psyche—usually as the result of some seemingly random mass school shooting of suburban or small-town (white) teachers and students by a fellow student—such violence is ultimately explained away through the tragic individual pathology of the white perpetrator (a recourse not allowed for African American youth who murder). Only rarely is such violence connected to the kind of astute analysis offered by Baldwin's critique of the American "state of innocence" that must reverberate in monstrous violence, much less connected to the logic of an incarceration nation.[17] The systematic brutalities of the U.S. mode of incarceration are not considered acts of violence because they are promoted by the state in the name of a victimized—and always innocent—public.

## Creating Culture across the Carceral Divide

If the deep structure of mass media and the form of the carceral narrative serve to protect "our" false innocence by preserving the false divide between "us" and "them," it is even more the case that the nature of U.S. state "corrections" as an institution insists on this divide as ethically just and inescapably natural. Just as enslaved humans had to be conceptualized and treated legally as domesticated animals ("chattel" deriving from the same root as "cattle"), so must the incarcerated be conceptualized in a similar way to justify their violent encagement. One wonders to what extent prison authorities have adopted their "corrections" technology not only from the administration of a slave economy but also from the herding and management of livestock in the way they cage, feed, taser, strip and probe to expose private parts, expose their toilet "business," and let prisoners "out into the yard."[18] Because the incarcerated are technically not citizens, hardly even resident aliens, virtually any treatment can be justified.

This process of stripping the rights of citizenship and residency is intended to signal and effect the state's authority to treat the prisoner as virtual animal, a creature without access to identifiable human culture. The prisoners' bodies are denuded to remind them that they have no private parts or properties, no private lives to protect—denuded for our common safety on the outside, where privacy correlates with an individual's right to cultural agency. This citizenship-stripping process, based in a lack of access to privacy, ripples out to other fundamental rights such as freedom of speech. In effect, the process seeks to disappear the imprisoned from "civil" discourse where the public arbitrates the collective fate of the imprisoned. The ultimate result is that the voices of the imprisoned tend to be heard—usually indirectly—only in moments of violent crisis within prisons, such as the sporadic prison uprisings that characterize the modern history of U.S. incarceration. Lack of access to "free speech" reverberates as the silence of the imprisoned exists amid the loud din of mass-media noises purporting to inform outsiders of life behind prison walls.

William Bennett Turner, for instance, relates the experience of Dannie Martin, an inmate in the federal prison at Lompoc who began to write a popular column on prison life—as a sort of foreign correspondent in the belly of the nation—for the *San Francisco Chronicle*. After Martin took on "the gulag mentality" of prison administration in an article of that name, he was placed in administrative isolation and then transferred to an out-of-state prison in an attempt to gag him. Turner points out that Bureau of Prisons rules—not always enforced—prohibit "a prisoner from conducting 'a business,' from receiving compensation 'for correspondence with the news media,' and from acting as 'a reporter' or publishing under a byline." When the newspaper and Martin joined in filing suit against the warden, the bureau released Martin on parole and requested that the appeals court dismiss the appeal.[19]

As we have seen across the twentieth century and into the twenty-first, many of the best cultural critiques of the carceral regime have come from the imprisoned themselves, in their own words: from Robert E. Burns's sensational 1932 *I Am a Fugitive from a Georgia Chain Gang!* to Mumia Abu-Jamal's 1995 memoir *Live from Death Row*, to cite only two of the most celebrated instances of this crucial kind of cultural expression.[20] Written from the perspective of "insiders" to expose the injustices of the carceral regime to the outside world, these narratives thus reproduce the carceral divide that the books themselves actually traverse. This long tradition constitutes a significant site of U.S. literary expression that routinely goes undertaught and underexamined as such. Despite its importance, or perhaps because of it, the right of prisoners to express and inform the public through their own words is not guaranteed. Moreover, their right to profit—monetarily as well as in the accrual of cultural capital—is closely surveilled (literally) when not strictly proscribed.

Ostracized from the public arena and also stripped of private rights, the imprisoned are forced into a cultural limbo, ostensibly not worthy of access to the public sphere, where culture is usually seen as appropriately shared and consumed. They are simultaneously and ostensibly barred from those private resources where cultural creativity is usually seen as being produced. How fortunate for us all that cultural productivity cannot be so easily squelched, even under the most vicious conditions. A conservative federal Supreme Court recently ruled California's prison industry[21] to be a "toxic" environment creating "unnecessary death and suffering." But even there, the imprisoned have managed to preserve their need for the right to cultural creativity.

## The Prison Vanguard

Given the extent to which African Americans have been targeted for punishment historically and for incarceration more recently, it is not surprising that within African American communities and black studies especially, there has been a long-held concern, rarely heard beyond these spheres, for the unbreakable cultural bonds that exist across seemingly impenetrable prison walls. The voices, philosophies, stories, tunes, and visions of prisoners are too often the ordinary stuff of African American life. African American literature, music, philosophy, fashion, visual art, grassroots politics, and social criticism are inseparable from the culture produced by, about, and for the imprisoned.[22] In this context, it makes sense that Point 8 of the Black Panther Platform and Program demands: "We want freedom for all black men held in federal, state, county and city prisons and jails"[23]—invariably for my students the most controversial of the ten points and the one they find most difficult to defend. In fact, the Panthers program as a whole is organized around the falsity of racialized punishment, from the starting point of learning the law to patrolling the patrollers in African American neighborhoods to the end point of fomenting revolutionary action once imprisoned (because eventual imprisonment is assumed as a badge of success against the patrollers).[24] The Panthers understood that to the extent that the imprisoned are pathologized, African Americans, like it or not, are also pathologized, particularly when pathology is understood as the attribution not only of social dysfunction to the mass, but also as the presentation of rare instances of exceptional individuals who prove the pathological rule.

The Black Panthers theorized the U.S. state as a regime of imprisonment for African Americans and conversely theorized the literal prison as a vanguard political *and cultural* space in the struggle for racial liberation. For African Americans, incarceration, both figurative and literal, is a crucial vehicle for the state's administration of racial injustice and accordingly for the struggle against that injustice. Huey Newton expresses as much in his autobiography, *Revolutionary Suicide*, in rather stark, hyperbolic terms: "Jail is an odd place to find freedom, but that was the place I first found mine" (99). Citing influence from Mahatma Gandhi's anticolonial strategy (101), he proceeds to narrate how solitary confinement especially clarified the stakes of the struggle:

> Soul breakers exist because the authorities know that such conditions would drive
> *them* to the breaking point, but when I resolved that they would not conquer my will,

> I became stronger than they were. I understood them better than they understood me. No longer dependent on the things of the world, I felt really free for the first time in my life. In the past I had been like my jailers; I had pursued the goals of capitalistic America. Now I had a higher freedom. (102)

Alluding to the slave breakers of the antebellum period, Newton heightens the sense of carceral enslavement by labeling it soul breaking. Newton extends this analysis from the political to the cultural sphere in emphasizing the import of language for the Black Panther ideology.

> The Black Panthers have always emphasized action over rhetoric. But language, the power of the word, in the philosophical sense, is not underestimated in our ideology. We recognize the significance of words in the struggle for liberation, not only in the media and in conversations with people on the block, but in the important area of raising consciousness. (163)

Newton is careful to locate the potentially expansive power of words, from their role in mass media to ordinary conversations on the street. We can see how Newton's understanding of himself as a political prisoner (even when not jailed) quickly extends to the role of culture for the figuratively and literally imprisoned.[25]

The Panthers' theorization of political and cultural agency as a struggle that must be engaged across the prison walls represents the culmination of a long tradition within African American writing, especially but not exclusively by men, across the Jim Crow and post–civil rights periods up to the present. Some of the most influential black male writers have experienced imprisonment, and many black male writers, whether imprisoned or not, have made imprisonment a central theme of their work partly because they have experienced directly the impact of incarceration in their communities, and frequently in their own families. They have refused to recognize or accept the ideological line that keeps the imprisoned culturally segregated from the nonimprisoned, for to concede such a line would in fact gag some of the most fertile cultural expression—in literature, music, philosophy, and social critique especially—helping to shape African American thought and art as the frontline of the struggle for liberation. The roster of such black male writers is far too voluminous to catalogue; a short list of those best known includes Langston Hughes, Claude McKay, Richard Wright, William Attaway, Chester Himes, James Baldwin, Ralph Ellison, Willard Motley, Ronald Fair, Martin Luther King Jr., Malcolm X, Bayard Rustin, James Baldwin, LeRoi Jones/Amiri Baraka, George Jackson, Huey Newton, Bobby Seale, Eldridge Cleaver, Iceberg Slim, Donald Goines, Nathan Heard, Etheridge Knight, Charles Wright, John Edgar Wideman, Joseph Beam, Ernest Gaines, Nathan McCall, Sanyika Shakur, Jarvis Jay Masters, and Mumia Abu-Jamal.[26]

The impact of imprisonment on individual writers, of course, varies greatly. Since the 1930s, however, the theme of imprisonment has been at the center of African American male narrative, both fictive and nonfiction. The influence can be as subtle as that of the New Negro Renaissance writer Wallace Thurman, who was arrested for public immorality (accepting a proposition for homosexual sex in a public laboratory) and spent three days in jail.[27] Thurman does not reference prison directly in his fiction, but I would suggest that the experience haunts his work, especially in the way racial oppression and sexual repression are intertwined claustrophobically as pressuring upwardly mobile characters toward the edge of utter self-destruction. As Thurman's biographer points out, it is probably only Thurman's newness to New York City, his anonymity, which protected him from the kind of scandal and stigma that befell other homosexuals exposed under such circumstances.[28] The high-yellow dissolute character Alva in Thurman's first novel, *The Blacker the Berry* (1929), embodies the horror of scandal, stigma, and a downward spiral resulting from an association with homosexuality, which in 1920s America is itself strongly identified with crime and punishment, with police entrapment, arrest, and imprisonment, as well as with the police corruption that kept mob-owned bars open for clandestine homosexual contacts.

Contrary to Thurman's furtive emplotment of the fear of crime and punishment, black male writing usually takes a more direct and even explosive approach in exposing the social, psychic, economic, and political import of the U.S. carceral regime for black men's everyday lives. The thematic figuration of imprisonment as emblematic of mass black men's experience comes to the fore in the 1930s with two influential texts, Angelo Herndon's 1937 autobiography, *Let Me Live*, and Richard Wright's 1940 best-seller novel *Native Son*. Herndon's autobiography was written during his time in and after being released from prison in Georgia, where he was arrested for interracial labor organizing based on a revised antebellum slave anti-insurrection statute. As Malcolm X and others would also do after him, Herndon exploits his prison memoir as a political platform—in his case, for labor organizing—as he represents not only himself as a political prisoner but also his fellow inmates. In a common strategy of the time, Herndon draws deep connections between slavery and labor exploitation. But taking a more novel approach, he also establishes links between imprisonment and labor oppression. Herndon details his life within and outside prison through a seamless interconnectivity with industrial workers, especially with coal mining, the work that he and his brothers experienced and from which their father had met a premature death.[29] In representing his prison experience, Herndon chooses not to emphasize the prison space as an abnormal and alien subculture, but rather insists on establishing its parallels to the outside life of industrial labor.

As is the case with other black male carceral narratives, Wright's *Native Son* was inspired by an actual death-row case in Chicago that he followed closely even after migrating to New York. The novel culminates with a prolonged exposé of the punishment system, from arrest to arraignment, from sentencing to impending execution. As many scholars have observed, the narrative interlinks the inside prison and the outside prison of the ghetto into a single condition of oppression for the protagonist, Bigger Thomas. Given the naturalist bent of the novel, its inexorable closure must move toward the place of most fatally extreme oppression, the jail cell as a harbinger of the electric chair. Ironically, in prison facing execution Bigger experiences the psychic transformation unavailable in the wider prison ghetto. Wright's formula has become so influential that it is still a touchstone of high literary work, popular and mass media, and of sociological studies; at times it seems that the fictional character Bigger Thomas embodies the real-life experiences of current young African American men ensnared in the punishment establishment. Not surprisingly, a 2006 report by the Joint Center for Political and Economic Studies, *A New Generation of Native Sons,* prefaces its findings with a discussion of Wright's 1940 novel.[30]

In scores of texts written across the Jim Crow era, other black writers adopted, adapted, and reacted against Wright's protest formula, in which the prison figures as the ultimate sign of black male desperation and injustice across the carceral divide. William Attaway's labor novel *Blood on the Forge* (1941), for instance, revises the Wright formula by having Big Mat, one of his black male worker-protagonists and a former inmate, rise to become a recruit of the steel industrialists only to meet his death fighting on the wrong side of the labor movement. The liberating conversion that Bigger undergoes in prison is mirrored in Big Mat, who ironically begins to feel like a powerful man at the very moment that he is clubbing to death his fellow steel laborers. For Attaway, the steel factory with its accompanying steel town is an inescapable prison-house of labor. As Mat's two brothers flee the steel town on a train, they hear explosive rumblings in the distance, a harbinger of what they'll encounter when they arrive in the even bigger industrial prison of Pittsburgh.

In her 1946 protest novel, Ann Petry revises the Wright formula by placing a woman in the role of criminally oppressed protagonist. Her young son is fated to be abandoned in juvenile detention after his mother commits a murder, ironically while attempting to acquire the money to get him released. She flees arrest by migrating from Harlem to Chicago, an ironic escape into Bigger Thomas's ghetto prison.

Even in the literary reaction against Wright's dominance, imprisonment as a place of racial injustice for all black people continues to hold sway. Despite

James Baldwin's forceful attack on Wright's protest formula, Baldwin's own fiction returns repeatedly to the prison as the central organizing figure of racial/sexual oppression for blacks inside and outside the prison walls. Himself briefly imprisoned in France, Baldwin made it the subject not only of an essay but also an inspiration for his second novel, *Giovanni's Room* (1956), whose eponymous character ends up, like Wright's Bigger Thomas, awaiting execution in prison.[31] As the Wright biographer David Leeming observes, "Prisons and prisoners were a significant part of Baldwin's personal experience," serving as a dominant metaphor for those "deprived of their birthright in the unfeeling and unseeing prison that was racism in America."[32] Going beyond Wright's curiosity about actual cases of crime and punishment, Baldwin became heavily involved in the attempt to free Tony Maynard, wrongly imprisoned for rape in New York City's notorious "Tombs."

Baldwin's frustrating experience with the criminal injustice system inspires his fifth novel, *If Beale Street Could Talk* (1974). Revealingly, Baldwin focuses not on the individual prisoner, Fonny, inside the Tombs but instead on the romantic relationships among Fonny, his girlfriend, Tish (the narrative point of view), and her family on the outside. Often criticized for idealizing Tish and her family for their commitment to the imprisoned, the novel actually represents Baldwin's own implicit commitment to Maynard, as well as his understanding of literal and symbolic kinship bonds that prevent many African Americans from ostracizing their imprisoned loved ones.[33] Baldwin witnessed this commitment in Valerie Maynard, Tony's sister. In the novel, Tish's pregnancy by Fonny represents the prisoner's ongoing creative influence beyond the prison walls. Furthermore, in fashioning his imprisoned character, Baldwin makes him a sculptor to emphasize the creativity and agency that the Tombs failed to destroy.[34]

Baldwin's grasp of imprisonment as the linchpin of U.S. racism goes beyond this constant representation of literal prisons and prisoners in his work. He saw the intractable ideology of social criminalization and punishment of the marginalized as integral to the pathology of racism infecting the American state of mind. His image of the nation's history as "house of bondage" is the subject of one of his last essays: "Thus, what the house of bondage accomplished for what we will call the classic white American was the destruction of his moral sense, except in relation to whites. But it also destroyed his sense of reality and, therefore, his sense of white people had to be as compulsively one-dimensional as his vision of blacks. The result is that white Americans have been one another's jailers for generations."[35]

If Baldwin seeks to shift the lens so that we can see the cultural agency and creativity operating within the imprisoned and across the carceral divide, another

key African American writer represents a quite different trajectory in the deconstruction of the divide through creative expression. Chester Himes starts writing
fiction while imprisoned in the Ohio State Penitentiary.[36] His first written novel,
published as *Cast the First Stone* (1953), is a gripping homosexual romantic tragedy
that rivals Baldwin's *Giovanni's Room*, except that the whole novel is set in prison.[37]
The model for an imprisoned author, Himes manages to turn his own experience
into memoir and fiction and cannily develops incarceration as a theme across his
work. In his first published novel, *If He Hollers Let Him Go* (1945), for instance,
his upwardly mobile protagonist ends up falsely imprisoned for raping a white
female coworker. Instead of meeting Bigger's fate, however, Bob Jones is given an
option: prison or the army. Having likened his everyday experience to living in a
racial war zone, Jones chooses the army, another racial war zone in a segregated
military. Himes is most famous for his popular series of mystery novels featuring
the cool Harlem detectives Grave Digger Jones and Coffin Ed Johnson. Unlike
contemporaneous detective fiction, where white male rationality keeps the detective above the fray of an anarchic criminal environment, Himes refuses the logic
that dictates that crime must end in fit punishment. Rather, he represents a city
whose criminal anarchy is fomented as much by the corrupt white downtown
police as by the denizens of Harlem, and where Harlem itself becomes a punishing prison that Coffin Ed and Grave Digger must negotiate like street-smart canny
inmates.

John Edgar Wideman is another major writer in this divide-crisscrossing tradition. His 1984 memoir *Brothers and Keepers* offers a radical revision of Capote's
*In Cold Blood,* for the inmate who is the imprisoned subject, Robby, is not a monstrous stranger but his own brother. In contrast with Capote, Wideman explores
his own liminality, existing on that carceral line, rather than securely on either
side, as enfolded in a broader flow of African American history and culture. Like
many African Americans, Wideman has been forced to deal with imprisonment
of a loved one not only in his own generation but also in the succeeding generation, as his youngest son's imprisonment is obliquely referenced in his 1990
novel *Philadelphia Fire.* As these brief instances establish, African American men
writers have fashioned different ways for narrating the central role that imprisonment plays in the everyday life of black communities while also straddling the
line constructed to gag insurgent cultural expression on both sides of the carceral
divide.

If African American literature tends to deconstruct the divide, carceral studies
based in the ethnographic/subcultural paradigm are strongly structured by it—
usually promoting the binary of a normative, rational "us" in the speaking figure
of the ethnographer versus a pathological "them" in the observed figure of the

imprisoned as objects to be investigated and corrected. Just as liberal, reformist-oriented mass media like the show *Oz* recognizes the need for a liminal figure like Augustus Hill who can allow us vicariously to cross that divide through a prisoner narrator, so ethnographic penologists recognize the need for such liminal figures and supply this need through the native-informant prisoner. Liberal by profession since their objective is the rational reform of the prison system ostensibly on behalf of the imprisoned, ethnographic penologists by training and method are required to cross the carceral divide. Their work therefore presents an interesting case in which that divide must be troubled in practice, even as in theory it grounds the fundamental distinction between the ethnographer's science (methods for interpreting the alien subculture) versus the prisoners' native knowledge (the alien subculture to be studied). Surveys, interviews, and case narratives provide access to the prison subculture while validating the artifactuality of it as a subculture. In being forced to cross, literally in most cases, into the prison fortress, ethnographic penologists nonetheless provide an unintentional, surreptitious acknowledgment of the lingua franca of African American communities—the inescapable crisscross between and across the inside and the outside in the constant re-creation of a common culture. I will touch on two brief instances of this ethnographic crisscross at work.

A groundbreaking, classic instance of ethnographic penology, the 1984 book *The Joint: Language and Culture in a Maximum Security Prison* announces its attempt to trouble the carceral divide on the title page itself with the attribution of a double authorship: Inez Cardozo-Freeman, Ph.D., the Ohio State University, "in collaboration with" Eugene P. Delorme, conspicuously uncredentialed.[38] In a foreword written by Simon Dinitz, Ph.D., the Ohio State University, we learn that Delorme is "native American, prisoner, leader, *good people*—a man predestined for Walla Walla as his autobiography attests" (ix). How else could Cardozo-Freeman claim to have, in the words of her mentor Dinitz, not only "successfully captured the standard lingo of the convicts in all its richness and subtleties" but also "successfully penetrated the minds and souls of her subjects, speaking their thoughts as though they are her own" (viii)? Dinitz appropriately lauds his junior colleague as not just a social scientist but also a creative artist, "a folklorist by profession" (viii). Significantly, convict Delorme's contribution to *The Joint* tends to disappear as the intellectual creation of the book crosses from "inside" the prison to its "outside" audience. The act of "penetrating" is done accordingly by the good doctor; she alone can deliver the final product to the outside world, in that Delorme remains locked behind prison walls.

As *The Joint*'s Augustus Hill, Delorme is necessarily a liminal figure, for his role in this liberal project is to provide interiority and individuality to the prisoners whose lives will be narrated, fragmented, flattened, packaged, exposed to public view, and reduced to scientific cases. Even when named, they remain an anonymous mass. As Cardozo-Freeman is "a penal reformer in the hallowed tradition of that term" (viii), devoted to cataloging the dehumanizing and degrading horrors of prison life, she needs Delorme as a go-between to penetrate the minds of men whose subculture is determined (and caused) by such horrors. "We recoil in horror as we realize that these men are being measured for sexual exploitation and victimization, for gang recruitment, even as they debark," Dinitz exclaims (ix). Of course, the measuring of new prisoners, revealingly, is being done not by the "corrections officers" but by other prisoners already adapted to the alien prison subculture. On the one hand, "even the coldest among us become less certain that the Walla Wallas in this country do anything well except inflict 'pains of punishment'"; on the other hand, "Inez Cardozo-Freeman makes it easy to forget that some of these men have committed the most heinous offenses" (ix). Through Delorme, the study negotiates the bifurcation between, on the one hand, the mass of anonymous prisoners and their violently degrading subculture, and on the other, the demand that the system, for at least some of these men, be reformed. The study also needs for Delorme, like Augustus Hill, to be a prisoner of color, as Cardozo-Freeman herself implies in the introduction: "He was able to interview or talk to men from every important group in the prison—black, white, native American, and Chicano" (xiv–xv). Presumably, if Delorme had been merely white, he may have had difficulty talking with everyone, but most crucially, in the lingo of prison subculture, he is "*good people*" partly because he is an "*old-timer.*" Like *Oz*'s old-timers, Rebadow and Busmalis, Delorme represents the reparable prisoner whose presence moderates the worst brutalities of the prison subculture.

An Isantee Sioux, in and out of prison since 1962, Delorme was "highly respected and trusted by the prison population," many of whom "referred to him as *good people*, a term used to describe a small number of men in the prison who are leaders exercising a positive influence in the population" (xiv). As a sort of organic intellectual—a respected leader and problem solver within the subculture— Delorme also occupies the position of tertiary authorship, as is indicated by being in the unusual position of being quoted within the introduction of his own book (see xv). The quoted paragraph that details "his methodology," as the primary author puts it, makes it clear that he is professional enough to do the fieldwork under her tutelage (inside the prison) but not professional enough (outside the prison) to coauthor the study itself. The final sentence of his quoted paragraph sums this up poignantly, "The guys I interviewed were typical, including me" (xv). Delorme is in the curious position of being both the atypical interviewer and the typical prisoner interviewed, a condition of carceral double consciousness that approximates W. E. B. Du Bois's influential understanding of the condition of the Negro in America: "this sense of always looking at one's self through the eyes of others, of measuring one's soul by the tape of a world that looks on in amused contempt and pity."[39]

*The Joint* is organized like a tourism primer for the wary traveler from the outside, and Delorme, as native informant, becomes a tour guide whose voice is fully swallowed up by the official interpretation. The chapters take us through the process as though *we* are being imprisoned, introducing us in chapter 1, "The Joint," to the layout of our new abode, and in chapter 2, "The Chain," to the transition process from free to prisoner, with succeeding chapters introducing us to the social roles/identities that various prisoners play/hold in the lingo of "the joint": "The Fish," "The Cons," "The Bulls," "Our Ladies," "A Punk in the Bunk." Finally, although *The Joint* makes a masterful effort to represent the prison through the eyes of the prisoners, as it endows the imprisoned with the capacity to create their own subculture, it inescapably also puts that subculture in its place as a deformed, degraded expression whose vitality is meaningless without the rational explanations provided by the greater cultural authority and creativity of the professional ethnographer. In this sense, prison subculture is a dependent, mimetic expression, not a genuine culture integral to the social scientist's own.

In the 2000 book *The Soul Knows No Bars*, we see a further step in the direction of attempting to trouble—and this time discredit—the carceral divide through the sharing of cultural authorship and authority crisscrossing that divide.[40] Part ethnography, part collective philosophical inquiry, *Soul Knows No Bars* is a collaboration between a philosophy professor (and volunteer prison instructor) and his imprisoned students in Baltimore's Maryland Penitentiary. The title page presents an image of the collaboration, with the professor's name, without accompanying credentials, standing above the mass of inmate authors in alphabetical order, but the professor's name almost bleeding indiscriminately into theirs. Chapter 1, "Getting into Prison," gives Professor Leder choice place among the voices, as he serves as a tour guide introducing us to the Pen, the guards, his students, the ritual of crossing the multiple sets of iron bars to get into the inside, and the trials and errors of conducting class within a high-security prison. Leder's understandable ambivalence about being on the inside is communicated tersely but powerfully: "As I descended a flight of stairs, voices echoed from the cell area to my right, resonating in the strange sound chamber made by so many cages in a row. It seemed a human zoo. I have been invited to visit that region of the prison, but in two years have never gone. Better to meet my students as men than to peer at them curiously through bars" (2). For this collaborative book of philosophical musings, it is appropriate that Leder concludes his introduction with an invitation to the reader metaphorically to cross that divide: "Another absent voice is that of you, the reader. . . . What might be the answer the discussants never found? You are in the dialogue. . . . As you hear us talk, listen to your own voice responding" (10). The book proceeds with brief biographies accompanying individual frontal photographs of the inmate philosophers and then a group photo of the class. There is no individual photo of the professor (and his bio is placed in the traditional position at the end of the book), but the class photograph exposes more blatantly what he tells us incidentally in the introduction: that he is a white professor volunteering to teach a class of all black inmates.

The racial dilemmas posed by *Oz's* and *The Joint's* outsider narrative authority is minimized here and recalibrated into playful camaraderie across not only the carceral divide but transcending the racial divide. When some of his students tease Leder about his "white man's gait," he responds in kind: "I knew this meant I was family. If they could mock the white man's gait, I could do my impression of the ghetto-blaster jive-stride and we'd laugh together. I grew up a scrawny Jewish kid, always with his (big) nose in the books. It felt good to finally be accepted by the tough boys. One of the gang" (7). That Leder is, of course, not "family," not "one of the gang," haunts and shapes the nature of this unique collaboration in philosophical authorship. We predictably get more of Leder's voice than that of the other authors. His voice frames each chapter, and we hear their voices only in the snippets of Socratic dialogue (classroom conversation) presented to us on each philosophical topic. As an experiment in crisscrossing the carceral divide through creative culture, *Soul Knows No Bars* is a refreshing relief from the ethnographic reduction of prisoners' cultural agency to a subcultural cage. The historical and high-cultural weight of philosophy, however, bears down on the inmates' own philosophizing, as their cultural expression is both produced and sublimated into the topoi, techniques, and social capital bestowed altruistically by the generous professor, whose academic discipline, of philosophy, is bestowed on the rest of us as an endowment of Western civilization that he, in turn, benevolently bestows on his black male student inmates from the "human zoo."

The dilemmas of mass media seem flimsy next to the determination of state "corrections" to enforce the alienation of the incarcerated from our common humanity, an alienation that contributes to the notion that either prisoners exist in a subhuman subculture or, even worse, have no culture at all—a great liability for the imprisoned given that humanness is so much defined by the power to produce (create) and consume (appreciate) a shared culture. Imprisonment can certainly deprive individuals of their most basic human, civil, and civic rights; it can even reduce an individual to a condition that seems sub- or nonhuman. Imprisonment cannot, however, prevent the imprisoned from making culture, nor can it cut off the sharing of culture that moves across the carceral divide. We need seriously to consider the impact of the imprisoned on culture at large, as well as the impact of the punishment industry itself on society's cultural health, where society here radically includes the imprisoned and the "free" as possessing a common culture across and despite the carceral divide.

## Notes

1. For a recent analysis of this global security regime and its consequences for cultural identities like race and class, see E. San Juan Jr., *In the Wake of Terror: Class, Nation, Ethnicity in the Postmodern World* (Lanham, Md.: Lexington/Rowan and Littlefield, 2007), particularly 1–21.

2. We cannot fail to note here how "inside" ironically denotes the most debased, marginalized sphere of social existence, whereas usually it signifies the most privileged site of power. The irony is multiplied when we realize that the violent power on display (or more accurately, hidden away from the nonincarcerated public) within prisons is an indirect arm of the influence of postindustrial capital and state-subsidized corporate power. For an instructive treatment of how prisoners tend to be staged to the outside world, see Mary Rachel Gould, who analyzes the annual rodeo held at Angola prison where the prisoners' bodies "become objects of desire, commodification, and control" for non-prison visitors. See "Discipline and the Performance of Punishment: Welcome to 'The Wildest Show in the South,'" *Liminalists: A Journal of Performance Studies* 7, no. 4 (December 2011): 1–31.

3. Most recent discourse of the sociopolitical establishment has been expressed as alarm over crime or over the *fiscal cost* of maintaining the imprisoned. A recent U.S. Supreme Court decision, *Brown v. Plata* (May 2011), provides some slight hope that there may be a shift in the dominant discourse away from basing the problem of punishment solely on the twin alarms of fear of crime and anger over the cost of housing prisoners. The 5–4 opinion held that overcrowding itself violates Amendment VIII of the U.S. Constitution's ban on cruel and unusual punishment, and ordered California to accord with the lower court's orders establishing population limits and deadlines for the state's prisons. Justice Kennedy's majority opinion is unusually aggressive in asserting the basic rights of prisoners (beyond access to health care, which had been the motivating cause of the plaintiffs), but Justice Scalia's dissent (joined by Thomas) continues to stoke the fear of crime, as well as antijudicial activism, as a rationale for the status quo. His dissent was so full of rage and vitriol that two in the minority (Alito and Chief Justice Roberts) decided to file a separate dissent. Scalia objected especially to the majority's exhibition of prisoner suffering—including deaths due to lack of access to health care—as a basis for their decision (see *Brown, Governor of California, et al. v. Plata et al.* at www.supremecourt .gov/opinions/10pdf/09-1233.pdf).

4. In *The Culture of Punishment: Prison, Society, and Spectacle* (New York: New York University Press, 2009), Brown makes the powerful move of forcing us to occupy the position of "penal spectator" from a critical perspective, rather than the more usual maneuver of a

nonprisoner attempting to occupy the place of the prisoner sympathetically or empatheti-
cally by reading or viewing cultural expressions created about prisoners (8–9; hereafter
cited parenthetically).

5. "Our" here refers to the customary notion that the nonimprisoned share a bond
together over against the interests of the imprisoned, whose identity is normally defined
through exclusion from the possessive plural that denotes a collective civility, as "they" are
seen instead to pose danger, stigma, abjection, and pathology.

6. David Garland, "Concepts of Culture in the Sociology of Punishment," *Theoretical
Criminology* 10, no. 4 (November 2006): 422; hereafter cited parenthetically.

7. Wacquant, *Punishing the Poor: The Neoliberal Government of Social Insecurity* (2004;
Durham: Duke University Press, 2009), xi–xii.

8. *Oz's* narrative liberalism is also indicated by showcasing an African American as the
prisoner-narrator. As John M. Sloop points out in *The Cultural Prison: Discourse, Prisoners, and Punishment* (Tuscaloosa: University of Alabama Press, 1996), the dominant representation of inmate violence focuses on black men, in tandem with the criminalization
of black inner cities in the post–civil rights period. He writes: "While the white male
prisoner remains forever open for rehabilitation and reunion, the 'other' male prisoner
divides. The products of this bifurcation, while both violent, take on opposite valences.
The violence of one is justified in that it emerges in reaction to an unfair social system that
imprisons the African-American male while it protects a racist society" (16). He further
points out that in popular discourse about prison, rape is foregrounded and racialized
with black male prisoners raping young white men, in accordance with his observation
that white prisoners are routinely represented in the "altruistic inmate" role versus black
prisoners, who are represented as violent exploiters within the prison (see 150–67). See
also Mark S. Fleisher and Jessie L. Krienert, *The Myth of Prison Rape: Sexual Culture in
American Prisons* (Lanham, Md.: Rowan and Littlefield, 2009), 23–24.

9. On the role of race and poverty in the emergence of carceral nationality, see Wacquant, especially chapter 6, "The Prison as Surrogate Ghetto: Encaging Black Subprole-
tarians" (195–208); and for an astute treatment of the role that plays in one mass-media
form—TV shows about small-claims court—see Valerie Karno, "Remote Justice: Tuning
in to Small Claims, Race, and the Reinvigoration of Civic Judgment," in "Punishment,
Politics, and Culture," ed. Austin Sarat and Patricia Ewick, special issue, *Studies in Law, Politics, and Society* 30 (2004): 261–82. Karno is especially enlightening on how such reality
TV invites public participation in matters of legal judgment beyond mere entertainment
while also creating "a vehicle for law to reinforce its legitimacy by cunningly inculcating
the evolving imagination of its utility and the possibilities for participatory citizenship
into the popular discursive will" (265).

10. Toward the end of the show's run, Rebadow fails to feel remorse in committing a
premeditated murder, and actually takes pleasure in it, requesting another assignment.
When refused, he attempts to murder Busmalis, his cellmate and best pal, but his circumstantial status is fully recovered as a white old-timer after doctors remove a tumor from his
brain and he is restored to his familiar role. This fungibility between choice and circumstantial criminality indicates the slipperiness of that dividing line within the prison, as
virtually every prisoner in the series crosses that line at some point, including the devout
Muslim leader Said, unlike the leaders of the Aryan Brotherhood and the Homeboys, who

remain intractably without interiority and without the capacity for movement across that line.

11. David Garland argues that in this sense the carceral establishment participates in the modern state's heightening of the modes of social control in the face of economic policies not consistent with increasing expectations of democratization across class, race, and gender in *The Culture of Control: Crime and Social Order in Contemporary Society* (Chicago: University of Chicago Press, 2001).

12. Jarvis, "The Violence of Images: Inside the TV Drama *Oz*," in *Captured by the Media: Prison Discourse in Popular Culture*, ed. Paul Mason (Cullompton: Willan, 2006), 157.

13. For another instance of a filmic attempt to work against the conventions of carceral narrative, see Jamie Bennett's analysis of Rex Bloomstein's use of cinema verité in his series of independent documentaries on the criminal justice system in Britain ("Undermining the Simplicities: The Films of Rex Bloomstein," in *Captured by the Media*, 122–36). "Alternative" forms like cinema verité often signal ideological dissent with mass-media conventions, but they cannot fully overcome the dilemmas posed by what Brown calls "penal spectatorship" and what Wacquant calls "penal pornography." In fact, by proceeding as though cinema can deliver a slice of truth by making the camera a sort of participant-observer, the technique installs another convention of spectatorship based on an inside/outside logic.

14. Baldwin, "Stranger in the Village," reprinted in *Price of the Ticket* (1953; New York: St. Martin's, 1985), 89.

15. Jarvis celebrates *Oz*'s numerical representation of the disproportion of inmates of color in the U.S. system, giving over the script unusually to the stories of minority characters (see 157); this same realism, however, also feeds into the identification of African American, Latino, and Italian males with unmotivated criminality. The creators of *Oz* thus find themselves in the classic liberal double-bind: making a spectacle of the suffering of (racial) others in order to garner sympathy, or at least understanding, for their plight tends to bind the racial other more insidiously to violent suffering as a coordinate of their cultural identity.

16. For instance, in campaigns to eliminate or cordon off violence from mass media (usually Hollywood film and hip-hop or rock music lyrics), the discourse is consistently couched as the need to protect the innocence of American children (meaning not the ones in the gang-infested black and Latino inner cities). It is the media that corrupts innocent youth, not a media that embodies the general violence of the nation-state. On the tendency for national discourse to erect the innocence of white middle-class youth as a basis for social policy, see Lauren Berlant's theory of "infantile citizenship" discussed in *The Queen of America Goes to Washington City: Essays on Sex and Citizenship* (Durham: Duke University Press, 1997). Berlant's theory—which focuses on gender, sexuality, race, and class—could usefully be extended to apply to the treatment of the incarcerated, especially in regard to jurisprudence that sentences black and Latino youth as adults at a glaringly disproportionate rate to white teenagers.

17. Michael Moore's 2002 documentary *Bowling for Columbine*, which takes the 1999 Columbine High School shooting as its jumping-off point, is a rare case where the connection to race is teased out relentlessly in a mass-media format.

18. The genealogy from slavery to the chain gang to modern incarceration has been

commented on by various scholars. See, for instance, Mark Colvin, *Penitentiaries, Reformatories, and Chain Gangs: Social Theory and the History of Punishment in Nineteenth-Century America* (New York: St. Martin's Press, 1997), 199–273; Edward L. Ayers, *Vengeance and Justice: Crime and Punishment in the Nineteenth-Century American South* (New York: Oxford, 1984), esp. 185–265; and Keally McBride, "Hitched to the Post: Prison Labor, Choice and Citizenship," in *Punishment, Politics, and Culture* (107–24).

19. See Turner, *Figures of Speech: First Amendment Heroes and Villains* (Sausalito: Poli-PointPress, 2011), 55. Turner served as Martin's lawyer for the appeals process.

20. Burns, *I Am a Fugitive from a Georgia Chain Gang!*, foreword by Matthew J. Mancini (1932; Athens: University of Georgia Press, 1997); Abu-Jamal, *Live from Death Row*, introduction by John Edgar Wideman (Reading: Addison-Wesley, 1995). In *Cruel and Unusual: Punishment and U.S. Culture* (London: Pluto Press, 2004), Brian Jarvis provides an incisive discussion of Abu-Jamal's text (112–14).

21. This language in the justices' majority opinion is actually quoted from the three-judge ruling of the Ninth District Court of Appeals (northern and eastern California), whose decision was upheld by the Supreme Court in *Brown v. Plata*.

22. I am not suggesting that the culture identified with imprisoned people should be equated with African American culture—only that each feeds the other to such an extent that any attempt to separate them would be undoable. I would also emphasize that a similar point could be argued, if not to the same extraordinary degree, for other marginalized groups with a long history in the United States of being disproportionately targeted for police surveillance, arrest, and imprisonment: Latinos, immigrants, the homeless, male homosexuals, and those deemed physically queer (phenotypically "ugly" or anatomically "deformed"). On the last category, a favored criminalized object in the late nineteenth and early twentieth centuries, see Ethan Blue's contribution to this volume, "Abject Correction and Penal Medical Photography in the Early Twentieth Century."

23. See Bobby Seale, *Seize the Time: The Story of the Black Panther Party and Huey P. Newton* (1970; Baltimore: Black Classics Press, 1991), 68; and Huey P. Newton *Revolutionary Suicide*, with J. Herman Blake (1973; New York: Writers and Readers Publishing, 1995), 117–18 (hereafter cited parenthetically).

24. In *Cruel and Unusual*, Jarvis makes a similar point concerning the ways in which African American prison writing of the 1960s and 1970s draws "critical analogies" between "specific punitive acts and a long history of white oppression" (79).

25. On Newton's theory of political imprisonment, see *Revolutionary Suicide* (258–62). Dylan Rodríquez has amplified this theory in conversation with the long-imprisoned Black Panther Marshall Eddie Conway (*Forced Passages*, 3–8).

26. A similar list of African American women writers could be made, though it would probably be considerably shorter. Consider, for instance, Angela Davis, Assata Shakur, Alice Walker, Toni Morrison, and Gayl Jones—all of whose work is indelibly marked by imprisonment.

27. On the details of Thurman's arrest, see Eleonore van Notten, *Wallace Thurman's Harlem Renaissance* (Amsterdam: Rodopi, 1994), 96.

28. See ibid. For a similar homosexual exposure that does end in scandal, consider the case of Augustus Granville, whom W. E. B. Du Bois fired when the assistant was arrested for homosexual solicitation (see Marlon B. Ross, *Manning the Race: Reforming Black Men*

in the Jim Crow Era [New York: New York University Press, 2004], 254–55). On Du Bois's discussion of his ongoing remorse over this firing, see his *Autobiography of W. E. B. Du Bois* (New York: International, 1968), 282.

29. See Marlon B. Ross, introduction to *Let Me Live* (1937; Ann Arbor: University of Michigan Press, 2007).

30. See Adolphus G. Belk Jr., *A New Generation of Native Sons: Men of Color and the Prison-Industrial Complex* (Washington, D.C.: Joint Center for Political and Economic Studies Health Policy Institute, Dellums Commission, 2006), www.jointcenter.org/sites /default/files/upload/research/files/FullBelk%20-%2060%20pages.pdf. See also Anthony J. Lemelle Jr., "A Reconsideration of Bigger Thomas: Afrocentric and Black Male Deviance," in *Black Male Deviance* (Westport: Praeger, 1997), 1–15.

31. On Baldwin's somewhat humorous but at the same time horrifying prison experience in Paris, see his 1955 essay "Equal in Paris," reprinted in *Price of the Ticket: Collected Nonfiction, 1948–1985* (New York: St. Martin's Press, 1985), 113–26.

32. Leeming, *James Baldwin: A Biography* (New York: Knopf, 1994), 323.

33. On the extraordinary lengths to which Baldwin went to help Maynard, see James Campbell, *Talking at the Gates: A Life of James Baldwin* (New York: Penguin, 1991), 237–38, 244–45.

34. In actuality, it was Maynard's sister, Valerie, who was the sculptor. It appears that Baldwin reimagined Valerie Maynard as the protagonist Tish, the pregnant girlfriend, rather than the sister of the falsely imprisoned youth.

35. Baldwin, "Notes on the House of Bondage," reprinted in *Price of the Ticket* (672–73).

36. See Himes, *The Quality of Hurt: The Early Years* (1971; New York: Paragon House, 1991), 64–65.

37. Himes was pressured by his publisher to make significant changes to the manuscript, including changing the characters from black to white. The original manuscript has been published under Himes's preferred title, *Yesterday Will Make You Cry,* introduction by Melvin Van Peebles (New York: Norton, 1998).

38. See *The Joint: Language and Culture in a Maximum Security Prison* (Springfield: Charles C. Thomas, 1984) (hereafter cited parenthetically).

39. Du Bois, *Souls of Black Folk* (1903; New York: Penguin, 1989), 5.

40. Drew Leder, *The Soul Knows No Bars: Inmates Reflect on Life, Death, and Hope,* with Charles Baxter, Wayne Brown, Tony Chatman-Bey, Jack Cowan, Michael Green, Gary Huffman, H. B. Johnson Jr., O'Donald Johnson, Arlando Jones III, Mark Medley, "Q," Donald Thompson, Selvyn Tillett, John Woodland, (Lanham, Md.: Rowan and Littlefield, 2000).

# 4 Life after Prison: Interviews

While the impact of incarceration on individuals can be quantified to a certain extent, the wide-ranging effects of the race to incarcerate on African American communities in particular is a phenomenon that is only beginning to be investigated. What does it mean to a community, for example, to know that three out of ten boys growing up will spend time in prison? What does it do to the fabric of the family and community to have such a substantial proportion of its young men enmeshed in the criminal justice system? What images and values are communicated to young people who see the prisoner as the most prominent pervasive role model in the community? What is the effect on a community's political influence when one quarter of the black men in some states cannot vote as a result of a felony conviction?

—MARC MAUER

Once you're in the system, they own you and that's the way it is.

—DEBBIE WALKER

# Jim Shea

*Interviewed by* JARED BROWN

JARED BROWN: Could you begin by introducing yourself?

JIM SHEA: My name is Jim Shea. I'm a retired university employee. I am also an alumnus of the university. I'm an ex-offender. I'm active in various political circles in Charlottesville. I'm an old guy with thirteen grandchildren.

JB: Could you elaborate on some of the political involvement that you spoke about?

JS: These days my partner of forty years, Brenda Lambert, and I, have been very active in the Dialogue on Race and in particular we are members of an action team within the Dialogue that is addressing reentry problems of ex-offenders trying to pull together. There're many elements in the city that address some aspect of these problems, and we're trying to pull it all together so that everyone is strengthened by what someone else is doing and so that we can generate some sense of movement on these issues.

JB: From your experiences with this movement that you are attempting to create, what have been some of the stumbling blocks or some of the obstacles that have deterred progress?

JS: Well, you're talking about progress for the movement or the progress of individuals trying to reenter? Those are two different things, actually.

JB: Perhaps you could elaborate on both.

JS: Okay. For individuals coming out of incarceration, there are many, many obstacles, and this is why the recidivism rate is so high. Because there're so many barriers placed in front of someone trying to put a life back together after they've been incarcerated—trying to put themselves on a solid economic basis, pull their family back together, and just establish themselves in a normal course of life because, in the very first place, it's very, very hard for people to get jobs. There's a great prejudice against hiring ex-offenders in the job market. Now, there are employers who will hire people, but there are many who just won't and so we get what amounts to a kind of a de facto kangaroo court that says to ex-offenders—you did your time, you paid your debt to society, as they say, but that's not good enough. We think you need to be punished further and so we consign you to the margins of society to live in poverty and you can take your children there with you, too, because, of course, if you can't get a job, your children suffer too, and this has a way of perpetuating, creating cycles, generational cycles.

JB: Well, perhaps I could ask you this—based on what you said, I've been thinking about the Fourteenth Amendment, the Equal Protection Clause which guarantees equal protection for people based on various factors such as race, sexuality, etc. Do you feel that the lack of protection for ex-convicts is a failure of the system?

JS: It is a failure of the system. I'm not a lawyer. I can't say that it technically violates the Fourteenth Amendment, but it certainly violates the spirit of the Fourteenth Amendment and violates any spirit of fairness that you would like to see in your community. Now, back in December, our action team presented the city council with a proposed resolution, which they adopted unanimously, declaring Charlottesville to be a City of Second Chances for ex-offenders, and the city has made a commitment to try to promote this cause. I said jobs. That's the biggest problem, but many ex-offenders can't get food stamps. They can't get access to public housing, although that may be about to change. If they owe fines or back child support, they can't get a driver's license, so they're just boxed in.

Now, if you can't pay your rent, you can't give money to the people raising your children, and you're sleeping on somebody's sofa, you might very well do something like you used to do to make a little money, and so a lot of people end up reoffending and back in prison.

JB: So the process of reoffending is a direct result of the infrastructure that is in place to disallow criminals, ex-criminals, ex-convicts, from having opportunity?

JS: It certainly does promote recidivism, the obstacles placed in people's paths, but I'll tell you something else. When you come out of incarceration, most people owe some fines or something of the sort, and if you cross your probation in any way, you may get sent back for that. For example, if you don't make timely re-payment of fines according to the schedule that's set by your probation officer, you can get sent back to jail. A very high percentage of people who go back to jail have not committed a new offense; they go back because there was some condition of their probation that they failed to keep. Maybe they failed a drug test. A lot of people go to prison these days, a very high percentage of people, who were involved somehow in drugs, and usually they were users, and many of them were people who were addicted in some way to something.

I want to mention a book to you that I think is one of the most important books written in the last fifty years in the United States. It's a book by Michelle Alexander called *The New Jim Crow,* and the thesis of this book—she's an African American legal scholar, she teaches at Ohio State University, she was a clerk for one of the Supreme Court judges when she was coming out of law school. The subtitle of the book is *Mass Incarceration in an Age of Colorblindness.* This book argues very persuasively that in the face of the civil rights movement and the gains that apparently were won as a result, people who wanted to keep matters as they were developed the "War on Drugs," and they targeted it at inner-city neighborhoods. As a matter of fact, drug use and drug selling in the suburbs and in the inner cities is about at the same rate, but arrests, prosecution, and incarceration in the inner cities is many times higher.

In some places, if you're a young black man, you have [a] thirteen times greater chance of going to prison on a drug charge than a white person living in the suburbs of the same city, although as you know yourself from your own observation, in a setting like this there're an awful lot of white people doing drugs just like everybody else. Everybody's smoking a little pot, doing a little of this, doing a little of that, but if you get stopped on the street because they see your brake light isn't working, they pull you over, you've got a much greater chance of getting arrested, convicted, and then you're marked as a felon for the rest of your life. [Alexander's] point is this: slavery held people by law as property, but after slavery was abolished, in a few short decades Jim Crow had reestablished this racial caste system that was challenged by the civil rights movement. When that movement finally succeeds in the 1950s and 1960s, within twenty years we've got a "War on Drugs" that is reestablishing the racial caste system so that a young black man today whose father and grandfather couldn't vote because of Jim Crow, had trouble getting jobs because of Jim Crow, whose great-grandfather couldn't vote because he was a slave, now this young man can't vote, can't get a job; now he is a state-certified victim of discrimination for life.

In Virginia, we have four hundred thousand people who can't vote because they're ex-cons. Fifty-five percent of them are African Americans, who can't vote for life until, one by one, they ask the governor to restore their rights. Four hundred thousand—that's almost 10 percent of the adult population of the state of Virginia.

I'm telling you these are the barriers. Some of them are barriers when you first come out, and some of them are barriers that go on forever. I know people who were convicted twenty-five or thirty years ago, who still when they go for a job . . . have to check that box indicating they've been convicted of a felony. What do you think that means about their application? In most places it's on the bottom or in the trash, and for many, many people. I've worked to help people get their voting rights restored, and I worked with a lot of people whose offenses were twenty years ago, thirty years ago, and some are still deprived of their political rights. They can't vote. They can't be on a jury. They can't run for public office if they wanted to—for life.

JB: So to continue, I'm interested in knowing—this denial of human rights—has it had an impact on you personally?

JS: Yes, it has, but I have to tell you, I'm the exception that proves the rule. My offenses were political offenses in the 1960s, and I eventually served some federal time. I have a felony charge—it's bail jumping actually. It was a failure to appear for incarceration when I was supposed to, so when all this happened, when I got out of custody, I was a white, middle-aged, middle-class, very well-educated person, so I was able to cope with some of these barriers better than many ex-offenders are. When I was incarcerated, I was in a federal minimum security prison, and my job was to teach in the school there while I was an inmate, and half of the people that came into that minimum security facility tested at grade five or below. Now, how do you think a person with a grade-five literacy level and, say, an African American and someone who doesn't have much in the way of a job history, how're they going to fare in the job market? Not so well.

I didn't fare so well myself. I had a lot of doors slammed in my face. I took work as a dishwasher in a restaurant, as a cook, and after six or seven years of that, I came back to Charlottesville. I finally got a job at the university in the library system and worked there until I retired. Now, I talked my way into a job at the library. They weren't going to hire me because I had marked that box, but I made a case for myself and they hired me at the lowest clerk level, so here I was with an Ivy League Ph.D. coming in to work at the University of Virginia Library, my alma mater as an undergraduate, and I was able to get that kind of a job, so I didn't really care. I just wanted to get a decent job at the university, but it certainly was well below my qualifications, so, yes, I had some difficulty and I had to apply twice to get my voting rights restored. But, even so, I think I had a lot easier time, an easier time than many people have, for sure.

JB: Could you perhaps elaborate about some of the racialized barriers you mentioned earlier? What specific barriers may be in the way of a minority or socioeconomically disadvantaged individual, that you may not have had to face?

JS: Well, in the first place, whiteness is, for some people, many people, a privilege, and although I grew up in a lower-middle-class family, I had educational opportunities. I grew up in the city of Petersburg, Virginia, and when I was ten years old, I went into the public library there and walked in and checked out some books, and I discovered on that day that black people in that city—this was about 1948—when they came into the library, they had to go into the basement. They had to ask someone at a desk in the basement, if there was someone there, to get a book for them. They couldn't go into the library to get a book. I was aware at the age of ten that being a white kid gave me privileges that, say, a black lawyer, a doctor, a minister, a school teacher, wouldn't have. As a kid, I could do that.

So, I mean, in the first place, and people often overlook this, white people, whites overlook this really, is that having white skin is an entitlement in this society, so I would say that my ability to get the education that I got was not unrelated to the fact that I belonged to the race of people for whom those doors were open.

So, when the harsher part of my life began, I had those assets that had come to me by virtue of my race. I'd say that's a major factor. I think people who believe that race isn't very important anymore are under an illusion. Race is important and we always have to take into account these considerations when we try to understand what the true elements of a situation are, so, yes, I don't know if that answers your question or not.

JB: Yes, it does. I think it does a great job in terms of allowing me to compare the experience of the white middle-aged male to the experience of a black male of any age group. I guess we could move on by talking specifically about your incarceration period.

JS: I want to back up a minute. You had asked me what barriers there are both in front of an individual and to a movement, and I want to say something about that. Of course, as a movement, we want to bring to public attention what many of these barriers are in a way that demonstrates their unfairness so that fair-minded people, as we saw in the civil rights days, there were people who were just quite content for things to go on as they were until they saw, until it was brought to their attention, how really wrong some things were that people were trying to address, and then they were energized and activated by that themselves and their minds were changed and they were not just tolerant but eager for some positive change to be made. So we have the indifference of people, the lack of information that people have, but there's another matter, too, and that is the underlying dynamic of racism that goes forward in our society today. It hasn't gone away. People think because we elected an African American president that we've reached a new era. We took a step we have never taken before, but the dynamic, the undercurrent of racism that has come to light since he was elected should tell us something.

In our local jail, I asked Colonel Matthews, the superintendent, "On an average day, what's the racial breakdown of the population of the jail?" He said, "80 percent black." Now, let's assume that it's in that order. We'll stick to that particular number, but this means that an awful lot of people coming out of incarceration are black men, for the most part, and all the old prejudices are still at work. Maybe they're not as bad as they used to be. I'm not so sure about that, but let me tell you, they're working, and it's easy, if somebody's been branded a criminal, you know. What are they, some low-life drug dealer or something? If you have been branded a criminal, that label just enables people's prejudices to come into play.

JB: Are you suggesting that white supremacy has not gone away but has evolved in new ways that make it more invisible?

JS: Yes, you don't hear people use openly racial language today. They don't call people names as they might have or brush people aside with some offhanded racial remark, so you could say that, just like styles change. Things that were acceptable at a certain time are thought to be bad form now, but that doesn't mean that the underlying motivations and inclinations have changed that much, if at all. I think that we still have serious problems of racial prejudice to contend with. That's why the Dialogue on Race, although it's an uphill battle all the way, we need to be undertaking initiatives like this at every opportunity to try to open people up a little bit, try to get them to look inside themselves and see what's not so pretty there that they might like to change if they thought about it.

JB: Do you feel that this language of color blindness functions to make race appear invisible?

JB: Yes, it does.

JB: Do you think that it is that color-blind dialogue that facilitates the criminal justice system and facilitates racially based oppression within the system?

JS: I think you've hit the nail on the head three times running there, Jared, and that's Michelle Alexander's thesis, and that's why I say this book is so important. I hope you'll read it. It's a powerful book, and it's a hard book to read. I couldn't read more than twenty or twenty-five pages at a time. It was so hard. It didn't tell me anything I didn't really know, but it put it all together in a way that made me think this was so awful, how are we going to change this? How are we going to do something about it? We thought we had done something, and here these people have sneaked in the back door.

After Martin Luther King was murdered and the riots broke out, there was a presidential commission appointed. Johnson appointed a commission to examine where the country was, and it was headed by a former governor of Illinois, a Republican named Otto Kerner, and the Kerner Commission's final report said that if steps are not taken to prevent it, that we are in the process of developing a permanent underclass based on race in this country. Well, of course, we had it for three hundred years already, but what this meant was, God, we thought we'd opened the doors to change. The Kerner Commission was actually saying, be careful, because the dynamics are all in place for a permanent underclass. In fact, that's what the "War on Drugs" has done, and when you read this book, you'll see that one of the great weapons of the civil rights movement was going to court, winning court cases. You can't do that anymore. The Supreme Court of the United States has undercut the ability to challenge the "War on Drugs" on the basis of racial discrimination. I'm not going to break the suspense for you, but read the book. You'll see. It is appalling.

JB: Do you feel that these particular steps that have been taken, some of which you've said have been taken by the Supreme Court to make sure that such cases are not brought forth on the basis of race, do you believe that that is a form of institutional racism at work?

JS: It is, yes. And the darling of the right wing of this country, they want to put his face on Mount Rushmore—Ronald Reagan. Ronald Reagan's administration was the administration that really put all this together. Let me give you an example of how this works. In 1970, there were three hundred thousand people in prison in the United States. Do you know how many people are in prison in this country today?

JB: I would probably say roughly 2 million.

JS: Two and a quarter million. All right. That's times seven. That means for every person in prison in 1970, there are seven people in prison today. The vast majority of these are people are in for low-level drug charges, and the vast majority of them are black and brown people, Latinos, and they're mainly drawn from the inner cities.

Now, how did this happen? Did people just step up and say I'll go, I'll go. No, indeed. The national government under Ronald Reagan began funding this "War on Drugs" by throwing money out and through federal agencies to the local police forces. Now, when I was growing up, we didn't have TAC squads anywhere. When these things started popping up, I thought, what in the hell is going on here? They militarized the local police forces of small towns, medium-sized towns, and big cities so that every significant municipality in the United States has got what amounts to a paramilitary unit in their police force, large or small depending upon the size of the city, and the funding for these and other programs like we have locally the Jefferson Area Drug Enforcement (JADE), every few months they're raiding somewhere and grabbing up fifteen or twenty people and sending them off; the money for these programs depends on maintaining a certain level of arrests. If your number of arrests drop, your funding drops. Yes, indeed.

JB: Which keeps incentive up.

JS: Indeed it does. Just any normal career-minded police officer is going to say, "Gee, we can't afford to lose that funding. You guys better get out there and . . ." The way we always say that the traffic cops have a quota for writing tickets for parking violations. In some way, this is similar. The police force has a quota that they need to maintain, and that's how we've got two-and-a-quarter million people. Do you know we have more people per capita in prison in this land of the free than any country in the world?

JB: Wow.

JS: That's right.

JB: I know another interesting statistic that I had noticed, and it is this, that America currently imprisons more black men than South Africa did under apartheid.

JS: That's right. And do you know that there're more black men either in custody or on probation in this country today than there were slaves in 1850? I mean, these are stark facts that are riveting, and I don't know what we can do about this. We've got to do something about it, and Michelle Alexander thinks that we've got to mount a movement, a multiracial—it needs to be a multiracial— movement to try to undo this, but, of course, her theory is this—every time you defeat the racial caste system, it finds a way to reinvent itself.

JB: Is that the manifestation of white supremacy?

JS: Sure, from slavery to the present. And, of course, in slavery times, the vast majority of white people didn't own slaves. They were working people, so that class comes into this. This always serves racial division, and setting working white people against black people serves the interest of people who operate by the principle of divide and rule. This was so of Jim Crow. And anti-unionism. All of this goes together.

The idea of insisting that unions be segregated. They were in South Africa, too. Except a couple of companies broke that rule. Ford was one that had an integrated union except I don't know how effective it was, but at least at Ford, black and white people were in the same union. Here in the South, it's hard to even have unions for working people of any color, so these caste systems, racial caste systems and divisions are a part of the political motives of first Nixon and then with Reagan. In the aftermath of the civil rights movement, Nixon developed a southern strategy. You've heard of this. In 1968, he saw how effective George Wallace was. George Wallace drew all these blue-collar white people into his movement. Well, in 1972, Wallace was out of the way and Nixon developed the southern strategy, which was to bring white southern Democrats who were against civil rights into the Republican Party and also union members, working-class white people in the major industrial cities of America, too, and so Nixon built the new majority, and Reagan solidified this even further. They still, to this day, think he was George Washington.

JB: So this new majority that has been created—my first question is, does that new majority still exist?

JS: I think when you look at the power of the Republican Party, when you consider that the Republican Party is so clearly, even more than the Democrats, a party that promotes the interests of the wealthiest people in the country, how [else] can they be as popular as they are? It's partly by zeroing in on issues like race, abortion, and the like and, of course, flag-waving. They're great flag-wavers. Certain Democrats are, too, but I think that the Republican Party has benefited from the Reagan redefinition of Republicanism and continues to profit from that to this day.

JB: . . . Could you speak briefly about the type of financial rewards that are provided for rural communities that are oftentimes the homes to various prisons, particularly here in the state of Virginia?

JS: Yes, well, everywhere. And another thing that goes hand in hand with that is the rise of the privately owned prison—

JB: It's called privatization?

JS: Yes. Well, I can't give you these figures, but I know that you can find them in Michelle Alexander's book, which shows what an enormously profitable business the private prisons are. You're right; they're often placed in some rural setting so that (1) they're out of sight of the population centers; (2) they provide jobs for people who live in those areas, mainly white country people, and this is a political boon to the people who represent that area, usually some Republican or conservative Democrat in Congress.

Another little sidelight to this, when the census is taken every ten years, people are counted as to where they live, so we have two-and-a-quarter million people in this country who are counted in the census where they're incarcerated. They can't vote, so remember, in the original Constitution, slaves couldn't vote but they counted as three-fifths of a person for the purpose of representation, so if we have, say, ten thousand people incarcerated in Albemarle County, which we don't have, but let's just say we did, that would count toward our congressional representation.

JB: So the three-fifths compromise in a sense has continued.

JS: Has reemerged in our time. Yes, indeed, in a less precise arithmetic manner, but it's there. So we have people incarcerated who count toward the representation in that area.

JB: But are not represented.

JS: They are not represented. They're in many ways alien from the people around them, and they can't vote. It's almost—I mean, it's so stark as to be almost comical what ironic twists there are to this business.

JB: What I find interesting is that these issues we have discussed are not invisible. They're very much so hypervisible, particularly for people who are interested in studying these things. What information is available, what type of role have the media and other entities played in terms of criminalizing people who are ex-convicts and in terms of upholding this type of system?

JS: Well, you watch television. You know what nighttime television does in promoting stereotypes. What kind of young black men are you finding on these police dramas? Right. You see it all right—this is powerful stuff. This is the way people are influenced without even realizing that they're being influenced. They're getting these images. They come to them just out of the ether, and it shapes people's expectations, their ideas. People who don't live in the inner city, where do they get their idea of what life is like in the inner city? And the media has not served us well. I would say that as a minimum, [the media] has not served us well. I think it's evident. I don't believe we have to belabor the point.

JB: I would like to move on to two more questions that are fairly essential. The first question concerns your experience of being incarcerated. I'm interested in knowing something about the people who were among you, about their mentality. What was going on in that space?

JS: Well, I really spent only nine months and fourteen days in custody, which interestingly enough is one gestation period. I spent about eight weeks in a jail awaiting sentencing on the bail jumping. I had already been sentenced for something else, and then I was six months or so in a federal minimum security prison. Then I was about ten weeks in a halfway house in D.C. Then I was out. So these were very different settings. It's never nice to be in jail. I'll tell you, it's not. After you're there a little while, you feel, gee, you realize that it's affected you, not just physically, but mentally. I know the first day I slept through the clanging open of the doors, I realized I'd been there a while. It didn't even wake me up anymore. It has a depressing effect, but it also works on your patience and your temper, so you may not be a very angry and violent person, but you may find you're right close to the edge of getting into a fight if somebody does something to you or says something to you that you don't like.

A federal minimum security prison is like being in the army of a third-world country. It's very meager physically. We had no heat in our dormitory, for example. Everything's pretty threadbare, but it's not the intense and on the edge of brutal environment as many prisons are, hardened prisons. But essentially anytime you're incarcerated, the essential element of experience you lose is liberty. You don't get to define anything except little things right around your person. You go where you're told. You do what you're told. You eat what you're given, and you associate with the people that you're just thrown in with. I found being in prison—I want to tell you that I found it in many ways a very interesting experience. I met people that I never would've met otherwise.

As I told you, I taught in the school in the federal minimum security facility, working with a friend of mine whom I taught the alphabet. This was a smart guy. He'd never been to school. How interesting is that? Here's a grown, smart guy. He knew one letter of the alphabet—his first and last names began with the letter *J*. He knew the letter *J*. He didn't know any other letters. He couldn't recognize any of the other letters. Well, in a few months he was reading at about the fourth- or fifth-grade level. He was a smart guy. It never came up for him.

So, there was a great racial diversity in the place where I was, and there were a lot of Latinos. There was a Cuban population that was by itself. A Mexican population, a Puerto Rican population. I found a lot of this really interesting, I have to tell you, but not so interesting that I wanted to stay longer than I was there. It was interesting. It was difficult in many ways. I never felt personally in danger in a place like that.

From there I went to a halfway house in D.C. where I was the only white guy in the facility, and there were a couple of people who were pretty hostile toward me there, and my approach was to try in my way to relax the situation and make some kind of accommodation with the people, and I was able to do that. It was tough, and the neighborhood that I lived in was in was very poor. Schoolkids chased me down the street throwing rocks at me one day. I mean, why not? I was white. That's all they saw. This was how prejudice works. They saw a white guy, and they had every reason in the world to be angry about that, so fortunately for me I was young enough to run fast enough where I could get away. I couldn't do it today. I would say that I learned a lot about myself and about human beings in general, the people I met.

I was locked up the year that Nixon was forced out of office, and there were a couple of Watergate people there, too, one who was a very solid guy and one who was awful.

It was hard coming out because, really, the guy running the halfway house kept sending me to government jobs, and I had an appointment, I wouldn't even get in for an interview. I'd sit in the waiting room all afternoon. One day I picked up the paper and I saw at the Mayflower Hotel they were hiring bus boys, and I went down there and got me a job as a bus boy at the Mayflower Hotel.

JB: Just so you could make ends meet?

JS: Well, I needed to have a job. It was the condition of my being there, so, yes, I learned about myself that I'm made of tougher stuff than I thought. I didn't buckle under humiliation or intimidation and came through with my head high so that was important to me. And I tell you, it also makes me feel a real kinship with people who go through worse than I went through and have faced worse than I did when I came out. I feel a kinship. I feel like a blood relation-ship, and I want to do what I can do to help them get a fair shake.

JB: I'll conclude with this question, which will end the official part of the inter-view. Afterwards, I will allow you to branch off into any subject that you'd like. If there's anything else that you would like to add, please do so. My question is this—corrections facilities, according to our government, are supposed to do exactly that—"correct" the individual. In your opinion, does this actually happen? If not, what happens?

JS: I think there's almost no pretense of rehabilitation in any correctional facility that I know about. Now, our local jail, on the other hand, has reentry pro-grams. They're trying very hard down there to help people get ready to walk out the door, but so many people who get locked up have never really worked for pretty obvious reasons. If you live in a certain kind of community and there's no work around, you're going to look for other ways to make money, so a lot of people who're locked up are people who made a little money selling a little drugs, doing a little of this, doing a little of that. They've never held a job so they haven't got these habits of work. There's nothing in jail that's going to teach them how to do that, how to show up every day, how to do what's ex-pected of you and to give you a skill that you can sell somewhere. There aren't training programs to enable people.

There are some programs, but they're very underfunded, underconcep-tualized. I know they don't teach people very much when they teach them anything at all. Yes, we need programs; we need these programs when people are young. We need them when people are in school, in high school, and af-terwards. We need training programs to give people skills that enable them to make a living before they ever go to jail. No, I don't think that rehabilitation is a serious element in the prison system anywhere that I know of. And so, of course, that just increases the chance that people are going to try to make a dollar in a way that's familiar to them.

These are correctional facilities only if you believe that punishment is a corrective. If you believe that pulling a person out of their family, out of their society, and throwing them in some place where they're in danger of one thing or another, if you think that's a corrective, then correctional facilities are cor-recting, but I think that by and large they're not. In fact, they're deepening people's habits and associations, unfortunately.

JB: Is there anything else that you would like to add before we conclude the in-terview?

JS: I would just like to thank you for doing this. And I understand that you're going to talk, if you haven't already, to some friends of mine in town who have not only a lot of experience to relate but who, I will tell you ahead of time, are men of great character and courage and perseverance, and I think you'll get good interviews with them.

JB: I'm very much excited.

JS: Thank you for doing this. This is such a big subject. It touches so many aspects of life in America, but I think it's time for us to take a book like Michelle Alexander's and get together, talk about it together, and figure out what in every locality we can do to turn the tide because one point I'd like to make that she also makes—during slavery and Jim Crow times, the oppression people experienced tended to pull them together. Not so in the present, in the new Jim Crow, because the oppression that's laid on people today makes them ashamed of themselves, makes their families ashamed of them, makes their families ashamed to admit that they're in prison and so forth, and that's something we've got to get over. We've got to stop letting shame that originates in oppression keep us apart. We have to pull together and be strong and bring about the changes we want to see happen. So thank you very much.

# Harold Folley

*Interviewed by* TSHEPO MORONGWA CHÉRY

TSHEPO MORONGWA CHÉRY: How did you get involved in Virginia Organizing?[1]

HAROLD FOLLEY: I got involved with Virginia Organizing through the Public Housing Association of Residents, a citywide organization that works on housing issues throughout the city of Charlottesville. There are seven public housing sites, and I was an organizer for them. Then I became an organizer for Virginia Organizing in 2007.

TMC: What's the connection between the public housing project and Virginia Organizing?

HF: Well, our concept at Virginia Organizing is a little bit different than the Public Housing Association of Residents. Public Housing Residents work on a small issue. They work on rent issues, they work on maintenance issues, and they work on issues within the Housing Authority. Virginia Organizing works on issues in Virginia, so we could be working on racial profiling, we could be working on living wage, restoration of [voting] rights, civil engagement. We could work on broad things [that] we can pull in housing authority residents to help us with, issues [that] affect them also.

TMC: What exactly is your role in Virginia Organizing?

HF: I am a community organizer, so I am the one who interviews people, which we call one-on-ones, and I'm the one who will find people. We tend to bring people as volunteers first, so they can get a look of what Virginia Organizing does. For instance, sometimes we bring people in to do phone banking, to make phone calls about Social Security or phone calls about Medicaid or when Governor Kaine was in office, calling folks to ask Governor Kaine to give rights back to all felons. So what I do is, I create leaders. I give people the leadership skills they need to become leaders in their community.

TMC: Can you speak a little bit more about the organizing surrounding ex-felons and restoration of rights?

HF: I believe maybe in my second year there at Virginia Organizing the issue about rights came up. So I had an opportunity to have some volunteers help me organize around restoration of rights. Folks like Jim Shea and his wife, Brenda Lambert, [were] so important in this process because they had the same vision I had—to get as many people their rights back and get as many people [the] opportunity to vote. We wanted to help folks who were paying taxes and not able to vote or not able to say what they feel about an issue in the state government or in the local government or in the federal government.

TMC: You said that you helped create leaders in different neighborhoods and different communities. How did Virginia Organizing create those leaders around this issue? What did the process look like?

HF: Charlottesville is a funny place. We have a lot of folks who are not felons but who are looking for things to do, who want something to do, so it was kind of easy. I remember [the] first meeting we had. We had over thirty people there ready to help out to get people their rights back, so it's an easy process and those folks are already leaders. They w[ere] just looking for extra stuff to do because they felt the need to help ex-felons get their rights back. We split folks up into five groups. . . . [W]e had thirty people. . . . [There were six] people [in each group]. We would go to Tonsler Park or Legal Aid or different places and have meetings. We wouldn't call them meetings but we would meet folks there and help them with their rights then and there. We even had someone from OAR [Offender Aid and Restoration] to help us by the name of Jason Ness. OAR is an organization that works with individuals who just got out of jail to help them find jobs, get their license if they need it, get their IDs if they need it. Jason Ness is the guy who helped us out. He [is] a notary public so if we filled the applications out, he could sign off right there and we could just stick them in the mail.

When we first met, we had big hopes and big dreams about helping folks get their [voting] rights back, but as we did those meetings, we found out that we had to reevaluate what we were doing because [out of four meetings] we might have gotten three people to come to those meetings. I'm talking about three ex-felons.

We did a lot of announcements on the radio, particularly 92.7, the black radio station here in Charlottesville. We did a lot of flyering. We put up stuff where [we] know that folks would hang out at, and then we did a meeting at Tonsler Park where it's predominantly African American, but we didn't get the numbers that we wanted. The folks helping [with the process] stopped coming to help the ex-felons with the process of the applications.

TMC: So the original thirty who you started with who are community leaders, many of them were not ex-offenders?

HF: No.

TMC: They were just community leaders, interested in this issue? Then they stopped coming? [Then] ex-offenders also stopped coming?

HF: Yes, and so then we had to reevaluate what we were doing, and we decided that we [were] going to do it on a one-on-one basis. What you have now is folks, ex-felons, who do know that I am doing this, and they stop me every so often. What I believe is some ex-felons do obtain jobs, and some of those jobs don't ask if you've been arrested or anything, so I have folks come to me in grocery stores whispering to me, it's like, "Can you help me get my rights back?" or pulling me to the side like, "I got this job but they don't know I'm an ex-felon, and I really want my rights back." . . . I realized then [why] a lot of people didn't come to us. A lot of ex-felons didn't come to us because of the shame, because society will look down on them as being ex-felons, so that's when Jim and I came and we reevaluated what we had to do, and like I said before, we decided to do the one-on-one thing, and we've been doing the one-on-one since I think about two years. So, say, for instance, since January, we might've had fifteen people who contacted me about getting their rights. Maybe out of the fifteen, ten [have had their rights restored], and so that's still good. That's a good number. It's become more recent now that folks want their rights back. I think with that happening, we're going to still need help eventually because if I get a list of ten people who can get their rights back, Jim cannot do ten people at one time, so I think once the ball starts rolling as far as folks knowing that they could get their rights back, it's going to be—I'm still going to need help with it.

TMC: Can you go back a little bit to this issue of privacy for ex-offenders and their former status? What did people say to you? Once you had that initial meeting, what do you think was the general consensus about this idea of hiding versus being open about [their] previous status? Was it specifically about a personal shame? Was it about maintaining employment?

HF: Mostly the folks who did come to me [were] more ashamed of their employer finding out they were ex-felons, and they felt like if their employers found out, they [were] going to get fired, so it was an economic reason for them because most of those folks were working maybe two or three years at that job, and they might've had a felony ten years ago, so it was mostly an economic reason.

TMC: You also said that you think you found more recently that people are more active about getting their rights. Why do you think that is?

HF: I think what's adding to that is, one, if you look at the status of how many people who live in Virginia or [how many] ex-felons are African American, you'll see that they feel proud that there's a black man as a president so they feel like they want to vote for someone who looks like them. One guy I talked to said his charge was in '85, and he's like, "I really want to vote," so it's people want to vote now. They want to get in the process. They want to be able to say, "I voted for him," and not knowing that once they get their rights back, they can go to speak to their member of Congress about issues that's relating to them, like lack of education, lack of employment.

TMC: What exactly is the process for ex-offenders to regain their voting rights, particularly in the state of Virginia?

HF: Well, the state of Virginia is the hardest place to get your rights back. Virginia is one of those good-old-boy states who[se] [leaders] back in the day realized that Jim Crow's not going to be here long, and so they decided to use mass incarceration to limit votes. So it's a two-pronged process. You have a process that's for felons that have violent felonies. Then you have a process that is for felons that have nonviolent felonies. What happened was in Warner's administration, nobody ever looked at them [ex-felons] when Mark Warner became governor. Before then, they would just throw them in a box and somebody'll see it, and it'll have cobwebs and dust on it, but when Mark Warner came in, he wanted to do something, and Mark Warner did do something. He made something happen where the process was faster. Instead of a thirteen-page application, he made it a one-page application, but what Mark Warner did was compromise, and he made drug offenses, which predominantly affect the black community, violent offenses, so that means instead of them doing the one-page application, they still have to do the thirteen-page application. So Mark Warner did something wonderful, but he compromised because he didn't want to feel like he was "soft" on drugs.

So, you have two applications. A one-page application for those who commit nonviolent felonies, then you have the thirteen-page, which is not really thirteen pages. It's thirteen pages, but it's got some application process that you have to do, some writing processes that you have to do, three letters of recommendation you had to get from folks, but I think the most difficult part for a lot of people, black or white, is the writing part. Then the other part is finding the information on your probation, on your parole, on your fines that you've had to pay, when you got out for probation, so it's a process that's so difficult that a lot of ex-felons don't even want to do it once they find out.

It's good to have Jim Shea there to say, "Come on, man, we can still do this, we can get this done." I had a guy who got his rights back I think maybe last year sometime. He was from Stuarts Draft, and his friend called me and said, "How you doing?" I said, "Hi." He said, "Mike — said you helped him get his rights back. I want to know if you can help me." I was like, "Yeah, no problem. I'm going to send you the application. Which one do you need?" He said, "Hmmm—I don't even have a sixth-grade education. I'm going to need some help," and to me, that's no problem. I don't judge anybody about education, their color or nothing as long as they can be able to help themselves. So I hooked him up with Jim, and I think he eventually got his rights back, but I think he might be still waiting for them. But like I said before, it's two applications, the long form and the short form. And the short form is very easy. You just fill it out with your name, the date of your crime, and you just send it in. The long form is very long, very redundant, and very scary from a point of view where you have lack of education, so that's it.

TMC: In what ways do you think disenfranchisement has affected ex-offenders in their reentry process into their own communities?

HF: The biggest thing I think is getting a job because every other application has that box asking, Have you committed a felony in the last five years, have you committed a felony in the last ten years, or have you ever committed a felony, and it always say it doesn't matter, but I'm an ex-felon, and I know it matters because I can remember applying for a job at the hospital, and my interview was so good. I mean, I'm a good interviewer. I know I am, and he got to the part where that box was, and the guy changed his whole attitude, and I was interviewing for a job just to mop floors and dump trash and maybe clean up some blood, and I was very young at the time so I didn't really understand what was going on. He looked at me and he said, "You know, I can't hire you because the nurses might think you steal drugs off the nurse's cart and it won't look right," and to me, I was upset and I walked out. I shook his hand, I wasn't mean or anything. I was like, "Thank you," but realizing that this guy was full of it because, first of all, the nurses do not know who is doing what or what they have in their files, and if I had known that, then I would've said, "No, the nurses wouldn't know anything about me."

But I can remember in the same year interviewing with UVA six times for a phlebotomist job. I decided I wanted to be a phlebotomist, and I went [and] took the phlebotomy course. I had to get my hundred finger pricks and a hundred sticks in the arms, and the only way I could do [it] is to be in a hospital setting, and so I had six interviews, and the last interview that lady said, "You know what, I'm sorry we gave you the runaround, but we're not going to hire you." So I looked at myself and thought, you know, this is so wrong. People judge me about what I did before but don't look at what I'm doing now, and so a lot of people I know feel so bad when that question comes up, particularly folks who have kids. It's worse because most of the folks who have kids are struggling, and if they're not living with their mother, they're probably paying child support and they need that job.

I hear a lot of my friends—because I got a lot of ex-felons who are my friends—say, you know, "It's hard for me to even get a job." I know one guy who's a friend of mine, he can't get a job so what he does is, he dumpster dives. He goes through dumpsters to get money to make sure that his kids have food on the table or they have school shoes. It's sad that so many folks look at criminals or ex-felons as criminals who're going to continue to be criminals, but no one ever give them a chance. The reason why I am who I am now is because somebody gave me a chance. Somebody looked at me and said, "You know what, I'm going to give you a chance." So I always feel if people who look at these applications say, "I'm going to give this guy a chance," then they wouldn't have to worry about people calling in or people saying they're sick or leaving early because most ex-felons are going to work 110 times harder because they know they're being looked at as someone who's going to do something wrong.

TMC: Currently, there're eleven states that bar ex-offenders from voting, among them Alabama, Delaware, Florida, Iowa, Kentucky, Mississippi, Nevada, New Mexico, Tennessee, Virginia, and Wyoming. Do you think that there's a particular impulse as to why these states in particular are limiting or barring voting rights? Is there something in particular that's going on in Virginia or the South or how are you viewing this particular regulation?

HF: To me, when you talk about the South, the South is what the South is. They have politicians who're always throwing the rhetoric out about being tough on crime, but is it surprising? It doesn't surprise me that it would be the southern states because if you look at the population of folks who are being incarcerated and losing their rights to vote, it is African Americans, and so it was a bigger plan to me. I'm not saying it's a conspiracy theory or anything, but I think it's a bigger plan to make sure. I'll tell you what happened in Florida. Governor Crist gave the rights back to all those felons two years ago, and the new southern governor came in and rescinded [them] and took, what, 500,000 or 300,000 people['s] right to vote, and you think about that. That's a big voting bloc right there. That can determine whether you're going to win something or you're going to lose something, so I think they know the numbers and they don't really care, because in Virginia if Governor Kaine had [given] back all the rights to ex-felons—that's over 250,000 people—who could vote, that was a valuable voting bloc for any candidate, so they know.

They deal with numbers all the time, and they know what that means so I think it's a bigger plan than what they say that it is because they could today or tomorrow, Governor McDonnell can write an executive order to give all rights back to ex-felons. I mean, he's doing some great things as far as reentry and making it easier for ex-felons to get their rights back and all, but . . . if he were to give rights back to ex-felons automatically, he know[s] they wouldn't vote for him. [*laughter*]

TMC: So what good things is [Governor McDonnell] doing in particular? You mentioned some of them, but what things are you viewing as good things?

HF: Well, the process is faster. If someone [applies], they'll get an answer back in ninety days. It used to be six months to a year, so they'll give an answer back to them in ninety days. He's putting money into reentry programs, so he knows that it's a problem, but it's [only] so much [he] can do about that because he is a Republican and his party would look at him as, you know, turning [his] back on the party if he does any more than what he has to do. I thought he was going to come in and do nothing, but he has done something good.

TMC: This issue of extending voting rights that's coming from governors in general, do you think that enfranchisement should be extended to current inmates, not ex-felons, but those who are incarcerated at the moment? Currently the states of Maine and Vermont are allowing inmates to vote. What might be some of the concerns for letting inmates vote in prison? I know you mentioned this voting bloc issue.

HF: That's another voting bloc if you think about it. I think in Virginia there's a million people locked up, so if a million people vote, they're not going to vote in a particular way. I don't know. I really don't know. That's something that would never happen in Virginia. They wouldn't even talk about that in the legislature because that would be a dream to inmates so I know that wouldn't dare happen here in Virginia.

TMC: You said it would be a dream to inmates. Do you think current inmates are thinking about voting rights, about their political presence?

HF: No, no, no, and the reason why they're not thinking like that [is] because they are thinking too much of their time, protecting their life in prison or making sure they have canteen, so, no, there is nothing in their eyesight right now, so to say. . . . [T]hey probably do talk political stuff, but a lot of people who do get out of prison don't really think about their rights until maybe five years if they're out of prison, maybe ten years.

TMC: So why do you see in the five-to-ten-year period people starting to think about their political rights and political presence?

HF: Because that give[s] them enough time to say, "I'm five years out of being in prison," so they probably got a job or probably getting back with their family members, the immediate family members, like the baby mommas or their kids, and they're establishing a life now.

Sometimes when you establish a life, your kids can be the drive for you to say, "Daddy, are you going to vote?" [A]nd if a child keeps saying that or people around said, "You know, did you vote today or are you going to vote?" that means they've changed their lifestyle. They're in a new culture of life now, and that's why I say five to ten years because everything changes. If you out that long, you're not hanging with the same people anymore so you either just hanging around people who are doing some stuff or you're just hanging with people who're doing nothing at all. I'm talking about crime stuff. And so the people that you are hanging with are mostly positive figures, so people who've been out five years, they mostly are churchgoing, and the pastors talk to them, and they [have] friends in the church and they [say] . . . "I went to vote" or saying "I voted for Obama." You know, so it kind of embarrasses you that you're not able to vote.

So, everything changes, and you sit there and think about like, "Man, maybe I should get my rights back," but then some people get false ideas about their rights. . . . I talked to a guy last night about his rights, and he said that his cousin told him that he can go to a judge and get his record expunged so he can get a job, and I told him, "That's not right; you have to get your rights back, then you gotta ask the governor to expunge your record." People think if they get their rights back, they can get a job also, and I always tell people, "You're getting your rights back; you're getting your rights back to vote. It might not help you get a job, but it'll give you an opportunity to make your voice be heard." Some people are like, "Okay, I'm still going with it," but some people are like, "You know what, I don't even want my rights back now if they're not going to give me a job." So it's about the money. If people can't put money in their pockets and they're ex-felons, they ain't going to care about voting, you know. Just point-blank.

TMC: So currently thirty-five states prohibit felons from voting while they're on parole. Thirty of those states exclude felony probationers as well. When is it appropriate for ex-offenders to get their rights?

HF: When they get out of prison. Once they finish their jail term, prison term. I think they should get their rights back automatically because when you're in prison, they give you money if you can't get to where you live; they give you money, they give transportation to get where you got to go, so why can't you get your rights back, too? So if an ex-felon get[s] out and he does good—say, for instance, he does wonderful. He get[s] out and get[s] a job on the first week he get[s] out and been out five years, paid all his probation and his stuff, why shouldn't he have an opportunity to have his rights automatically?

TMC: Many proponents of disenfranchisement argue that those who commit felonies have essentially given up their rights to actively participate in civil society, so they argue that disenfranchisement acts as a deterrent for future crime, so have you found that disenfranchisement has acted as a deterrent in any way for any ex-offenders or, in fact, is it quite the opposite?

HF: It's the opposite.

TMC: How so? Because people are saying essentially that if you commit a crime, then you have actively given up your rights and you should never get your rights back, and this is part of the punishment. That's what you suffer as having committed those crimes. That's the argument that they're saying. Furthermore, other people are saying beyond that, it helps people say, "Okay, I'm not going to commit."

HF: No, that's just a myth.

TMC: Those are the major arguments that people are putting forth.

HF: I mean, the numbers tell you for yourself if you look at it. People lose their rights every day, and 60 percent of those people who lose their rights get out of prison [and] go back to jail, so it's not a deterrent.

TMC: Two questions then. Since you were talking about the recidivism rate because people come out and then there are some people who are successful and are able to change their lifestyle, as you said, but then there're some people who don't have the opportunity to excel partially because of how society has structured things, so then what do we do with the issue of rights? Do they continue to get them? If [their rights] are bestowed [on them] immediately when they're out of prison, is that the process you think should constantly be like that?

HF: I think so. I mean, I think what people are looking for is opportunity. Most people who got their rights back know it's so important just to have their voting card in their pocket, so it's like a whole different change in people's attitudes. Even that person who gets out and decide[s] they want to change their life, that person decided that he don't want to go back to jail once he got out of prison. Or if that person fifteen years later decided he wants his rights back, that person still decided that they don't want to go back to jail, so it's not about the rights. This is about people's decisions . . . [and their] attitudes about opportunity.

TMC: Since you are with the Virginia Organizing Project, do you see something very unique in terms of the demographics of ex-felons and organizing happening in Charlottesville, or do you think there're similar problems and they're being addressed in similar ways throughout Virginia?

HF: With the ex-felon thing, it's spotty, you know, say, for instance, I haven't got a call for two months about somebody wanting help to get their rights back, and all of a sudden now, I got ten people who want their rights back and then probably later on in 2012, I might get fifty people just because they want to vote. That's another thing, too. Folks only vote when there's a presidential election, so we'll probably get more people who want their rights back, and that's good. We accomplished what we had to accomplish, but I think it's just spotty. I think folks don't know. I had people call me, it's like, "Somebody told me I could never get my rights back," and so folks do not know what their rights [are].

The only thing that Charlottesville has [is] the University of Virginia because the University of Virginia drives the liberal state of mind in Charlottesville. If you lived in Danville, it's a whole different thing because Danville doesn't have a liberal-type school there. They have the good old boys, and they're not going to do too much rallying around ex-felons, so it's hard in different communities to really organize folks, but we still do it. At Virginia Organizing, we decided that we're going to do this in every place we have an organizer to say we're doing this. If someone in Danville comes to someone and say, "Hey, I need my rights back," the organizer in Danville has a place in Danville where they can go send them to get their rights back, so we refer people. What we do is, though, we take the opportunity to say, "Hey, you don't have a job, so why don't you come with us and go to this rally about jobs?" So we know we can get people connected in some other kind of way if they're ex-felons where we can give them the leadership they need to continue to fight to be citizens that can vote in the state of Virginia because . . . most people who lost their rights to vote are living in a lower economic spectrum. . . . They probably [don't] have the income capability to send their kids to school if they want to. They don't probably have the economic ability to go to school themselves, so what we do is we engage them [by saying] . . . "Why don't you come with us to see how other people are doing stuff?" so organizing is about showing people where the dots are and how you can connect the dots.

## Note

1. Virginia Organizing is a statewide grassroots organization dedicated to challenging injustice by empowering people in local communities to address issues that affect the quality of their lives. Virginia Organizing especially encourages the participation of those who have traditionally had little or no voice in our society. By building relationships with individuals and groups throughout the state, Virginia Organizing strives to get them to work together, democratically and nonviolently, for change.

# Eddie Harris

*Interviewed by* TSHEPO MORONGWA CHÉRY

TSHEPO MORONGWA CHÉRY: This is an interview with Mr. Eddie Harris from REAL Dads.[1] Can you please describe how you got involved with the [REAL Dads] program?

EDDIE HARRIS: Well, actually I got involved with REAL Dads when I was facing a criminal situation and I needed a job. I was working at a carpet-cleaning place doing some telemarketing, and a friend of mine suggested [that I] contact the folks at Children, Youth & Family Services. They were doing some outreach in our community, and they felt like because I know the community so well that that would be a pretty good fit for me, so I started off actually working on the Parenting Mobile, doing outreach in different communities, and then we got here. We started to shape and form and talk about forming a program that would serve men incarcerated or men with incarcerated type of lifestyles, you know, high-risk, low-income fathers that don't seem to get the type of support. So that's pretty much how I got involved in it.

TMC: REAL Dads, where did the idea come from?

EH: The idea came from myself, along with my supervisor Hilary Nagle and a gentleman that still works here—his name is Josh Stewart. We got together and started like bouncing some ideas off of each other, and we went to other staff people, other people in the community. I did about two months' worth of interviews with people and just asking them about their view of fatherhood, what would they like to see in a program, and just getting a feel from the people that I probably wouldn't be serving or outreaching to, and we put all of that together and we're still like shaping and molding it. So it was something that was created here at Children, Youth & Family Services by us, by myself.

My supervisor plays a really big part in it. We reached out to the people at the jail, got involved with that, and it's been molding and shaping since then pretty much.

TMC: How does the program function?

EH: REAL Dads is really an acronym. REAL means Responsible Evolving Available Loving men in the lives of their children, and the way it works is that I first was going to the jail. I felt like, you know, well, we felt like that's an underserved group of people, fathers, almost like the forgotten father. You go to jail, the only thing you can look forward to is having a high child-support bill when you come out. Nothing like support or anything like that was available, so we started really looking at that, and we got in touch with the jail people, Colonel Mathews and Phyllis, who's the program director over there, and they were very good about letting us come in and they've been good about us doing—

We did a little short DVD film of the fathers to send to their children, so the way it works is that guys get in my group in the jail or guys have been in my program out here in the community, and I serve them. It's not like a 120-day program. It's like a lifetime program if you're going to stay involved in it, and I see guys in the community once a week. I go to the jail on Mondays. We do a group, a six-man group, so it doesn't get all big and bulky and people get lost in it. We want to keep it intimate for trust issues so guys can speak freely about some issues that might be bothering them and, at the same time, learn to trust other individuals with some of their stuff, so I mean, it works like that.

When they transition out, if they want to remain a part of REAL Dads, I continue to outreach them, continue to see them; even if they don't want to formally be in the program, I will stay in touch with them. I will keep reaching out to them, and it's just something that's going to tie into the rest of the things that are going on in the community with Second Chance, peer support network, and different things that's going to be in place to help guys who are transitioning back to be a part of the community, be a part of their family, be a positive part in their neighborhoods.

TMC: Can you give me an example of when you meet with people who are in the community, what does a meeting or a group meeting of REAL Dads do?

EH: Like in the jail? Or in the community?

TMC: Either one or both.

EH: It's different. In the jail, we use this curriculum called InsideOutDads, and all of the guys have a manual, and what I've been doing is letting each group member go through the book and pick what page we're going to focus on for the next week, so they will do the lesson, and we'll have a group discussion about whatever the lesson was. We'll go over the questions together. Everybody gets a chance to participate in it and engage with it. It's something that all guys normally [get] engaged [with] in the group. We have a set of group rules that we follow about the profanity thing and cross-talking thing. We like to keep that down to a minimum, and that way we get more work done, and then we'll set up who's going to pick the topic for the next week. We have a group discussion. Unless someone has something that's really bothering them, then we'll shut that down and we'll focus on whatever it is that they're going to bring to the group and in the community; it basically changes from individual to individual because each individual is dealing with a different set of things that they're really focusing on.

I mean, one guy I'm dealing with right now is basically homeless. He's going from like place to place to live. He's been on my case load since '08, though, and he's going through substance-abuse issues and all of that. I still meet with him once a week, and his issues are quite different than the guy that I meet with that owns his own business, you know, and probably the most common thing that I see is that a person has to decide when they're going to respond to whatever life is bringing them different. You know, the guy that's got the substance-abuse issues and the homeless issues, he basically knows what the answers are. He has a solution process inside of himself. He's going to have to decide when he's going to start implementing it. I'm always there to help him, to assist him. I can walk with you, but I'm unable to walk for you. We can walk together.

The other guy, he's got control issues and he knows it. However, until he decides to address it in a good, responsible way, he's going to draw people to him and he's also going to run people away, and I think he's learning what that looks like now, so each meeting with each individual is different. The guys in the community don't work like the guys that's incarcerated. They [the incarcerated guys] have a manual. So many distractions in the community it's been hard for me to form a group in the community because everybody's doing so many different things at so many different times and can't find the right time, so there are other groups that are forming, and what I'm hoping to do is to be able to tag onto one of those groups and maybe bring some of this information into it, into [another] group setting. OAR is doing stuff, probation and parole is doing stuff, and you have a couple of peer support network groups that are forming, and I'm hoping to tag onto those and bring some of this information to them, just the general public.

TMC: What have you found have been the biggest obstacles for the people that you are working with, the people who are actually incarcerated right now?

EH: It's so many. If it was like just one answer, I think it would be so much easier to deal with, but I think it's a whole process [involving] all areas of a guy's life. It might be a combination between him dealing with the mother of his children, and he may have four, three, four different mothers of his children that he has to deal with, dealing with the employment issues of the day and maybe substance-abuse issues. If not that, you've got lifestyle issues because I didn't used to use but maybe I used to sell, and maybe this is how I got my money and maybe I've really got a fear of doing an interview because I don't have a lot of practice in doing that, so all these lifestyle areas, all these areas in life, you know, it's what guys are up against.

They may come out with a child-support noose around their neck. The child-support enforcement people may say, "Hey, you owe us this amount of money and if you don't get that to us right away, you're going to be in court and possibly going to be reincarcerated." Then you have your probation officer that's saying, like, "You owe $696.00 fines ,and you owe $1,200 cost of court. When can I get it?" So those are situations that people face, and depending on what kind of practice they have, responding to those and how they feel about reaching out for help plays a big role in what the result's going to be. If my relationship with instant gratification is like high up on my list, well, then I may not be willing to wait for the work at McDonald's, so I have to put myself in places, probably different places, than I'm used to being, but it takes a willingness.

First, I got to be honest and say the way that I was doing things didn't work. Then I have to be open enough to listen and try something different. I've got to be willing to show up for myself. All of that is so complicated, though. I wish it was just a matter of a simple answer, but it's spread out so far and it's got so many legal ends, and the way the community responds to these people plays a big part in it also because, I mean, when I perceive somebody is responding to me a certain way because I may have a record or I may be a certain color, something like that, it does something to my insides, and I imagine it does to anybody. I think community attitude plays a big part in it also, the way these guys that are transitioning or women that are transitioning, the way that the community responds to them plays a big part in what the direction they go in also.

TMC: What are the specific ways that REAL Dads helps with the transition back into the community, the reentry process?

EH: Well, right now what REAL Dads does is, it's like a resource kind of a bank. I had a guy that just got out day before yesterday, and my thing is [to let him] know . . . what's available, to find out what their needs are. Hopefully what we try to do is get some kind of aftercare situation worked out for them, let them work it out when they know that they're getting ready to transition, so those things can be in place. I can contact the folks that I may need to contact to help them because this particular guy is trying to get into Piedmont and take some classes. I don't want [to have getting] into Piedmont to be [a] stumbling block. . . . So, I was making bus passes available to him or setting up a contact with someone that he knew, someone that he felt comfortable with that would transport him to these different places.

What REAL Dads really does is like collaborate with different people like people like Mr. Dickerson that works over at the Haven, Mr. Foley, anybody that may have community connections to whatever these guys' particular issues might be. If they've got substance-abuse situations going on, I get them linked up with the twelve-step community. If they [are] homeless, I get them linked up with the people at the Haven that deal with that. Just getting them plugged in with the proper resources is mostly what REAL Dads do, and then we continue to work on whatever their parenting goals are and how we're going to be able to fulfill those in the midst of all these other responsibilities. We don't want to lose sight of our main mission to help guys identify some goals for themselves and to support them in reaching those goals, but a big part of that is, is a guy really doing what he needs to do as a man?

TMC: What does that look like? When you say, "doing what he needs to do as a man," I know there might be different representations of it for people, but what types of goals are people thinking about?

EH: I've never actually met a guy since I've been doing this work that wanted to be [a bad] father. All guys—most guys that I speak with—want a better relationship with their children. They want a job so they can support themselves and their family. Most guys want to map out a future for themselves and their family, you know, not like a day-to-day existence, something like a future. In talking to these young men and older men, too, when we start talking goals to them and visions . . . "What would you like for your future to look like? What are you passionate about?" These are sometimes questions that they haven't touched on in a while because a lot of the dreams, goals, and aspirations that they have may be underneath a big pile of whatever, so to get back in touch with that, it's great because you see the light come on, but then we have to support that. We have to nurture that because just like that light was on before, it got dimmed out, so we have to support that and help them follow through because a lot of these guys, they got goals of being a good person, a productive person in the community. Not everyone has the practice of being receptive to things that are not quite fair or things that they perceive like, "I didn't deserve that," and it's a difficult road, man, you know. It's a difficult road.

TMC: You've identified some of the key ways that agencies and non-profits in Charlottesville are helping ex-offenders, but I'm wondering what have been some of the obstacles that you've faced in trying to create these systems of support?

EH: I think one of the biggest obstacles is the fear, and it's the community buy-in because I can give all the tools in the world, and I can have a guy ready to face the world, but if the world is not ready for him? As, you know, Charlottesville signed a proclamation to be a City of Second Chances, [but] you've got the people in the community saying, "I don't want them people over here. This is my business, I don't want him working for me," you know. So does that support an underground lifestyle, if you have all the employees feeling like, "No, I'd rather not? No, he has this on his record." But he's in our community so what do we do with them, you know, is this the new Jim Crow? I don't know.

TMC: How do you think imprisonment in particular affects ex-offenders' or inmates' relationships with their families?

EH: That's hard. On both sides you have expectations. If I'm incarcerated, if I'm the one that's incarcerated, I have expectations of my family—Are they going to come visit me? Are they coming to visit or they're going to send me money, and some of those expectations I have on that side of the fence are unreal because I've got to realize that they still have to pay bills, they still have to work, they still have to take care of things, and they can't like receive phone calls from me every day and still be able to send me money and still be able to live, so that affects that relationship, and it can build resentments on that side.

  Then when I transition out, my family's got some expectations of me or for me, and when I don't live up to those, that can create some resentments. I think the biggest thing that can help to turn that down is just like some real communication and getting the family involved. If we're going to do like transition-type things, I like to try to get as much of the family involved in it as possible so everybody can be in the same book and close to the same page so everybody can get the healing. There's a lot of healing that needs to go on, and if I'm just the only one healing and you've been hit, too, so I've got bandages and iodine and all that stuff on me, but you're sitting in the chair with your head gashed open and still bleeding and everything's supposed to be cool . . . that's not really real to even think that it's going to be that way. Yeah, [incarceration is] really hard on both parties, and it's a family destroyer.

I speak on that from personal [experience]. When my son left, his daughter was like one. She'll be twelve before he gets home. He gets home in September, and even though they've been in communication, she's been going to visit him and all of that, it takes so much away from that man, the man part, and it takes so much away from that child. It's a lose/lose when we don't support those situations because people get reincarcerated.

I would actually love to see people talk more about these men becoming entrepreneurs, these men talk about business ownership rather than if I could get a job over there. Yeah, that's fine, you know, but when we start owning our own businesses, we can employ and we have power. [Reentry] is definitely a social problem. It's definitely like a human rights problem. It's also an economic problem, you know, and we have to look at it from that aspect because that's the real part of it. Those elements are what make up like a real community.

TMC: How do you get the families involved in the process, whether they're in the community or they're incarcerated?

EH: Well, what I attempt to do, and this has worked out a couple of times to where I was seeing the male person in the family, and we have home visitors here [Children Youth and Family Services] that deal with the female part of it.

We actually [have] some strengthening-families programs. My coworker, Beth, does a great class that involves the whole family, getting them involved in stuff where they can kind of learn how to talk things in the family and build a unit back up. The family is like very, very, very [shot] up, you know; the family is almost like nonexistent, and to try to heal that and try to repair that, you need everybody at the table and a couple of classes that she offers, that she does, give everybody an opportunity to kind of voice it in a nonchaotic way, you know, in an orderly way. Everybody's voice, the kids' voice can be heard, the father can kind of like get back in his square. And that's one of the major resources that I use.

Then there's other things in the community that's offered. Region 10, OAR, different programming like that. If I can, I try to hook people up with somebody that they can meet with almost like on an individual [level]. I feel like a lot better about that.

TMC: Historically, at least in terms of the public consciousness, African Americans have generally not been receptive to psychological examinations, to therapy sessions, so has that been a challenge in convincing people to be a part of that, or are there other alternatives that you've presented?

EH: For me, it's not really that challenging, and the reason why is that I know a lot of people in the community, first of all, and I'm not coming in like I'm the expert in the room. I'm coming in [like], "I want to know how I can serve you."

TMC: I mean the things that you've talked about outside from you, so some of these classes that you're talking about?

EH: How receptive are some of the people? Well, they're not as receptive to it as I would like. Yeah, you hit it because a lot of people don't take that step. I've had like maybe one or two that tried it. One family tried it and finished one aspect of it, but that was like one family out of all the ones that I suggested it to. Then they tried another portion of it, and they didn't complete that. I think they maybe went to like one or two groups, and I think that's a real disconnect right there because the resources are not really actually getting to the people the way that I would love to see them get to them.

TMC: I was going to ask you that next, why [do] you think people don't want to participate?

EH: Well, it's comfort, I think. It's like we're doing this interview, you know, before we started, we got to know each other a little bit better, and I got comfortable with you. I'm not sure that these classes are being presented that way to where it's like either you come or you don't, or I don't know how that's presented, you know, so I don't want to judge him or anything like that.

TMC: Not even [just] these particular classes in Charlottesville because this seems to be a larger problem.

EH: Definitely so. It's got stigma to it, attached to it, and I think my experience is that I can't approach everybody the same way, you know, some people have to—I mean, if it's not working, if I'm not drawing the people that I know I could serve on a national level, so maybe I should look at my process. Maybe my process is flawed somewhere because I'm not getting the people in that I know will best be served by some of these measures, and for me just to say it was available and you didn't come, but I'm a service provider, a national service provider, so what am I supposed to be doing? Providing a service, right? So sometimes we have to meet the people where're they at, and I don't know. I don't know. It is a problem, and it's a big problem. It's too big of a problem. I don't like it. [laughter]

TMC: In terms of young men, the children of ex-offenders, are there any services or any specific things that you're targeting with them because just even in terms of the literature, there's this whole discussion about a cyclical family, a family [in which] one generation is incarcerated and the next generation has a higher risk of being incarcerated and so on? I focus on young men, but, of course, it's obviously young girls as well that might be at risk.

EH: The guys that I deal with in the group, what I normally do and what I have been doing is getting like stats to them about incarceration numbers and all that and the effects that it has on the children, just to bring the awareness up on that, and at one point we had like a little reader's list going on. Guys were getting transferred so quick that some of the books got—because I was basically buying these books myself . . . and bringing books from my personal library for them to read and for them to take a look at. I had this book, *Why Are So Many Black Men Incarcerated?* and I thought that was something good for them to read. It was a little statistic heavy, but I thought it was good for them to take a look at.

There was another book that was written by this young man and the title really caught me. [It was] *Hustle to Win,* something like that, you know. It was almost like, how you can win hustling, right? And if anybody that's hustled, they'd be like, "What? They got a book on that?" But the title was totally different than what you may have thought because when you get into the book, it gets into aspects of how you're living your life and how to really look at what it is that you're doing and are you really hustling, and I thought that was a really good book and guys connected with it because they connected with that element, that hustle element of it, so I try to get them to read those type of books.

There was another book that we had on our reading list, *Know Thyself,* because I'm really big on self-acceptance, and I'm really big on self-awareness, and I'm really big on guys getting a relationship with themselves and whatever God that they serve where they have some power greater than them or however they want to view that, but to get those relationships straight and then they can get some other relationships in their lives straight. And just try to pass that type of information on. The *Science of the Mind* book or *The Spirit of a Man* by Iyanla Vanzant. I thought that was a powerful reading and just sharing those types of readings with them, but like I say, a lot of that came like books that I had and I was like, "You want to check a book out?" and I got permission to do it so I could just put the little sticker in the book and they could read it, but they weren't coming back because they don't know when they're going to get transferred and when somebody says pack your stuff up, I mean, the last

thing that you're thinking about is like, "Oh, I gotta get this book to —." You
might carry it with you or you might have loaned it to somebody in the block,
and you was going to get it back and bring it back to class, but it never got a
chance to happen, so the book is somewhere floating around and at least it's
floating, you know. But I would like, you know, I've started it again on a small
level like circulating one book around, and so far it's like it's got to two guys.
One guy read it in a week, which I was pretty impressed by that, and I'll see
where the other guy's going to go with it. I do some work with artists. Right
now, I'm working with a music artist. He does rap, and he's going to be coming
out with a song pretty soon that he didn't write . . . with Second Chance in
mind or peer support network in mind, but the song fits so much what I see
that these movements are trying to capture. It fits it so well so and he's . . . I've
watched this guy transition. He's an ex-offender. He's been out for about like
four years. Went in at seventeen, got out at twenty-seven, so he did like ten
years. He's got a son that's like fifteen. He's got a little daughter that's like a year
and a half, and he's just learning to live life and bigger than the music, it gives
me an opportunity I think to have an impact on this young man's life. I can
share with him what was so freely shared with me when I was growing up, you
know, the real things and the true things and the things that you can hold onto,
the things that you can hang your hat on, and I've seen it actually coming off in
the different things that he's talking about in his music. [The way] he's viewing
life now is much different than it was when we first met because we actually
first met, his cousin had asked me to help him with doing a rap project so I
helped him with the one project, and I noticed he had a very good work ethic,
and he was really like creative, and he was more into it for the art than he was
for like throwing money and all the glamorization and all of that, so that was
interesting to me and the independent aspect of it because I think so many
folks . . . When I think independent, I think free, you know, so why wouldn't
I want to be free? But I would rather sign a contract to give my freedom up
[*laughter*], you know, so I think about that, and me and him are working on
several other projects now because of the way I think about independence, and
I think the way that he sees independence and the freedoms of that, and hopefully it's an opportunity [to use] music to kind of like promote the other things
that's really important like fatherhood and giving guys an opportunity. Even
though it may not have been given to me, but being willing to give somebody
an opportunity and creating some situations and some opportunities for some
men where they can feel welcomed coming back to our community, so they
feel a part of their community, so they won't feel like they want to take away
from the community, their family, their neighbors, you know, they feel like,

"Oh, I'm a homeowner," so when you're a homeowner or you feel like you own something in the community, you're going to protect that.

But if everybody's got me in this little underclass, this little subculture in a different culture, so I think it's important, and I'm just saying be on the lookout for this music from this kid because he's got a song that's called "It's Time" and it's powerful. It gives me hope because some of the music that I listen to I'm like, "Oh, God, we're lost," you know, and then to hear that and to hear that come out, you know, I'm like, "Wow, that's a good message. That's a message that needs to be heard," so I just wanted to add that.

### Note

1. The mission of REAL Dads, sponsored by Children, Youth, and Family Services in Charlottesville, Virginia, is to improve the quality of children's lives by supporting fathers in becoming more Responsible, Empowering, Available and Loving men in the lives of their children. The program provides fathers with encouragement and support, as well as resources and information to support their parenting goals.

# Debbie Walker

*Interviewed by* TSHEPO MORONGWA CHÉRY

TSHEPO MORONGWA CHÉRY: Can you tell me a little bit about yourself and your experiences with the prison system, and how you became involved in the fe-Male Perspective?

DEBBIE WALKER: I moved up here [Charlottesville] back in March from Danville. Because of my involvement with the prison system, I made a strong decision in my life not to go back. Once you become an offender, it's really easy to go back, whether it's two years from now or whether it's ten years from the time you're released, it's just really easy to get caught back up in that, and there were people and places and things around me there that weren't good for me, and so I reached out to my mother, and she come and got me. I was here for about a week, and there was a special on public access [television] through the fe-Male Perspective. They were having teenagers come in to do interviews with [other teens] about, "Is jail cool?" Apparently some of the area teens thought jail was cool. I [later] got a call at my mom's house and was asked to [be a part of this program]. That's when I was introduced to Michelle Bates, [the executive director of the fe-Male Perspective]. I did interview the kids and explained to them that [jail] is not cool. Once you're in the system, they own you, and that's the way it is.

From there I spoke with Michelle and got really involved in the program. Then the Re-entry Summit [was held here in Charlottesville], and I became really passionate about that because the prison system makes it so hard for an offender to come out and readapt to society. You get anxiety attacks. You get like where you can't breathe because you feel so overwhelmed, like you have to pay your fines, you have to see your probation officer, but yet you have to find a job and no one wants to give you a job because you have to check that box that says you're a felon. Michelle and [the group at the fe Male Perspective] have been my support system as well as my family. You know, getting everything back in line where I can have my children and be around them and be around my granddaughter, you know, things that I had missed and still be able to have that trust. It's really hard for family members and people that don't know you to trust you or to love you for really who you are as a person, not the person that committed the crimes. When you're on drugs and you're out there, you're not the same person.

When you're in jail, you have time to reflect on everything and everyone that you hurt, including yourself, so having an organization like the fe-Male Perspective embrace me and not say, "You know what, we just want to use you just for a minute or talk to you just for a minute." It wasn't like that at all. It's like they embraced me as family so I thought, "Well, okay, if these people that don't even know me can embrace me, then I have to get back out there and just be myself," because that's all I was doing was being myself with them. I don't hide my incarceration because that was part of my life, so in order for someone to want to, like, not talk about it, I don't want to be that person anymore. I'm not that person anymore, but at the same time, that was part of my life, so I feel like being more open about it can lead more people not to do it, and so that's what I'm doing now.

TMC: I just want to take a step back and hear your story about Danville and your period of incarceration. You're originally from Danville?

DW: Yes.

TMC: When you were released from prison, where did you go and what was that experience like in terms of just reentry, first in Danville and then now in Char-lottesville/Albemarle?

DW: Well, it's a little bit more extensive than that. I was born in Danville, and I was raised in Louisiana. My mom and dad split up when I was thirteen. I stayed with my dad. My mom, I didn't even talk to her again until I was seventeen. At that point in my life, I wasn't using drugs. I didn't do anything like that. Then I moved to Arizona. I got married when I was seventeen. I graduated in June and got married in July and, yeah, and then I had my oldest daughter [Nina] when I was nineteen, almost twenty. I remember I was working in Arizona at a truck stop. Nina's dad was barely working at all, and a truck driver came in and handed me some speed. I didn't even know what it was, and someone told me what it was, which led me on a path of destruction, really.

So I got divorced and then was really trouble-free. I went to college for two years to try and obtain my associate's degree in criminal justice. Ended up getting in trouble and was in prison by the time I was twenty-nine. I turned thirty in prison. I got out. I did good. Got on drugs again in 2004 and got in trouble again, but that whole path led me from Texas to Georgia back to Virginia. I was actually on the run when they caught me in Virginia the last time. And I ended up having to do time here, and then I had to go back to Georgia and do time there. So that being said, when I got out in Georgia, they weren't going to pay my way back to Virginia, so I had a friend that actually drove fourteen hours. She drove down to Georgia, took her six hours to come and get me, and I had to be at the probation office that Friday. She came down on Thursday evening. I had to be in the probation office that Friday morning in Danville at nine o'clock. This is what they give you, so you don't have a way home. They didn't have any way of knowing anything. They just said you're going to be in the office Friday morning at nine o'clock, so at this point, I didn't even know where I was going to stay, so [her friend] brought me up there. I went to the probation officer and we talked about that night, and it was agreed that I would stay there so that I could be close to my daughters.

TMC: Staying in Virginia?

DW: In Danville, yes. It took me like six months to find a job in Danville. That's ridiculous, you know, but that's how long it took. Then once I got a job, I was paying half of the bills there at the house. We had no rent but we had utilities and all this stuff, so I'm paying half the bills. She's still telling me who can call the house and who can't call the house, who can come to the house and who can't come to the house, so I felt almost like, you know what, this is not how life is supposed to be either. If I had forty dollars left after I paid the bills, she wanted twenty dollars of that, so it was like I was never going to get up, you know. It was like she was moneying me to death, and at the same time, I felt like I was better off to be in prison almost because she was clocking me, you know.

So, it basically came to a breaking point one night. She and I both had had some drinks and we got into an altercation. I couldn't take it anymore, and it was like eleven o'clock at night, and I called my momma crying, and I was like, "I got to get out of here. I can't do this." You know, once you've done drugs, it's like really easy when things crash down on you to run that way because it's a means of escape, of escaping reality. I cried out so—it makes me want to cry now—because I didn't want to go back down that road again and it scared me, you know, because it was like, all it was, was a phone call, so which phone call do I make? I called my mom, thank God. That's when I came to Charlottesville.

It was like that quick. Even my probation officer there; she was so under-standing.

It's really important for ex-offenders to develop a rapport with their P[robation] O[fficer], because that is the person that you have besides your family and the people that are really close to you in your life. That is the person that you really have to be the most honest with and really tell them this is what's going on. I had already told my PO, you know, [about] issues troubling me [in Danville], [so] when I walked in and she saw my mom sitting there with me, she looked right at me and she said, "You going to Charlottesville, aren't you?" She already knew, you know, so not everything in the justice and the correction system is bad, you know, but it's how you handle yourself. You know, if you keep going down a path where you're lying to people and you're lying to your POs and you're lying to your family, you know, yeah, you're going to go back, but because I've been honest with myself as well as with the people around me, I've been able to overcome a lot of stuff, but it's been hard. It's not easy at all, especially being a female. I'm not African American or whatever, but it's really hard. I'm in the same box. They put me there, and it's like up to me to get out of it by myself.

TMC: So, you mentioned that the reentry process is really difficult and there are some family members and friends who can be supportive at times and problematic at other times. Can you tell me a little bit more about that? You mentioned your friend who helped you move from Georgia to Virginia but then became an issue in terms of your living situation. What about other family members?

DW: Well, like my sister made the comment one time when I got out and I went to see her, like, "How long are you out this time?" I had a nephew come down last week. He was in the Marines and he's dealt with a lot of pain[ful] issues himself when he has had too much to drink. He started [to] throw up my past, my drug use, my this, my that. People will put things in your face, and it's up to you how you deal with it. For example, the old me probably would've confronted him and argued with him. I'm not going to do that anymore. I understand that I have to develop trust with them, but at the same time, I don't owe them anything. I did my time. But it took me a long time to realize, to get to that point.

Michelle and the other people in our program [the fe-Male Perspective] have really helped me to know [that] I don't owe any explanations to those people, to my family. I know I hurt them by being incarcerated, but at the same time, I did my time. Now, let me move on with my life, and you don't have to keep throwing it back up. A major hurdle for reentry is just reentry into your own family, you know, and them trusting you again. It's not even about society. Sometimes it's easier for me to deal with someone that I don't know than it is for me to deal with someone in my own family or someone that I've been close to for years and years.

TMC: Why is it more difficult to deal with somebody that you know very well versus someone that you don't know?

DW: I think that even though I've forgiven myself, it's a process, and you really do it while you're incarcerated, well, I know I did. I wrote letters to my mom, to my kids, to my sisters. The people that I had hurt—apologizing. By the time I got ready to get out, I had already forgiven myself. I didn't know if they'd forgiven me, but it's up to them; that's not on me, you know.

TMC: I'm interested in following up on [the matter of] reent[ry]. You've talked about different relationships, [but] you haven't touched upon your daughters. You said you wrote them letters and then eventually you came back and offered yourself, so how has the process been in terms of trying to re-create these relationships with your daughters, who might have [during your incarceration] grown up a lot and changed?

DW: With my oldest daughter, at the beginning, she was real optimistic because she's twenty-one, so she's seen a lot more than my youngest daughter has. She's nine. With my youngest daughter, she just wanted to be there with me and just be with me. That's all she wanted, and so I was working toward, okay, let's get a place, let me get this straight, you know. Still I'm working trying to make a life to where I can say, "Okay, Summer, this is us. This is me and you. But I haven't even been out a year, so I was able to have her over the summer, and I don't want to disrupt her school and things like that, so at this point, she is still going to have to go back to her dad and stay. She doesn't want to go, but I can't be with her as much as I would like to be with her right now. If I brought her home to stay with me constantly, she would spend more time with her grandmother (my mom), more than she would me because of the way that I have to work.

Now, my oldest daughter and I—I'd like to think [we are] at a point where she trusts me again and we talk, [but] in the beginning when I first got out, it wasn't like that. It was more like she was more smart-alecky and basically disrespectful to me. Like she didn't owe me any respect because of me not being there for her or whatever, and I sat her down one day and I was like, you know, if you have some issues that you want to talk to me about, we just need to talk about it. I told my nine-year-old the same thing, because I might have done the things I done and for whatever reason I done them, I'm not going to make an excuse, I'm not going to say it was to try and give you all a better life because it ended up not doing that at all, so I'm not going to say that anymore, but you will respect me because I'm your mother, and I'll be there for you forever. You think that you can just talk to me any kind of way, I'm just not going to tolerate that, so whatever issues that you need to get off your chest or if it's something that makes you angry, if you want to write it down, whatever you want to do. In doing that, they said some things that night but not much. Over a period of weeks, I got more feedback from them, and we talked out the issues, and so now I feel like I've got my little girls back. You have to address the problems and issues that your family has with you as well as what you have with them.

TMC: It seems you're saying that reentry is a really complicated situation—[especially] with the people who are close to you. You mentioned that [reentry] can also be a very difficult process in the larger society. What obstacles [have you] faced [as a woman reentering society]?

DW: Well, [for] one thing, my appearance has changed. While I was incarcerated I messed my teeth up and couldn't get [them] fixed there. Then I got out here, and I couldn't get [them] fixed. It actually happened while I was in DOC [Department of Corrections], but once you're released, you're not their problem anymore. I'm dealing with things on a different level because I'm older and because of my appearance and because of my record. For example, even though I've been a waitress and I've worked in the restaurant industry for years, they won't let me serve tables, you know. I wash dishes or I work in the back, which is okay with me because really I don't even want to deal with people on that level anymore, but to have it as society telling me you can't do it anymore, it makes it harder.

There [are] some kids that work where I work now, and they come and talk to me, I think because I'm older, old enough to be most of their moms. We'll be talking, and it'll come up and then they're like, "Well, I did some jail time," you know, for like [public drunkenness] or whatever. You spend four hours [with them], and I'm like, "Don't do it again, because those little things are what leads up to big things." I talk to them so that they don't label people that are incarcerated or have been incarcerated as bad, because if I hadn't shared [my imprisonment] with them, they wouldn't have known. Some of them changed the way they talk to me, like some of them don't even talk to me anymore because of that.

TMC: What other obstacles have there been?

DW: Well, when I was immediately released in Danville, I had nowhere to live. If my friend hadn't [given] me a place to live, I wouldn't have had a place to live, you know, and as I said before, just in Danville, it took me six months to find a job. When I moved to Charlottesville, the same day because I'm persistent, you know, I'm just, like, when I set my mind to do something, that's what I'm going to do, so I got on the bus in Charlottesville that morning at like nine o'clock, and I think by three o'clock in the afternoon I had a job. But I had went—I started out downtown and I went all over town filling out applications that day, and I wasn't going to stop until I got something positive, and if I didn't get anything positive that day, I would've went out the next day.

TMC: And you went by bus?

DW: I went by bus and walked and just kept going different places. The whole reentry thing [is] about, for me—I didn't have distribution charges or anything like that. Distribution charges [are for] actually distribut[ing] drugs, which is something that I had done before, but I never got charged with it, so I was lucky in that [respect]. And I don't want to say they couldn't catch me, because they kept trying, but that's basically what it boiled down to. They never could catch me, but once you get a distribution charge, it can be . . . It doesn't even have to be on housing property. When you get a charge like that, because of the federal government and the hold that they have put on people that are distributing drugs—it can be twenty dollars' worth of cocaine. It doesn't have to be a multiple quantity, but when you get out of prison, you're not eligible for housing anymore and you're not eligible for food stamps anymore because of that distribution charge. So what you're doing, as society, [is] putting out a person that has offended coming out of prison, and they can't find a place to live or can't get any food, so what are they going to do? You know, they're going to go right back out there and they're going back to selling drugs, because that's the only way they're going to survive, unless they try and find a job and try and do right, you know, but it's really hard to just adjust to society coming out of prison.

It took me like three months before I actually went in a store, I mean, like a big store like a grocery store before I would go in there and actually shop. I would go like in one of these little country stores or like a little mini-market or something like that and get a pack of cigarettes or whatever, but to actually put me in a Wal-Mart or anything like that? I couldn't do it.

TMC: And can you explain why that was difficult for you?

DW: Because I felt like I was at a place, you know, like you get—Prison life is so structured, you know. They tell you when to get up, they count you, like you do five standing counts a day. Your movement is structured. When you move from one building to go to your job, when you move from your job to go to chow, everything is structured, so just getting out of that mind-set was difficult for me to adjust, even though I knew that I was free, at the same time in my mind, you know, I felt uncomfortable because there was no structure and I was used to this structure. Now everything is just like chaotic almost to me, so I just—It took me a little while to adjust, you know. This is life and this is prison life.

TMC: How did you adjust? How did you create that change from prison life to life outside of prison?

DW: Well, actually I had to go to a doctor, and I had to tell her. I had been prescribed Xanax before for anxiety but I was trying really not to do it, but I had to, and so she ended up having to prescribe me Xanax again, and that's how I cope. I still get anxiety attacks, you know, especially when I'm feeling really passionate about something. It's like I'll stutter or I can't get it—I can't even get it right now, you know, it's like I can't explain to people the difference, how my life would be if I had never got in trouble and what it is now because it is what it is now, so what I do with that is up to me. I still get anxious sometimes, and I worry because even though I'm not doing anything to go back [to prison], I still worry. I never want to go back, so I think that I have this guard that keeps me from really entering into society.

I mean, I do things with the program, but that's because the organization I'm in treat[s] me as family so whenever we go do something, we're together, so it's not even like I'm—I can do more things with them. They make me stronger than I can [be] with just trying to do it by myself.

TMC: Can you tell me about what you do with the fe-Male Perspective?

DW: I work with the community, [with] the Ladies & Gentlemen program for Charlottesville High School. I love that.

TMC: Tell me what that is.

DW: It's an after-school program. We have meetings on Wednesdays and Thursdays at Charlottesville High School, and we try and do things with them or come up with ideas for things for teenagers to do so that they can stay out of trouble, [to] get them more introduced into how to act in situations, you know. I don't really know how to explain it, but like we were going to take a trip to the "I Am America Tour" with Tavis Smiley. Something happened and it didn't work out [because] of time constraints. [We asked the kids, "What do ya'll want to do today because we're going to spend the day with ya'll?" They were like, "Let's go to the mall," and so we all went to the mall and even though it's in town, we'd spent the day with them. We took them home, and, I mean, they were just so pleased that we just spent the day with them. Like a lot of the kids, they just want somebody to spend time with them, which is the same thing that my kids wanted. If I can do that, if [someone] just need[s] me to talk to them to keep them from doing something that maybe they're going to regret, then that's what I do with the fe-Male Perspective.

TMC: And then do you have a particular role in terms of reentry into the community because I heard that that's one of your big passions?

DW: Yeah, it is. I guess you could call me like the reentry coordinator, and I'm program assistant also, but the reentry thing I'm very passionate about because I know the challenges that these men and women face when they come out. A lot of people in Charlottesville are trying to do these things and they've never even been locked up, you know, or they're trying to say that we're going to do this little meeting every [week]—Okay, the last thing that a person really wants when they come out is meetings because they don't want to be made to go to another meeting because you get a lot of meetings while you're incarcerated, but you're made to do those things. Sometimes when you just have somewhere to direct that person when they come out and have somewhere for them to come and talk to somebody, if they need to, that's what they need—someone that they can trust that's not connected to DOC, that is not connected to OAR [Offender Aid and Restoration], that's not connected to the courts at all—just someone to come and say, all right, so, what you dealing with today? It may be a female dealing with the same issues that I was dealing with when I got out, but yet she wants to go really get high or something like that. You don't want them to do that so sometimes they just need somebody to talk to and direct them. This is what I did—I got on a bus and I went and looked until I couldn't walk anymore that day, and if you really want to find a job, you can find a job, but you just have to help them to want to help themselves. That's why I'm really passionate about it because it's hard for people to understand what it's like to be locked up and come out and [no one], including some of your family, even want[s] to talk to you.

For the city or anyone to take on a reentry project, I feel strongly that there should be someone in place that really understands *what* they're dealing with and *who* they're dealing with, because over behind the walls of a prison, it's almost like a sorority, and unless you're really part of that sorority—I used that maybe because of the college thing—but it really is, it becomes like a sister-hood or a brotherhood.

You know these women. I know some of the women that I was locked up with better than I know some of the people in my family, so when they come out, I can tell if they're telling the truth. I can tell if somebody is lying. I can tell if they're trying to play somebody. These are all things that you learn from interacting with people. You have to be able to differentiate what somebody is really thinking even though they might be saying something else, and so being an ex-offender and being incarcerated and dealing with the people that I had dealt with in my life through the drugs, through everything, it has given me more insight [into] society as a whole, you know. I can tell when people really don't want to be bothered with me, and it's [not] by the way they say anything; it's that it's all in the eyes or in body language, so, that's why it's like I think that I'm the person to do this reentry thing and I'm really passionate about it because I don't want the reentry program to fall onto the wayside. If you really want to help [ex-offenders], then have people in place that can help them, that can direct them to better ways of living.

TMC: Earlier in our conversation, you said that there are some things that you thought worked in the prison system and then there're other things that didn't, so what works? You said something about your PO.

DW: Well, I was saying not all the people [or all] things in the correctional system are bad. But prison life is.

TMC: Or anything associated with it, so not just the prison life but you talked about your parole officer.

DW: Well, the parole probation system works as long as you develop that relationship with your PO and you let them know what's going on in your life. You don't have to tell them like on a day-to-day basis—this is what I'm doing, this is what I'm doing, this is what I'm doing—but if you're having issues with something that is going to lead you down another road or another path, than what you're trying to achieve in your life. At the same time, when you're in prison, that doesn't work. Prison, to me, doesn't work. What it does do is it'll give you time to sit down and think about all you've done and how you want to correct your life, but as far as rehabilitating you, basically you do that for yourself. They don't do it for you. When you go in, you're just a number except for some of the COs [correctional officers]. When you're there a while, you develop—because of the type of person that I am, I picked at them, too. I picked at the COs. I'd be like, "You ain't doing nothing. I'm down here loading all these trucks with all this laundry. You're just getting to sit there in the air-conditioning all day," you know, or something like that. I'd pick at them, but as far as rehabilitating you, the only relationships that you have with anyone in the prison system is a person that you're in your cell with or the people you're on your hall with or you work with or the COs. They have these little programs that you go to. They have a prerelease program that they're getting ready to do away with, which to me was crazy because I got so much information from that program so the good things that [the system] [is] doing [are being] replac[ed] with something else.

TMC: What is the prerelease program?

DW: The prerelease program that I did at Goochland was six weeks, and you went from eight thirty in the morning until like three in the afternoon. Speakers would come in from like Social Security, from housing, from social services, even from probation and parole, and just people would come from the community outside to try and give you some information on things that could help you out when you get out. Some of those things aren't even in place. But the thing was, it's like it gave you ideas on some kind of mapping out what you needed to do. I knew that when I got out I wanted to volunteer and work with people and try and just keep somebody else from going down the same road, so [the reentry program] gave me information on who to volunteer with even though those places aren't there anymore.

Within six weeks of your release, you're already feeling that anxiety. You're already worrying—What about my kids? How'm I going to do this? How'm I going to get to work? How'm I going to get a job? You're already worrying about things, so when you actually read the information that you're given, it helps you develop some kind of goal. You might want to say, "Okay, this is what I want to do, and this is what I'm going to do, and by this time this is what I want to be doing," so that's what the prerelease program was for me. Now, what it is to everyone else I don't know, but it helps you just to get ready to reenter the society. It doesn't take the anxiety away by any means, but it does help you try and adjust, to focus on what you need to do and [on] the resources that are out there to help you.

TMC: As an ex-offender now working with the fe-Male Perspective, have you noticed that women ex-offenders have had [unique experiences], both in the prison and then outside? You worked with both men and women and young people, too, so I'm wondering if you've noticed different experiences?

DW: I have. I've actually ran into a few women since I've been in Charlottesville that I was incarcerated with. Several women that I was incarcerated with in Danville, once I was out on the streets, and I [could] say that working with the fe-Male Perspective for me has probably been the best thing that could've happened to me because if you don't get out and you don't get involved, you're going back. If you don't get involved with something, whether it be a job or whether it be an organization or whether it be good people, you have to surround yourself with positive people in your life. And by that, I mean the men and women that I was locked up with in Danville, I will tell you right now, I'll just give you an example.

Say there's ten of us, including myself. Eight of them are back, so out of ten people, only two of us are still out. I actually counted on my fingers the other day, and I think it was eleven, but just say nine of them are back, back in the system, and it's because they chose to come out and [to] think that [they could] be strong and go out here and do it by yourself. You can't, and that's the whole point of reentry. Like I'm lucky enough to where I have my mom and I have my daughter and I have Michelle and I have these people; if you don't have that, then find that. Get in a church or get into a organization. If you don't want to go to church, get into something that's positive because life in itself is so overwhelming anyway just for the normal person that's not been incarcerated, but for the person that's been incarcerated, you can multiply that times a hundred and just the challenges that you face on a day-to-day basis are crazy.

TMC: So do you think there're differences in how women experience prison versus men?

DW: Yeah. Oh, yeah.

TMC: In what ways?

DW: Well, on the inside, I think that the women share more. They open up more and develop more friendships than the men do. You know, men, I'm not saying they don't develop friendships because obviously I'm sure they do, but men seem to get focused on just doing their time, where women are more focused on going home. You understand the difference? Like the mind-set, and I can say that because I had pen pals. I wrote to people from other prisons, and so like we had developed friendships and stuff through letters even though you're not supposed to write each other. People that I was locked up with in Danville, once they got down the road, we continued to stay in contact even through family, like what you would do is you send a letter to—like I would send a letter to you and you'd send the letter to the prison for me, so that way it's not stamped, so their focus and my focus was two different things, like they were focused on just doing their time, and they didn't really talk about what they wanted to do when they went home or even what was going on at home. My letters would be more like, well, I've got pictures of [Lily] today—that's my granddaughter—or Summer got AB Honor Roll in this, this and this, you know, so it was different focus [on forming] goals.

TMC: And even when they've come out, have you seen a difference in just how people deal with these obstacles with reentering society and families, so how women deal with [reentry] versus how men deal with it?

DW: The women tend to want to go on the straight path. I'm not saying all of this applies, but I know that in the beginning, all those women reported to their POs, they were clean, and they were getting jobs and they were doing well, where I know men right now that got out and never went in that PO's office and actually within three days you're supposed to report to your PO, within three days of your release. They never went at all, and then they wonder why they get violations. Well, they didn't go to their PO. If they're not going to their PO when they get out, they're not even going to try and do right, and they're out and doing the same thing they were doing before they went in.

TMC: Why do you think that is? Why do you think they have different mentalities coming out?

DW: From my perspective, I would say for children and for family and everything, I think that even friends and stuff, it's easier for a man to feel left out of the loop and feel better if he stays out of it. In other words, if a man's been out of his children's lives for X amount of years and really never been there, he doesn't feel appropriate stepping in now. And if most of that time that he has been incarcerated and, say, his daughter or son was two or three, you know, the mother has moved on and remarried, and so he doesn't fit anywhere. For women, it's harder to let go. It's harder to let go of your daughter. It's hard[er] to let go of your mother than it is sometimes for a man that's really never been in your life anyway, and so they tend to probably reoffend because they don't fit in anywhere else. That's just my view on it.

TMC: You have mentioned the way religion can play a part in prison and also outside of prison, so can you tell me how religion functions in prison?

DW: For me, it helped me get that inner strength that I had lost within myself, you know, like to know that I wasn't going to use drugs again, no. 1. You know, all these things, when you've used drugs, literally, you will lay there when you get incarcerated and you will actually dream about using, so for me, I had to pray really hard for God to take that from me before I stepped back out on the streets again. And so that, and then just you pray for strength and you pray to be able to help other people to be able to get where they feel like what you feel.

There's a lot of women I was with [in prison] that had no hope at all, you know, and I would just tell them, you know, just pray.

You don't really want to push the Bible or anything, but just pray, just prayer because you don't know if that person may be Muslim or they may be Christian so you can't say, well, read your Bible, so what I would say is like, "Meditate within yourself. Get with yourself and get with God, whichever way you want to do it, and it's going to happen and it does." I mean, it's like miraculously. When you know that there is a higher power is when you're at your lowest moment and you think that you're not going to get up, like literally the strength came within me, well, I didn't even think about drugs anymore. I didn't think about getting high. I can sit here and talk to you about it. It doesn't bother me. I can be in a room with it. It doesn't bother me. Those total temptations, even though the devil is out there and he's working hard, it doesn't even bother me. It's almost like I can just brush my shoulder off and it goes.

Now, there are times people, places, and things that aggravate me, and so that's something that I'm working on.

# Contributors

JUAN BATTLE is Professor of Sociology, Public Health, and Urban Education at the Graduate Center of the City University of New York. He is coeditor with Sandra L. Barnes of *Black Sexualities: Probing Powers, Passions, Practices, and Policies* and coeditor with Michael Bennett and Anthony Lemelle of *Free at Last? Black America in the Twenty-First Century.*

ETHAN BLUE is Assistant Professor of History at the University of Western Australia and the author of *Doing Time in the Depression: Everyday Life in Texas and California Prisons.* His work on the histories of punishment have appeared in *Law, Culture, and the Humanities, Journal of Social History, Humanities Research, Pacific Historical Review, Radical History Review,* and elsewhere. He is currently researching the history of deportation.

JARED BROWN is a doctoral candidate at the University of California, Berkeley.

TSHEPO MASANGO CHÉRY is Assistant Professor of African and African Diasporic Studies at the University of Texas at Austin. Her first book project reexamines the racial contours of black nationalism and religious activism by linking together the political ambitions of South African Ethiopianism, North American Garveyism, and East African radicalism. Her work has been supported by the Fontaine Society, the Annenberg Foundation, the University of Virginia's Carter G. Woodson Institute for African American and African Studies, and the John L. Warfield Center in African and African Diasporic Studies at the University of Texas at Austin.

MARY ELLEN CURTIN is Assistant Professor of History at American University in Washington, D.C. She is the author of *Black Prisoners and Their World, Alabama,*

1865–1900 and served as a consultant and interviewee for the PBS Documentary *Slavery by Another Name*. She is currently working on a biography of Texas congresswoman Barbara Jordan.

HAROLD FOLLEY is a community organizer and a resident of Charlottesville, Virginia, where he serves on the staff of the Virginia Organizing Project.

CLAUDRENA N. HAROLD is Associate Professor of African American and African Studies and History at the University of Virginia. She is the author of *The Rise and Fall of the Garvey Movement in the Urban South* and is completing a manuscript on the history of New Negro activism and thought in the Jim Crow South during the interwar period.

EDDIE HARRIS, a resident of Charlottesville, Virginia, is affiliated with Children Youth and Family Services, where he directs the REAL Dads program, which works to improve the quality of children's lives by supporting fathers in becoming more Responsible, Empowering, Available, and Loving men in the lives of their children.

ANNA R. HASKINS is a doctoral candidate in sociology at the University of Wisconsin–Madison. Her current work focuses on the intergenerational effects of mass incarceration on young children's educational outcomes and academic trajectories and has been funded by the National Science Foundation, the Ford Foundation, and the American Sociological Association.

CHERYL D. HICKS is Associate Professor of History at the University of North Carolina at Charlotte. Her work addresses the intersections of race, class, gender, sexuality, and the law. She is the author of *Talk With You Like a Woman: African American Women, Justice, and Reform in New York, 1890–1935*.

CHARLES E. LEWIS JR. is President of the Congressional Research Institute for Social Work and Policy, an independent nonprofit organization supporting the mission and goals of the Congressional Social Work Caucus. He is Adjunct Professor at the Howard University School of Social Work. He is coeditor with W. Wilson Goode Sr. and Harold Dean Trulear of *Ministry with Prisoners and Family: The Way Forward*.

MARC MAUER is Executive Director of the Sentencing Project, a nonprofit research and advocacy organization based in Washington, D.C. He is the author of

*Race to Incarcerate* and the coeditor with Meda Chesney-Lind of *Invisible Punishment: The Collateral Consequences of Mass Imprisonment.*

DEBORAH E. MCDOWELL is Alice Griffin Professor of English at the University of Virginia and Director of the Carter G. Woodson Institute for African American and African Studies at the University of Virginia. She is the author of *Leaving Pipe Shop: Memories of Kin* and *"The Changing Same": Studies in Fiction by Black American Women;* co-editor with Arnold Rampersad of *Slavery and the Literary Imagination;* period editor of the *Norton Anthology of African-American Literature;* and founding editor of the Beacon Black Women Writers Series.

ANOOP MIRPURI is Assistant Professor of English at Portland State University. His work centers on race and American culture, and he is currently working on book manuscript entitled "Resisting Ordinary Punishments: Towards a Black Radical Posthumanism."

CHRISTOPHER MULLER is a doctoral candidate in the Department of Sociology and a doctoral fellow with the Multidisciplinary Program in Inequality and Social Policy at Harvard University. His dissertation examines racial disparity in incarceration in three periods of U.S. history.

MARLON B. ROSS is Professor of English and African American Studies at the University of Virginia. He is the author of *Manning the Race: Reforming Black Men in the Jim Crow Era* and is completing a sequel entitled "The Color of Manhood: Imaging Black Masculinities in the Civil Rights Era and Beyond."

JIM SHEA, a resident of Charlottesville, Virginia, is currently active in ex-offender reentry issues and other issues of racial and economic justice.

JONATHAN SIMON is the Adrian A. Kragen Professor of Law at UC Berkeley. He is the author of *Governing Through Crime: How the War on Crime Transformed American Democracy and Created a Culture of Fear* and *Mass Incarceration on Trial: The Constitution and the Future of Imprisonment.*

HEATHER ANN THOMPSON is Associate Professor of African American Studies and History at Temple University. The author of *Whose Detroit: Politics, Labor, and Race in a Modern American City,* she is currently completing the first comprehensive history of the Attica prison uprising of 1971.

DEBBIE WALKER, a resident of Charlottesville, Virginia, is affiliated with The fe-Male Perspective, Inc., a nonprofit organization in Charlottesville that works to recommend culturally relevant solutions to "break the chains" of systemic and cyclical inequity and injustice through empowerment. She works with the group assisting the formerly incarcerated to meet the challenges of reentry from prison.

CHRISTOPHER WILDEMAN is Assistant Professor of Sociology, Faculty Affiliate of the Center for Research on Inequalities and the Life Course, and Resident Fellow of the Institution for Social and Policy Studies at Yale University. His forthcoming book, coauthored with Sara Wakefield, is entitled *Children of the Prison Boom: Mass Incarceration and the Future of Inequality.*

# Index

*Figures and tables are indicated by "f" and "t" following page numbers.*

Contagious Disease Acts, 115

convict lease system: abolishment of, 8, 20; in Alabama, 7; competing with free-world miners, 50–51; in Florida, 50; in Louisiana, 218; in plain sight, 49; in postbellum South, 47–48, 67n23; in Texas, 31

Cozart, Reed, 219

crack cocaine mandatory-sentencing policies, xi, 72n106, 194, 203, 207n16

Crane, Jonathan, 170

Craven, Walter, 142

creative culture. *See* aesthetic imagination

crime and crime rate: compared to prison rate, vii, 2; distinguishing from warfare, 136; meaning of, 139; Nixon campaign (1968) on, 200–201; preemptive action against, 202–3; response to increase in, xi, 137; rise and decline in, xi–xii, 2. *See also* deterrent effect; drug-related offenses; "hard back" of mass imprisonment; murder; sentencing; "soft underbelly" of mass imprisonment; "War on Crime"

Crist, Charlie (governor of Florida), 285

Critical Resistance, 63, 137

"Critical Resistance South: Beyond the Prison Industrial Complex" (conference 2003), 213

critical theory on relation between prison and society, 11

*Cruel and Unusual* (Jarvis), 261n24

cruel and unusual punishment, 56, 61, 146–47, 148, 258n3. *See also* prison brutality

*Cultural Prison, The: Discourse, Prisoners, and Punishment* (Sloop), 259n8

culture: across carceral divide, 246–48; African American culture separate from imprisoned people's culture, 261n22; creative culture's relationship to carceral nation, 240–41; of dissemblance, 76

Cummins prison farm, Arkansas, 55

Cunningham, Randy "Duke," vii

Currie, Elliott, 1

Curtin, Mary Ellen, 7, 29, 46

Daniel, Pete, 29

Davis (Superintendent of Bedford), 88

Davis, Angela Y.: as activist, 225, 228; on blues women singers, 100n15; critique of liberal reformism, 130; on disproportionate numbers of prisoners in U.S., 1, 2; on exploitation of prison labor, 23n16; on fear as part of racism, 24n28; imprisonment and trial of, 141, 261n26; at penal reform conference (2003), 213; on pornography, 124n12; and radical prison movement, 11, 139

Davis, Katharine Bement, 87

Davis, Mike, 15

Davis, Stephen, 226

Dayan, Colin (Joan), 147

dead prez (musical group), 16, 214, 216, 230–31, 232

death penalty: execution of prisoner at San Quentin, 108–9; for homicide, 196, 197; Supreme Court review, 56, 197, 202

Delorme, Eugene P., 254–55

depersonalization of prisoner, 243–44

detective novels, 253

deterrent effect: of disenfranchisement, 287; of education, 231; of punishment, 137, 153n23, 229

Diallo, Amadou, 229

Dialogue on Race, 265, 270

Diedling, Rudolph, 88

Dinitz, Simon, 254–55

"Discrimination in the Criminal Justice System from 1910–1955" (NAACP papers), 7

disenfranchisement. *See* voting

District of Columbia Court Reform and Criminal Procedure Act of 1970, 223–24

Douglass, Frederick, 49

Doyle, Aaron, 231

drug reduction strategies, 15, 195

drug-related offenses: African American and Latinos imprisoned for, 206n3;

arrest quotas for, 272; crack cocaine policies, xi, 72n106, 194, 203, 207n16; effective ways to reduce imprisonment for, ix; and race, 203–4; Rockefeller drug laws (1973), 207n14; sentencing for, 207n14. *See also* Rockefeller Drug Laws (New York); "soft underbelly" of mass imprisonment

drug treatment, 194

Du Bois, W. E. B., 7, 49, 52, 256, 261n28

due process violations, 54

Dylan, Bob, 211, 226

early intervention policy, 200

economic consequences of incarceration, 159–76, 178. *See also* employment

economics of mass incarceration system, ix, 2–3, 20; benefits to cashing in on public obsession with crime and punishment, 16–17, 24–25n30; prison industrial complex, 21n3, 174, 228; and privatization, 274; in rural settings, 274; using black men for labor, 49. *See also* convict lease system

Edin, Kathryn, 169, 170

education system, criticisms of, 231

Eighth Amendment, 56, 146–47, 258n3

Ellis Island, 117

Ellison, Ralph, 249

Ellwood, David T., 170

Elmira State Reformatory, 52

Embree, Frank, 120

employment: as factor in crime trends, 20; Fragile Families Study, 162–68, 164t, 166t, 168t; labor-market outcomes, 13, 20, 160–68, 172–76, 194, 266, 306–7; and marriage prospects, 168–70

environmental protections, 204–5

Equal Protection Clause, 39, 266

*Estelle v. Gamble* (1976), 56

ethics of medical testing in prison, 60–61

ethnic differences. *See* racial/ethnic differences

ethnographic penology, 17, 253–54

eugenics, 111, 113–14, 127n24

evidence-based research, ix, 137, 160, 169, 178, 185, 187–88

exposés of prison conditions, 55, 63–64, 237

extradition cases, 37

Families Against Mandatory Minimums (FAMM), 63

Families of Prisoners, 63

family consequences of incarceration, 13–14, 168–72, 171t, 295–96, 304–6

Fanon, Frantz, 134, 230

Farrington, David, 186

Fausto-Sterling, Anne, 128n34

fear: of black male in popular white imagination, 215; of crime generally, 201–2, 205, 258n3; of crime tied to fear of black people, 24n28; of deviant sexuality, 113; of violent crime, 15, 192, 195–96, 199, 202, 206, 207n10

Federal Bureau of Prisons, 60

female activism. *See* women

fe-Male Perspective, 301, 302, 304, 308–9

Fifteenth Amendment, 39

Florida prison system: employment and earnings following incarceration, 162; investigation of Tabert's death in prison, 50

Folley, Harold, 17, 18, 279

Folsom Prison, 138

Folsom Prison Manifesto, 11–12, 141–46

Foster, Holly, 185, 187

Foucault, Michel, 111, 131, 137–38, 150, 153n23, 240

Fourteenth Amendment, 39, 56, 266

Fragile Families Study, 160, 162–69, 164t, 166t, 168t, 170–72, 171t, 173, 185, 186

Franklin, Howard Bruce, 222

fraud and crimes involving breach of trust, 161

Freedman, Estelle, 104n90

freedom of speech, 246

Freeman, Richard B., 161

*Free Will* (Scott-Heron), 216

"frontlash," 201

232–33; for long prison sentences, 196; racial implications of, 45, 59; and social turn to political right, 62, 149. *See also* sentencing

Putname Lumber Camp, Florida, 50

Queeley, Andrea, 215

*Race Rebels* (Kelley), 22n8
*Race Traits and Tendencies of the American Negro* (Hoffman), 6
racial/ethnic differences: drug-related offenses, 203–4; hyperpolicing of marginalized groups, 261n22; illegal drug use, 194; makeup of prison population, vii, x–xi, 3, 45, 159–60, 177, 206n3, 206n6; marital and cohabitating relationships, 169; types of crimes, 199; whiteness, entitlement of, 269. *See also* African Americans; Latinos
racism: against black prisoners, 33; of criminal justice system, 38–40, 214, 229, 248–58; in free world linked to racism inside prisons, 56; in hip-hop music, 215; prison racial segregation, 65, 87–89, 193; and punishment, 8–9, 48, 53, 222–23, 252; structural racism, 193–94, 205; United Nations Convention on Elimination of All Forms of Racial Discrimination, 65; and War on Drugs, 192; white supremacy as invisible factor, 270; young black women's sexual behavior as, 75, 79. *See also* civil rights movement
radical prison movement, 11, 131–55; Folsom Prison Manifesto, 11–12, 141–46; and sense of crisis, 136–41; and violence, 146–50. *See also* Attica Prison
radical social movements, language of, 138
Rafter, Nicole Hahn, 106n109
Raiford camp, Florida, 36
Rainey, Gertrude "Ma," 83
Ramsey State Prison Farm, Texas, 32, 35–36

rape. *See* sexualized violence
rap music. *See* hip-hop
rates of incarceration: African American disproportionate numbers, 1–2, 3, 13, 59, 159, 177–78, 179t; African American musicians protesting, 227–33; black vs. white males in U.S. prisons, 2–3, 59, 159, 177–78, 179t, 259n8; international comparison, ix, 15, 177, 272; juveniles, 230; reasons for increase in, xi–xii, 4, 151n11; in U.S., vii–ix, 2, 45, 58, 151n11, 177, 178f, 271–72
Reagan, Ronald, 204, 224, 227, 228, 271–73
REAL Dads, 290–300, 300n1
reality TV calling for participatory public, 259n9
Rebadow, Bob (*Oz* character), 243, 255, 259n10
recidivism, 5, 265, 266, 287, 303–4
Re-entry Summit (Charlottesville), 301
rehabilitation: abandonment of, 20, 25n34, 59, 277; adoption of policy of, 52; prisoners' view of, 134; public opinion on (1971), 58; of white vs. black prisoners, 259n8; of women in Bedford, 74, 87, 103n69
Rehnquist, William, 147
reintegration into society, xii, 10, 17–21; Folley interview, 285; Harris interview, 291–96; men vs. women, 312–13; Shea interview, 268–69, 276–77; Walker interview, 301–10
Reitz, Kevin, 58
release of prisoners: parole boards, 197; racial divide in, 196–97
religion, 83–84, 313–14
Republican Party, 227, 273
resistance by prisoners to their mistreatment, 40–43. *See also* prison activism
restoration of rights, 18, 268–69, 280–89
restraints, use of, 61
*Rethinking Juvenile Justice* (Scott and Steinberg), 230
*Revolutionary Suicide* (Newton), 248

Thurman, Wallace, 250
Tocqueville, Alexis de, 1
*To 'Joy My Freedom* (Hunter), 22n8
Torres, Jose Campos, 224
Torture Convention, 65
*Towards Freedom from Fear* (Nixon campaign 1968), 200
trust, 291, 302, 304
trustee guards, 53
Tucker prison farm, Arkansas, 55
Tully, Jim, 118, 122
Turner, Ed, 47, 48
Turner, William Bennett, 247
Tzeng, Jessie M., 169

underground economy, 13, 165, 167, 295
unions. *See* labor unions
United Kingdom: incarceration rates, 177; parental imprisonment's effect on children's behavior, 186
United Nations: Convention against Torture, 65; Convention on Elimination of All Forms of Racial Discrimination, 65; Declaration on the Rights of the Child, 61; Minimum Rules for the Treatment of Prisoners, 134
United Network of Organ Sharing, 60
United States: first prison crisis in, 50–53; rates of incarceration in, vii–ix, 2, 45, 58, 151n11, 177, 178f, 271–72; reasons for increase in incarceration rates, xi–xii, 4, 151n11; spaces of captivity in, 139; Tocqueville and Beaumont tour of prisons in (1831), 1. *See also* carceral crisis; historical context; rates of incarceration
Universal Declaration of Human Rights, 65
University of Virginia conference (2009) on carceral state in U.S., 64
urbanization, 15, 128n29, 205

vagrancy, 46, 74, 80, 85, 218
Valdosta, Georgia, prison camp, 36
*Vampire That Hovers over North Carolina, The (Negro Rule)* (1898), 215

venereal diseases, 85–86, 115, 116, 117
Vietnam war, 136–37
violence: campaigns against media depiction of, 260n16; legitimatized by prison, 10–11; in media portrayal of carceral narratives, 245–46; in reaction to unfair social system, 259n8
violent crimes. *See* "hard back" of mass imprisonment
Virginia: ex-felons' voting rights in, 268, 282–84; model prisons in, 19, 19f
Virginia Organizing, 279–80, 288, 289n1
voting: inmates allowed to vote, 285–86; loss of voting rights due to criminal records, 25n31, 268; restoration of rights to felons, 18, 268–69, 280–89

Wacquant Loïc, 5–6, 227, 241, 260n13
Wakefield, Sara, 186
Waldfogel, Jane, 169
Waldfogel, Joel, 160–62
Waldrep, Christopher, 29
Walker, Alice, 103n62, 261n26
Walker, Debbie, 17, 18, 263, 301
Wallace, George, 201, 273
Warner, Mark, 282
"War on Crime," 5, 14, 15, 195, 196, 200–203
"War on Drugs": and fear of crime, 15; and hyperpolicing, 267; and incarceration rates of African Americans, viii, 5; racial caste system established by, 192, 267, 271; racial critique of, 194–96, 203–4; Reagan's launch of, 227, 228; and women's imprisonment, 14
Washington, Booker T., 49
*Washington Post:* on Louisiana State Penitentiary (Angola) conditions (1951), 218–19; on waterboarding (1968), 145–46
water torture, 145
Watson, James "Bluebeard," 118
Weathermen, 201
Weaver, Vesla M., 201
Welch, Robert "Guitar," 221
welfare benefits, 204, 307

Western, Bruce, 12–13, 160, 161, 169, 172, 173
White, Deborah Gray, 78
White, S. G., 47
white masculinity: presumed to be model of normality, 112; threats to, 128n29
whiteness, entitlement of, 269
whiteness literature, 127n24
white supremacy as invisible factor, 270
*Whitley v. Albers,* 147
Whitman, Charles, 201
Wideman, John Edgar, 249, 253
Wildeman, Christopher, 13–14, 173, 177, 186–87
Williams, Robert, 220
Wilson, William Julius, 170
Winship, Christopher W., 170
Wisconsin prison mistreatment, 48
*Wolff v. McDonnell,* 21
women: African American females in prison system, 3, 7, 9; as black blues singers, 77, 83, 100n15; as black incarcerated authors, 261n26; cult of true womanhood, 105n95; ex-offenders, female vs. male experience, 311–12; increase in incarcerated population, 3; interracial attachments among female inmates, 78, 89–96; labor-market participation, effect on divorce and decline in fertility, 169; maternal imprisonment of African Americans, 14; mental problems of female inmates, 172; New York City working-class black women in early twentieth century, 8, 73–107; prison racism's gendered dimension, 39–40; reconnection with children after maternal incarceration, 18
Wonder, Stevie, 222
Wood, Robert G., 170
Woods, James, 92
Woods, Sarah, 82
Work, Monroe, 7
Wright, Paul, 25n30
Wright, Richard, 17, 249–52

Zobel, Alfred J., 116

## Recent Books in the Carter G. Woodson Institute Series

Midori Takagi, *"Rearing Wolves to Our Own Destruction": Slavery in Richmond, Virginia, 1782–1865*

Alessandra Lorini, *Rituals of Race: American Public Culture and the Search for Racial Democracy*

Mary Ellen Curtin, *Black Prisoners and Their World, Alabama, 1865–1900*

Philip J. Schwarz, *Migrants against Slavery: Virginians and the Nation*

Armstead L. Robinson, *Bitter Fruits of Bondage: The Demise of Slavery and the Collapse of the Confederacy, 1861–1865*

Francille Rusan Wilson, *The Segregated Scholars: Black Social Scientists and the Creation of Black Labor Studies, 1890–1950*

Gregory Michael Dorr, *Segregation's Science: Eugenics and Society in Virginia*

Glenn McNair, *Criminal Injustice: Slaves and Free Blacks in Georgia's Criminal Justice System*

William Dusinberre, *Strategies for Survival: Recollections of Bondage in Antebellum Virginia*

Valerie C. Cooper, *Word, Like Fire: Maria Stewart, the Bible, and the Rights of African Americans*

Michael L. Nicholls, *Whispers of Rebellion: Narrating Gabriel's Conspiracy*

Henry Goings, *Rambles of a Runaway from Southern Slavery*, edited by Calvin Schermerhorn, Michael Plunkett, and Edward Gaynor

Philip J. Schwarz, ed., *Gabriel's Conspiracy: A Documentary History*

Kirt von Daacke, *Freedom Has a Face: Race, Identity, and Community in Jefferson's Virginia*

Deborah E. McDowell, Claudrena N. Harold, and Juan Battle, eds., *The Punitive Turn: Race, Prisons, Justice, and Inequality*